A Good Year to Die

A GOOD YEAR TO DIE

THE STORY OF THE

GREAT SIOUX WAR

Charles M. Robinson III

University of Oklahoma Press
Norman and London

Library of Congress Cataloging-in-Publication Data

Robinson, Charles M., 1949–
  A good year to die : the story of the great Sioux War / Charles M.
Robinson III.
     p.   cm.
  Originally published: New York : Random House, c1995.
  Includes bibliographical references and index.
  ISBN 0-8061-2890-9 (alk. paper)
    1. Dakota Indians—Wars, 1876. 2. Dakota Indians—Government
relations. 3. Dakota Indians—Land tenure. 4. Black Hills (S.D.
and Wyo.)—History—19th century.   I. Title.
E83.876.R63   1996
973.8′2—dc20   96-21423
                                                                    CIP

The paper in this book meets the guidelines for permanence and durability
of the Committee on Production Guidelines for Book Longevity of the
Council on Library Resources, Inc.∞

Oklahoma Paperbacks edition published 1996 by the University of Oklahoma Press, Norman, Publishing Division of the University. Published
by arrangement with Random House, Inc., 201 East 50th Street, New
York, New York 10022. Manufactured in the U.S.A. First printing of
the University of Oklahoma Press edition, 1996.

        1   2   3   4   5   6   7   8   9   10

To the valiant of both sides

It is a good day to die!

—L<small>AKOTA BATTLE CRY</small>

The art of war among the white people is called strategy or tactics; when practiced by the Indians it is called treachery.

—M<small>AJ</small>. G<small>EN</small>. N<small>ELSON</small> A. M<small>ILES</small>

EXPLANATIONS

IN RETROSPECT, THE GREAT SIOUX WAR IS CONFUSING BECAUSE IT not only pitted white against Indian but Indian against Indian as well. At the time, those in government service were classified as "friendly," while those who opposed the government were "hostile." For the sake of simplicity, I have continued to use the word *hostile* for those at war with the government, to distinguish them from those on the government side. It does not imply any criticism, for indeed the government had given them much to be hostile about.

From the very beginning, the Crows, Arikaras (also known as Rees), Shoshones, Utes, Pawnees, Nez Percés, and Bannocks were allied with the government, and remained so throughout the war. The Crows, Rees, and Shoshones in particular performed valiant service as military scouts.

The antigovernment Indians consisted of the western Sioux, or Teton Lakota Nation, and their allies, the Northern Cheyenne Nation. They were supported to a limited extent by individual groups of Santee Sioux, Yanktoni Sioux, and Arapahos. However, the antigovernment Indians were never completely unified, and to understand who was or was not fighting against the government, the war must be divided into three phases.

In the earliest period—from about January through April 1876—most of the opposition came from free-roaming bands of Lakotas and Cheyennes outside the reservation; the reservation Indians were largely neutral. Beginning in late April 1876, however, hundreds of reservation Lakotas and Cheyennes went over to the hostile side, joined by the Yanktons, Santees, and Arapahos, although the majority of the Arapaho Nation continued to maintain neutrality. By late September 1876, the tide had turned against the hostiles; many of the Lakotas and Cheyennes still on the reservation declared for the government, as did the majority of the Arapahos. After the hostile Cheyennes were defeated in November 1876, large numbers of their warriors changed sides and served with the government forces for the remainder of the war.

"RESERVATION" AND "AGENCY" ARE TWO DIFFERENT THINGS. A reservation is an area of land set aside by the government for the exclusive use of an Indian tribe or group of tribes. An agency is the administrative seat of a particular area, and was the location at which Indians were entered on government rolls, and government rations were issued. Smaller reservations were served by a single agency. On larger reservations with several tribes, more than one agency might be necessary. At its height, the Great Sioux Reservation had nine different agencies independent of each other.

Lodge and tipi are used interchangeably, as both denote a form of housing. Tipi describes a particular type of lodge, a conical structure covered with hides or canvas, whereas lodge might mean any type of shelter.

A PECULIARITY OF THE PERIOD WAS THE ARMY SYSTEM OF BREVET rank among officers who had served in the Union Army. A brevet was a temporary rank given to Union officers during the Civil War as a reward for meritorious service. Its purpose was twofold: to honor the recipient in a quick, efficient manner, and to create an officer corps sufficiently large enough to handle the emergency. When the war ended, officers who opted to remain in the army often were required to take reductions in rank and pay. As a courtesy, however, they were addressed by their brevet ranks. Thus Custer, Mackenzie, and Miles were all called "general," in deference to their Union Army service, although in reality, Custer was a lieutenant colonel, and Mackenzie and Miles were colonels.

I have referred to all officers by their permanent ranks, using the brevet only in quotes.

UNTIL 1889, WHEN THEY WERE PARTITIONED TO FORM SEPARATE states, North and South Dakota were combined into a single federal administrative area known as Dakota Territory. The territorial capital was at Yankton on the Missouri River. Since the events in this book largely occurred in 1876–77, I generally have referred to the region as Dakota Territory. Sometimes, however, when I found it necessary to specifically locate a particular place or event, I have used the modern state name.

ACKNOWLEDGMENTS

MANY INDIVIDUALS AND ORGANIZATIONS WERE INVOLVED IN THIS project, and to all of them, I owe a debt of gratitude.

The Ken Graves family of Red Fork Ranch, Kaycee, Wyoming, allowed me to visit the site of the Mackenzie–Dull Knife fight on their ranch. Cheri Graves and daughters showed me through the area of the fight, pointing out where specific actions occurred.

John Yellow Bird Steele, president of the Oglala Sioux Tribe, Pine Ridge, South Dakota, took time to discuss the Indian perspective, even though he was especially busy that day, and I gave him no advance notice. While we did not agree on all points, the conversation gave me a feeling of being more personally involved with the Lakota-Cheyenne side of the war, which otherwise I might not have had.

In Montana, Kitty Belle Deernose of the National Park Service spent several days locating material on the war in the extensive archives of the Little Bighorn Battlefield National Monument, and has since answered a substantial amount of my letters on the subject. Paula West Chavoya and the staff of the Wyoming State Museum in Cheyenne have likewise located material during my visits and answered correspondence since.

Thanks also to the Montana Historical Society, Helena; U.S.

Military Academy Library, West Point, New York; Jim Court, Hardin, Montana; Thomas Gilcrease Institute, Tulsa, Oklahoma; National Archives, Washington, D.C.; Library of Congress, Washington, D.C.; Nebraska Historical Society, Lincoln; Minnesota Historical Society, St. Paul; San Benito, Texas, Public Library; Interlibrary Loan Department, University of Texas-Pan American Library, Edinburg; and to my wife, Perla, who ran errands and hunted up files in various archives, and did not start screaming when I bought a McClellan saddle at a roadside shop in Nebraska on our anniversary; and to the many friends we made on the road.

I wish to express special appreciation to the staff of Fort Union National Historic Site, New Mexico, for their quick response when my wife became ill, and to the emergency room staff of Northeastern Regional Hospital, Las Vegas, New Mexico, who understood the symptoms and effects of Takyasu's arthritis and treated accordingly.

Finally, to Robert D. Loomis, my editor, for all his help, encouragement, and patience on this project.

Grateful acknowledgment is extended to the following publishers and holding institutions for granting permission to quote from various sources:

American Heritage Center, University of Wyoming, Laramie: Thaddeus Capron Collection; Gerhard Luhn Collection.

Henry E. Huntington Library and Art Gallery, San Marino, California: Walter Schuyler Collection; Frank Baldwin Collection.

Little Bighorn Battlefield National Monument, Crow Agency, Montana: Walter Mason Camp Collection; Fred Dustin Collection; Journal of Private Eugene Geant.

Montana Historical Society, Helena: Edwin M. Brown Diary.

Nebraska State Historical Society, Lincoln: James Frew Diary and Letters; Eli Ricker Collection.

The Newberry Library, Chicago: Richard Irving Dodge Diary.

Old Army Press, Fort Collins, Colorado, and University of Oklahoma Press, Norman: *Centennial Campaign: The Sioux War of 1876* by John S. Gray.

Presidio Press, San Rafael, California: *The Freeman Journal: The Infantry in the Sioux Campaign of 1876* edited by George A. Schneider.

Reference Publications, Inc., Algonac, Michigan: "She Watched Custer's Last Battle," from *Custer on the Little Bighorn* by Thomas B. Marquis.

Scribner's, an imprint of Simon & Schuster, Inc., New York: *I Fought With Custer* by Frazier Hunt and Robert Hunt. Copyright 1947 Charles Scribner's Sons; copyright renewed © 1975 Frazier Hunt and Robert Hunt.

Special Collections Division, U.S. Military Academy Library, West Point, New York: John Gregory Bourke Diaries.

University of Nebraska Press, Lincoln: Permission to quote from the many, many works published by Nebraska Press and listed in the bibliography.

University of Oklahoma Press, Norman: Permission to quote from the substantial number of works published by Oklahoma Press and listed in the bibliography.

Wyoming Department of Commerce Cultural Resources Division, Wyoming State Museum, Cheyenne: "The Indian Border War of 1876" by Cynthia J. Capron.

CONTENTS

LIST OF MAPS

INTRODUCTION

THE YEAR 1876 WAS A PIVOTAL ONE. THE UNITED STATES PREpared for its centennial with an extravagant exposition in Philadelphia. During that hundred years of national existence, the industrial revolution had changed the face of the planet, and man's capabilities seemed limitless. The focal point of the exposition would be the halls of arts and industries, with exhibits of technological achievement from every major nation on earth.

The United States itself had grown from thirteen agrarian British colonies hugging the Atlantic coast to one of the world's leading industrial and economic powers. The Atlantic and Pacific were linked by rail and telegraph. In 1876, Alexander Graham Bell invented the telephone. John D. Rockefeller was organizing the businesses that would ultimately become Standard Oil. Andrew Carnegie was making Pittsburgh synonymous with steel.

Nor did the nation lag behind in art. Winslow Homer, John Singer Sargent, and James McNeill Whistler were establishing American painters as equals to their European counterparts. The American stamp in letters was even greater. In 1876, Samuel L. Clemens published *The Adventures of Tom Sawyer,* a timeless story of boyhood that confirmed its author as a giant of American literature, and shook the literature itself from its British roots giving it a national character all its own.

Baseball had become a national passion since its invention almost thirty years before, and in 1876, the five-year-old National Association of Professional Base Ball Players reorganized itself as the National League.

In the South, the bitter years of Reconstruction were drawing to a close. Most states had reestablished their sovereignty, and only a few remained under military rule.

Not everything was bright, however. Four years earlier, General Ulysses S. Grant, the Civil War hero, had been overwhelmingly elected to a second term as president, only to find himself mired in scandal. First, the Credit Mobilier, involving high officials in government, nearly destroyed the Union Pacific Railroad on which the nation depended for coast-to-coast transportation. Then the Whiskey Ring, equally well connected, defrauded the government out of millions of dollars in liquor tax revenue. The administration of the Indian agencies had long been a national disgrace, and Congress was becoming suspicious of Grant's sacrosanct War Department. Aggravating the situation was one of the worst economic depressions in history. Thousands went hungry and homeless, while politicians enriched themselves at public expense.

The nation in 1876 was only one third of its present area. Although the United States was second only to the British Empire in North American possessions, much of it was "territories," a polite republican word that essentially meant "colonies." The territories were outside the national boundaries, and administered according to the will and pleasure of the federal government. Although it was presumed that eventually all would be admitted as states, they were dependent possessions whose people had only limited voice in territorial affairs, and none at all on the federal level. The primary recourse for action was public opinion in the nation as a whole and, with the tacit support of the army, territorial citizens manipulated public opinion.

Except for Texas, Kansas, and Nebraska, the eastern United States ended at the 95th meridian. West of that line were millions of square miles of territories—Dakota, Montana, Wyoming, Colorado, Indian Territory, and more—until one reached the states of

Nevada, California, and Oregon. So remote were these territories that people living in them often referred to "the States" as if they were a distant foreign land.

Although Colorado entered the Union in 1876, many of the remaining territories were still unsettled. Large tracts of the western Dakotas and eastern Montana and Wyoming were unexplored, their features unknown, never seen by any member of the white race. Scientists, scholars, and government officials knew less of these areas than modern schoolchildren know of Saturn.

Most of the people who lived in this land were the nomadic tribesmen customarily called American Indians. Like many primitive societies, they were warriors. The greatest of these were the Teton Lakota or western Sioux. Fearless in battle, their fighting men would cry, "It is a good day to die!"

For the United States Army, 1876 was a good year to die; for that year, an extraordinary number of soldiers did die at the hands of the Sioux and their allies—1876 was the worst year for the army since the close of the Civil War. It was the year of the Great Sioux War.

Like most wars, the Great Sioux War was expected to resolve permanently a situation that both sides found intolerable. And like most wars, it created more problems than it solved, problems that have continued to haunt the national conscience.

The complicated nature of Indian-white relations has been oversimplified throughout our history. Until the 1960s, the whites were thought to represent progress and civilization whereas the Indians were viewed as bloodthirsty savages. Since then, the Indians have been depicted as virtuous custodians of nature; the whites have been vicious despoilers of the land and environment. In reality, neither side was essentially good or essentially evil. More than anything else, they were different. As national development threw white and Indian into ever increasing contact, the differences became more apparent until they were irreconcilable.

Perhaps the greatest difference was an attitude toward land. The Plains Indian concept of private property was restricted to personal possessions. Tribal lands were held in common. As a seminomad who existed largely by hunting, the Indian thought it absurd that anyone could claim individual ownership over the bounty of nature. To the whites, however, property essentially meant land, and the right of individual ownership was one of the cornerstones of white civilization.

Land was a key issue in the government's Indian policy, and that policy was less than noble. Tribes were invited to sign away their land in treaties they did not understand, in exchange for goods that often were of no use to them. The goods were frequently less than promised, because government officials routinely plundered the Indian appropriation. Treaties were broken. When the Indians rebelled at this treatment, troops were sent to restore order.

There were those in the East, particularly among the religious groups, who viewed the entire policy as a travesty. Exactly two weeks after Custer's defeat at the Little Bighorn, Rev. D. J. Burrell, a Chicago minister, told his congregation that the government had brought the disaster upon itself through its historic indifference to the rights of Indians as human beings.[1]

Despite their good intentions, however, the religious groups offered no viable alternative to existing policy. For seven years prior to the Great Sioux War, the government had allowed churches to administer the western Indian agencies and work with the tribes. The churches failed, largely because they neither understood nor respected the indigenous Plains Indian cultures. Their goal was to "save" the Indian by destroying his very existence as an Indian. Their primary method was to force agriculture on a warrior society, ignoring not only the social upheaval it brought but also the even more important fact that Indian reservations were often located on land totally unsuited for farming. When the Indian failed to respond in what the missionary/Indian agent considered an appropriate manner, he was allowed to starve, much as white children of the period were sometimes starved to guide them toward the Victorian ideal of virtue.[2] (The Indians were, after all, children of the "Great Father" as the president was called.)

Religious groups aside, many easterners adhered to the "noble savage" concept of eighteenth-century European author-philosophers, such as Jean Jacques Rousseau and Alexander Pope. Although Pope died in 1744, and probably never saw an Indian, nineteenth-century easterners nevertheless quoted a stanza of his *Essay on Man,* which begins:

Lo, the poor Indian! whose untutored mind
Sees God in clouds, or hears him in the wind.

Ironically, this passage was also quoted by western frontiersmen, as a sarcastic comment on eastern idealism. The phrase, "Lo, the poor Indian," was so well known that "Poor Lo," "Mr. Lo," or just plain "Lo" became common western slang names for the average Indian.

Words and ideals did not alter the situation on the plains. The seemingly endless warfare did, however, alter public opinion, even in the East. As white casualties grew, many citizens came to agree with Gen. William T. Sherman, commander of the army during much of the Indian wars, who observed, "The more we can kill this year, the less will have to be killed in the next war, for the more I see of these Indians the more convinced I am that they all have to be killed or be maintained as a species of paupers. Their attempts at civilization are simply ridiculous."[3]

Sherman was frustrated; initially, he had hoped for a peaceful settlement of white-Indian differences and saw those hopes drowned in bloodshed. Far from being a Hitlerian Final Solution, his comment was actually the most extreme expression of a profound dilemma—the basic conflict between a technologically advanced society and a primitive, tribal society. In such a situation, where both occupy—or wish to occupy—the same area, the less advanced society must yield.[4] How to make the less advanced society yield, yet preserve its rights and integrity until it can become fully integrated (as eventually it must), is a problem that continues to trouble the nations of the world.

In the nineteenth century, however, the government rarely concerned itself with Indian rights. The "civilization" of the Indian, and the expansion of mainstream America into Indian lands became a quasi-divine mission. For those citizens who might have pangs of conscience, the officials in Washington created elaborate subterfuges, placing the moral burden upon the Indians. With or without war, the seizure of the Indian lands would have ultimately occurred. War simply speeded the process.

The United States Army of that period very closely resembled the French Foreign Legion. It was a largely mercenary force, whose recruiters asked no questions when someone sought to enlist. Almost half the soldiers were foreign born, and had already fought in nationalist uprisings in Europe, or imperialist expansion elsewhere. Others were former Confederates—often former officers—forbidden by law from holding a U.S. Army commission, but willing to serve in the ranks in order to follow the only profession they knew. A substantial number of soldiers were Germans, and the Irish constituted such a high percentage that army anecdotes and songs of the era are often in brogue.[5]

Officers went to the Indian frontier indoctrinated by West Point to fight an organized predictable enemy. The Indian was not—by West Point standards—organized, and was predictable only in his unpredictability. Of all the senior officers who served in the Great Sioux War, only three, Ranald Mackenzie, Nelson Miles, and, to a lesser degree, George Crook, went west with the idea that they could learn from their foes. And it should be noted that these three officers brought the war to its successful conclusion.

Just as the army did not understand the reality of Indian warfare, it was likewise woefully unprepared for a major conflict. The United States was still recovering from the Civil War, which not only imposed a direct economic burden on the government but also disrupted American commerce. After the initial postwar demobilization of 1865–66, economic expediency dictated further cutbacks in the early 1870s.[6] By 1876, the army was little more than a national police force, fixed by law to a maximum number of 25,000 officers and men. Its principal combat unit, the regiment, consisted of ten to twelve companies. In theory, each company had 100 officers and men. In practice, however, few companies exceeded 40 or 50. The army sent to fight what the Grant administration hoped would be a quick, easy war was a shadow of the force required. Only after a series of blundering spring offensives, followed by serious defeats at the Rosebud and the Little Bighorn, did Congress authorize the strength necessary to vanquish the Indians.

The greatest single problem facing the army was terrain. Although sporadic fighting occurred over large portions of Nebraska, Wyoming, Montana, and the Dakotas, most of the action occurred in a rugged, mountainous area overlapping northeastern

Wyoming, southeastern Montana, and western South Dakota. The main geographical feature of the region is the awesome Missouri River, which flows eastward then southeastward, in an arc through the entire area on its way to join the Mississippi just above St. Louis. Its three main tributaries are the Platte in the south, and the Little Missouri and Yellowstone in the north.

The Platte follows a broad valley through Nebraska until it forks in the western part of the state, with the North Platte leading into Wyoming, and the South Platte into Colorado. The Little Missouri runs northeast from Wyoming, flowing into the Missouri just above Bismarck, in North Dakota.

Although the Platte and Little Missouri are of some interest to the Great Sioux War, most of the story involves the extensive system of the Yellowstone River. Beginning in Yellowstone Lake in far western Wyoming, the river flows northeast across Montana to its juncture with the Missouri River just inside the North Dakota line. Its own tributaries are born in the snowmelt of the Bighorn Mountains of northern Wyoming, traveling northward into Montana where they empty into the Yellowstone. Looking on a map, some of the more important tributaries are the Bighorn in the west, then the Rosebud, the Tongue, and, in the east, the Powder River. This network is so vast that even these rivers have tributaries of their own. The Crazy Woman and Little Powder feed the Powder, and together their waters travel north to the Yellowstone. The Bighorn is fed by several other rivers, one of which is called the Little Bighorn.

Each of these rivers flows through its own narrow valley, cut off from the other waterways by broken ridges, hills, and mountains. A traveler going from one valley to another must struggle over the divide separating the two.

In the northernmost areas of the war zone, the Northern Pacific Railroad ran from St. Paul, Minnesota, only to Bismarck. Beyond that point, troops had to follow the most rudimentary existing trails or make their own. The entire east-west route is broken by streams and small rivers running into the Yellowstone and Missouri. To assist the soldiers, daring steamer captains took their boats up the Missouri and into the uncharted waters of the Yellowstone and Bighorn. In autumn, however, the water level fell, closing much of the region to navigation, and in winter heavy snows often blocked the Northern Pacific line; the region was effectively isolated six months out of the year.

In the southern sector of the war zone, the Union Pacific ran from Omaha, Nebraska, to San Francisco, via Cheyenne, Wyoming. But Union Pacific had only an east-west main line, with no feeders, so that anyone traveling north of Cheyenne used horse, wagon, or foot. Thus the five-hundred-mile trip from Omaha to Cheyenne was about twenty-four hours by train, whereas the ninety miles from Cheyenne to Fort Laramie took the better part of two days by horse.

Covering this vast and difficult country, infantrymen generally marched with about fifty pounds of equipment on their backs. Cavalrymen packed their gear on their mounts, but in addition to personal equipment, each cavalryman had to carry ten to fifteen pounds of grain for his horse.[7] Unlike Indian ponies, government horses could not live off the land, and required supplemental feeding. On long marches, when the supply of forage was exhausted, horses began to wear out, and many cavalrymen ended up on foot. Extra food, forage, and ammunition were carried in wagons where the terrain allowed, and packed on mules when it did not. Often the mule train fell behind the marching column, a problem that hindered military operations throughout the war.

In 1873, the army standardized weapons so that soldiers in the Great Sioux War generally were issued two basic arms: the .45-caliber Colt Single Action Army revolver; and the Model 1873 Springfield rifle, in caliber .45-70 long rifle for infantry, and .45-55 light carbine for cavalry. The Springfield was a single-shot, breechloading weapon that fired a metallic cartridge. It could be loaded and fired much more rapidly than its predecessors, and had twice the range of repeating rifles such as the Winchester, Henry, or Spencer. Despite its advantages, the average soldier was not sufficiently trained to make maximum use of the rifle's superiority, and many gave themselves a psychological edge by supplementing their government-issue arms with weapons purchased with their own money.[8]

The improvement in firearms forced a dramatic revision of cavalry tactics. This revision, adopted in 1874, recognized that in the face of these weapons, the classic, sabre-wielding cavalry charge was suicidal. Under the new tactics, the mounted charge was used only for initial shock, the weight and speed of the horses creating confusion among the enemy, and giving the cavalryman an advantage in choosing his ground to fight. Once engaged, however, the cavalry unit dismounted and formed a skirmish line using squads of four men each. Three men with carbines placed themselves on the line, while the fourth remained on his horse behind the line, holding the horses for the others. When several companies were engaged, as was the case in most instances during the Great Sioux War, one company was held in reserve about 150 yards behind the line.[9]

Indian weaponry was a collection of whatever could be accumulated by barter, capture, theft, or various other means. Studies of cartridge cases recovered in archaeological investigations of the Little Bighorn show the Indians carried at least forty-one different kinds of firearms in that fight, and it is estimated at least 25 to 30 percent were armed with modern, sixteen-shot Winchester and Henry repeating rifles. After the fight, they also armed themselves with captured Springfield carbines, many of which were surrendered to Crook and Miles the following year.[10] Aside from firearms, the Indians carried traditional weapons, such as bows and arrows, hatchets, tomahawks, and war clubs.

The average Indian thought almost entirely as an individual, and not as part of a larger organization. Strategy, communications, even numbers of people in a particular location—essential to any white history—were seldom noted because they did not affect most Indians as individuals.

This basic difference in cultural experience—the collective view of the whites opposed to the individual view of the Indians—has slanted most accounts of the Great Sioux War. History recognizes only a few chiefs, such as Gall or Crazy Horse, ignoring the rank-and-file warriors actually responsible for the success or failure of a battle. This is partly because the white experience centers on leadership and partly because the army could not accept losing to what appeared to be rowdy, undisciplined tribesmen. Defeat was more endurable at the hands of an aboriginal Napoleon or Alexander, a born military genius with the ability to exercise command at the critical moment.

Unfortunately for white egos, this simply was not the case. On the northern plains, a chief—or more often a group of chiefs in council—devised a general set of tactics. These tactics it was hoped would be implemented successfully by the warriors. Yet Indian fighting power, once committed to battle, became highly personalized—each warrior more concerned with his own actions, and those immediately around him than with the overall plan.

In 1877, after interviewing many of the Indian combatants, one officer wrote:

> Great prominence has been given Crazy Horse and Sitting Bull in this war; the good fighting strategy and subsequent muster by retreats being attributed to them, whereas they are really not entitled to more credit or censure than many others so far as plans and orders were concurred. . . .[11]

Certainly, great native generals did occur, but they were primarily Apaches such as Victorio or Cochise, leaders in a more authoritarian society, heading small subsistence bands over whom they could exert control. Among the wealthy, populous tribes of the northern plains, such leadership was neither feasible nor desirable, and the role of a paramount battle chief was largely symbolic.

An Indian Alexander or Napoleon is missing from this book, simply because there was none.

The Great Sioux War was different from other American conflicts. Despite the fact that the government won, the war is remembered primarily for Custer's defeat at the Little Bighorn. Many of the leaders remembered today as heroes are those whom the government had designated as the enemy. And, while the outcome was a forgone conclusion, it was long and bloody.

The tragedy of the war is that despite their many cultural differences, the Indians and whites were so much alike. With few exceptions, the Indians were neither noble mystics nor savages. They were people. In particular, the thoughts, dreams, and problems of the young Indians strike a chord in today's young people throughout the world. Many younger warriors lived at home with their parents. They had household chores, which they tried to duck. They were not necessarily obedient if something distracted them.

They found the girls from the next camp circle more fascinating than those from their own. They stayed out too late. They got into trouble. If, after a fight, even the small children seem too preoccupied with scalps and plunder, it must be remembered that a world close to nature is not the idyll so often portrayed. It is a violent, uncertain life that breeds violent responses. Still, after the Little Bighorn, there was no rejoicing in the Indian camps. Their losses had been too heavy. They were mourning and praying.

The very nature of the war makes its story difficult to tell from both sides. Although Indian sources are used whenever possible, the recollections contained in this book are largely those of whites. Given public outrage after the Little Bighorn, and the glorification of Custer that lasted another eighty-odd years, few Indians spoke of their roles in the war. When they did, they were often careful to tailor their remarks according to what they thought the whites wanted to hear. Well into this century, their fear of government reprisal, while unfounded, was very real.[12]

PART I

THE QUEST FOR LAND

1

The Indians and the Land

BEFORE ANYTHING ELSE, THERE WERE THE BLACK HILLS, DARK and cool on the horizon, overlapping the boundary between South Dakota and Wyoming. "Hills" is a misnomer for, in fact, they are loftier than the Appalachians or Ozarks; Harney Peak, their pinnacle, is the highest point in the United States east of the Rockies.[1] Neither are they black, but lighter colors, ranging from off-white to blue-gray to red. From a distance, however, they appear black, because of the deep green leaves of the young ponderosa pines that cover the slopes.

The southern half of the hills, below Rapid City, South Dakota, is a series of sheer peaks, separated by narrow, winding valleys. Above Rapid City, the mountains give way to more gentle hills with wide, sheltered meadows, before one final northern upheaval among the rugged, tortuous Slim Buttes. The central part, with its hills and meadows, offers a haven from the severe northern winters, and was a refuge of Plains Indians for hundreds of years.

The region abounds in natural resources. Deer, pronghorn antelope, and elk provide meat. Fox, beaver, and marten yield their pelts. The soil produces grass for grazing. The native stone is excellent for building. There is quartz—and gold. Although men have known about the gold since earliest times, it did not have significance until the middle of the last century. Gold was not important to the Indians of the northern plains.

It is believed the Crow Indians lived in the Black Hills in the beginning of the eighteenth century, but were expelled by more powerful tribes.[2] In recorded history, the first to possess the hills were the Kiowas, who settled the vicinity during the middle of the eighteenth century. The Kiowa occupancy lasted only a generation, for about 1770 they came into conflict with two larger, more powerful peoples, the western Sioux and Cheyennes.[3]

The word *Sioux* does not refer to a tribe, but rather to a language group and culture shared by several related peoples. The word is derived from a French corruption of the final syllable in *Nadowe-is-siw,* the Chippewa name for this group.[4] Over the years, the Sioux became divided into three distinct nations, based on dialect and region: the eastern Sioux or Santee Dakota; central Sioux or Yankton Nakota; and the western Sioux or Teton Lakota. It is the Teton Lakota whom we generally mean when we say Sioux, for they are the classic Sioux of the plains.

The Lakota Nation was composed of seven distinct tribes, the largest of which was the Oglalas, followed by the Brulés. In the nineteenth century, these two tribes lived south of the others and had the greatest range, roaming from Kansas to Wyoming. The northern tribes, the Miniconjous, Two Kettles, Hunkpapas, Sans Arcs, and Blackfeet,[5] wandered in the Dakotas and Montana.

Within those regions, each tribe had its own territory, and spent most of the year camping and hunting in that area. From time to time, they would meet with one or two adjacent tribes to trade and perform rituals, but the great gathering of all Lakotas generally occurred each summer, when the entire nation assembled at some central location for council. This annual meeting of the seven tribes represented the basic national cohesiveness of the Lakotas, regardless of where they might be the remainder of the year. They would hold a great Sun Dance, and the chiefs and elders would meet to act on matters that affected them as a whole.[6]

The Sun Dance was their great spiritual event, and the council of the chiefs of all the tribes, their legislature. Presiding over the council were the Shirt Wearers, four head men selected from the outstanding chiefs of all the tribes. They recommended national policy, endorsed or condemned actions of the individual tribal chiefs during the preceding year, judged offenses against the peace and dignity of the nation, and approved or disapproved proposals of subordinate chiefs. The decisions of the Shirt Wearers constituted advice more than mandate. Nevertheless, they carried weight and were an important consideration when the full council deliberated.[7]

The chieftaincy itself was theoretically hereditary, but the actual power of an individual chief was based on prestige he brought to the office through wisdom, valor, and generosity. Within a tribe, there were different chiefs for different areas of responsibility. Political chiefs oversaw government, while war chiefs led the warriors in combat. Occasionally, the lines would overlap in versatile men of outstanding ability, such as Red Cloud and Crazy Horse, war chiefs whose leadership gave them political responsibility as well. Besides political and war chiefs, most Plains Indians had "old man" chiefs, elders whose opinions were sought and respected for the wisdom that comes from age and experience.

Originally a southern people, the majority of the Sioux migrated north and, in the sixteenth century, settled in the marshes and lakes of northern Minnesota, on the headwaters of the Mississippi River. There they lived in permanent lodges, raised crops, hunted and gathered food in the marshes, and traveled in birch canoes.

Sioux occupancy of the Mississippi headwaters was contested by native Algonquian tribes, the most powerful of whom were the Crees. In intertribal warfare, the numerically superior Sioux held the advantage until the 1670s, when the Algonquian tribes obtained metal weapons and firearms through trade with the whites in Canada. With the advantage of modern arms, the Crees and their allies gradually forced the Sioux peoples into southern Minnesota. Over the years that followed, the Sioux drifted out onto the buffalo plains to the west, becoming the Indians familiar to nineteenth-century whites.[8]

By the mid-eighteenth century, the Lakotas had also acquired firearms from Canada, which allowed them to push as far as the upper Missouri River, overwhelming all who opposed them. But the outbreak of the French and Indian War in 1753 disrupted the supply of arms and ammunition, and Lakota battle efficiency suf-

fered. Further westward expansion was also blocked by the
Arikaras—the Rees—whose permanent, fortified villages with-
stood their assaults. A stalemate ensued until the 1770s, when
three successive smallpox epidemics devastated the Rees, and the
Lakotas gained the upper hand. The Rees were driven from their
lands, dominated and despised by the Lakotas, and forced to the
very edge of their own country, where they waited for a chance to
even the score. A century later, it came.[9]

Never as populous as the Lakotas, the Cheyennes are among the
westernmost of the Algonquian peoples, originally living far to the
east of their nineteenth-century territories. Tribal legend speaks of
a great water, probably Lake Superior or Lake Michigan. Like the
Lakotas, the earliest Cheyennes were an agricultural people who
lived in fixed villages. They appear to have been driven from their
homes by Crees and Assiniboines, a division of the Yankton Sioux
who had come to terms with the Crees. They, too, wandered out
onto the plains.[10]

At some point in their wanderings, the Lakotas and Cheyennes
entered a permanent, if loose, alliance. The acquisition of horses,
which occurred in the second half of the eighteenth century, gave
them greater mobility, and together they expelled the Kiowas permanently from the Black Hills, which henceforth they regarded as
their own. The hills became sacred to them, and, while they might
wander the plains of the Dakotas and the mountains and valleys of
Wyoming and Montana, both Lakotas and Cheyennes saw the
Black Hills as their spiritual home.

The Kiowas and the Rees were not the only people to suffer from
the Lakota-Cheyenne alliance, and the Black Hills and the plains
of the Upper Missouri were not the only areas seized. The Pawnees
were driven south of the Platte River in Nebraska. The Crows lost
their ancient homeland in eastern Montana, and were driven west.

The Crows also remembered this seizure of their land and, like
the Rees, would ally themselves with the federal government in
1876 to get it back.

Secure in their new territories, the Lakotas and Cheyennes un-
dertook a nomadic existence that would be a key factor in the wars
that led to their destruction. With thousands of people to support,
it was obvious that the seven individual tribes that composed the

Lakota Nation could not remain consolidated even within their own areas. Had they tried, the game of the vicinity soon would have been hunted out, and the ground stripped bare of wild turnips and other vegetables. Consequently, during most of the year, not only did the nation disperse into tribal areas but also each tribe broke into smaller, local bands, the nucleus of which was the chief and his immediate relatives. Beyond the family, the size of a particular band depended on its leadership. No Lakota was bound by unconditional loyalty to an individual chief, and people naturally gravitated toward renowned war leaders. Indeed, the reputation of a particularly competent chief, such as Sitting Bull or Crazy Horse, might spread beyond his own band and tribe, giving him a commanding position among the Lakotas as a whole.[11]

The Cheyennes had tribal units, but because they never had the vast population of the Lakotas, these divisions had no real bearing on their organization. Dull Knife, the greatest of all their chiefs, was first and last a Cheyenne. Among the Lakotas, by contrast, Sitting Bull was a Hunkpapa, and Crazy Horse, an Oglala.

One significant division, however, did occur among the Cheyennes about 1830, when they began separating into northern and southern groups. This split soon became so profound that within a few decades, the Northern and Southern Cheyennes became two distinct nations.[12] Although friendly contact remained, by 1860 their history becomes totally separate. What affected the Southern Cheyennes did not necessarily concern the Northern Cheyennes and vice versa. The Northern Cheyennes were spared the disastrous massacres of their southern cousins by white soldiers at Sand Creek, Colorado, in 1864, and along the Washita River of Oklahoma, four years later, and did not share in the ultimate defeat of the Southern Cheyennes during the Red River War of 1874–75. In 1876, the northern group still considered itself at peace with the federal government.

During the warm months, Lakotas and Cheyennes wandered through their ranges, following the game and harvesting wild vegetables in the classic fashion of a hunter-gatherer society. The bands were fluid. Since the Cheyenne range was close to those of the Oglalas and Miniconjous, they met often, and frequently intermarried. One could nearly always find a few Cheyennes in an

Oglala camp, Oglalas in a Cheyenne camp, and Miniconjous in both. Among the Lakotas themselves, there was mixing between Oglalas and Brulés. As white settlement pushed the Santee and Yankton Sioux farther west, they visited the camps of the various Lakota tribes. While the great summer council was essentially a Lakota affair, the alliance gave the Cheyennes input on the deliberations, and Santees and Yanktons were welcome if they chose to attend.

Both the Lakotas and Cheyennes had warrior societies, fraternal organizations that gave identity in battle and functioned as civil police in camp. Each had its own officers, rules, battle regalia, and traditions. Membership in a particular Lakota or Cheyenne society was generally by invitation to the prospective candidate. The candidate was a boy or young man who had shown initiative, daring, and willingness to cooperate.

The Cheyennes more than the Lakotas seemed to attach importance to warrior fraternities. Cheyenne societies were responsible for planning battle and were consulted by the chiefs in both political and military affairs. Lakota societies on the other hand functioned as police and combat units, leaving battle plans largely to the war chiefs. While six of the seven Cheyenne warrior societies were, like those of the Lakota, open to any able-bodied, ambitious man, the seventh, the Chief Soldiers, was restricted to the forty-four chiefs of the entire nation. A Cheyenne warrior was identified by the society to which he belonged, while a Lakota was more likely to be identified by his tribe.[13]

Despite their warrior culture, the Indian attitude toward white Americans was friendly during much of the first half of the nineteenth century. Most whites were travelers. They did not crowd anyone, and the Lakotas welcomed and assisted them in their journeys.

Visiting a Miniconjou Lakota chief in the 1830s, artist George Catlin remarked on the kindness and hospitality he received. But Catlin realized he and other whites were in the territory because the Lakotas chose to allow it. He estimated their total population at 40,000 to 50,000, of whom 8,000 or 10,000 were warriors. At least half those warriors were six feet or more tall. They had ample power to resist intrusion.[14]

The first whites to settle in this country were fur traders who purchased buffalo robes from the Indians, often on behalf of corporate employers. Chief among the corporations was the American Fur Company that, in 1841, built a trading post called Fort John, but which was popularly known as Fort Laramie because of its location on the Laramie River. Most trading companies had no intention of dispossessing the Indians, partly because their business depended on native goodwill. But the fur trade introduced a particularly vile form of cheap whiskey called Taos Lightning, and alcoholism became rampant among the tribes.

Peace is a relative condition. Just as the conflicts of the Cold War often originated between nations nominally "friendly" through diplomacy and trade, so the peace between Indian and white was punctuated with sporadic fighting. If the Lakotas and Cheyennes from time to time chose to retaliate against cheating by unscrupulous traders, this did not necessarily mean they regarded the peace as broken.

So long as the white population consisted of fur traders and itinerant artists, writers, and adventurers, this condition of relative peace remained intact. The establishment of the Oregon Trail, however, brought huge numbers of emigrants westward, unsettling Indians, particularly the Oglalas, Brulés, and Cheyennes, whose territory they crossed.[15] In the 1840s, Francis Parkman noted, the Indians

> could scarcely believe that the earth contained such a multitude of white men. Their wonder is now giving way to indignation; and the result, unless vigilantly guarded against, may be lamentable in the extreme.[16]

The "result," initially, was horse stealing. Emigrants brought horses, highly prized by the Indians, and the Lakotas raided wagon trains to get them. As more people moved west, however, the wagon trains became larger, and the Indians more cautious, although they continued to steal horses and occasionally rob and kill stragglers if the opportunity presented itself.

The whites, naturally, resented this, but the grievances were not one-sided. The now continuous movement along the trail upset the wildlife on which the Indians depended. The buffalo, in particular, could not coexist, and moved out of the North Platte River area. By 1845, their disappearance from the Platte Valley forced the Lakotas to hunt west of the Laramie mountains of Wyoming, far beyond their normal range. When explorer John Charles Frémont visited them that year, they were angry.[17]

The danger of open warfare was enough to prompt the federal government to order a council that convened on June 16, 1845, on a meadow three miles up the Laramie River from Fort Laramie. Col. Stephen Watts Kearny, with five companies of dragoons and seventeen wagonloads of provisions and gifts, met with a thousand or so Lakotas. After expressing the Great Father's love for his children—red and white—Kearny warned them against whiskey and other corruptions. Then he came to the point: The emigrant roads must remain open, and the whites traveling on them must not be disturbed. Interested more in the Great Father's wagonloads of presents than his instructions, the Lakotas agreed.[18]

Like most Indian treaties, this document was unworkable. It had no legal or moral power under Indian tradition because no individual chief or group of chiefs could bind the tribes; the treaties were binding only on individuals who signed them. Among the whites, the treaty terms were observed only as long as they were convenient. Within a year, the promises were forgotten by both sides. Visiting Fort Laramie in 1846, Parkman noted the "dangerous spirit" of the Lakotas, and said that unless Fort Laramie was garrisoned by troops, travel would become dangerous.[19] Recognizing the seriousness of the situation, the government purchased Fort Laramie in 1849, and sent soldiers.

The military occupation of Fort Laramie was symptomatic of a chain of events that began to alarm government leaders. The altruistic superintendent of Indian Affairs, Thomas H. Harvey, believed the existing white contact, with its liquor, disease, and concubinage of Indian women, was corrupting, and should be replaced by beneficent white influences of permanent settlement and honest toil. But instead of easing the Indians into the mainstream of society, he advocated placing them under an "efficient administration," which would introduce missionaries and establish vocational schools.

According to Harvey, the need was immediate because the buffalo herds were being rapidly depleted by settlement of their normal ranges. The tribes dependent on them would compete for hunting grounds. Since many of these tribes were already hostile to each other, Harvey feared large-scale intertribal warfare would erupt, and whites would be caught in the middle.

In September 1851, the various northern tribes convened at the government's request on Horse Creek, a few miles from Fort Laramie. There the mutually antagonistic nations, such as Crows and Lakotas, agreed to suspend hostilities, remain in their own specific ranges, and acknowledge the right of the government to establish roads, military posts, and such other facilities as might be necessary. They also agreed to make restitution for any depredations against citizens of the United States lawfully passing through their respective territories. In return, the federal government would pay an annual annuity of $50,000 for fifty years, "in provisions, merchandise, domestic animals, and agricultural equipment."[20] The entire program would be administered by agents, whose offices would be in the various tribal territories. In binding the Indians to a set of concepts they barely understood, and insisting they take farm animals and implements for which they had no use, the government was setting the stage for war.

THE THIRTY-SIX YEARS OF BLOODSHED COLLECTIVELY KNOWN AS the Sioux wars began on August 19, 1854, during the annuity issue at Fort Laramie. The Lakotas and Northern Cheyennes were camped in a broad valley a few miles east of the post. There were an estimated 600 lodges, which represented between 4,200 and 4,800 people. This gathering worried the military authorities, since it concentrated a large number of warriors in one spot.

On August 18, a cow strayed from a passing party of Mormons. Wandering into the Indian camp, it was killed, butchered, and eaten. Attempts by the chiefs to negotiate restitution were unsuccessful, and the following day Lt. John L. Grattan, a swashbuckling young officer out to make a name for himself, received permission to take twenty-nine soldiers and a civilian interpreter to the Indian camp, and arrest the Indian who killed the cow. There was a cautionary note to Grattan's orders: If the Indians refused to surrender the suspect, he was to avoid a fight unless absolutely certain of success.

A more experienced soldier would have given these orders careful consideration. Grattan, however, is said to have remarked that he "hoped to God they would have a fight." Such attitudes by ignorant young officers cost the lives of scores of soldiers over the next two decades.

Grattan's party went out to the camp the next morning. The Indians refused to surrender the suspect, and Grattan refused to discuss restitution, and the argument became increasingly bitter. Gunfire erupted, and when it was over, Grattan and all but one man were dead, and that one was mortally wounded.

The Grattan Massacre was the first time since the army's organization in 1775 that a military unit had been completely annihilated, and the public demanded a scapegoat. The army's answer was to blame the Lakotas, and plans were soon under way for retaliatory measures that would last for decades.[21]

Among those witnessing the Grattan Massacre was a young Oglala Lakota boy who was called Curly. As an adult, he would gain immortality as Crazy Horse.

2

Defeat and Duplicity

NO ONE WHO SAW CRAZY HORSE COULD FAIL TO BE IMPRESSED by him. Capt. Azor H. Nickerson, Gen. George Crook's senior aide-de-camp in the Department of the Platte during the Great Sioux War, summed up the opinions of many when he wrote:

> There was something peculiarly fascinating in the personality of Crazy Horse. He was the finest looking Indian I ever saw. . . . In repose, his face and figure were as clear-cut and classical as a bronze statue of a Greek God. When he moved, he was as lithe and graceful as a panther, and on the war-path, he was as bold as a lion, and as cruel and bloodthirsty as a Bengal tiger.[1]

Jesse M. Lee, an army officer who was with Crazy Horse the day he died, called him "the ideal Captain, who was not only in touch with his soldier braves, but who fired their souls with his own martial ardor."[2]

A solitary, mystical figure who kept apart from most of his people, Crazy Horse generally was acknowledged as "the strange man of the Oglalas." Even his physical appearance was different. Frank Grouard, an army scout who knew him well, recalled: "He had sandy hair, and was of a very light complexion. He didn't have the high cheek bones that the Indians generally have, and didn't talk much."[3] About five feet, eight inches tall, with a slight build, he was smaller than Sitting Bull or Gall, but those who knew him considered him more striking. Later in life, his cheek would be scarred by a bullet wound, inflicted by his wife's jealous former husband.[4]

His baby name, Curly, referred to his light, wavy hair. Although some people mistook him for a white captive, he was in fact Lakota. His father, also named Crazy Horse, was an Oglala Lakota holy man. His mother was a Brulé Lakota, the sister of Spotted Tail, the great chief of that tribe. He was born in the vicinity of Bear Butte, near the present site of Sturgis, South Dakota, in the early 1840s.[5]

Young Curly's early training came from his father and a warrior named High Back Bone, whose nickname was Hump. Hump, who had seen Lakotas arrested and carried off in chains for various violations of white law, always said it was better to die a fighting Indian of the plains than to live in chains under the whites. The boy always remembered this.

Curly was about twelve when the Grattan Massacre occurred. Over the next several years, whites and Lakotas skirmished, each undertaking punitive raids against the other. During times of truce the traders' whiskey so corrupted the Indians that the elders despaired of finding a great man among the adult generation.

After watching a particularly bad drinking binge, the senior Crazy Horse told his son that the next great man of the Lakotas would be one who had no part of these troubles, and would lead by example, rather than words. He and the other elders then built a sweat lodge and invited the boy to sit with them. Surrounded by the counselors of his people, Curly told them of a vision he had seen.

There are at least two versions of this story, the most famous of which was recorded by Mari Sandoz in her classic work, *Crazy Horse, the Strange Man of the Oglalas*. According to Sandoz, Curly saw a warrior riding on a horse that changed colors many times, and seemed almost to float on the air. The rider, who likewise floated on the back of the horse, wore plain blue leggings and a white buckskin shirt. He had no paint. A single feather was tied in his long hair, which hung loose to his waist. He wore a few beads in his scalp lock. A small brown stone was tied behind his ear. There were no scalps on the warrior's belt, apparently an injunction against taking them.

Enemy shadows came at him, but he rode into them. Their arrows and bullets streaked toward him, only to disappear before they reached him. His own people tried to catch his arms, but he would shake them off and ride on. Behind him was a thunderstorm, and as it rolled in a streak of lightning appeared on the man's cheek. His clothing disappeared until he wore only a breechcloth. There were spots on his body like hailstones. The spots disappeared and a small, red-backed hawk flew over him. Then the warrior vanished.[6]

The second account was related by William Garnett, a frontiersman from the Dakotas, who apparently heard it from Crazy Horse himself.

> Crazy Horse told the story that he was near a lake. A man on horseback came out of the lake and talked with him. He told Crazy Horse not to wear a war bonnet; not to tie up his horse's tail . . . so Crazy Horse never tied his horse's tail, never wore a war bonnet. It is said he did not paint his face like the other Indians. The man from the lake told him he would never be killed by a bullet, but his death would come by being held and stabbed.[7]

Whatever the details, Old Crazy Horse pondered his son's vision, and said the boy must become the man on the horse. When he went into battle, he must always think of the vision and dress and act like the ethereal warrior. Henceforth, the boy tried to do as the vision directed. He was also given his father's name, becoming Crazy Horse.

While the young Crazy Horse was learning the ways of a warrior, the full effect of the Grattan Massacre was being felt. The Lakotas spent the next year terrorizing the Oregon Trail through the Platte Valley in Nebraska and Wyoming. The government responded by sending Brig. Gen. William S. Harney to restore order. On September 3, 1855, Harney attacked a band of Brulés, killing 136, and capturing the survivors. Using the prisoners as bait, he forced the Sioux tribes to reaffirm the 1851 treaty and concede the right of a road connecting Fort Laramie with Pierre, in Dakota Territory.

To avoid Harney, the Oglalas withdrew from the area. Because they made up the bulk of Lakota fighting power, the Platte Valley became quiet. The tranquillity remained undisturbed during the 1862 Sioux uprising in Minnesota, since that involved the Santees, and few Lakotas probably even knew about it. The Lakotas, however, were affected by the discovery of gold in western Montana in 1862. This flooded the region with emigrants, and their interfering presence was too much for the Indians who once again began terrorizing the trail. By 1864, there was a full-scale war in southern Nebraska.

The war spread west when John Bozeman blazed a new trail north and west from Fort Laramie to Virginia City, Montana. Popularly called the Bozeman Trail, the Montana Road was the shortest route. But it led directly through the Oglala hunting lands of the Powder River, and the Indians reacted by attacking emigrants with appalling ferocity.

The federal government understandably was concerned about security on the Bozeman. The influx of gold from Montana would provide a much needed boost to the economy and rebuild government cash reserves badly depleted by the Civil War. In March 1865, Congress passed an act authorizing construction of a wagon road along the trail, and that summer Gen. Patrick Connor established a post in the Powder River area of northern Wyoming, which became Fort Reno (no connection with Maj. Marcus Reno, who would gain notoriety during the Great Sioux War of 1876). Beyond Fort Reno, however, there was no protection, and emigrant trains literally had to fight their way through to Virginia City. The situation in the Platte Valley was even worse, for various military expeditions to the Powder River country had driven many Indians south, where they harassed travelers along the Platte.[8]

Unable to provide protection and embarrassed by public outcry over a recent massacre of peaceful Southern Cheyennes at Sand Creek, Colorado, the government began new negotiations with the Indians. In the fall of 1865, treaties were signed with chiefs representing nine different bands among the Sioux, Cheyennes, and Arapahos. These chiefs, however, had signed treaties before. Their people had long since opted for peace and now hung around Fort Laramie living on handouts. As such, they were known contemptuously to soldier and Indian alike as "Loafer Indians" or "Laramie Loafers." Not a single chief involved in the raids signed the new treaty.

Nevertheless, government officials convinced themselves they had secured the road to Montana. In the spring of 1866, Col. Henry B. Carrington was sent to make that feeling of security into reality by replacing Civil War volunteers at Fort Reno with regular troops, and building two new posts, Fort Phil Kearny in northern Wyoming, and Fort C. F. Smith in southern Montana.[9]

Carrington's party arrived at Fort Laramie in the midst of yet another treaty council. This time it was an effort to win over the chiefs who had not participated the year before. Its lack of success was summed up in a single paragraph by Carrington's wife.

> [The chiefs] "The Man afraid of his Horses" and "Red Cloud" made no secret of their opposition, and the latter, with all his fighting men, withdrew from all association with the treaty-makers, and in a very few days quite decidedly developed his hate and his schemes of mischief.[10]

Until now, Red Cloud was probably a distinguished warrior, rather than an actual chief. This act of defiance, however, combined with his leadership in the ensuing months, made him a power to be reckoned with. For the remainder of the nineteenth century, and until his death in 1909, Red Cloud would be the most enduring force in Lakota politics.

This remarkable Oglala was born in 1822, probably in southwestern Nebraska around the forks where the Platte River divides into northern and southern streams. His father and grandfather were both called Red Cloud, as was a deceased cousin, making him, in effect, Red Cloud IV. (The same principle of hereditary names also applied to Little Big Man—which simply means the younger Big Man—Sitting Bull, Man-Afraid-of-His-Horses, and Crazy Horse.)

Not much is known of Red Cloud's youth other than that his father died shortly after he was born. Presumably he was a typical

Oglala boy who as he grew older became a particularly fierce warrior. He took his first scalp in a fight with the Pawnees. On a raid against the Crows, he killed their pony herder and made off with fifty head. During an expedition against the Utes, he dragged an enemy warrior out of a stream, and scalped him alive. He even killed the chief of a rival Oglala faction during an internal dispute.

The hallmarks of Red Cloud the warrior were tactical skill, valor, and cruelty. Physically, he was tall and sinewy. The many photographs taken during the last fifty years of his life show a stern man, with high cheeks, firm jaw, tight lips twisting down at the corners, and long, hawklike nose. His eyes were heavy-lidded, but the right one glared piercingly.

Like most Lakotas, Red Cloud initially appears to have been friendly toward the whites, as long as they were trading or just passing through. However, he was one of the first to realize that nothing but evil would come from the whiskey trade or the growing number of emigrants on the trail. His initial status was not enough to influence his people toward war, but by 1865 the Oglalas were ready for someone to lead them in a general uprising. Red Cloud only needed the opportunity, and this presented itself in the person of Colonel Carrington.[11]

Carrington's expedition largely consisted of infantry armed with muzzle-loading rifles, augmented by cavalry equipped with Spencer repeating carbines. These troops—not quite 700 in all and mostly raw recruits—were to be scattered among Forts Reno, Phil Kearny, and C. F. Smith. Phil Kearny was a good sixty-five miles northwest of Reno, and C. F. Smith, another ninety miles northwest of Phil Kearny. More troops were promised, but by the time they finally arrived, months later, they were too late to do anything but die.

After relieving the volunteers at Fort Reno, Carrington pressed on to establish and construct his headquarters at Fort Phil Kearny, sending the remainder of his column to build Fort C. F. Smith. The division of his force among three posts left him critically shorthanded.

On June 16, several Cheyenne chiefs appeared at Fort Phil Kearny. They knew every detail of Carrington's march so far, as well as the disposition of his troops. All this had been told to them by Red Cloud, whose name cropped up frequently during the discussion. The Cheyennes had no quarrel with the whites, and after an amicable visit they departed. That left Red Cloud as the enemy, and Carrington realized that now the Oglala chief knew considerably more about him than he knew about Red Cloud.[12]

The Red Cloud War began at 5:00 A.M. the following day, when the Oglalas ran off horses from the post, then attacked the pursuit party. Two soldiers were killed and one wounded. On their way back to Fort Phil Kearny, the troopers found a nearby trading camp sacked. The trader and five others had been massacred.[13]

Over the next several months, the soldiers at Fort Phil Kearny were under siege. Through scouts and friendly Indians, Carrington learned Red Cloud now led a large number of Oglalas, Brulés, Miniconjous, and Hunkpapas, along with some Cheyennes, Arapahos, and Gros Ventres. Even the Crows were invited, and some joined. Soldiers and travelers were often attacked within plain view of the fort. Carrington had no idea how many hostiles he faced; he only knew that the 345 officers and men at Phil Kearny were badly outnumbered.[14]

More than once, attacks were driven back only by explosive shells from one of the howitzers at the post. Artillery was still new to the Indians, and the flying metal from shellbursts proved deadly in the first few encounters. They soon adjusted, however, scattering when the guns fired, and rendering cannon ineffective in most subsequent campaigns.

On November 3, sixty-three additional cavalrymen finally arrived at Fort Phil Kearny. Among them was Capt. William J. Fetterman, an arrogant, ambitious officer with an enviable Civil War record. New to the plains, Fetterman openly criticized Colonel Carrington for not taking the offensive against the Indians. The captain went so far as to state that with only eighty men, he could ride through the entire Sioux Nation. Fetterman was expressing what several officers already felt, and his words aggravated a growing anti-Carrington faction that polarized the command.

Only one month after Fetterman's arrival, Carrington himself had a near-miss with disaster. A band of warriors lured a company of soldiers led by Carrington out of range of the fort, and cut them off. The soldiers managed to fight their way back to safety with only two losses.

The action appealed to Red Cloud, who believed that with refinement a similar scenario could be used for a single, decisive battle that would break the government's will. An all-or-nothing engagement between two opposing forces went against the entire Lakota military tradition of hit-and-run attack. Yet it was typical of Red Cloud's innovative genius. The plan was simple. A small group of warriors would lure the soldiers over the ridges, beyond the view of the fort and out of range of the howitzers. Once the soldiers were out of sight, the main body of warriors would come out of concealment and cut the troops to pieces.

The first attempt came on December 19, when the Indian decoys attacked a wood train returning from the post sawmill with construction material. A relief force was sent under Capt. James W. Powell who, remembering the earlier fight, went directly to aid the wood train and did not pursue the Indians.

Two days later the Indians again attacked the train. Fetterman, using his army seniority, demanded the right to lead the relief force. Carrington assented, cautioning Fetterman to do just as Powell had done—relieve the train and escort it back to the post, avoiding all pursuit of the Indians.

Instead, Fetterman chased the Indians. The decoy party, which included young Crazy Horse, led him about two miles beyond several ridges until the troops found themselves completely surrounded. The soldiers fought for an hour, but when it was over Fetterman, who had boasted that with eighty men he could ride right through the Sioux Nation, was dead. His command had consisted of exactly eighty men besides himself. Once again, an entire military force had been annihilated by the Sioux. The action was led by Crazy Horse's old mentor, Hump. Red Cloud himself was not present, but there is little doubt that he planned the victory.

The army demanded vengeance for the Fetterman Massacre. Gen. William T. Sherman, commanding the Military Division of the Missouri—an administrative area that included the entire war zone—wanted an immediate punitive campaign to carry the war to the Indians. Realistically, such a campaign was impossible. The army had declined in both strength and quality after the Civil War, and many units were on Reconstruction duty in the occupied South. A disproportionate number of soldiers on the frontier were fresh recruits, and only a few were properly trained.

It made no difference, because Congress was not ready for such a campaign. As Red Cloud had anticipated, a military defeat, together with constant guerrilla warfare along the trails, had worn down the government. The Bozeman Trail was blocked by the Indians. Communication between military posts was difficult. Bands of raiders led by Crazy Horse and Small Hawk surrounded Fort Reno, and Red Cloud kept Phil Kearny under constant surveillance. The Wells Fargo agent in North Platte, Nebraska, was convinced no freight would reach Montana from the east in 1867. Freight rates to Forts Reno, Phil Kearny, and C. F. Smith became exorbitant, and even then the army had difficulty procuring contractors.

Yet another peace commission was organized to negotiate a treaty. Officially, its aim was to secure the same concessions as all previous treaties, among them, safe passage through Indian country.[15] In reality, its primary role was to ascertain the conditions under which Red Cloud and the other hostile chiefs would end the war.

It took time to get the chiefs to the peace conference, but on April 29, 1868, the agreement was signed. Officially known as the "Treaty with the Sioux—Brulé, Oglala, Miniconjou, Yanktonai, Hunkpapa, Blackfeet, Cuthead, Two Kettle, Sans Arcs, and Santee—and Arapaho, 1868," it is commonly called the Fort Laramie Treaty.

Under its terms, both sides agreed to end the war and maintain peace. The government was obligated to punish persons under U.S. jurisdiction who committed offenses against the Indians. The Indians promised to deliver up any offender of any race under their jurisdiction, who committed any offenses against the United States, or to pay an indemnity to the injured party. Although the Bozeman was to be closed, the Indians agreed to allow such other roads, railroads, and forms of transportation as the government deemed necessary, and not to restrict travel on those routes. The usual provisions were made for annuities, education, and allocation of farmable land at 160 acres per person, with implements, in the consistently vain hope that the Indians would make a 180-degree shift to farming. Two articles of the treaty, however, are worthy of special attention.

Under Article 2, the United States established a reservation comprising all of what is now the state of South Dakota west of the Missouri River, including most of the Black Hills. It stated that aside from those persons authorized under the treaty or permitted by the Indians with the consent of the government, no one "*shall ever be permitted to pass over, settle upon, or reside in the territory.* . . . [italics added]."

Article 16 was equally significant. Its full text states:

> The United States hereby agrees and stipulates that the country north of the North Platte River and east of the summits of the Big Horn Mountains shall be held and considered to be *unceded Indian territory,* and also stipulates and agrees that *no white person or persons shall be permitted to settle upon or occupy any portion of the same; or without the consent of the Indians first had and obtained, to pass through the same;* and it is further agreed that within ninety days after the conclusion of peace with all the bands of the Sioux Nation, the military posts now established in the territory in this article named shall be abandoned, and that the road leading to them and by them to the settlements in the Territory of Montana [the Bozeman Trail] shall be closed [italics added].[16]

Simply put, this article recognized that the Indians retained possession of vast tracts outside the reservation boundaries, and that the tribes had not ceded them to the federal government. This "unceded" land (which included large sections of southern Montana and northern Wyoming) was, in effect, an independent state under Indian control. Along with the Black Hills, the unceded land would be a key point of contention in the next major war.

While the federal government had the legal authority to grant the land exclusively to the Indians, in reality it lacked both the civil and military power necessary to keep others out. No one saw this more clearly than the generals. Years of experience had taught them that the white tide could not be stemmed, regardless of government edicts. Settlers would occupy the unceded lands, indeed the reservation itself, presenting the government with a fait accompli. The Indians would resist, and the army would be called in to clean up the mess.

For the time being, however, the War Department adhered to the terms of the treaty. The Bozeman was officially closed. Forts Reno, Phil Kearny, and C. F. Smith were abandoned, and the structures burned, either by retreating soldiers or advancing Indians, the record is not clear.

With the inauguration of President Ulysses S. Grant in 1869, General Sherman was elevated to command of the army, while Lt. Gen. Philip H. Sheridan succeeded him as commander of the Military Division of the Missouri. Like Sherman, Sheridan advocated a policy of force, insisting that no meaningful peace could be concluded until punitive expeditions had impressed the Indians with the power of the government. As a former departmental commander within the division, he had led a successful winter campaign on the southern plains, and so had field experience in Indian fighting. And knowing white settlement of the Indian lands must ultimately occur, the generals decided to take advanced precautions, penning the tribes into the reservation proper, regardless of treaty guarantees of the unceded lands.

On June 29, 1869, at Sherman's direction, Sheridan issued a general order acknowledging the jurisdiction of the agents and the Department of the Interior within reservation boundaries. But he added, "Outside the well-defined limits of their reservations [i.e., on the unceded Indian lands] they are under the original and exclusive jurisdiction of the military authority, and as a rule will be considered hostile."[17]

Barely a year after it was signed, the Fort Laramie Treaty became worthless.

3

Black Hills Fever

ULYSSES S. GRANT WAS A MAN OF PERSONAL INTEGRITY BUT NO
political acumen. He tended to fill many key positions with relatives and old Union Army cronies, some of whom were inept, dis-
honest, or both. The War Department and the Department of the
Interior were special plums because the vast network of military
and Indian supply contracts offered unbounded opportunities for
graft and outright theft.

Much of the military corruption centered around Secretary of
War William W. Belknap, to the disgust of his immediate subordinate, General Sherman. Barely on speaking terms with the secretary, and repelled by what he considered the moral and social
decay of Washington, Sherman removed army headquarters to St.
Louis, communicating with Belknap by telegram and only when
necessary.

Below Sherman, the country was divided into three army administrative regions, the largest of which was the aforementioned
Military Division of the Missouri. Headquartered in Chicago, this
division covered approximately the central two thirds of the
United States and its territories. Its commanding officer, Lieutenant General Sheridan, was responsible for the main theater of
the Indian wars and answered directly to Sherman.

The division itself was separated into four geographical departments—Texas, the Missouri, the Platte, and Dakota—each commanded by a brigadier general responsible to Sheridan. The areas affected by the Fort Laramie Treaty were in the Departments of Dakota and the Platte, which would be the scene of the Great Sioux War. The Department of the Platte, with headquarters in Omaha, and initially commanded by Brig. Gen. E.O.C. Ord, included Iowa, Nebraska, Wyoming, and Utah. The Department of Dakota, headquartered in St. Paul, Minnesota, and commanded by Brig. Gen. Alfred H. Terry, was composed of Minnesota, Dakota Territory (the modern states of North and South Dakota), and Montana. Within these departments were local districts and subdistricts, temporary administrative units created as needed by the department commanders and abolished when no longer necessary.

Despite corruption, poor training, and troop cutbacks, this vast military structure functioned more or less as the government intended. The same, however, could not be said for the Department of Interior's Indian Bureau, where a system of thefts and payoffs created shortages and unrest at the agencies.

Even in the best of situations, the agencies were a complex operation. They dealt directly with the Indians, administering government programs, distributing all payments, and implementing all treaty guarantees. It soon became obvious that given the size of the Great Sioux Reservation, and the immense population it was supposed to serve, the single agency provided in the Fort Laramie Treaty was not adequate. In all, nine agencies were finally established for the Sioux Reservation alone. The most important were the agencies that primarily served the Oglalas and Brulés, the two most populous Lakota tribes. These agencies were named Red Cloud and Spotted Tail, respectively, after the men with whom the government dealt as paramount chiefs.

Initially, the Red Cloud Agency was located on the North Platte, just west of the Nebraska-Wyoming line. The Spotted Tail Agency was on the Missouri River, twenty-three miles above Fort Randall in what is now South Dakota. The Brulés detested the site. The hot, humid climate on the Missouri was unhealthy to the Indians, who were accustomed to cool mountains and dry plains. The proximity to white settlement also caused friction and provided the Indians

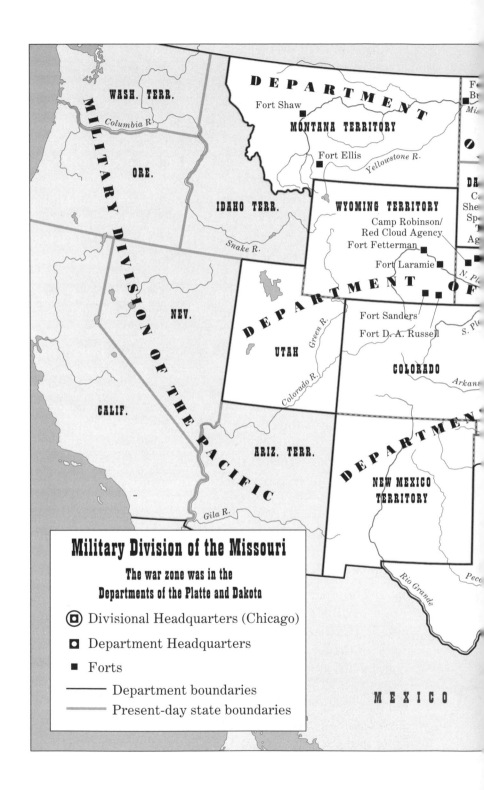

WASH. TERR.

Columbia R.

ORE.

IDAHO TERR.

Snake R.

NEV.

CALIF.

D E P A R T M E N T

Fort Shaw

MONTANA TERRITORY

Fort Ellis

Yellowstone R.

WYOMING TERRITORY

Camp Robinson/
Red Cloud Agency
Fort Fetterman

Fort Laramie

Green R.

UTAH

Colorado R.

D E P A R T M E N T   O F

Fort Sanders
Fort D. A. Russell

COLORADO

Arkans

S. Pl

N. Pl

Mis

DA

C

She

Sp

T

Ag

O

F

B

ARIZ. TERR.

D E P A R T M E N

NEW MEXICO
TERRITORY

Gila R.

Rio Grande

Pec

MEXICO

Military Division of the Missouri

The war zone was in the
Departments of the Platte and Dakota

◉ Divisional Headquarters (Chicago)

▣ Department Headquarters

■ Forts

— Department boundaries

— Present-day state boundaries

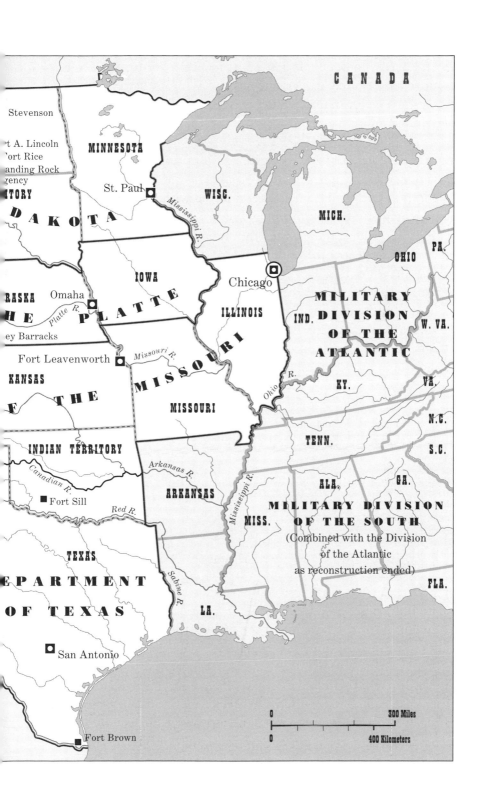

CANADA

Stevenson

t A. Lincoln
ort Rice
anding Rock
gency
TORY

MINNESOTA

St. Paul

WISC.

MICH.

DAKOTA

IOWA

PLATTE

Chicago

ILLINOIS

IND.

OHIO

PA.

MILITARY
DIVISION
OF THE
ATLANTIC

W. VA.

RASKA
HE

Omaha

Platte R.

KY.

VA.

ey Barracks

Fort Leavenworth

Missouri R.

THE

MISSOURI

R.

Ohio

KANSAS

MISSOURI

N.C.

TENN.

S.C.

INDIAN TERRITORY

Canadian R.

Arkansas R.

ALA.

GA.

Fort Sill

Red R.

ARKANSAS

MILITARY DIVISION
OF THE SOUTH
(Combined with the Division
of the Atlantic
as reconstruction ended)

MISS.

TEXAS

EPARTMENT

OF TEXAS

Sabine R.

LA.

FLA.

San Antonio

300 Miles

Fort Brown

0

0

400 Kilometers

with easy access to liquor. In 1871, the federal government agreed to remove the Spotted Tail Agency to the White River country of northwestern Nebraska, 225 miles west of the Missouri, which the Brulés found more agreeable. Eventually the Red Cloud Agency was also moved to the White River country.[1] The new agencies, both of which were outside the reservation proper, were protected by two new military posts, Camps Robinson and Sheridan.

In addition to the nine agencies connected with the Sioux Reservation, which served the Sioux Nations, Cheyennes, Arapahos, and affiliated groups, there were other reservations in the northern part of Dakota Territory, and in Montana. Chief among these were the Gros Ventres, Piegan Blackfeet, Blood, and River Crow Reservation, served by the Fort Peck Agency in the east and Blackfeet Agency in the west, with a central subagency at Fort Belknap; the Arikara, Mandan, Gros Ventres Reservation, with an agency at Fort Berthold; and the Mountain Crow Reservation, whose agency was about a hundred miles west of the present Crow Agency near Hardin, Montana. Like Red Cloud and Spotted Tail, most of these agencies had some sort of military presence, although Fort Berthold, an abandoned military post, was used only for Indian purposes; the army was located nearby at Fort Stevenson, a new post.

Despite corruption in the Indian Bureau, it might be said of this period that the Indians' worst enemies were their friends—the social engineers of the East who, in their misguided sense of wisdom and Christian charity, presumed to dictate the best interests of a people about whom they knew nothing. President Grant unwittingly contributed to the problem when, in an effort to remove the Indian Bureau from congressional patronage, he turned the agencies and their superintendencies over to religious groups.

Now in power, the "friends of the Indian" flexed their muscles, and began mandating government policy.[2] Their programs to "civilize" the Indians were many and varied. The most insidious, however, was an implied plan to starve them until they abandoned their culture and adopted the white way of life. And when the buffalo began to disappear from the Midwest under the weight of expanded settlement and commercial hunting, so did the Indians' means of self-sufficiency. They became more dependent on government rations issued at the agencies, and the government rations became leverage to enforce obedience.[3]

To the whites, this was the only way to save the Indian from himself. There was no middle ground. Grant himself summed up the feeling at the beginning of his second term in 1873, when he said:

> My efforts in the future will be . . . to bring the aborigines of the country under the benign influences of education and civilization. It is either this or war of extermination. . . . The moral view of the question should be considered and the question asked, Can not the Indian be made a useful and productive member of society by proper teaching and treatment?[4]

The Indian, of course, already considered himself a useful and productive member of his own society. He was productive—hunting, making weapons, breeding and breaking ponies, and any number of other activities vital to a nomadic, tribal people. The president and his associates, however, meant labor according to white standards, specifically agriculture. Farming implements were sent to the reservation, and the Indians were expected to learn to use them, earning their way by "honest" toil.

Most Indians viewed this with undisguised contempt, drawing away from the agencies except at ration time. Those who tried to comply suffered from the same vagaries of nature—drought, grasshopper plagues, and soil unsuited to agriculture—that had frustrated white farmers in the region, which is to say west of the 100th meridian. It was essentially a problem of geography.

As conditions at the agencies deteriorated, and agency rations failed to meet the needs of the people, more and more Lakotas looked to the rich hunting grounds of the north, where the Hunkpapa chief, Sitting Bull, called out

> Look at me and see if I am poor, or my people either. . . . You are fools to make yourselves slaves to a piece of fat bacon, some hardtack, and a little sugar and coffee.[5]

Now that Red Cloud had come to terms with the whites, Sitting Bull was emerging as the most influential leader of the non-treaty

Indians. He was, according to a Cheyenne warrior who knew him, "the most consistent advocate of the idea of living out of all touch with white people. He would not go to the reservation nor would he accept any rations or other gifts coming from the white man government."[6]

Younger than Red Cloud, Sitting Bull was not exactly certain of his age or place of birth, although most evidence indicates he probably was born in March 1831, on the Grand River a few miles below what is now Bullhead, South Dakota. He was the only son of Returns-Again, a noted Hunkpapa warrior who had changed his own name to Sitting Bull upon seeing a vision of a buffalo bull. As a child, the son's careful, deliberate manner earned him the name Slow. According to Stanley Vestal, one of his first biographers, the boy called Slow inherited the paternal name, Sitting Bull, after counting his first coup on an enemy warrior.

The coup was the ultimate act of daring, and originated in the days when Lakotas fought at close quarters for the simple lack of long-range weapons. Even after the development of bows and arrows and the acquisition of firearms close combat remained the only truly manly form of battle, particularly after improved weapons increased the dangers of a hand-to-hand fight. Thus the tradition of the coup emerged, by which prestige went to the first warrior to "count" or physically touch an enemy, living or dead. The total number of coups counted by an individual warrior did much to determine his social position among his people.

For counting his first coup, against a Crow at the age of fourteen, young Sitting Bull was allowed to wear a white feather. The following year, at fifteen, he received a red feather, indicating he had been wounded in combat. In the ensuing years, the number of white and red feathers grew.

Despite his reputation for valor, Sitting Bull's main hold on his people was his "good medicine." He seemed able to predict victory, and know when to fight and when to withdraw. By the late 1860s, Sitting Bull's prestige was such that the Lakotas took an unprecedented step—the creation of a single, paramount chieftaincy to replace to traditional autonomous tribal structure.

The idea was devised by Four Horn, one of the four Shirt Wearers, or head chiefs within the Hunkpapa tribe. Approximately one third of the entire Lakota Nation had rejected the reservation created under the Fort Laramie Treaty, and the Hunkpapas made up a disproportionate share of that group. Four Horn determined the non-treaty Lakotas of all tribes needed unified leadership to counter the influence of Red Cloud, Spotted Tail, and other chiefs now cooperating with the government. Although Sitting Bull was not from a chiefly family, he had more prestige than any other non-treaty leader, making him the logical choice.

Four Horn's idea appealed to powerful chiefs of other tribes, among them Crazy Horse of the Oglalas, Makes Room and Lame Deer of the Miniconjous, and Spotted Eagle of the Sans Arcs. Even the Cheyenne leaders were ready to support Sitting Bull, though Lakota politics ordinarily did not interest them. Meeting in council on the Rosebud River of Montana, the leading chiefs formally proclaimed Sitting Bull paramount chief of the Lakota Nation.

Despite support from the chiefs, and the obvious strategic practicality, Sitting Bull's elevation was regarded as a usurpation by many Lakotas, especially those realistic enough to understand that the old, nomadic existence was drawing to a close. Rather than unify, it created a permanent breech between Sitting Bull and Red Cloud, and divided even the Hunkpapas into pro– and anti–Sitting Bull factions.[7]

As early as 1871, Sitting Bull was regarded as leader of the Lakotas who were disillusioned with Red Cloud's tolerance of the government. This faction abandoned the Red Cloud Agency, prompting the commissioner of Indian Affairs to observe: "Unless carefully managed, these seceders, reported to have 800 lodges, may cause great trouble to the Government." Military leaders were quick to point out that unless the Indian Bureau could control the Montana bands, hostilities would erupt.[8]

Among the generals, Sitting Bull had a worthy adversary in Phil Sheridan, commander of the Division of the Missouri, and the army's sole lieutenant general. Sheridan has been described by biographer Paul Andrew Hutton as "the perfect soldier for his times." His ability to grasp a situation was almost uncanny. One field officer of the period wrote:

Sitting in his distant office in Chicago, he was so thoroughly informed that he could order out his cavalry to search through a region hitherto known only to the Sioux and tell them just where they
would find the highway by which the vast hordes of hostiles under
Sitting Bull were receiving daily reinforcements and welcome supplies of ammunition from the agencies three and four hundred miles
to the southeast.[9]

Like Sitting Bull, Philip Henry Sheridan did not know exactly
where or when he was born. For official purposes, he listed Al-
bany, New York, March 6, 1831, although he probably was born
in County Cavan, Ireland, shortly before his parents emigrated.
While he was still an infant, his parents settled in Somerset, Ohio,
where he lived until 1848, when he was appointed to West Point.
Sheridan's western, working-class Irish Catholic background made
him feel out of place in the patrician, eastern, largely Episcopalian
military academy, and a fight with an upperclassman led to a one-
year suspension. He returned to graduate thirty-fifth in a class of
fifty-two in 1853, and was posted to the western frontier. He was
in Portland, Oregon, when the Civil War broke out and propelled
him to greatness.

Sheridan viewed the United States as a single, continental nation
rather than a collection of autonomous states and territories, and
he would fight any adversary—southern white, striking industrial
worker, or western Indian—to make it so. He put down strikes in
Chicago, and pursued the Indian wars on the frontier with the
same cold inflexibility with which he had devastated the Shenandoah Valley during the Civil War.

A bachelor until relatively late in life, Sheridan was hard drinking, high living, and profane. His odd physique—a large, stocky
body set on short, stumpy legs, the whole surmounted by a can-
nonball head with close-cropped hair—led people to call him "Little Phil."[10]

The northern plains were not foremost in Sheridan's mind during the first half of the 1870s, for Texas, Oklahoma, and Kansas
had been aflame for decades with vicious fighting between the
Kiowas and Comanches on one side, and the whites on the other.
The situation in Texas was particularly critical, since the conflict

was passed down through generations, and both sides viewed it as a war of extermination. This hereditary hatred came to a head with the outbreak of the Red River War in June 1874 and, although Ranald Mackenzie won a decisive victory at Palo Duro Canyon, Texas, in September, the army was still mopping up isolated pockets of resistance in late spring 1875.

While fighting raged on the southern plains, the Indians on the Great Sioux Reservation suddenly found themselves affected by an unrelated event in the East. As is often the case after a long, exhausting conflict, the eight years following the Civil War were an era of unbounded optimism and speculation, particularly in gold, railroads, and paper money. In 1873, however, the prosperity collapsed. Businesses failed. Unemployment rose to one of the highest levels in history. Paper money lost value. And, much to the satisfaction of Sitting Bull, railroad construction on the plains halted.

The annual annuity to the Sioux was $1.25 million, which a discouraged public and its elected Congress increasingly grudged. At the same time, these Indians blocked access to the Black Hills, which offered new opportunities for settlement and—more important for a sagging economy—gold, rumored in the hills for more than a decade.[11]

By 1874, the depression had reached the point where rumors could no longer be ignored. Despite government policy and treaty guarantees, companies began organizing to send prospectors into the Black Hills.[12] Although these expeditions were disbanded under orders from the army, it was obvious that some sort of scientific survey of the Black Hills was needed, and in June 1874, Lt. Col. George Armstrong Custer led an expedition into the Black Hills. Officially it was a reconnaissance to consider sites for new military posts. There is little question, however, that the rumors of gold constituted an unofficial reason since, in addition to engineers, topographers, and other specialists needed for purely military purposes, the entourage included two veteran prospectors.

Custer was a thirty-four-year-old native of New Rumley, Ohio, who grew up in the home of a half-sister in Monroe, Michigan. He was appointed to West Point where, after a lackluster career, he graduated last in a class of thirty-four in 1861. Small by modern standards, and sparely built, Custer was pale and prone to freckles from prolonged exposure to the sun. Early in his career, he cut a dashing figure, riding into battle with his long, strawberry blond hair flowing behind. As he grew older, he wore it shorter, and cut it very close for field service.

For all his failings at West Point, Custer rose rapidly in the Civil War, and within two years became the second youngest general in the army. His military success often depended on panache and that phenomenal good fortune that the soldiers came to call "Custer's luck." Unimaginative in combat, he preferred an all-or-nothing cavalry charge, which worked more often than it failed, although he and his troops had some very narrow escapes.

After the war, Custer took a reduction from brevet rank, and in 1867 was appointed lieutenant colonel of the newly organized Seventh Cavalry. Officially second in command, he was de facto field commander of the regiment, because successive colonels were usually on detached duty elsewhere.

Custer's first experience in Indian fighting came in 1867 during a brief, mismanaged campaign known as Hancock's War, which served only to alienate erstwhile peaceful Indians. Because of several serious errors in judgment, the campaign ended with Custer suspended from rank and pay for one year, under sentence of court-martial. Phil Sheridan intervened and got the sentence lifted so that Custer could join him for an expedition against the Kiowas and Southern Cheyennes along the Washita River of Oklahoma in the winter of 1868–69.

In the Washita fight, an incident occurred that cost Custer the confidence of at least half his officers and no doubt influenced events at the Little Bighorn. After the main fight, Maj. Joel Elliott took a detachment to pursue fleeing Indians. As Custer prepared to withdraw from the field and return to camp, he was informed that Elliott had not returned. He shrugged it off and only later learned Elliott's detachment had been killed to the last man only a few miles away, and easily could have been saved. This seeming betrayal of a fellow officer split the Seventh into two factions: the so-called Custer clan, of close friends and relatives with whom he surrounded himself, and those who hated him and found their leadership under Capt. Frederick W. Benteen.

Despite his limitations as a field commander, Custer's writings and his wide variety of interests suggest an intelligence far above the average. But like many brilliant people, he could not channel his energies down a single path. His personal life was like his military career—disjointed and devoid of any clear goal. He lived from one day to the next, spontaneously and thoughtlessly, reacting to circumstances rather than creating them. This trait kept him in a great deal of trouble, and ultimately destroyed him.[13]

The proposed reconnaissance into the Black Hills was perfectly suited to Custer, who enjoyed camping and hunting. It was also perfectly suited to the failing economy, for the two prospectors did find gold. "Black Hills Fever" swept the country, and a gold rush was soon under way. Within weeks, General Terry, in the Department of Dakota, advised Sheridan that corporations were organizing at Yankton, Dakota Territory, and Sioux City, Iowa, to send mining expeditions to the hills.

Sheridan's response was to direct Terry, and General Ord in the Department of the Platte, to use force if necessary to prevent incursions into the reservation. On the other hand, Sheridan wrote, "Should Congress open up the country to settlement by extinguishing the treaty rights of the Indians, the undersigned will give cordial support to the settlement of the Black Hills."[14] By stating in advance his position on a congressional act that had not occurred and—at that time—was not even contemplated, Sheridan made his feelings on the matter very clear.

Far from being callous, Sheridan's attitude was simply realistic. Despite formal military opposition, prospectors and miners began moving into the Black Hills, and it was difficult for the poorly manned and equipped army to do much about it. Given the lure of gold and the high unemployment rate, General Terry anticipated the hills would soon be overrun. "Every part of it which is left unguarded will be invaded," he reported to divisional headquarters.[15]

In 1875, the Black Hills gold rush boomed. President Grant advised army headquarters:

> All expeditions into the portion of the Indian Territory known as
> The Black Hills Country must be prevented as long as the present

treaty exists. Efforts are now being made to arrange for the extin-
guishment of the Indian title, and all proper means will be used to
accomplish that end.

   If however the steps which are to be taken toward opening The
Country to settlement fail, those persons at present within that territory, without authority, must be expelled.[16]

By "steps," of course, Grant meant yet another treaty in which
the Indians would surrender the Black Hills. He did not seriously
expect failure in acquiring the hills by fair means or foul, any more
than he expected the military to keep prospectors out. A new government expedition to the hills, in the summer of 1875, found miners already staking claims. Some showed off gold to a *New York
Herald* correspondent accompanying the survey, who wrote,
"They emphatically assured us that there was plenty of gold all
along the stream and quartz lodes containing it in the hills." With
such reports reaching the economically depressed cities of the East,
the Indian position in the hills was hopeless.[17]

   Moreover, a recent change of command in the Department of
the Platte made the prospectors and settlers more optimistic than
ever. They knew the Indians would not surrender the Black Hills
without a fight. Already some were retaliating, and prospectors
had been killed. When the war came, the gold seekers wanted a
firm military commander with an established reputation for Indian
fighting. They believed they got it that spring, when Brig. Gen.
George Crook replaced Ord as commander of the Platte.

   An able commander during the Civil War, Crook had proven
even more successful in recent campaigns against the Apaches in
Arizona. It was fully expected that "Arizona" Crook would handle the Sioux just as he had handled the Apaches.[18]

4

The Road to War

THE MOVE TOWARD WAR ACCELERATED IN THE AUTUMN OF 1875. IN September, General Crook reported that Indian livestock raids had become commonplace in Wyoming, Nebraska, and Colorado, and the trails of stolen animals often led to the Great Sioux Reservation. The hostiles also obtained supplies, firearms, and recruits among the Indians at the various agencies on the reservation.[1]

That same month, as part of Grant's effort to "extinguish" Indian title to the Black Hills, a government commission convened at the Red Cloud Agency to negotiate purchase not only of the hills themselves but all the unceded lands of the Powder River and Bighorns as well. Its members included Sen. W. B. Allison, chairman; General Terry; S. D. Hinman, a Sioux missionary; G. P. Beauvais, a trader who had spent years dealing with the Sioux; and several easterners with no Indian experience at all.

The Fort Laramie Treaty stipulated that any future agreements must be ratified by a three-quarters majority among all adult Sioux males, and couriers began carrying summonses to every camp they could find. This was the first mistake. The proud Lakota Sioux, particularly those of the non-treaty bands, resented being ordered to a council in their own territory. When a courier arrived in Sit-

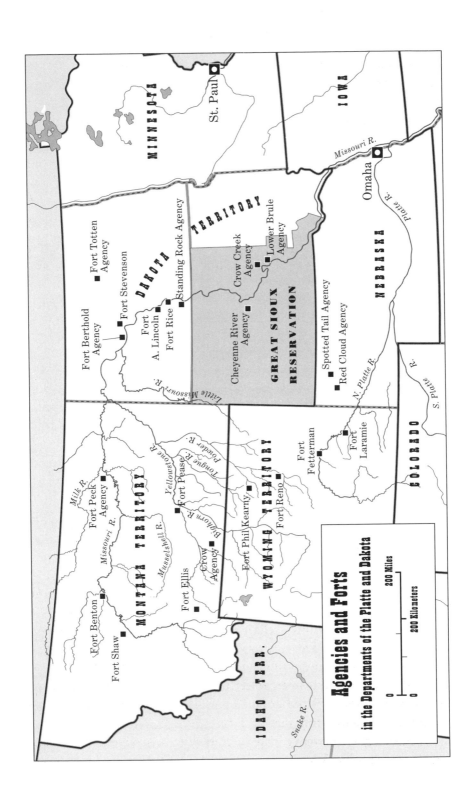

Agencies and Forts
in the Departments of the Platte and Dakota

0   200 Miles

0   200 Kilometers

MINNESOTA

St. Paul

IOWA

Missouri R.

Omaha

Platte R.

DAKOTA TERRITORY

Fort Totten Agency

Fort Stevenson

Standing Rock Agency

Crow Creek Agency

Lower Brule Agency

NEBRASKA

Fort Berthold Agency

Fort A. Lincoln

Fort Rice

Cheyenne River Agency

GREAT SIOUX RESERVATION

Spotted Tail Agency

Red Cloud Agency

Little Missouri R.

N. Platte R.

S. Platte R.

COLORADO

Fort Fetterman

Fort Laramie

Milk R.

Fort Peck Agency

Missouri R.

MONTANA TERRITORY

Musselshell R.

Yellowstone R.

Powder R.

Tongue R.

Fort Pease

Bighorn R.

Fort Phil Kearny

Fort Reno

WYOMING TERRITORY

Fort Ellis

Crow Agency

Fort Benton

Fort Shaw

IDAHO TERR.

Snake R.

ting Bull's camp, the chief expressed the feelings of the non-treaty Sioux, asking:

> Are you the Great God that made me? Or was it the Great God that made me, who sent you? If He asks me to come see Him, I will go, but the Big Chief of the White men must come see me. I will not go to the reservation. I have no land to sell. There is plenty of game here for us. We have enough ammunition. We don't want any white men here.[2]

Most non-treaty bands boycotted the council, sending word that any chief who agreed to the sale did so at his peril. Nevertheless, representatives came from throughout the Sioux reservation. One commissioner estimated at least 20,000 were present. The Indians were angry and quarreling among themselves, and as the days passed the commissioners began to sense the negotiations were doomed to failure.

The government was prepared to offer $6 million for outright title to the Indian lands. Years of dealing with whites, however, had sharpened Lakota business skills. For a century, since they had first occupied the Black Hills, they had valued the region as sacred, and they reasoned the white insistence on owning them meant they were even more valuable. This perception was strengthened when the agents for Red Cloud and Spotted Tail, genuinely interested in the welfare of the Indians, told them the true value of the area was forty to fifty million. Still, a large, vocal minority, composed of virtually all the fighting men, refused to consider sale at any price.

After arguing for two weeks, during which the various Lakota factions frequently came close to going at each other with weapons, nothing had been accomplished. Toward the end of the conference, fights broke out among the Indians, and the warrior police societies formed a protective cordon around the commissioners. Young Man-Afraid-of-His-Horses, son of the older Man-Afraid and a respected warrior in his own right, ordered the crowd to disperse until it cooled down. That night, more than half the Indians left the gathering, further diminishing hope of an agreement.

A meeting with twenty leading chiefs the following day brought no better results. Red Cloud demanded that in exchange for the

Black Hills, the government feed and clothe the Lakotas for seven generations, as well as make a cash payment of $600 million, an arbitrary amount whose enormity he probably did not even comprehend. Each of the other chiefs set his own price, giving notice that his particular figure was not negotiable. The commissioners then decided to ask for a lease on mining rights at $400,000 a year. Even this was unacceptable. There had been enough concessions. The government could not have the Black Hills. To Agent E. A. Howard at the Spotted Tail Agency, the future appeared "cloudy and threatening."[3]

On November 1, Edward P. Smith, commissioner of Indian Affairs, observed that the non-treaty Sioux had never recognized the authority of the government, except to occasionally draw rations at an agency. The non-treaty Sioux would have argued whether even the draft of rations constituted recognition. By refusing to sign the Fort Laramie Treaty, they had made it very plain they did not acknowledge any government jurisdiction over themselves or the land. If the government was willing to issue them rations anyway, that was entirely the government's affair. The fact that the non-treaty Sioux drew rations did not obligate them to anyone. The government saw it differently. Having accepted federal largesse, Washington officials rationalized, the Indians had become government wards, treaty or no treaty. Smith was determined to impress that point on them, saying it would probably be necessary

> to compel the northern non-treaty Sioux, under the leadership of Sitting Bull . . . and such other outlaws from the several agencies as have attached themselves to these same hostiles, to cease marauding and settle down, as the other Sioux have done, at some designated point.[4]

President Grant no doubt welcomed this assessment. That same week, he met privately at the White House with Secretary of War Belknap and Generals Sherman and Crook to discuss Indian affairs in general, and the Black Hills situation in particular. As the meeting progressed, Grant summoned Secretary of the Interior Zachariah Chandler, Assistant Secretary B. R. Cowan, and Commissioner Smith. The fact that the president initiated the meeting with the secretary of war and the generals, not calling the ranking members of the Interior Department until midway through, indicates Grant had already made up his mind that military action was necessary.

The conference itself was not recorded, and is known only through discreet leaks to the press, and remarks to close associates by the participants. It appears that at some point during the discussion, Crook pointed out miners were entering the hills from every direction, and it was impossible to keep them out. By the time the meeting ended, it was agreed the government would no longer interfere with gold seekers in the Black Hills.[5]

Almost immediately, justification presented itself for military action against the Indians. On November 9, Indian Inspector E. C. Watkins reported 30 to 40 lodges under Sitting Bull, "who has been an out-and-out anti-agency Indian," and a band of some 120 lodges under Crazy Horse from the Red Cloud Agency did not accept the government's reservation policy, and continued making war on both friendly tribes and settlers. Watkins recommended troops be used to subjugate them. Acting as though they had not already come to a similar decision in the White House conference, the generals used Watkins's and similar reports from the Department of the Interior to justify their own calls for action.[6]

On December 6, Commissioner Smith, acting on Interior Secretary Chandler's instructions, directed the agents at the Nebraska and Dakota agencies to advise Sitting Bull and other "hostile" Indians that the government required them to be within the bounds of the reservations on or before January 31, 1876. The fact that Sitting Bull and the other non-treaty chiefs were not obligated to be on a reservation, and that any Indian had a legal right to be on the unceded lands, was no longer relevant. Couriers began taking the ultimatum to the various bands on December 12, and would continue to do so even after the deadline, until February 4. Having set the stage for war on instructions from his superiors, Smith became a scapegoat for the failure of the Indians to remain within the reservations, and was bundled off to Canada in a diplomatic post. He was replaced as Indian commissioner by another Smith, this one being John Q.

John Q. Smith later would attempt to justify the war by stating "no regard" was paid by the Indians to the government's order. Initially, however, some agents were optimistic that the Indians would cooperate and comply with the terms. On December 31, John Burke, agent to the Hunkpapas at Standing Rock, wrote that he was sending runners to the various bands under his jurisdiction. Many of those who could be contacted had already indicated they would come in by late winter or early spring.[7] Burke did not point out that late winter or early spring was after the deadline, apparently assuming that his superiors would understand that such a large-scale effort at communication, and large-scale effort in response, was not feasible in the dead of winter, when blizzards swept the northern plains and drifting snow blocked the trails and mountain passes.

At the Spotted Tail Agency, Howard was more confident than Burke. He believed the ultimatum had time to reach the northern camps by January 3, 1876, well before the deadline, and that Sitting Bull was fully aware of the government's intentions.[8]

Chandler, however, had already put the army on notice that he would request military intervention if the Indians refused to come in to their "assigned" reservations by the January 31 deadline. In response to Sherman's request for an assessment of military preparedness, Sheridan polled Crook and Terry. Crook felt he could undertake operations whenever the Indian Bureau deemed necessary. Terry believed Sitting Bull's band was encamped at or near the mouth of the Little Missouri River, and that a quick movement against it could be decisive in winter. There were already sufficient troops in the Department of Dakota to do the job. On the other hand, Terry tried, as gently as possible, to warn the volatile Sheridan that weather increasingly would be a determining factor. Operating alone, his cavalry units would be able to carry rations and forage for only a few days in the field, totally inadequate for the hundreds of miles they would have to cover; they needed supply wagons, which would bog down in snow and mud once the full force of winter set in.

Failing—or refusing—to grasp the full implications of Terry's report, Sheridan convinced himself that the two generals were advocating a large-scale winter campaign, one of his favorite tactics.

The southern plains, where he had personally exploited the winter, offered little shelter from the arctic blasts sweeping down from Canada, and Indians gathered in protected bottomlands where they stayed the entire season. Fast-moving cavalry operating from closely spaced forts caught the Indians in camp, destroying their lodges, pony herds, and food stores, exposing them to the elements and breaking their will to fight.

"As the commands of these two officers embrace all the Indians against whom military action was contemplated," Sheridan told Sherman, "it will be seen that the movement is considered practicable, and I earnestly request, should operations be determined upon, that directions to that effect be communicated to me as speedily as possible, so that the enemy may be taken at the greatest disadvantage."[9]

Sheridan seemed to ignore Terry's subtle references to the northern winter. Not being familiar with those latitudes, Sheridan did not know that it was the troops who were confined to their isolated posts by weather, while the Indians moved with relative freedom along chains of sheltered valleys surrounded by vast, high mountain ranges. The winter of 1875–76, which would be particularly long and severe, had not yet completely set in. By the time word came to commence hostilities, the season had unleashed its full fury. Although Crook would be able to begin his march northward through Wyoming, Terry's troops in Montana would be frozen in place, cut off from their supply sources until the spring thaws, and Terry would be asking for time to get them into the field.[10]

NOT ONLY DID THE FREE-ROAMING INDIANS BALK AT REPORTING to their agencies, but the agency Indians grew restless as their food gave out. As early as March 1875, Custer had reported shortages at Standing Rock. "The supplies received from the Government constitute the entire support of the Indians belonging to the Agency . . . and the condition of the Indians at Standing Rock is such to entitle the subject to fair and proper treatment," he complained.[11]

The Standing Rock Agency was not alone. By the end of 1875, the situations at the Red Cloud and Spotted Tail Agencies were becoming critical. Upon arriving at Red Cloud in December, newly appointed Agent James S. Hastings initially found the agency Oglalas reasonably quiet, and well disposed toward the government. After all, the order was directed toward non-treaty bands, and did not affect them. A month later, however, both Hastings and Howard reported supplies of flour and beef, on which the reservation Indians subsisted, would be exhausted by March 1. Hastings also pointed out any attempt to convert the Indians to agriculture was doomed to failure, since the climate was not suitable. He and Howard both recommended Congress authorize emergency appropriations to feed the Indians for the remainder of the winter.

Congress took no action, and the Oglalas and Brulés at the agencies grew hungry. In agencies with garrisons nearby, Indian women sold themselves to the soldiers, as one agent put it, "for something to cover their limbs and for food for themselves and their kin." Discontent mounted, and people began slipping out to join Sitting Bull.[12]

By January 21, 1876, only ten days before the deadline, some of the agents still had not reported on the Indian response. With the exception of Agent Howard, who felt the non-agency Indians were aware of the order, the agents who did reply felt more time was needed. Nevertheless, the new Commissioner Smith was satisfied that

> enough has been done to fully commit the [Interior] Department to the policy of restraining by force of arms, any further outbreak or insubordination on the part of these defiant and hostile bands should they refuse to comply [before January 31] with the demands then made upon them.
>
> Certainly I can conceive of nothing more damaging to the authority of the government, not yet fully recognized by other bands of Sioux, than a failure to execute threats of Military operations so clearly made.[13]

Secretary Chandler sent Smith's memorandum to Belknap, who forwarded copies to Sherman, Sheridan, Crook, and Terry. Upon reading his copy, Sheridan commented, "The matter of notifying the Indians to come in is perhaps well to put on paper, but it will in all probability be regarded as a good joke by the Indians." Sherman agreed.[14]

Not everyone was laughing. At Standing Rock, Agent Burke had experienced a serious disruption in communications, which made him increasingly uneasy as the expiration date approached. On January 30, with only one day left, he reported that couriers trying to deliver the ultimatum to bands not already contacted had been delayed because of fighting between the Sioux and Gros Ventres. He requested an extension of the deadline, pointing out that intertribal warfare aside, weather prevented timely delivery to all the bands affected by it.

No single document deserved more careful consideration than Burke's brief but realistic appraisal of the situation. Had the government acted on this message and been a little more patient, perhaps a general war could have been averted. On February 7, Hastings at the Red Cloud Agency wrote that Crazy Horse and Black Twin were at Bear Butte, and reportedly were en route to the agency with between 3,000 and 4,000 people. Hastings's report, however, did not reach Washington for over a week, and was not sent to the War Department until February 17. By then it was too late.

Although the government machinery, by both accident and design, was rapidly destroying any chance for peace, Sitting Bull himself now contributed directly to the problem. He was apparently attempting to keep the whites off balance with a series of confusing messages that only clouded the issue. He maintained regular contact with the Sioux and Assiniboines at the Wolf Point and Fort Peck Agencies, and in early February sent word through them that he did not want war. Instead, he wanted to visit Fort Peck and confer with officials there since, he said, the rumors about his hostility were exaggerated. A similar message was sent to the agency at Fort Berthold, through two Indians who had been with them since summer. Sitting Bull likewise stated his intention to visit Berthold, this time to trade his accumulation of buffalo robes and dried meat. But the two Indians also repeated rumors circulating in Sitting

Bull's camp that once the trading was completed, the Sioux would continue on to the Black Hills and drive out any prospectors they found.[15]

This was what the officials in Washington wanted to hear—that the Sioux planned to attack whites in the Black Hills. The government was in no mood to be realistic or patient, or to try and figure out what was on Sitting Bull's mind. The war had been planned for months. The military machinery for waging the war had already been set into motion. Sherman was ready for a showdown, and throughout the frontier officers were eager for any action that might bring promotion. On February 1, Chandler formally turned the non-agency Sioux over to the War Department, advising Belknap that the Indians were now the army's affair.[16]

Oddly enough, no immediate action was taken. Frustrated, Sheridan advised that success was impossible unless orders were issued immediately. He pointed out a winter campaign was imperative to take advantage of the weather, which slowed Indian movements.[17] Exactly why the winter would slow the Indians enough for attack by Sheridan's troops but would not impede their efforts to comply with the government's ultimatum was not explained.

The army was finally authorized to move against the Sioux on February 7. The following day, confidential messages were sent to Terry and Crook, instructing them to commence hostilities as soon as possible. Sheridan knew that Crook, who could move on short notice, planned to operate in the country of the Bighorn Mountains in northeastern Wyoming, near the headwaters of the Powder, Tongue, Rosebud, and Bighorn Rivers, a favorite Indian hunting ground. He now sent a telegram to Terry, inquiring about the status of his preparations, and his plans for the campaign.[18]

Terry was in a bind. Winter had brought his department to a complete standstill, and Custer, whom he felt he needed, was winding up a five-month leave in the east. He could only respond:

Sitting Bull has left the Little Missouri for the Yellowstone, probably as high up as [its confluence with] Powder River. I report this not for the purpose of making objection to any orders I may receive, but to put the Lieutenant General in possession of all the information which I have. I suggest that Colonel Custer be directed to report here on his return to [Fort Abraham] Lincoln.[19]

This meant Sitting Bull was miles from his last known position. He could move northward, away from Crook, without hindrance, since Terry's troops would be unable to block him at least until early spring. Furious at Terry, and perhaps with himself for not grasping the implications of Terry's earlier references to weather, Sheridan replied in frustration:

> I have no specific instructions to give you about Indian hostilities. If Sitting Bull is not on the Little Missouri, as heretofore supposed to be, and cannot be reached by a quick march, as you formerly contemplated, I am afraid that little can be done by you at the present time. I am not well enough acquainted with the character of the winters and early springs in your latitude to give any instructions, and you will have to use your judgement [sic] as to what you may be able to accomplish at the present time or early spring.[20]

On that sour note, the Great Sioux War began.

PART II

THE OPENING GUNS

5

The Army Takes the Field

AT THE BEGINNING OF 1876, THE GOVERNMENT ESTIMATED THE
war would involve no more than 3,000 non-treaty Lakotas, of
which only 600 to 800 were warriors.[1] Terry's intelligence indicated most were in the Powder River country straddling the line
between southeastern Montana and Wyoming. Sheridan's plan, as
analyzed by Col. John Gibbon, commander of the Western District
of Montana under Terry, was to

> have in the field a number of columns, so that the moving Indian vil-
> lages cannot avoid all of them, and have these columns cooperate
> under some common head [in this case, Sheridan in Chicago]. Each
> of them being strong enough to take care of itself, the Indians, if
> successful in eluding one, will in all probability be encountered by
> one of the others.[2]

Like the winter campaign, the converging columns had been
used successfully against the southern Plains Indians, and Sheridan
incorporated them into his plan. There would be three: two from
Terry's department and one from Crook's.

Terry's troops were concentrated in two general areas hundreds
of miles apart, around Forts Shaw and Ellis in western Montana,

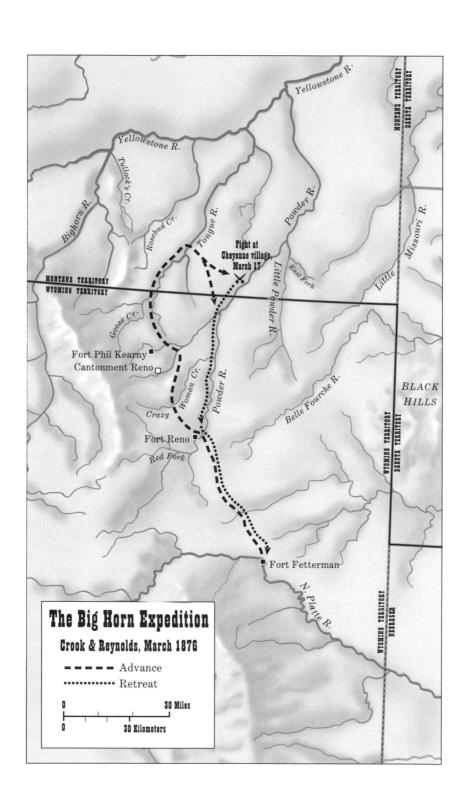

Yellowstone R.

Yellowstone R.

MONTANA TERRITORY
DAKOTA TERRITORY

Tullock's Cr.

Bighorn R.

Rosebud Cr.

Tongue R.

Powder R.

Missouri R.

Little

East Fork

Fight at
Cheyenne village,
March 17

MONTANA TERRITORY
WYOMING TERRITORY

Little Powder R.

Goose Cr.

Fort Phil Kearny
Cantonment Reno

Woman Cr.

Powder R.

Belle Fourche R.

BLACK
HILLS

Crazy

Fort Reno

WYOMING TERRITORY
DAKOTA TERRITORY

Red Fork

Fort Fetterman

N. Platte R.

WYOMING TERRITORY
NEBRASKA

The Big Horn Expedition

Crook & Reynolds, March 1876

- – – – Advance
- ·········· Retreat

0   30 Miles

0   30 Kilometers

and among the forts along the Missouri River in Dakota Territory.[3] Colonel Gibbon would lead the Montana troops eastward along the Yellowstone River, ultimately linking with the Dakota Column moving west under Custer. In Crook's department, most of the soldiers necessary for Sheridan's plan were in southeastern Wyoming, and would move north toward the other two columns.[4] If all worked well, Gibbon and Custer would force the Indians southward toward Crook's men, who, in turn, would drive them north again. Caught between these forces, they would be battered back and forth until they had no choice but surrender, as had happened in the Red River War on the southern plains.

Alfred Howe Terry, the man responsible for the two northern columns, was the only departmental commander in the Division of the Missouri who was not a West Pointer. A wealthy New England bachelor, he was an attorney by training, who spoke several languages and was well read in art and literature.

During the Civil War, Terry enlisted as a ninety-day volunteer, but remained for the duration. He so distinguished himself that he was promoted to major general of volunteers. His capture of Fort Fisher, North Carolina, in 1865, closed the last major Confederate seaport and hastened the end of the war. For this, Congress voted him a special resolution of thanks, one of only fifteen such honors extended to Union soldiers. After the war, he accepted a commission as a brigadier general in the Regular Army.

Terry was placed in command of the newly created Department of Dakota in the midst of the Red Cloud War. This gave him experience administering an Indian Campaign, although he did not exercise actual field command.

In 1876, Terry was almost fifty years old. He stood six feet tall, with a straight bearing. His receding black hair had a knife-edge part. His cheeks were clean-shaven, but he wore a mustache, and his chin was covered with a thick, black beard. He was a respected and popular commander, who cooperated with superiors, equals, or subordinates. But his good nature sometimes prevented him from adequately controlling younger, more ambitious officers.[5]

The war in Terry's department began almost immediately. The preceding year, a group of traders from Bozeman, Montana, had established a post called Fort Pease, in the wilderness on the banks of the Yellowstone near its confluence with the Bighorn, almost 250 miles to the east. During February 1876, several parties from Fort Pease arrived in Bozeman, saying the stockade was under virtual siege. Forty-one men remained at the post, and could probably hold off the Indians long enough for a relief column to reach them.

Bozeman was near Fort Ellis, commanded by Maj. James S. Brisbin who, under orders from Terry, left for Fort Pease on February 22, with 14 officers, 192 enlisted men, and 15 civilians. Reaching the Crow Agency, near the present site of Columbus, Montana, the relief column was joined by 25 civilians, and 54 Crow Indian scouts, who knew the country and were hereditary enemies of the Lakotas.[6]

Brisbin reached the trading post on March 4, and evacuated nineteen survivors, eight of whom were wounded. Of the others, six had been killed and the remainder had made night escapes. "No Indians were seen . . . but war lodges were found representing a force of about sixty Sioux who had fled southward," Terry noted.[7]

Brisbin's march of twelve days from Fort Ellis to the stockade was comparatively easy, considering Terry's overall problem of getting his forces into the field. Winters on the northern plains are dangerously erratic. Although the season is generally cold, there are warm spells where the temperature may get as high as 60 or 70 degrees. This warming can be followed by sudden, blinding snowstorms that last for days and send the thermometer plunging well below zero. The wind picks up light snow, mixing it with blowing dust to fill the air with a brownish muck, reducing visibility to almost nothing. When spring finally arrives, the snow melt turns the slow, shallow rivers into raging torrents.

The war zone was in the eastern half of Montana, a sparsely settled region with few roads or trails. The troops who were to form Colonel Gibbon's column were scattered among posts in the heavily populated western part of the territory, and the simple task of consolidating them for the operation posed a significant logistical problem. The military post nearest the zone of operation was Fort Ellis, which would serve as Gibbon's main base. Ellis, however, was 183 miles south of Gibbon's headquarters at Fort Shaw. After marching through snow and mud from Fort Shaw to Fort Ellis, he would then have to go about a hundred miles east to the Crow Agency, where he planned to establish his advance depot.[8] It was another 140 miles from the Crow Agency to the trading post at Fort Pease, which was the closest place Gibbon could expect to encounter hostile Indians. This meant some of the Montana troops would travel more than 400 miles over icy trails and mud with horses, mules, and wagons before even nearing the area where they might expect to fight. Distance and weather combined to make an early start impossible. Nevertheless, on March 8, Gibbon wrote Terry from Fort Shaw that every effort was being made to get moving.

"It will take ten days to get to Ellis if we have *no storms*," Gibbon said, but added a heavy snowstorm had been blowing for the past two days, which had delayed wagons contracted directly to Fort Ellis. It was imperative to cross the mountain ranges east of Fort Ellis before thaws turned the roads to mud, but even with good weather, Gibbon now doubted he could get started before April 1.

Once he did get under way, Gibbon planned to march east along the Yellowstone to its confluence with the Bighorn River, near old Fort C. F. Smith, one of Colonel Carrington's ill-fated posts. After that, he would move against any camps or wandering bands of Indians he encountered in the vicinity. "There must be some, tho' I hear most of them are about Tongue River," he wrote, adding he might have to go south, up the Bighorn, or continue east along the Yellowstone. The route finally adopted would depend on information from guides and Indian scouts hired at the Crow Agency.

Since both he and Crook planned to use Indian scouts, Gibbon worried that an unexpected encounter between the two groups of government Indians on the trail ahead of the two columns might start a fight unless they had a means of recognition. Gibbon planned to mark his scouts with red rags tied around their left arms, a method also adopted by Crook.[9]

IF SHERIDAN STILL ENTERTAINED ANY VISIONS OF A WINTER CAMpaign, Gibbon's predicted starting date of April 1—weather permitting—ended them entirely. Likewise, he could harbor little hope of a coordinated movement. Only Crook appeared capable of getting into the field in a timely fashion, and then only because winters in the Department of the Platte were less severe. It was the beginning of many frustrations Sheridan would endure in this war.

The lieutenant general would have been even more frustrated had he known the opinions among Crook's veteran staff officers, who were far less sanguine than Gibbon. In his diary, Lt. John Gregory Bourke, one of Crook's aides-de-camp, observed:

> We are now on the eve of the bitterest Indian war the Government has ever been called upon to wage: a war with a tribe that has waxed fat and insolent on government bounty, and has been armed and equipped with the most improved weapons by the connivance or carelessness of the Indian Agents.[10]

Bourke's candid appraisal came from four years already spent at Crook's side. At forty-six, George Crook was one of the best Indian fighters in the army. His experience went back to the 1850s when, as a young lieutenant, he participated in the Rogue River and Yakima Wars in the Northwest. There and later in the Union Army, he emphasized training and marksmanship, two concepts considered novel in the United States Army of the period. Returning to the Northwest after the Civil War, his pacification of the Shoshones and Paiutes earned a resolution of thanks from the Oregon Legislature. His greatest innovations, however, occurred against the Apaches in Arizona, where he perfected the use of Indian scouts as trackers, on the theory that "it takes one to catch one." He also refined the pack mule train, giving his troops far more speed and mobility than they had with the slow, lumbering wagon trains. For these accomplishments, he was jumped two grades from lieutenant colonel to brigadier general and given command of the Platte.

Crook was six feet tall and, like Terry, had an erect carriage. At 170 pounds, he was lean and sinewy. His cheeks were ruddy, and his blue-gray eyes prompted the Indians to call him "Grey Fox."[11]

Despite his achievements, Crook's tactics were erratic, and his campaigns often seesawed between brilliance and stupidity. There were times when he seemed almost mentally lazy. Still, he was a great commander when he applied himself, and his overall record of success was the best of any general on the frontier.

There was, however, a less attractive side to Crook. One officer who served under him during the Sioux War called him a "somewhat cold-blooded warrior, treating his men perhaps too practically in war time. . . ." He carefully cultivated the press, making sure friendly reporters accompanied his expeditions, and ostracizing unfriendly ones. His staff was selected largely on the basis of unquestioning loyalty.

Although he and Sheridan were boyhood friends and had roomed together at West Point, professional jealousy on Crook's part irreparably damaged the relationship, so that by 1876 it had deteriorated into pure hatred. Crook openly ridiculed Sheridan's physique, which he blamed on what he considered the lieutenant general's dissipated personal life. In fact, it often seemed as though Crook deliberately tried to irritate Sheridan, both personally and professionally. Sheridan, who had not sought the quarrel, respected Crook as a soldier but privately returned the animosity with a vengeance.

In the field, Crook ceaselessly questioned his officers for information, but rarely shared his thoughts. Conferences were primarily statements of the general's final decisions, without any discussion. He issued broad, general instructions, allowing his commanders to work out the details, but while this gave them wide freedom of movement, the exasperated officers sometimes got so little information they did not really know what he wanted them to do. Indeed, it occasionally seemed as if newspaper reporters knew more about the general's plans than the regimental commanders. This failure to communicate would seriously hamper operations as the Sioux War progressed, so that what little success Crook enjoyed in this war would be due entirely to subordinates such as Anson Mills and Ranald Mackenzie.[12]

Crook and his staff had left departmental headquarters in Omaha for Cheyenne, Wyoming, on February 17, accompanied by Ben Clarke, a guide from the Indian Territory of Oklahoma. Clarke's employment was no doubt prompted by Sheridan, who knew him as one of the most able guides on the southern plains, and apparently reasoned he could advise the field commanders for an equally successful campaign in the north.

Arriving in Cheyenne, Crook found troop and equipment preparations well advanced, in contrast to the Department of Dakota, where Terry's troops were still hibernating in their snowbound forts. Tom Moore, an experienced civilian contract packer, had a well-equipped mule train waiting to take to the field. Five companies of cavalry—roughly 250 men—at adjacent Fort D. A. Russell were also prepared to go.[13]

The only problem was heavy transportation. Although Crook planned to employ pack mules in actual field operations, supplies would be carried north to the various depots by wagon. But wagons were hard to find because Cheyenne was gripped with Black Hills fever. The town was on the direct line from Colorado to the gold in the hills, and a new iron bridge over the Platte River at Fort Laramie, about ninety miles to the northeast, made the Cheyenne road more practical for gold seekers from the Midwest than the shorter, more rugged routes through Sidney and North Platte, Nebraska. As a result, almost every vehicle in town was already chartered for freight. Procurement of wagons took time, but was more of a nuisance than a damaging delay.[14]

Crook seemed to have little confidence in Sheridan's overall concept of a pincer movement, for his plan was that of a commander operating alone. His careful preparations had three goals: to strike a quick, sudden blow, which would demoralize the Indians; to do it in winter, which would cause far more hardship than in late spring or summer; and, because of the small number of troops at his disposal, to knock out some of the hostile bands immediately so that he would encounter less resistance during the summer.[15]

As a brigadier general and departmental commander, Crook was theoretically an administrative officer who had little to do with day-to-day operations and—officially at least—would accompany the column as an observer. Col. Joseph J. Reynolds, Third Cavalry, an aging veteran with a good Civil War record, was assigned to command the field force, which was designated the Big Horn Expedition. The objective was the Bighorn Mountains, which run northwest through northeastern Wyoming and into Montana, straddling the Departments of the Platte and Dakota.

"It is the intention to move in the lightest marching order possible hence everything not absolutely needed in the way of clothing, and equipage and bedding is to be rejected," Lieutenant Bourke noted.[16]

The staging point was Fort Fetterman, 130 miles north of Cheyenne and the limit of military protection for the Wyoming settlements. On February 21, the main cavalry contingent left Fort D. A. Russell for Fetterman, to be joined by two more companies of horse soldiers departing simultaneously from Fort Sanders, near Laramie City. The following day, Crook departed for Fort Laramie, where he would pause for a couple of days and pick up three additional companies of cavalry, before continuing on to join the main contingent at Fort Fetterman.[17] After a forced march of fifty-four miles, he reached the Chugwater River, where he spent the night at the ranch of John "Portuguee" Phillips.

A true pioneer who had spent many years as a government scout, Phillips had ridden 236 miles through a blizzard to Fort Laramie in 1866, carrying word of the Fetterman Massacre and a plea for help from the battered and besieged garrison of Fort Phil Kearny. He probably knew the area of Crook's intended campaign as well as any white person, and gave a blunt assessment of the situation. If the war lasted into the summer, he said, the Indians would continue leaving the reservation and consolidating, until they ultimately numbered at least 18,000 to 20,000 people in aggregate, and could field nearly 4,000 warriors. He had no doubt they would fight; he had seen them do it on several occasions with far less provocation than the government had given them now. Unless they were concentrated in one spot, where an immediate, decisive blow could be delivered, he believed the war would drag on into several campaigns before they would be forced to sue for peace.[18]

With this sobering thought, Crook resumed his march early the next morning. He arrived at Fort Laramie later in the day, having traveled a day and a half over rolling plains from Cheyenne. The post was alive with excitement over the prospect of war, as well as the influx of argonauts for the Black Hills. At the fort and on the road, the soldiers saw large numbers of people heading toward the hills, heavily provisioned, with new wagons drawn by strong, fresh horses. Some, however, were on foot, begging their way from ranch to ranch, indicative of the hard economic times in the East.[19]

Crook spent February 23 studying maps and interviewing scouts and guides. He already had Ben Clarke, described by one of his fellow guides as "one of the most modest and brave plainsmen in the country."[20] At Fort Laramie, he added Louis Richaud, called "Louie Reeshaw" from the French pronunciation of his name; Baptiste Pourier and Baptiste Gaunier, called "Big Bat" and "Little Bat" respectively; and Frank Grouard.

The most striking of this group was Grouard, a thick-set, muscular man who weighed over 200 pounds. He was swarthy, with a wide face, and dark, wavy hair and mustache. Grouard's origins are disputed. Some Indians, including a woman who claimed to be his half-sister, said his father was French Creole and his mother, Oglala. His enemies called him a mulatto. The most commonly accepted story—although possibly fabricated by Grouard himself— is that he was born on September 20, 1853, in the Friendly Islands of Polynesia, the son of an American missionary and an island noblewoman.

Frank said that when he was two years old, his father took the family to San Bernardino, California, where even that climate proved too severe for Mrs. Grouard. She returned to the South Pacific with all the children but Frank, who was placed in the care of a foster family. In 1865, Frank hired out to a freight transporter bound for Helena, Montana. It is reasonably certain that during his Montana experience, he was captured by the Oglalas, and lived with them for six years. He learned their language and customs, and got to know Crazy Horse so well that the two men intensely disliked each other, although Grouard, who pretended affection for the chief, never specified why.[21]

Crook was fascinated by Grouard, and asked him if the Lakotas could be caught in winter camps as Sheridan wanted. Grouard said it was possible with proper planning and troop deployment. The general hired him at $125 a month, about $25 above the going rate for guides and scouts.

In all, thirty scouts were contracted at Fort Laramie.[22] To Bourke, they were "as sweet a lot of cut throats as ever scuttled a ship. Half-Breeds, squaw-men, bounty-jumpers, thieves, and desperadoes of different grades from the various Indian agencies composed the outfit." The only ones who seemed to impress him were Ben Clarke, Grouard, Louis Richaud, and Big Bat Pourier. Maj. Thaddeus H. Stanton, nominally a paymaster but who often served as troubleshooter and chief of scouts, was placed in charge of this outfit, a position that won him Bourke's deepest sympathy.[23]

Finishing his business at Fort Laramie, Crook left for Fort Fetterman. Arriving after a two-day trip over barren, rocky country, he found some Arapahos under Black Coal, a minor chief, who said Sitting Bull was on the Powder River below old Fort Reno. This was some eighty miles north of Fetterman and in the line of march.

On February 27, the five pack trains, whose 400 mules would bear the bulk of the load, arrived at Fetterman from Cheyenne in good order. The wagons would follow the column until a base was established, after which the mules would take over.

To coordinate movements between his department and Terry's, Crook telegraphed Custer (still en route back to Fort Abraham Lincoln from extended leave in the East) that the Wyoming Column would leave for the Bighorn country in a few days with ten companies of cavalry and two of infantry, but advised that plans would have to be formulated based on terrain and scouting reports during the march.[24] Altogether 883 soldiers, civilian scouts, guides, and packers would accompany the expedition.

On March 1, the Big Horn Expedition marched out of Fort Fetterman and headed north, the first of Sheridan's three columns to enter the field.[25]

6

Collision Course

DESPITE HIS OFFICIAL STATUS AS AN OBSERVER, CROOK SOON made it clear he was actually in control of the Big Horn Expedition, and that Col. Joseph Reynolds would command in name only. Crook's own explanation was that he had been told an Indian campaign in the northern plains was impossible during winter and early spring, and he "accompanied" the troops to personally determine whether this was so. He implied there were other reasons, but did not elaborate.[1]

Reynolds's age may have been a factor. He was fifty-four, and despite a good Civil War record, some of the younger officers did not feel he was up to the rigors and deprivations of an Indian campaign. More probably, however, Crook did not trust him. Several years earlier, when Reynolds commanded the Department of Texas, Mackenzie accused him of corruption because of questionable financial transactions involving Fort McKavett, a west Texas post that Mackenzie then commanded. Now, in 1876, Reynolds's name was cropping up again as the graft in the Belknap War Department began to surface.[2]

The expedition itself was remarkable for the number of first-hand accounts it produced in the form of newspaper articles, letters, and diaries. Indeed, the Great Sioux War was one of the best documented conflicts of the nineteenth century. Officially, the press on the Big Horn Expedition was represented by Robert Strahorn of the Denver *Rocky Mountain News,* who also corresponded for the *Chicago Tribune,* Omaha *Republican,* Cheyenne *Sun,* and *New York Times.* Strahorn, who wrote under the pen name, "Alter Ego," was only twenty-four years old, but already had ten years in newspapers. He quickly won respect from the officers and soldiers on the campaign.

Although Strahorn was the only professional journalist with the expedition, he was not the only correspondent for the *Chicago Tribune.* Capt. Andrew Burt, an infantryman who joined the column at Fort Laramie, also wrote for that paper, as well as for the Cincinnati *Commercial.*[3] In fact, officers and enlisted men in both Crook's and Terry's commands supplemented their army pay by selling accounts to newspapers. Had the Indians subscribed, the outcome of the war might have been different. Security was nonexistent in 1876, and virtually every aspect of the military campaigns was published in great—often accurate—detail.[4]

Diaries of the Great Sioux War were kept by men with varying degrees of education, from near illiteracy to accomplished stylists. Some are little more than observations on the weather, and itineraries. Many, however, exhibit an understanding of the historic significance of the campaign, and contain perceptive observations of terrain, events, and people, and even keen insight into personalities.

Most impressive of all is the diary kept by Lieutenant Bourke during fifteen years at General Crook's side. Born in Philadelphia in 1846, John Gregory Bourke ran away from home at sixteen to join the Union Army. After the war, he was appointed to West Point, graduating in 1869. Posted to Arizona, he joined Crook's staff in 1872.[5] Bourke's position as the general's aide gave him an insider's view of a pivotal time in national history, and his diary is filled with detailed notes, newspaper clippings, photographs, maps, and sketches. He was also interested in anthropology, and kept careful records on the ways of the Indians he fought. His published findings brought him recognition not only as a soldier but also as a scientist. It is a tribute to Bourke's thoroughness and his great ability as author, observer, and analyst that more than a century later, several of his books on military affairs and Indian culture are still in print.

AS THIS EXPEDITION OF SOLDIER-WRITERS HEADED NORTH, FOL-lowing the old government road through eastern Wyoming, the Indians signaled its progress with mirrors from hilltop to hilltop. Seeing the flashes of light, the troops presumed they were Lakotas, although they may have been Cheyennes. Like the Lakotas, many Cheyenne bands refused to live on the reservations, preferring instead the freedom of the unceded Indian lands. So long as they allowed whites to travel through their territory en route to or from the various settlements, they understood the army would leave them alone. Since these travelers rarely interfered with their activities, they were perfectly willing to let the whites pass.[6] Lately, no one had bothered the Cheyennes, and they did not consider themselves at war with anyone.

During the winter of 1875–76, the non-reservation Cheyennes and Oglalas camped near each other, staying close as they moved from place to place. When Crook took to the field, both were on the west side of the Tongue River in southeastern Montana. Among them was an eighteen-year-old warrior named Wooden Leg, whose recollections provide one of the few eyewitness Cheyenne accounts of the early stages of the war. Although he was tall and thin, Wooden Leg was noted for his stamina, and received his name because he could walk long distances without tiring, as though his legs were made of wood. He had proven himself in battle the year before, when he distinguished himself against Crow horse thieves.[7]

This year, however, his mind was not on fighting, but on the pleasant life of the winter camp. True, coffee, sugar, and tobacco were scarce, but these were sometimes obtained from agency Cheyennes, or traded back and forth with the Lakotas. The shortages were a small price to pay for the freedom of the unceded lands by the Tongue.

The tranquillity of the camp was disrupted at the end of February when Last Bull, a leader of the Fox Soldier Warrior Society, came to the camp with his family and reported that the army had been sent against all Sioux and Cheyennes off the reservation, although he did not know from which forts the soldiers would come or who their commanders were.

Most Cheyennes thought Last Bull was simply passing along an unfounded rumor. But the report was confirmed several days later, after the Cheyennes had separated from the Oglalas and moved east to the Powder River. Spotted Wolf, Medicine Wolf, and Twin, three respected chiefs, arrived at the new location and advised them to head south to the reservation. After a two-day council, the chiefs of the camp decided to stay in place. If the soldiers came, the Cheyennes would run off their horses so they couldn't fight. The camp, which now consisted of forty lodges (about 320 people), was put on full alert. Every hunting party was told to look for soldiers or for the trail of a military column. The women and old people were ready to flee immediately if the camp were attacked.[8]

IN WYOMING, CROOK CONTINUED HIS MARCH NORTH. THE TEN cavalry companies led, followed by the two companies of infantry, then ambulances, wagons, and pack trains—almost 900 men in all. A herd of sixty or seventy beef cattle brought up the rear, to be slaughtered as needed for fresh meat until time came to cut loose from everything except horses and pack trains.[9]

Although there had been a snowstorm the night before the column left Fetterman, the sky had been clear ever since. Temperatures hovered at about thirty degrees. Even so, the soldiers realized that a sudden storm could plunge the thermometer to more than forty degrees below zero, and preparations were made accordingly.

The infantry was in less danger of freezing, since the constant walking with arms swinging in time kept up circulation in the extremities. The real risk was to the cavalrymen, who sat in their saddles for hours on end, motionless except for an occasional pressure of their knees or tug on the reins to guide their horses. For protection, they wore layer upon layer of wool, buckskin, and fur, so that they hardly looked like a military unit, since virtually nothing of the standard campaign uniform was visible.

The chief obstacle was forage for the animals. So long as the snow did not fall in the valleys and river bottoms of northern Wyoming, there was a year-round supply of rich grass, which lessened the demand on the grain supply. But snow covered the grass and compressed into ice, so the horses could not graze. On the hills, cold winds dried the grass, and prairie fires burned it off. The eighty wagons accompanying the first legs of the march were all loaded with grain, as were any ambulances not needed for medical supplies or other uses. Grain was also the main burden of the pack mules. Where grass could be found, no grain was issued. And when grain was passed out, the horses only received half to three quarters of the full ration.[10]

Initially, marches were short, to accustom men and animals to the pace. On the second day, the Black Hills appeared, seventy miles to the northeast but visible in the clear air. That night, the column went into camp on the South Fork of the Cheyenne River. There was abundant grass for the horses, and cottonwood for fires. Two veins of bituminous coal cropped out of some nearby bluffs, and samples were collected.[11]

About 2:00 A.M. the third day, the camp suddenly rang with shouts, rifle shots, and Indian whoops. The troops grabbed their arms, but it was not an attack. The Indians had shot one of the beef herders and stampeded forty-five head of cattle. The herder, who was not critically wounded, said he had seen two or three Indians creeping toward him through the brush, and shouted an alarm. The Indians opened fire, wounding him and stampeding the cattle before help arrived.

Since a night pursuit was useless, a cavalry detail waited until dawn before following the trail. After about six miles, the scouts saw the trail split, the nervous Indians apparently abandoning the cattle, which then appeared to be homing toward Fort Fetterman. Assuming that most of the animals would get to the post and at least feed soldiers there rather than Indians, the detail broke off pursuit.[12]

Despite its dangers, the old government road offered great

beauty. Later in the day, the snowclad peaks of the Bighorns loomed ahead and slightly to the left. Remarking on them, correspondent Strahorn wrote:

> We could see almost the whole of the resplendent range stretching off for over a hundred miles along the northwestern horizon, its loftiest peaks appearing white, fleecy and ethereal enough to belong to cloud-land—yet too beautifully grand to be spared by even a beautiful earth. In most harmonious contrast [to the] great banks of glittering snow—banks of burnished silver they looked to us—were the long, purple-tinged pedestals upon which they rested. These were unusually rugged foot-hills, and they received their rich coloring from dense forests of pine which covered them from base to summit.[13]

This wild and scenic land, which would become cruelly familiar to Crook and his men over the coming months, was virtually unknown in March of 1876; except for trappers and scouts, few whites had ever ventured off the government road to explore it. Even the rivers were named by the Indians—Tongue, loosely adapted from "Talking River," because voices echoed off its rock bluffs; Powder, from the powdery soil that lined its shores; Crazy Woman, because, according to legend, there lived along its banks a woman who was either insane or promiscuous (the Indians used the same word for both).

Moving deeper into this terra incognita, the troops saw a pony trail not quite twenty-four hours old. The growing signs of Indians, and the loss of the beef herd, prompted extra security precautions, and sentinels were posted around that night's camp and on adjacent hillsides. The local water was tainted with alkali, but melted snow was drinkable. Wood for fires was scarce.

The next morning there were many lodgepole trails headed for Fort Fetterman or Red Cloud.[14] These trails were made by the two main poles of a tipi, which were strapped on either side of a horse to form a travois on which Indians packed belongings when moving from place to place. It was obvious that, as word of the government ultimatum reached them, the Indians were starting toward the reservations. None of this was reported to Crook's superiors. Sheridan in Chicago, and the Interior and War Department officials in Washington continued to believe that no further effort at peace was necessary, and it was not the duty of Crook or Reynolds to report signs of Indian compliance. The government had decided on war. The army had been ordered to prosecute that war. It was the job of the generals and their subordinates to carry the war to any Indians they found still in the field.

More lodgepole trails were encountered and the troops sometimes saw smoke signals. One day, two young warriors appeared far ahead, sitting motionless on their ponies. They waited until the column was within a thousand yards, then turned and fled. The soldiers let them go under orders from Crook who, to save wear on his animals, had forbidden pursuit of small Indian parties until deep into their country. He also theorized that failure to pursue might mislead the Indians into thinking the soldiers feared them. Then they would become overconfident, let down their guard, and Crook could surprise them in their camp.

On March 5, the weather turned foul, with leaden skies, high winds, and snow. In camp, about 8:00 P.M., a sentry saw three mounted Indians approaching. Presuming it was another stock raid, and having no orders to challenge before shooting, he opened fire. The Indians shot back, and suddenly a fusillade opened up from warriors concealed in the brush on both sides of the camp. The campfires, still burning, were extinguished immediately, but the Indians had already used them to find aiming points for their rifles. Not being able to see, the soldiers waited until a rifle flashed from the brush, then shot at the flash point. After thirty or forty minutes, the Indians broke off and left. The only army casualty was a corporal grazed on the cheek by a bullet.[15]

Despite the stir it created, the officers were almost pleased that the attack had occurred. The soldiers, many of whom were fresh recruits, now had been in their first fight of the campaign, and no longer faced the terror of the unknown. Well drilled, they had reacted instinctively, every man in his assigned position, doing what he was supposed to do. Morale was high.[16]

By noon the next day, the cold had passed, the temperature was almost at summertime level, and the heavy clothing became oppressive. It was typical of the freakish weather in those parts that the Crazy Woman still had ice thick enough to hold both horses and riders as they crossed. Smoke signals were visible throughout the day, and the scouts twice saw mirror flashes. In the distance, there was a great column of dust, presumably a large band of Lakotas or Cheyennes trying to get away from the soldiers.

Five days and almost eighty miles out from Fort Fetterman, the command reached the ruins of Fort Reno, which would serve as Crook's depot. Little remained of the once large post, located slightly east of what is now Kaycee, Wyoming. The only evidence of any human habitation was part of the bake oven, chimneys from the trader's store, and one or two chimneys where the officers' quarters had been. A storm broke just as they arrived, and the troops pushed onward through the blowing snow, going into camp several miles up the road at a site that offered the first good water since leaving Fort Fetterman, as well as plenty of dry cottonwood for fuel. There was, however, no grass for the animals.[17]

That night, Crook called a meeting of his officers and scouts. The wagons would be sent back to the depot at Reno, and the infantry would accompany them. From here on, everything would depend on the mules. Each officer and enlisted man was allowed only the clothes on his back. For bedding, there would be one buffalo robe or two blankets per man. Instead of eating separately, company officers would now mess with their men, and staff officers with the pack train personnel. Each officer was allowed one tin cup and one tin plate. For shelter, each enlisted man could carry one section of pup tent. Officers were allowed one piece of canvas each, or one tent fly for every two officers. Each man would carry one hundred rounds of ammunition on his person, with another hundred on the pack train. Rations for fifteen days would consist of bacon, hardtack, coffee, and sugar. Henceforth, marches would be made at night.[18]

From that point, the expedition underwent the misery that characterized Crook's campaigns for the remainder of the war. Snowstorms continued for the next several days, and at times, Frank Grouard could not see fifty yards ahead.[19] The pup tents, nothing more than two pieces of canvas buttoned together, offered little protection from this kind of weather. The soldiers went to sleep on freezing ground, wrapped only in their overcoats or blankets, and woke to bitter, pelting snow. Frozen bacon and frozen coffee were the fare. Still, they pushed on. Sixty miles northwest of Reno, they crossed Big Piney Creek near the ruins of Fort Phil Kearny. Mustaches and beards were coated with rime where the moisture from their breath condensed and froze. On the afternoon of March 9, the temperature dropped to six below zero.[20]

A PARTY OF YOUTHFUL CHEYENNE SCOUTS LOCATED CROOK'S column one night, just as the soldiers were breaking camp to resume their march. Most of them had never seen so many troops in the field and the sight made them nervous. Separated from each other in the darkness, and wandering in small groups, one party of jittery Cheyennes shot at some movement, starting a chain reaction of gunfire. Later, they learned they had spent the night shooting at each other long after the soldiers had moved on.[21]

On returning to their own camp on the Powder River, some sixty miles to the northeast, the scouts were questioned by their leaders about what they had seen. Then the chiefs and old men deliberated. Two Moons, who at thirty-three was a distinguished warrior and ranking chief, argued they should seek protection at Fort Laramie, following remote river valleys to get there. "I wished to miss the soldiers on the way," he later explained, saying an army on the march had trouble distinguishing friend from foe. "They fight any Indian they run onto."[22] The council accepted Two Moons's advice, and a herald was sent through the camp ordering the people to prepare for a move far up the river, in the general direction of Fort Laramie over 200 miles to the south.

With hunters and scouts watching for the soldiers, the Cheyennes relocated to a point just above the confluence of the Little Powder River and the main stream of the Powder in eastern Montana, near the Wyoming line. The soldiers, meanwhile, were reportedly moving away from them, westward toward the Tongue River. The Indians relaxed, thinking that perhaps the soldiers were not even looking for them.[23] Peace had been maintained.

*   *   *

THE SOLDIERS MARCHED THROUGH THE LONG, COLD NIGHTS AND into the bitter mornings. At 8:00 A.M., March 11, the temperature dropped to minus twenty-two, the lowest register on the thermometer, and the mercury was compressed into the bulb. Now following the Tongue, the column pushed north into Montana where Crook wrote, "The snow and wind were so blinding that everything beyond a few yards from us was obscured from view." Some minor cases of frostbitten fingers and ears were reported.

The general would have preferred waiting for a break in the weather, but food was growing short and they had not yet located any hostile camps. Although the mercury was now stuck in the bulb of the thermometer, he ordered the march to resume.[24]

The bad weather lasted for two more days before the sun came out. The air was cold, but there was no wind and the sky was clear. At 7:00 A.M., the thermometer registered minus ten. By 10:30, it had risen to twenty-four degrees above zero, and by 3:00 P.M., it was thirty-two. Thus far, they had not sighted any hostile Indians and, to avoid pointless marching, Crook kept the troops in camp until the scouts reconnoitered ahead. They arrived back in camp with six deer, which were turned over to the enlisted men for supper. Again, they had seen no Indians, but a large number of trails led eastward to the Powder River, convincing Crook that Sitting Bull and the other hostile chiefs were camped at its confluence with the Little Powder.

He resumed the march, doubling back toward the east. The soldiers had gone only a short distance when Col. Thaddeus Stanton and the scouts sighted and chased two young warriors who had run into the column while hunting. Crook called an immediate halt for coffee, hoping the Indians were watching and would presume he was resting his men before pushing on down the Tongue Valley toward the Yellowstone. If this happened, a forced night march would bring the troops to the Indian camp, taking it by surprise. He ordered one day's rations distributed to each man, and grain for the horses. The mules would remain behind; their shoes had worn so smooth, he was afraid to take them into the rough country where he expected to find the village. Since an unguarded train invited attack, he himself would also remain with four companies of cavalry. Reynolds would take the other six companies and the scouts, and follow the trail of the two young hunters. If it led to a village, he was to attack, capture, and hold it until Crook arrived with the rest of the troops. Otherwise, the two sections would re-group and make new plans.[25]

Shortly after dark, Reynolds moved out, on a collision course—with the friendly Cheyennes.

7

"The Soldiers Are Right Here!"

FRANK GROUARD REMEMBERED THE NIGHT OF MARCH 16 AS THE
coldest he had ever experienced on the frontier. The wind blew
without letup, and flurries of snow cut into the faces of the men.
The command marched through this bitter night, Stanton and his
scouts in the lead, with Grouard, Big Bat, Little Bat, and one or
two others working ahead of the rest. The path was tiring for the
horses. The ground was hard and slippery, and the rolling country
of the previous day had given way to a maze of little ravines and
gullies, not more than three or four feet deep.[1]

At 2:30 A.M., March 17, Reynolds called a halt, ordering the
troops to conceal themselves in a dry ravine while Grouard and
some of the scouts looked for further Indian signs. To keep from
freezing as they waited, the men walked up and down the sides of
the ravine. Occasionally a soldier would lie down in the snow to
sleep, the prelude to freezing to death, and his friends would shake
him loose and get him moving again. Officers went through the
ranks, keeping the men on their feet.[2]

While the army scouts searched for the Indians, Cheyenne scouts
also looked for the soldiers. The two young warriors seen the day
before had returned to the village and given the alarm, and ten
young warriors were sent out to find and track the column. That

night most of the Cheyennes slept, confident their scouts would warn them if anything was amiss.[3]

Meanwhile, Grouard returned, reporting that the trail showed the two warriors belonged to a hunting party of about thirty or forty. He believed Reynolds could follow their trail to the village. It was almost daylight when the command got under way again. The clouds broke up and the sky began to clear, but the cold grew more intense. Reynolds called another halt to rest men and horses.

Ahead once again, Grouard came to a ledge over a valley filled with fog, which hid everything from view. He had descended about halfway when the fog lifted, revealing the Indian village directly below him. He could hear talking, and from the cries of the herald he determined they had sent their own scouts to look for the troops. A short distance away was a large pony herd. With this information, he went back up the cliff and returned to the command.

Reynolds, who had no previous experience with Indian combat, seemed uncertain about his next move.

"Fight them Indians," Grouard told him. "I suppose that is what you want."

"What can I do?" Reynolds asked.

"Fight them Indians," Grouard repeated. "That is all you have to do."

At Grouard's suggestion, the column was divided into three battalions of two companies each. Battalion commanders were Capt. Henry E. Noyes, Second Cavalry; Capt. Anson Mills, Third Cavalry; and Capt. Alexander Moore, Third Cavalry. Stanton and his scouts functioned separately. Bourke and Strahorn, not attached to any unit, volunteered to go with Capt. James Egan's company, which was part of Noyes's battalion.[4]

The soldiers moved up to a ridge overlooking the valley. Some questioned Grouard excitedly, while others fidgeted, impatient to get started. After all their labor, they could hardly believe that finally they had reached their goal—a hostile village. Some experienced troopers checked their weapons and saddle girths.

As the remaining morning fog evaporated, they got a good view of the village, set against a line of broken ridges slightly to their left and perhaps two miles ahead. The Indians later said there were 65 lodges, while soldiers' estimates went as high as 130. But even the low Indian count meant at least 450 people, about one third of whom were warriors. Some of the lodges were erected in the shelter of shallow caves and overhanging ledges. In front of the village, a low, rocky plateau sloped down toward the bottomland in a bend of the Powder River. The river itself was lined by a grove of cottonwoods with a dense undergrowth of wild plum bushes. Although the soldiers and the Indians were on the same side of the river, they were separated by a steep ravine, ten to twelve feet deep and fifty feet or more wide, which curved down from the ridges to the river. The troops would have to cross this ravine, since the bluffs protected the Indian rear. Young Indians were moving among the tipis, while the horses and mules grazed quietly on the banks of the river.[5]

Reynolds detailed Noyes's battalion to descend to the riverbank on the right, and work up to the big ravine. There, the battalion would divide into two companies. One, under Noyes, would capture the pony herd on the river, while Egan's company crossed the ravine and charged the village, firing pistols at close range.

As Noyes and Egan moved toward the village, Captain Moore's battalion would occupy the ridge directly behind the village, cutting off any escape with gunfire from the height. Moore was excited about his assignment, and bragged he would give them a "blizzard" and get "a bucket full of blood." None of the other officers were amused.[6]

Told his battalion would be held in reserve, Mills objected, saying Egan's initial assault "would just scare" the Indians, and they would escape past Moore and out the far end of the valley. He asked Reynolds "to let us all dismount and creep in among them." The colonel told Mills to stay put, then apparently changed his mind, ordering him instead to support Moore on the ridge.

Mills's battalion followed Moore's out onto the ridge, until he was motioned not to come any closer. Dismounting, Mills walked over, and told Moore he had been ordered to bring support. Moore replied there was no point in it; a deep gully blocked any further advance, and it was impossible to reach the assigned position on the height directly behind the village.

Walking up to a rise, Mills saw the village still ahead, beyond the range of the cavalry carbines. When he tried to offer suggestions, however, Moore told him to keep his battalion out of the way. Disgusted with Moore, Mills decided to ignore orders and go down to the village and back Egan, whom he figured would eventually need help.

This disagreement was typical of the Third Cavalry, which was notorious throughout the army for the bitter factionalism among its officers. With Moore failing to take his assigned position, and Mills forced by indifference to act on his own, the attack was doomed before it even started.[7]

Unaware of the problem and assuming Moore would cover them, Noyes and Egan had already descended into the valley and were working up the riverbank. After riding two miles through troublesome little ravines and gulches, Noyes led them into the long ravine by the village, which kept them concealed while offering a fine view of the target. Some young Indian boys were driving the pony herd to the river for water. Suddenly Bourke noticed a boy not ten feet away, and leveled his pistol. The youth wrapped his blanket around himself and stared at Bourke, waiting for the bullet.

"Don't shoot," Egan commanded. "We must not make any noise."

The boy fled, letting out a whoop that rang from the bluffs but, incredibly, did not disturb the village.

The troopers were impatient, but Noyes kept them in line, determined not to charge before ascertaining the terrain. Big Bat went out, looked around, and reported that once the advance began, the Indians would be forced out the other end of the village. There they would be caught by Moore's men, firing down at them from the bluffs, and effectively trapped—assuming, of course, that Moore was in his assigned place.

With Egan in the lead, the mounted battalion moved out in columns of twos, until it emerged from the ravine. On the command, "Left front into line," the forty-seven troopers of Egan's company formed a line and moved toward the village, leaving Noyes to isolate and capture the pony herd once the shooting started. Because the horses were too tired for a lengthy run, Egan's men would approach at a walk until they entered the village or were discovered, then charge at a slow trot. When they were close enough, they would open fire and storm the village.[8]

They were discovered—by an elderly Cheyenne looking for a knoll for sunrise meditation or prayer, as was customary among the old men. He had wandered a short distance from the village and begun his ritual. Then he saw the troopers and began shouting toward the camp, "The soldiers are right here! The soldiers are right here!"

Now less than 200 yards from the nearest tipi, Egan shouted, "Charge, my boys!" and the soldiers on their matching grays rode in. Indians came bounding out of their tipis and scattered. The troopers fired at random from one side to the other and bullets tore through the lodges. Women screamed, and old people hobbled to get out of the way.

It took only a moment, however, for the Cheyennes to recover from the initial shock. They grabbed their weapons and dived for cover in the plum bushes. The soldiers fired into the undergrowth, forcing them farther in among the trees. From there, however, the Cheyennes opened a steady return fire. Bullets whistled past the troopers, wounding horses, cutting reins, and tearing through clothing. Amazingly, only three soldiers were wounded during the three or four minutes of near continuous gunfire.

"The beautiful gray horses were a splendid mark for the Indians," Strahorn wrote, "and four or five dropped before we got through the village, Captain Egan's own animal being among the number."[9]

Wooden Leg had loaned his pistol to a cousin who had gone out with the scouts the night before, and so now had only a bow and arrow. He and several other young Cheyennes managed to reach the pony herd before Noyes, leaped on the first ponies they saw, and rode back to the fight.

"I shot arrows at the soldiers," he said. "Our people had not much else to shoot. Only a few people had guns and also ammunition for them."[10]

When the Indians realized there were less than fifty troopers, they counterattacked, rushing to cut off retreat and trap the soldiers inside the village. Egan ordered his men to dismount and form a skirmish line with their carbines. Still thinking Moore was in position, the desperate soldiers scanned the ridges, waiting for his troops to cover them. But the blustering Moore, who wanted buckets of blood, was nowhere to be seen. Noyes came up from the rear but, ignoring Egan's plight, cut to the right and took possession of the now isolated pony herd. He obeyed his orders to the letter, but it was small comfort to Egan's hard-pressed troops in the village. Without waiting for orders, Stanton sent his scouts in to support Egan, and slowly the soldiers began pushing the Indians out of the village and into the rocks of the sheltering bluff behind it.

About half an hour after the attack began, Moore's troops finally opened fire, having moved no closer than the point where Mills had left them. As Mills had predicted, they were too far away, and their spent bullets fell among Egan's men. Without Moore's covering fire to force them back toward Egan, the Indians began shooting from the rocks. Cheyenne marksmanship, wild in the initial confusion, improved steadily. Troopers began to fall.

Having worked his way down from the ridge, Mills finally arrived in the village with his battalion on foot at a run. These troops held the Indians at bay while Egan's men searched through the abandoned lodges. Still, the area left open by Moore allowed the Cheyennes plenty of room to move among the rocks and gullies at the base of the very ridge he was supposed to have occupied.[11]

In the meantime, once Wooden Leg had snatched a pony from the herd, he rode back into the village, trying to reach his lodge. "I wanted my shield, my other medicine objects, and whatever else I might be able to carry away," he remembered. Women were struggling to escape with such belongings as they could gather. Some carried or dragged children.

One woman was running with a pack on her back, her younger daughter under one arm, and the older daughter, a ten-year-old, holding her free hand. When she could run no farther, she hid in a thicket. Seeing her there, Wooden Leg rode over and lifted the ten-year-old up behind him on the pony. Farther on, he saw a woman struggling with her pack, a baby on her back, two small children under her arms, and an eight-year-old boy. He pulled the boy up in front of him, guiding his pony as best he could with the two clinging children. The pony shied and bucked, but he managed to get the children to safety, then rode back to the fight.

He encountered Two Moons and Bear Walks on a Ridge, and followed them to cover, where Two Moons stood his repeating rifle on end, passing his hands over the barrel to make medicine.

"My medicine is good," he announced. "Watch me kill that soldier."

He fired and missed. Then Bear Walks on a Ridge took careful aim with his muzzle-loading rifle and stunned the soldier with a shot across the back of his head. The three Cheyennes ran over and, together with a fourth, beat and stabbed him until he stopped moving. The fourth Cheyenne took the man's carbine. Wooden Leg got his blue tunic, the others took whatever they wanted, and they fled into the rocks.[12]

Reynolds, who had remained behind to oversee the attack, now arrived on the scene, and, with the Indians beaten back to the bluffs, Mills reported the village was secured. The colonel ordered him to burn it as quickly as possible so the command could be moved to a safe camp. Mills replied it was a large village, and destruction would take time. It was also heavily provisioned with meat and robes, which could be taken back to the pack train to resupply the expedition and extend its range. He suggested, therefore, that their own camp be established on the village site to allow sufficient time to destroy the Indian lodges and load the meat and robes. Reynolds agreed, and detailed two lieutenants to help oversee the burning of the lodges.

Meanwhile, Moore's column had withdrawn from its useless position on the ridge, and had descended into the valley behind the rest of the troops. As Mills deployed skirmishers to cover the detail burning the lodges, the Cheyennes began moving up the bluffs and along the ridge where Moore had been, then down the slopes to attack from behind. Alarmed, Mills sent a lieutenant to inform Reynolds that Moore had retreated. The colonel replied not to worry, that Noyes would be along directly. Twice more, Mills sent officers to tell the colonel that control of the ridge had been lost, exposing the troops to sniper fire and attack. Each time he received the same reply.

About that time, one of Egan's men fell mortally wounded. Mills ordered him carried to the rear for the surgeon. Wandering up, Reynolds noticed the men with the wounded soldier and asked how badly he was hurt. On being told he was almost dead, the colonel ordered him left where he was.

Mills finally found Moore, all his officers, and twenty or thirty enlisted men behind a clump of trees. He pleaded with them to move forward and cover his left, but Moore did not even answer him.

Fortunately, Mills was about to receive help from another quarter. Returning to his own men, he encountered Egan, who offered him extra troops to assist in burning the village. Soon a couple of Egan's squads came to cover the fire detail. Then Noyes, having captured the pony herd and placed it under guard, arrived with the long-awaited support.[13]

From a distance, the Cheyennes watched the soldiers burning their homes and all their possessions. From time to time, one of the lodges flared up as a supply of powder caught fire, and they occasionally heard the pop of rifle cartridges. Wooden Leg had only the clothes on his back and the dead soldier's tunic. He was not alone. The Cheyennes were left destitute, their children crying from cold and terror.[14]

Had they known it, they might have taken grim satisfaction that the soldiers were hardly better off. To move more rapidly, they had brought no rations. Their heavy clothing had been left with the pack train, and they wore only field uniforms against the bitter weather. Incredibly, Reynolds now ordered everything destroyed. Tons of meat, robes, blankets, and other provisions that the troops desperately needed were fed to the flames.

With Moore out of the fight, the Cheyennes now had total control of the rocks and ridges, giving them command of the field. Those with rifles opened fire with devastating effect. Soon, they were ready to counterattack.

Elsewhere, the Cheyenne scouts sent out the night before had found the soldiers' trail and guessed its implications. They tried to rush back to warn the village, but their tired ponies gave out, despite being whipped. Now at last they arrived and joined the fight.[15]

Realizing his position was no longer tenable, Reynolds ordered the village abandoned. As Mills withdrew, Pvt. Lorenzo E. Ayers got a bullet through the thigh, which broke his leg. Another private, Jeremiah Murphy, and the company blacksmith, Albert Glavinski, picked him up and were carrying him off when he was shot again, this time in the arm. The blacksmith ran for help while Murphy stayed by the wounded man. Glavinski caught up with Mills, reporting Ayers was in danger of being left behind. Overhearing the conversation, Reynolds interjected nothing could be done and ordered Mills to continue withdrawal. Noyes's battalion was still in the village, however, and Mills told Glavinski to "ask him in my name to try and recover" Ayers.

If anyone planned to rescue the wounded man, they waited too long. Six Cheyennes had already found the two soldiers. One fired point blank at Murphy, hitting the stock of his carbine and snapping it in two. His weapon useless, Murphy had no choice but to flee. Another group of Indians rose out of the bushes ahead of him, but Murphy managed to dodge them. They then ran over to the others who were dancing around Ayers. The last Murphy saw, they were scalping him alive.[16]

The abandonment of the dead and wounded brought muttering among the soldiers. Their resentment was compounded by the general knowledge that whatever the risk Indians recovered their own dead and wounded. "Retreating slowly, as they did after our first onslaught, and nearly always close to cover of some kind, they had no difficulty in removing every body from one position to another," Strahorn said. Neither officers nor enlisted men ever forgave Reynolds for abandoning their comrades.[17]

The troops now retraced their trail of the previous night, herding some 700 captured ponies, their rear protected by a strong skirmish line that exchanged a few shots with the Indians. After a twenty-mile march, they went into camp shortly after sunset. Officially, four soldiers died in the fight, and six were wounded.[18]

Everyone was hungry. Some of the officers had grabbed a little dried meat before the Indian stores were destroyed. Others had managed to save a few spoonsful of coffee and tea. Searching their saddlebags, several found hardtack crumbs. Combined, this made for a miserable supper. The meat, roasted in the ashes of the campfire, was handed around, each man getting one bite. There was enough coffee for one cup, and this, likewise, was passed around, each person taking a sip. The enlisted men, with empty stomachs and frostbitten extremities, named the place Camp Inhospitality. No guard was placed over the herd of 700 captured ponies, which were allowed to stray.

There was, nevertheless, a certain satisfaction to the fight, albeit a misguided one. They thought they had attacked a Lakota camp. The scouts reported that while searching the Indian village, they found an elderly, bedridden woman who told them the village belonged to Crazy Horse and Little Big Man, and was made up primarily of Oglalas and Miniconjous, with a few lodges of Northern Cheyennes and agency Indians.[19]

There can be little doubt the scouts were repeating exactly what the woman told them. But they were expecting to find a village of hostile Lakotas, and perhaps mentioned Sitting Bull or Crazy Horse while questioning her. Immediately comprehending, the old woman told them what they wanted to hear, a common trait among Indian prisoners. Possibly, she also lied to conceal the true nature of the village, mentioning Northern Cheyennes to explain her own presence. Regardless of how it happened, the soldiers were convinced they had carried the war to Crazy Horse, and so it was announced to the world.

The next morning, Dr. C. E. Munn, the expedition surgeon, treated the night's cases of frostbite, painting toes, feet, noses, and fingers with iodine. The camp routine was getting started when a small party of Indians slipped up and recaptured the pony herd. One of the scouts reported the herd was still in sight, and could be taken by cutting across a ridge and heading it off. Reynolds rejected the idea.

The recovery of the ponies restored mobility to the Indians, and with the weapons saved during the fight, they might begin to resupply and reestablish themselves. In short, the entire march and fight had been for nothing.[20]

The officers had had enough. They now openly accused their colonel of incompetence. All pretense of courtesy and respect for rank vanished. As far as they were concerned, Reynolds was an idiot, and Moore, a coward. Even the normally soldierly Bourke commented in his diary, "Reynolds' imbecility is a very painful revelation to many of us." General Crook was now bringing the pack train to meet them, and everyone eagerly awaited his appearance so they could air their grievances.[21]

Crook arrived that afternoon, and must have suspected something was wrong, for earlier in the day he had encountered Indians driving some of the ponies. A brief fight ensued, and perhaps a hundred animals were recaptured by the soldiers. Bourke noticed that as Crook listened to reports from Reynolds's officers, he "appeared annoyed" over the abandonment of the dead and dying "like carrion to the torture and mutilation of the Indian's scalping knife." He was also furious that the Indians had managed to recover and keep 600 ponies. He meant to get Reynolds and Moore. As Captain Nickerson, the senior aide-de-camp, noted, "Nothing would appease him, but the verdict of a court martial. . . ."[22]

For now, however, Crook's wrath would have to wait. He moved the camp eight miles to the banks of the Powder, where there was wood, water, and grass. The men were given a hot supper, and the surgeons passed out brandy. With the troops assigned to Gibbon and Custer still snowbound in their stations hundreds of miles away, Crook saw no point in lingering in the wilds of southeastern Montana. On March 19, two days after the fight, the command began the long march back to Fort Fetterman, arriving eight days later.

At Fetterman, Crook's first act was to file charges against Reynolds, Moore, and Noyes for the failings of the expedition, which he summed up:

> 1st. A failure on the part of a portion of the command to properly support the first attack.
> 2nd. A failure to make vigorous and persistent attack with the whole command.
> 3rd. A failure to secure the provisions that were captured for the use of the troops, instead of destroying them. . . .[23]

The charges against Reynolds and Moore were easy to understand. In Noyes's case, however, it was simply a matter of being too obedient. He had followed his orders to the letter, concentrating on the pony herd, when Egan's desperate situation was clearly visible, and common sense should have told him to assist. Instead, Egan had been saved by the scouts, acting without orders, and by Mills, in disobedience to orders.

Reynolds argued he had made a good faith effort to carry out all orders and instructions, and should not be subject to court-martial. But Crook insisted the entire action needed to be examined, and responsibility for mistakes assigned.[24]

Almost a year would pass before Reynolds went to trial. For now, however, the opening phase of the Great Sioux War was finished. It had accomplished nothing except to force the erstwhile indifferent Cheyennes into the hostile camp. Crook's forces—men and animals—were worn out by cold and hunger, and needed rest and reconditioning. In the north, Gibbon's soldiers were only now beginning to peer out from their forts. For a decisive, energetic commander like Sheridan, it was all so frustrating.

8

The Indians Consolidate

AFTER DRIVING REYNOLDS FROM THEIR DEVASTATED VILLAGE, THE
Cheyennes found only one tipi still standing. Inside was the bedridden old woman who had been interrogated by the army scouts. She
had been left unmolested, and allowed to keep her tipi for shelter.
A head count showed everyone present except those known to
have been killed. The Oglala, He Dog, who had been visiting when
the attack occurred, now suggested the Cheyennes take refuge with
his people. After salvaging as much as possible, the Indians started
for Crazy Horse's Oglala camp on the East Fork of the Little Powder River, fifty miles east of where the soldiers supposed.

"Three nights we slept out," Wooden Leg remembered. "Only a
few had robes. There was but little food, only a few women having little chunks of dry meat in their small packs."

During the night, the wet ground froze, and by day, the sun
melted it to a cold slush. The food gave out, and the women and
children became almost too weak to travel. On the morning of the
fourth day, they reached the Oglalas.[1]

AS THE CHEYENNES TREKKED TOWARD THE OGLALA CAMP, THE
Oglalas were still debating whether to obey the summons from the

agencies. Crazy Horse opposed any concessions to the government. Realistically, he knew that the white tide was irreversible, and that the old ways were dying. He had pondered all of this long and carefully. He understood that after twenty years of war, many of his people were exhausted and ready for peace, even if it meant the agencies. He never hid the fact that as a boy he had played with white children, and once considered whites his friends. When the government ultimatum went out, he initially appeared ready to cooperate. The more he considered it, however, the more he realized that he could never adjust to the life of a Loafer Indian at the agencies, dependent on the mercy and charity of the whites.

A few days after the Reynolds fight, a runner came from an Indian camp near Fort Fetterman with the news that the soldiers said Crazy Horse's village had been destroyed. The Oglalas thought this was funny, until it became obvious a big Indian camp really had been attacked and destroyed. But whose camp? As they argued the possibilities, a scout signaled from a hilltop that a large number of people were approaching. They moved slowly, mostly on foot, showing signs of hard travel.

Realizing something was wrong, Crazy Horse sent the herald around the camp telling the women to start preparing hot meals. Then he and the other warriors packed horses with meat and robes, rigged travois for the sick, old, and wounded, and headed out to meet these strangers.

Moving down a little slope, they first encountered He Dog, with the Cheyenne, Two Moons. Behind them straggled men, women, and children, many with their feet wrapped in pieces of blankets. Mounted warriors rode the flanks and the rear, guarding the others and helping the boys herd the worn-out ponies that they had recovered in the raid on Reynolds's camp.

Food was distributed on the spot. Those no longer able to walk were loaded on travois. When they got to the camp, the Oglalas began doubling up their own families among relatives to make room in their lodges for the newcomers. From the cooking fires, people called out, "Cheyennes, come here! Come and eat here!"[2]

The Cheyennes rested for the remainder of the day. That night, the chiefs of the two nations called a council. After the pipe was passed around, Two Moons rose and addressed the group.

Friends! The pony soldiers have fired on my people. They have broken our friendship. They have driven our women and children into the hills to go hungry and cold. They have burned our homes, stole our horses, and now have our hatred. They are coming here to fight you, and we have come to you as friends. Give us arms and horses and we will fight. Give our women robes and food for our children, until we can supply them, and my warriors will fight [the whites] to death. Stay with us and we will stay with you. We will fight with you until we are all killed or they are driven back.

One by one, the Cheyenne warriors rose in support. As Two Moons remembered, "It was war, war, war."[3]

THE RESOURCES OF CRAZY HORSE'S OWN VILLAGE WERE STRAINED by the arrival of the destitute Cheyennes. They would be better off joining Sitting Bull's Hunkpapas, who had more provisions. The next morning, the Oglalas and Cheyennes started toward the Hunkpapa camp near Chalk Butte, some thirty-five miles to the north. The Oglalas turned their spare ponies over to the footsore Cheyennes, so no one had to walk. It took them a day to reach the enormous village, which contained more Hunkpapas than Oglalas and Cheyennes combined.

Although the Hunkpapas had no warning the Oglalas and Cheyennes were coming, preparations to take care of them began as soon as they were sighted approaching from the south. Two giant lodges were erected in the middle of the village, and the Hunkpapa women put meat to boil. The heralds went about calling, "The Cheyennes are very poor. All who have blankets or robes or tepees [sic] to spare should give to them."

People brought blankets, robes, spare tipis, even ponies. Within days, the Cheyennes were burdened with gifts, and each family was installed in its own lodge. It was as if the Reynolds fight had never happened.

"Oh, what good hearts they had!" Wooden Leg remembered, years later. "I never can forget the generosity of Sitting Bull's Uncpapa [sic] Sioux on that day."

It was especially remarkable since this was the first time most

Cheyennes had ever seen the Hunkpapas. A large, free-roaming
tribe of hunters, the Hunkpapas' normal range was far to the north
and east. The Cheyennes knew them only through stories passed
on by the Oglalas and the Miniconjous, who sometimes hunted
and intermarried with the Cheyennes. By coincidence, a large band
of Miniconjous under Lame Deer was at that moment also in the
village and, between them and the Oglalas, the Cheyennes found
many familiar faces among the strange, near-legendary Hunkpapas. Altogether there were perhaps 235 lodges—over 1,600 people—in this immense camp.[4]

Like the Cheyennes, the Miniconjous had little previous trouble
with the soldiers, but Sitting Bull was determined to rally them all.
Calling a council, he said:

> We are an island of Indians in a lake of whites. We must stand to-
> gether, or they will rub us out separately. These soldiers have come
> shooting; they want war. All right, we'll give it to them.

Runners were sent to all Sioux, Cheyenne, and Arapaho camps
and agencies west of the Missouri. Sitting Bull was summoning
them to the Rosebud River, where he would host the great annual
council of the Lakota Nation in June. There, he hoped to plan a decisive battle that would break the whites, just as Red Cloud had
done with Fetterman almost ten years earlier.[5]

SITTING BULL'S CALL TO ARMS AGGRAVATED AN ALREADY SERIOUS
division among the Indians at the agencies. On April 6, Congress
finally authorized an emergency appropriation of $150,000 for ra-
tions at Red Cloud and Spotted Tail, but by then many were starving. So far, the majority of the agency Indians wanted to cooperate.
They were not friendly; they were frightened. At the agencies, they
had associated with whites long enough to understand the real
power behind the government—something Crazy Horse and Sitting Bull did not. They knew the vacillations and appeasements
were signs of indecision, not weakness, and if Washington decided
on a war policy, the ability to pursue it was limitless. They feared
if Crazy Horse and Sitting Bull persisted in their resistance, everyone would be dragged down with them.

Despite these fears, there was an active war faction at the Red Cloud Agency, and it was headed by none other than Red Cloud himself, who had lost faith in the government. Far from being cowed, he wanted to fight and had already permitted his son, Jack, to leave the reservation. Although the agency Oglalas managed to convince Red Cloud to stay, many others slipped out of the reservation, aggravated by starvation, encouraged by Sitting Bull, and with Red Cloud's blessings.[6]

PHIL SHERIDAN WAS NOT YET AWARE OF SITTING BULL'S MESSAGE to the tribes, but he nevertheless realized that the war, which should have ended victoriously by now, was only beginning. Crook's campaign had accomplished nothing except to unite the Indians. From Cheyenne to New York, the newspapers were beginning to criticize the attack on the Indian village—labeling it "Crook's Chagrin," and his "partial failure."[7] Frustration led the Cheyenne *Daily Leader* to suggest that Terry's command should share some of the responsibility. Custer and Gibbon were supposed to have worked in concert with the Big Horn Expedition, but the *Leader* charged they appeared more interested in parades and pageantry, leaving the actual fighting to Crook.[8]

This was hardly fair, since Terry's troops were only now digging themselves out of the snow. Still, it looked bad when, so far, the only successful effort in the Department of Dakota was Brisbin's relief column to the Fort Pease stockade, which finally returned to Fort Ellis on March 17, the very day Reynolds hit the Cheyenne village.

Sheridan was also perturbed that Crook was now sniping with the agents at Red Cloud and Spotted Tail. In his initial report of the Reynolds fight, Crook claimed his troops had discovered "a perfect magazine of ammunition, war material and general supplies . . . every evidence was found to prove these Indians to be in copartnership with those at the Red Cloud & Spotted Tail agencies & that the proceeds of their raids upon the settlements have been taken into those agencies & supplies brought out in return." He urged that the agencies be relocated to the Missouri River as soon as possible.[9]

Crook did not detail his "evidence" for the simple reason he had none. The two agents—Howard, at Spotted Tail, and Hastings, at Red Cloud—challenged him immediately. Hastings counter-charged Crook's "complete failure" had created a dangerous situation at the agencies, since it might demonstrate to otherwise peaceful Indians that the whites could be defeated, and provoke a general uprising.[10]

Despite his personal animosity toward Crook the man, Sheridan was inclined to believe Crook the soldier. An uncomplicated person, Sheridan saw everything in simple terms of black and white, good and evil—and he, of course, was always on the side of virtue. To Sheridan, every Indian was a savage, who never missed an opportunity to scalp white men and rape white women. Indian agents were, at best, misguided altruists, and, at worst, thieves.

At this point, though, Sheridan's main concern was getting Terry's forces in Montana and Dakota into the field. Colonel Gibbon, who had finally managed to reach his departure point at Fort Ellis, was to march east, keeping north of the Yellowstone River until he linked up with Custer, who was coming west from Dakota. Unaware that the hostiles were moving west toward the Rosebud, the generals believed they were heading north. Thus if Gibbon marched along the Yellowstone, he would stand between the Indians and the Missouri River, denying them access to the northern reservations.

The error of that plan became apparent on March 30, when Gibbon wired Terry in St. Paul that Indian trails showed them to be well south of his assigned sector. Since he would have the only force in the field, he wondered if he was still restricted to blocking off the reservations, or could he engage Sitting Bull wherever found?

Terry told him to remain north of the Yellowstone until he determined Crook's plans, and until Custer started west from Fort Abraham Lincoln. By the time Gibbon reached the Bighorn River, Terry would have more information. In the meantime, he said Gibbon could strike hostile bands anywhere, provided he continued to block their access to the Missouri River and the northern reservations.[11]

Gibbon's task looked easy on the maps at Terry's headquarters in St. Paul. Unlike the Cheyennes encountered by Crook and Reynolds, however, any hostiles Gibbon might meet would be expecting trouble, and could readily avoid a large military column operating alone. So long as he had to stay north of the Yellowstone, patroling the approaches to the Missouri while working toward Custer, Gibbon's chances of finding a major hostile village were slim to none. But 1876 was a freakish year, in which the unlikely happened frequently. When Gibbon did meet the Indians, he would prove even more inept than Reynolds. Reynolds, at least, had fought.

ON APRIL 19, A GROUP OF HALF-BREEDS ARRIVED AT THE CHEYenne Agency with information that demolished the last vestiges of achievement Crook might have claimed for his Big Horn Expedition. They said Crazy Horse was nowhere in the vicinity of Reynolds's fight. Instead, the village was predominantly Cheyenne, with only a few lodges of Oglalas. According to the half-breeds, the attack outraged the Indians, who were threatening an equally swift and sudden reprisal against the whites. Sheridan forwarded the report to Crook without comment.[12]

The meaning was clear. Through his own vanity as much as the blundering of his officers, Crook not only failed to accomplish his objective but also had made a complete fool of himself. Crazy Horse was still out there, somewhere, and had new allies in the Cheyennes. Neither Crook, Bourke, Frank Grouard, nor anyone else connected with the expedition ever admitted the mistake; until their dying days, they insisted they had attacked and destroyed Crazy Horse's village.

As the implications of Crook's failure were being absorbed, a new complication arose. The summer wanderers, who habitually spent the winters near the agencies of the Great Sioux Reservation, were ready to leave for their seasonal hunt. Nomads at heart, they were disdainful of the sedentary Loafer Indians who remained close to the agency, and were likewise indifferent to the government ultimatum.

The summer wanderers had followed the same pattern for years, leaving the reservation to attend the annual council and hunt on the unceded lands of Montana and Wyoming guaranteed them in the Fort Laramie Treaty. This year, however, they were going in unprecedented numbers. Living apart from the agency Indians and government officials, they understood almost nothing of federal policy and believed they would be attacked if they remained on the reservation. They watched while whites invaded their territory and moved into the Black Hills. As hunters, they were less affected by short rations than those directly tied to the agencies, but nevertheless were growing hungry as their meat supplies from the previous year gave out. Throughout the winter and spring of 1876, their fear and resentment grew and, as Agent Hastings had predicted, Crook's fiasco encouraged their new defiance.

Because their ponies grew lean and weak during the winter, the summer wanderers always waited to begin their annual migration with the new growth of grass in the spring for the ponies. In 1876, the new grass began in the last week of April. The various tribes and bands began moving out to the prairies on the western edge of the reservation. After a couple of weeks there, the ponies would be strong, and the summer wanderers could get under way in time to participate in the great council.[13]

The stirring of the summer wanderers was noticed almost immediately. On April 27, a Sioux scout at the Standing Rock Agency told government officials that most of the young men were leaving with their best ponies to join Sitting Bull. Five days later, Maj. Marcus Reno, commanding Fort Abraham Lincoln in Custer's absence, notified Terry that several hundred lodges had been reported between the fort, on the Missouri River near Bismarck, and the Yellowstone. Although Reno could not have known about the great council, it was obvious the Indians were beginning to consolidate. Reno also confirmed, through scouts, that the Cheyennes attacked by Crook and Reynolds were now with Sitting Bull.[14]

Already this mass movement was being felt by the civilian population. A growing number of settlers and gold seekers reported attacks. By and large, however, the frontier was still relatively peaceful considering the number of Indians roaming the area. Most of them wanted to reach the great assembly and fight the decisive battle planned by Sitting Bull.

9

Blundering Along the Yellowstone

IT WAS IMPOSSIBLE FOR THE COMBINED CAMPS OF THE HUNKPA-
pas, Oglalas, Miniconjous, and Cheyennes to remain in one place
for any length of time. The game would soon be hunted out and
the horses would eat all the grass. The chiefs decided to move
north, following the game and fresh spring grass of the sheltered
valleys until time for the great council. Then they would turn west,
crossing the mountains and establishing their camp along the
Rosebud.

The Cheyennes led the march, sending scouts ahead. The
Oglalas and Miniconjous were in the middle, their fighting men
guarding the flanks, while the Hunkpapas were last, some of their
warriors staying well behind to make sure no one followed.

As they traveled, they met up with the Sans Arcs, and later with
the Blackfeet. Both of these groups brought fresh horses, which
were distributed where they were needed. They were even joined
by some Santee Sioux, refugees who had fled to Canada after the
ill-fated 1862 uprising in Minnesota, and had ultimately arrived in
Montana. The Santees were the poorest of all, having few goods
and no horses. They even used large dogs as draft animals.

At the Powder River, they met a large band of Cheyennes under

Lame White Man, who had been looking for Sitting Bull since leaving the White River Agency. More Cheyennes joined on the Tongue River, bringing ammunition, sugar, coffee, and tobacco. There were now six tribal circles, each tribe with twice as many people as when the march began.[1]

There was no particular destination other than the general vicinity of the Rosebud, which Sitting Bull had designated for the annual council of the Lakotas. The immediate route was determined by the availability of game and forage. Scouts reported large herds of buffalo by the Rosebud, so this vast gathering of Indians worked slowly north, following the Tongue Valley until they could conveniently turn west, across the narrow strip separating that valley from the Rosebud.[2]

MEANWHILE, COLONEL GIBBON WAS MOVING EAST OUT OF FORT Ellis on a line that would intersect the Indian march. Known to the Indians as "No Hipbone" because of a crippling pelvic wound received at Gettysburg, the fifty-year-old Gibbon was a distinguished veteran whose service dated back to the Mexican War. At the outbreak of the Civil War, he was named brevet brigadier general of volunteers and, in subsequent battles, Gen. George McClellan called Gibbon's troops "equal to the best soldiers of any army in the world."

In 1866, he accepted the permanent rank of colonel in the Regular Army and, three years later, was given district command in Montana under General Terry. Although he approached this campaign with such caution that his men wondered about his courage, Gibbon was no slacker. Yet he privately suspected that the Indian situation was more serious, and the number of hostiles far greater, than most other ranking officers believed and this, in the long run, affected his judgment.[3]

Gibbon's column left Fort Ellis in staggered units, the first being a party sent ahead on March 23 to establish a field supply depot by the new Crow Agency. On April 3, Gibbon wired Terry: "Expedition finally off today. Total of 409 men and 27 officers."[4] As a matter of fact, by that date most of the troops had already reached a rendezvous designated Camp Supply, on the north bank of the Yellowstone, only eighteen miles from the Crow Agency depot.[5]

Gibbon arrived in camp on April 7. The following day, he went to the agency and hired some young, militant Crow warriors as scouts. Lt. James H. Bradley was appointed chief of scouts, in perhaps the only intelligent decision Gibbon made during the entire expedition. The thirty-one-year-old Bradley had a talent for analyzing conflicting reports and drawing the right conclusions.

A native of Sandusky County, Ohio, Bradley was slim and handsome with long, well-groomed hair brushed back over the tops of his ears, and a carefully trimmed mustache. He was an enlisted volunteer during the Civil War and, in 1866, was commissioned as second lieutenant in the Eighteenth Infantry. He first fought Indians while serving at Fort Phil Kearny, and Indian fighting would occupy most of the remaining eleven years of his life. Transferring to the Seventh Infantry in 1871, he fought in the Modoc War in California, two years later, and was a first lieutenant at Fort Shaw when the Sioux war broke out.[6]

Bradley's first move was to hire twenty-five-year-old Thomas Leforge as chief scout in charge of the Indians. A white who had spent his entire adult life among the Crows and knew the country, Leforge was then on the agency payroll as a blacksmith. Bradley also hired Barney Bravo, a former soldier of the Twenty-seventh Infantry, who had lived among the Crows for nine years.

The scouting detachment included twenty-three Crow warriors, Leforge, and Bravo. Except for a few middle-aged men, most were young. One, Curly, was about seventeen.[7] In addition, there were civilian guides Henry S. Bostwick, post interpreter at Fort Shaw; Michel (Mitch) Boyer, a half-Santee Sioux who lived among the Crows; and John W. Williamson, H. M. (Muggins) Taylor, and George Herendeen, members of the Fort Pease group. Of these men, Boyer was probably the most competent; according to Gibbon, he had "the reputation of being, next to the celebrated Jim Bridger, the best guide in the country."[8]

The Crows, guides, teamsters, and packers brought the command up to 477 people. It also had a twelve-pound Napoleon field piece and two Gatling guns, although there is no record that anyone besides Gibbon believed these heavy, clumsy weapons would be of any use.

On April 13, Gibbon's Montana Column finally began its long-awaited march along the Yellowstone. The alkali soil was soft and powdery, which, together with the snow, hindered the wagons, often forcing the column to halt and wait. The wagons, Capt. Walter Clifford noted, "must always be kept in sight by the men to guard against a sudden attack by our watchful enemies."

The usual in-service rivalry between horse and foot soldiers expressed itself in various ways. During one halt, the cavalry rode past the resting infantrymen, and one cavalryman noticed a foot soldier's pet dog fitted with a wire muzzle.

"Look at that dog with a nose-bag, Bill," the horse soldier called to a companion. "What do you suppose they put that on him for?"

"That's to keep him from eating cavalry-men," an infantryman shouted.[9]

On April 21, courier Will Logan arrived with mail and newspapers, carrying "bad news" of Crook's failed expedition in March. Logan also brought a message from General Terry, informing Gibbon that his force was alone in the field, and directing him to march no farther east than the mouth of the Bighorn River, unless he was sure of striking a successful blow.

Pondering this order, Bradley wrote:

It appears that General Crook has not yet retaken the field and will not before the middle of May, and that General Custer will not start from Fort Abraham Lincoln until about the same time. We were to have acted in conjunction with these forces, but we are now, when well advanced in the Sioux country, left unsupported. General Crook's victory was not so decisive as we have regarded it, while the fighting seems to have demonstrated that there are heavier forces of warriors to encounter than had been counted upon. General Terry fears that the Indians may combine and get the better of us; and we are therefore to cease our advance for the present and remain in this vicinity until further orders . . . unless sure of striking a successful blow.[10]

That afternoon, the column moved down the river and went into camp at the abandoned stockade of Fort Pease. The soldiers found most structures intact, and the flag still flying overhead, indicating hostile Indians had not been there. The only occupant was a greyhound, apparently abandoned when Brisbin removed the traders, who was overjoyed at seeing humans again.[11] The troops began putting the fort back in order and storing supplies in the buildings.

Over the next three weeks, Gibbon scattered his men in several directions. On April 24, Capt. Edward Ball took two companies of Second Cavalry to scout the Bighorn River country. After six days of routine marching, Ball arrived in the valley of the Little Bighorn, where he found the remains of the Lakota Sun Dance circle from the previous summer. One of the Crow scouts made some charcoal drawings on an empty cracker box, explaining he was telling the Lakotas they would be defeated by the soldiers. Then, he filled the cracks in the wooden box with green grass as a sign it would happen that summer.

Encouraged by the Crow's prophecy, Lt. Edward J. McClernand remarked to the scout, Herendeen, that it would be just as well for Ball's two companies to meet and fight the hostiles. Herendeen disagreed, saying the Lakotas might beat them. The entire scenario had an eerie, unreal quality, for not quite two months later Custer would engage the hostiles at almost the exact spot, and Herendeen would be one of the survivors.[12]

Bradley, meanwhile, had sent four Crows out to scout the area along the Rosebud. They found nothing, but created a minor stir, when they rushed back toward Fort Pease in a panic on May 1, having mistaken Ball's returning cavalry for a party of advancing Lakotas.[13]

With no information on the hostiles, Gibbon could do nothing but wait. Bored with the inaction, the Crows had been slipping away until, now, six were missing. Barney Bravo and an influential Crow named Little Face were sent back to the agency to convince the six deserters to return.

But where were the Lakotas? The question made Dr. Holmes Paulding, expedition surgeon, particularly anxious:

> I wonder where they are? Probably have gone north of the Missouri to their "Agencies" or across the line [into Canada]. I wish we

would go somewhere away from here instead of *purposelessly* fool-ing around in sage brush bottoms all summer.[14]

The location of the soldiers was very well known to the Indians, however. A group of Cheyennes under Two Moons was just out-side the camp at Fort Pease, watching every move. On Tuesday night, May 2, Two Moons slipped down into the camp, his blan-ket wrapped entirely about his body so that only one eye showed, and he could pass for a government Indian. Peering into a tent, he saw a group of officers playing cards. Security was lax. Encouraged by Two Moons's report, the Cheyennes crept in among the horses.

The next morning, when the guide Henry Bostwick went to get his horse and mule from their grazing area just outside the sentry line, he found them missing. The Crows rushed to their grazing area on a little island just above camp, and found all thirty-two of their ponies gone, too. The Crows wept openly in humiliation and outrage. They saw themselves as master horse thieves, and now they had been beaten at their own game, and in the presence of whites.

Recovering their composure, they began trailing the ponies until, about eight miles downstream, the trail crossed the river. As they started to cross, warning shots were fired from the other side, and they fled back to the military camp. To Bradley, this indicated that the hostiles "were not very anxious to get out of the way and had little dread of pursuit. . . . Of the seventeen Crows now with us, not one has a horse."[15]

The next day, two scouts—Half-Yellow-Face and Jack Rabbit Bull—borrowed two government horses, and continued along the trail until they jumped three hostiles presumed to be Sioux. They chased them until the hostiles abandoned their mounts and fled into rocky ground by the river. The Crows took their ponies and returned triumphantly to camp.

"It was a daring deed," Bradley admitted, "for the three Sioux they saw might have been merely lookouts for a heavy force near at hand."

Encouraged by the exploit, Bradley himself rode out on May 7, at the head of seventeen soldiers, four Crows, Bostwick, and

Leforge, and picked up the trail again. About six miles from camp, they found fresh pony tracks, showing hostiles were "hovering around." Deploying his troops against attack, Bradley pushed on throughout the day and into the night. After midnight, the Crows discovered a recently abandoned camp for some thirty warriors.

Bradley's party rode on until daylight, when they found where a party of hostiles had crossed the river. Continuing onward, they discovered a trail about two days old, which kept to the left—or south—side of the Yellowstone. Examining the hoofprints, Bostwick recognized the shoes of his mule. Bradley surmised that after the raid on the camp, the hostiles—whom he still presumed were Sioux—had split up, one group moving ahead with the captured animals, while about thirty remained behind to watch the troops. The three who had lost their horses to the two Crows were obviously outriders, and their discovery prompted the entire group to retreat.

The location of another abandoned camp only confirmed that wherever the main concentration of hostiles might be, it was south of the Yellowstone. Bradley turned his detachment back toward Fort Pease, arriving May 9, without seeing any further signs of hostiles.[16]

Bradley's report at last stirred Gibbon. Since all signs indicated Fort Pease was too far upriver for effective action, Gibbon decided to move farther down. On May 10, the command started off with Captain Clifford's company of infantrymen in three boats that had been left at Fort Pease when Brisbin removed the traders. The remainder of the troops and wagons marched along the riverbank.

"It is really remarkable that the Sioux have permitted us to march so far into their country without offering to molest us," Clifford noted. "Small parties of them are frequently seen, but their camps are well hidden if they have any in this vicinity."[17]

In fact, the Crows were beginning to find substantially more evidence of hostiles than they related to Bradley. Many of these signs were not reported because, Leforge explained,

> To do so might have caused merely a fruitless sally of troops—or, worse, a disastrous encounter. Our observations convinced us that

there were many more Sioux in the country than our present forces could handle.[18]

Bad weather so hampered the march that the column spent practically every second day in camp. A particularly severe storm struck on May 14, when large chunks of hail stampeded the horses. The hail was followed by high wind and rain, knocking down tents, flooding some parts of the camp with almost a foot of water, and soaking the food just as the men were settling down for supper. A party of Crows, sent out the day before, was forced back to camp after the storm obscured a trail they were following.[19]

The next day, the ground was too muddy for marching. Nevertheless, Bradley obtained permission to lead a scouting expedition. The detail consisted of twelve of his own troops, eight infantry volunteers, Barney Bravo, and five Crows. Three days' rations were drawn, and that evening the men left camp one by one so as not to draw attention from watching hostiles. Based on the Crows' observations, Bradley believed he could find the main hostile village on the Tongue River.[20]

In the late morning of May 16, Bradley found the trail that the Crows had lost in the storm, and determined it led to the Tongue, fifteen or eighteen miles above the mouth. "We were now pretty sure of finding a village, and it became necessary to travel with the utmost caution, keeping concealed as much as possible," he wrote.

About 4:00 P.M., two Crows signaled from a ridge that they had found something. Hiding his men in a depression, Bradley rode ahead and joined the Indians. Looking at the valley below, he saw the Tongue about five or six miles in front. Although much of the view was obscured by bluffs, columns of smoke rose from the timber along the river, then came together in a single cloud over the valley. Thousands of buffalo were quietly feeding. As Bradley watched, however, the buffalo suddenly began stampeding, and the Crows concluded Lakota hunters had startled them.

Weary of inaction during the past six weeks, the scouting soldiers wanted to attack. Bradley, however, convinced them that the village contained at least 400 lodges—meaning 800 to 1,000 warriors—and that a fight would be suicidal. The detail hurried back toward Gibbon's camp, putting some distance between themselves and the hostile village before resting their mounts.[21]

Based on Bradley's report, Gibbon decided to move against the Indian village, which was only thirty-five miles away. Excitement stirred the camp. No one was more eager than the Crows, who had been frustrated since losing their ponies. One company of infantry was left in charge of the camp, while the rest moved out.

All together the fighting force was now 392 officers, soldiers, Crows, and civilian auxiliaries. The mounted infantry would cross the river first, followed by the cavalry, after which the foot infantry would be ferried over in boats. The plan was for everyone to be across the river by dark and, with a forced night march, reach the village by daylight.

A mounted infantry detail plunged into the river, the soldiers swimming their horses across, holding on by the mane or tail. When the regular cavalry's turn came, however, everything went wrong. The troopers entered the boats, leading the horses, which were to swim behind. The animals panicked, struggling in the water, and after an hour only ten horses made it to the other side.

The horses were then tied in tandem to drive them across the river. But they stampeded several times and had to be rounded up. Near sunset, several animals drowned. This was enough. After an entire afternoon of effort, only one company of cavalry had reached the opposite bank. Gibbon canceled the move, and ordered those on the other side to recross.[22]

Pvt. Eugene Geant, who had the usual enlisted man's opinions on the wisdom of officers, reflected in his journal, "It looks to me that whoever was in charge did not understand his work or did not care to cross the river."[23]

Gibbon's decision to stop has remained controversial ever since. His stated reason was the problems in crossing. But a large group of hostile warriors, undoubtedly from the village on the Tongue, appeared during the day, and watched the troops from the bluffs overhead. Surprise was lost, and now a move against the village appeared pointless.[24] The confidence of the hostile warriors, who did not bother to conceal themselves, was also unsettling.

On May 19, Gibbon received a message from Terry informing him of the acquisition of steamboats for transportation and supply. Apparently, Custer was in some sort of trouble, because Terry was assuming direct command of the Dakota Column. The message reiterated the general's position that Gibbon was to stay on the north bank, continue moving east, and keep the Indians from crossing.

"If they can be confined to the south bank," Bradley wrote, "some of our column will be pretty sure to strike them, whereas, if they escape into the vast, difficult country to the north, they could more easily elude pursuit, if necessary, crossing the line into the British possessions."[25]

Capt. Lewis Thompson took two companies to block the mouth of the Tongue. Four Crows also left on foot, in hopes of stealing horses from the Lakotas. A heavy rain was falling on May 20, and Gibbon decided to remain in camp that day. At 8:00 A.M., however, the four Crows returned, saying they had seen a formidable war party of several hundred Lakotas, riding toward the Rosebud. On their way back to camp they later heard firing to the east in the direction of Thompson's companies.

Fearing Thompson was under attack, Gibbon took the remaining cavalry and five companies of infantry to find him. After moving down the Yellowstone several miles beyond the mouth of the Rosebud, Gibbon was satisfied the hostiles had not crossed, and bivouacked the command, sending Bradley ahead to look for Thompson. Thirteen miles beyond the bivouac, Bradley discovered a cavalry trail, which he followed until he found indications that soldiers had prepared for a fight. The rain, however, had obliterated the trail and it was getting dark, so he returned to the camp.

Thompson returned the following morning, confirming that he had seen a party of about forty or fifty hostiles on the south bank of the river. He stationed his troops in ravines on the opposite bank, to catch them if they tried to cross, but the Indians remained on the south side. Hoping to steal some horses, Mitch Boyer and one of the Crows swam the river, and stumbled into Lakota scouts. Startled by the encounter, both sides fled, and Boyer and the Crow managed to get back across to the troops. Thompson then quietly withdrew the command and continued his march.[26]

Gibbon found his current bivouac preferable to the previous site, and sent for the remaining men and equipment. No sooner had the troops settled in than two soldiers and a civilian were killed after slipping out of the new camp for some unauthorized hunting.

Any nervousness the men might have felt over the deaths of the three hunters was largely forgotten later that day, when Col. J. D. Chestnut, a Bozeman trader, arrived in a Mackinaw boat with vegetables, butter, eggs, tobacco, and other goods to sell. He also brought a keg of beer for the officers, who promptly drank it.

Although Chestnut reported no encounters during his trip downriver, at dark a party of warriors appeared on the opposite bank, one wearing a large war bonnet, which he shook in defiance. Gibbon immediately took additional precautions for security. The cannon was rolled up to the bank, to fire on anyone attempting to cross the river, and each company was assigned to a position in case of a fight. And since they believed Indian attacks occurred just before dawn, the command was ordered henceforth to fall out at 2:00 A.M., remaining on station until daylight.[27]

On May 24, the now-routine Indian appearances abruptly stopped. Gibbon took their sudden disappearance with misgivings and, after three days, sent out the indefatigable Bradley to find them.

After marching fourteen miles, Bradley halted while Leforge and the Crow scout White Man Runs Him ascended a height, which gave them a view of the Tongue and the Rosebud.

"Indian lodges were strung along the Rosebud for a distance of two miles," Leforge recalled. "It appeared the valley and adjacent foothills were solid with grazing horses."[28]

They signaled to Bradley, who joined them. After confirming his line of retreat was open, the lieutenant "passed about half an hour watching the camp and studying the probabilities." This obviously was the same village he had seen on the Tongue, thirty-five miles from Gibbon's earlier camp. But instead of moving north, as the soldiers presumed it would, it had shifted west to the Rosebud. The large war party observed by the four Crow horse hunters had been the advance guard. With Gibbon's last move, the distance between the two camps was now reduced to eighteen miles. "The fact that they had moved down within easy striking distance seemed to prove that they held us in no awe," the astute Bradley observed.

Bradley reported back to Gibbon, who decided against a move on the village. Terry was now in the vicinity, and Gibbon later said he interpreted the general's orders as directing him to establish contact as soon as possible. Manpower was also a problem. With one company and several smaller detachments out on various errands, his effective fighting force was reduced to about 350 troops against between 800 and 1,000 warriors.

Despite the odds, most of Gibbon's officers wanted to attack; some later came to think it would have prevented the even greater gathering that massacred Custer only a month later. "On the other hand," Bradley acknowledged, "we might ourselves have been massacred."[29]

Perhaps. Unlike Custer, however, Gibbon knew the location, direction, and approximate strength of the Indian camp. Of all the columns in the field (for by now Terry was moving into Montana and Crook had formed a new expedition), Gibbon's alone had repeatedly come into contact with the main hostile band, which was much farther west than military intelligence had indicated, and was moving still westward. And his scouts had determined they were working toward the divide between the Rosebud and the Little Bighorn.[30]

Gibbon did nothing, and the war dragged on.

10

The March of the Dakota Column

TERRY TOOK PERSONAL COMMAND OF THE DAKOTA COLUMN BE-
cause Custer, through incredibly bad judgment, had incurred the
wrath of the President of the United States.

There had been no reason to suspect that Custer might fall from
grace when the Indian campaign was being organized. On extended leave in the East when the government ultimatum expired,
he reported to departmental headquarters on February 15, to find
nothing had been done to prepare for the operation in his sector.
With Terry, he drew up mobilization plans that factored in the delays caused by winter, and determined April 6 the earliest possible
date on which the Dakota Column could head west from Fort
Abraham Lincoln. His business with Terry finished, Custer sought
transportation to the fort, so he could begin preparations.[1]

Snow blocked the Northern Pacific track beyond Fargo, and
trains to Bismarck, the station for Fort Abraham Lincoln, would
not begin running on a regular schedule until April. To facilitate
Custer's timetable, the railroad assembled a special train fitted
with two snowplows and three locomotives. Forty railroad crew-
men were loaded on board to shovel snow too deep for the plows.
Freight cars contained coal and baggage, and army officers and recruits for the expedition were placed in several day coaches. Mind-

ful of the need to make a profit, even on this run, Northern Pacific also filled some passenger coaches with miners headed for the Black Hills. Custer and his wife, Libbie, were given the paymaster's car, which had its own kitchen, sitting room, and other amenities.

The train left Fargo for Bismarck on March 7. Drifting snow often blocked the track, and sometimes the trainmen had to get out and shovel. Finally, only sixty-five miles from its destination, the train encountered a massive drift that buried the snowplows and one locomotive. After several days of fruitless digging, Custer found a telegrapher among the passengers. The main line running parallel to the track was spliced, and Custer wired his brother, Tom, an officer at Fort Abraham Lincoln. Tom Custer arrived with a mule-drawn mail sleigh and took Custer, Libbie, and the colonel's inevitable pack of hounds back to the post. They arrived on March 13, having taken six days to make a trip normally requiring only a few hours.

Thawing weather finally freed the special train, which rolled into the station at Bismarck a week later.[2] By then, Custer had taken a stagecoach back to Fargo. He had been at Fort Abraham Lincoln only two days before he received a summons to appear in Washington before a congressional committee investigating the War Department.

The congressional investigation centered around Secretary of War William Belknap, who had reaped a fortune selling military contracts. Among the beneficiaries was Orvil Grant, the president's brother. These abuses, the subject of grievances within the army for several years, finally became public through a series of exposés in the New York Herald in 1875. The Democrats, out of power for fifteen years, smelled blood, and in February 1876, the House Committee on Expenditures in the War Department began investigating the secretary of war.[3]

Belknap resigned to avoid impeachment, but the House proceeded against him anyway. Custer, who habitually complained about corruption among military contractors on the Upper Missouri, was summoned as a witness in the congressional investigation.

In his testimony on March 29, Custer mixed rumor and fact concerning Belknap's sale of the post trader contracts, and the economic hardships the system imposed on officers and enlisted men who were required to purchase goods exclusively from the traders. The Indian agency trade was operated by a different department of the federal government,ᵉ but Custer claimed the corruption between the two was often interrelated, and the result was hunger among reservation Indians.

So far, so good. Now, however, Custer began implicating Orvil Grant. Although Orvil had already admitted influence peddling in the Belknap operation, the mention of his name by a lieutenant colonel was more than his brother, the commander-in-chief, was willing to tolerate. President Grant decided to ruin Custer.

Custer left Washington on April 20 (two weeks after his column was supposed to have departed from Fort Abraham Lincoln, and seventeen days after Gibbon marched out of Fort Ellis), but he was summoned back to face accusations of perjury and character assassination. Although General Sherman, who had returned army headquarters to Washington from St. Louis after Belknap's departure, tried to support Custer, Grant instructed interim Secretary of War Alfonso Taft to notify General Terry that someone else should lead the expedition. Sheridan decided Terry himself must do it.

Custer tried to meet personally with Grant and resolve the situation, but the president refused to see him. Finally, on May 1, he started for Fort Abraham Lincoln.[4]

But in Chicago, Custer was placed in detention on Grant's orders. Then he was allowed to continue to Fort Abraham Lincoln, but was told to remain on post, and "not to accompany the expedition supposed to be on the point of starting against the hostile Indians, under General Terry."[5]

In a tearful interview in St. Paul, Custer sought Terry's help to at least keep field command of his regiment. The written personal appeal to Grant, although composed in Custer's name and signed by him, was entirely Terry's work.[6] The letter acknowledged Grant's orders, but respectfully pointed out Custer's own responsibility to the Seventh Cavalry as senior officer of the regiment in the Department of Dakota.[7] Closing, Custer said, "I appeal to you as a soldier to spare me the humiliation of seeing my regiment march to meet the enemy and I not share its dangers." No doubt it was also Terry who, aware of the president's sentimental weakness

for former officers of the Union Army, prompted Custer to sign the
letter with his Civil War brevet rank. Grant relented and allowed
Custer to go as field commander of the Seventh, but with Terry in
charge of the expedition.[8]

Custer was elated. Once before, in 1873, he had been subordinate—to Col. David S. Stanley during a railroad surveying expedition to the Yellowstone. Then he had managed to break away from
the main column, strike out on his own, skirmish with the Lakotas, and enhance his reputation as an Indian fighter. Now, on the
way back to his hotel from Terry's office, he ran into Capt.
William Ludlow, departmental chief engineer. Excitedly, Custer
told Ludlow he had his regiment again, and soon would "cut
loose" and move out on his own. He said he "got away with Stanley and would be able to swing clear of Terry." Believing Terry
should know he had been deceived, Ludlow repeated the information to his superiors. But by the time it went through army channels, the general and Custer were already en route to Fort
Abraham Lincoln, where troops were assembling to form the third
arm of Sheridan's oft-postponed pincer.[9]

The column's departure was set for May 15. By now, Gibbon
had been marching sporadically eastward along the Yellowstone
for almost six weeks, and Crook was preparing for another push
north from Wyoming. After a two-day delay because of bad
weather, the long-awaited Dakota Column moved out of Fort
Abraham Lincoln at 5:00 A.M., May 17. The Seventh Cavalry, in
the lead, was distinctive in its color-coordinated horses, one of
Custer's whims. Company A rode blacks; B, D, H, I, and L, bays;
companies C, G, and K had sorrels; and E, grays. M was the only
company with mixed colors.[10]

As the two-mile line of troops and support services marched out,
those left behind at the fort saw an eerie phenomenon. The early
morning sun began to burn through the haze, creating a mirage
that obscured the horizon. It appeared as though the Seventh was
riding up into the sky.[11]

During the first day, the column was accompanied by Libbie;
Custer's niece, Emma Reed; and his younger sister, Margaret Calhoun, whose husband, Lt. James (Jimmi) Calhoun, was acting
commander of Company L, of the Seventh. Other members of the

family traveling with the regiment included brothers Tom Custer, a two-time Medal of Honor winner who was captain of Company C, and Boston Custer, signed on as a scout in a blatant case of nepotism; and eighteen-year-old nephew Armstrong (Autie) Reed, Emma's brother, along as a guest. Collectively, this group, together with loyal officers, was called the Custer clan.

"The column . . . seemed unending," Libbie Custer wrote. "The grass was not then suitable for grazing, and as the route of travel was through a barren country, immense quantities of forage had to be transported. The wagons themselves seemed to stretch out interminably. . . . The number of men, citizens, employees, Indian scouts, and soldiers was about twelve hundred. There were nearly seventeen hundred animals in all."[12]

The march of the Dakota Column was the first time in nearly ten years since the Seventh Cavalry's creation that all twelve companies were serving together; previously the regiment had been scattered throughout the frontier and as far east as Kentucky. Aside from the fully assembled Seventh, the column included a battery of Gatling guns; two companies of the Seventeenth Infantry; one company of Sixth Infantry; and a detachment of Ree Indian scouts under command of Lt. Charles A. Varnum, Seventh Cavalry.

As the Dakota troops had no experience with pack mules, 150 wagons were used to carry supplies. Terry, however, had ordered 250 pack saddles loaded on the wagons so that, in case of emergency, the wagon mules could be unharnessed and packed for transportation. Maj. Orlando Moore was already at the rendezvous at Glendive Creek, with three companies of infantry and additional supplies sent up the Missouri River by steamer.[13]

Unlike Crook, who gloried in press coverage, Terry carried only one newspaperman, a shadowy figure named Mark Kellogg, an employee of the *Bismarck Tribune* who also sent dispatches to the *New York Herald.* Although Kellogg was the only accredited correspondent, Terry's adjutant, Capt. Edward W. Smith furnished dispatches to the *St. Paul Pioneer-Press,* and Custer himself authored several unsigned dispatches to the *New York Herald,* which the paper attributed to "a prominent officer."

While there was little publicity, the Dakota Column had its share of diarists, ranging from General Terry himself to a civilian scout named Charles Alexander Reynolds, called "Lonesome Charlie" for his solitary habits. Unlike the verbose men of Crook's column, however, these chroniclers kept their diaries short and to the point, making them primarily itineraries—records of miles marched and weather conditions.[14]

In camp the first night, the soldiers of the Seventh Cavalry were paid. Much to their resentment, the money had been withheld until now, to avoid their debauching themselves in the saloons and bordellos of Bismarck before the march.

The following morning, May 18, the Custer women were escorted back to the post by the paymaster, while Terry's expedition continued its march toward Montana. As she watched the column ride off, Libbie Custer had an uneasy feeling of impending doom.[15]

Libbie was aware of the factionalism that had permeated the Seventh since Custer had left Maj. Joel Elliott's command to be massacred during Sheridan's Washita Campaign in 1868. From that day forward, Frederick W. Benteen, commander of Company H and senior captain of the regiment, despised Custer as a soldier and a human being, and became the leader of the anti-Custer group among the officers.

A Virginian, the pipe-smoking Benteen opted for the Union Army at the outbreak of the Civil War, and by 1865 had been breveted to colonel. He had been with the Seventh since its organization, participating in every major fight involving the regiment since then. Born in 1834, he was five years older than Custer, silver-haired, and known for his irascible disposition, and occasional drunken binges.

Custer respected him professionally but hated him personally. He also appears to have feared Benteen, who, at least once, called his bluff on a threat. The two men tended to avoid each other except as duty required.

The unknown factor in this regimental in-fighting was Maj. Marcus A. Reno, second in field command after Custer himself. Oddly enough, the two men did not know each other well. Reno was assigned to the Seventh in 1869, and with the various companies scattered along the frontier, he and Custer had never served at the same post until this year.

Reno attended West Point, where his excessive—almost deliberate—accumulation of demerits delayed graduation from 1855 to 1857, and he narrowly avoided dismissal. Despite this dismal start, he distinguished himself during the Civil War, ultimately attaining the brevet rank of colonel. After the war, feeling his abilities unappreciated, he began a letter-writing campaign that antagonized superiors ranging from the superintendent of West Point, where Reno served briefly as an instructor, to President Andrew Johnson. This brought a series of out-of-the-way assignments until he reached the Seventh. After Custer got in trouble in Washington, Reno had tried to obtain command of the Dakota Column. The effort, quickly squelched by General Terry, was typical of Reno, and was resented by Custer. "It was pretty clear that there wasn't much love lost between the two men," Pvt. Charles Windolph recalled.

Cold and aloof, Reno did not carry himself well in society. That, combined with more or less chronic drinking, made him unpopular among the officers. Dr. James DeWolf, a contract surgeon on the expedition, summed up the feelings of many when he wrote his wife: "Reno who commands my wing I cannot like. . . ." Reno and Benteen also disliked each other, although it did not approach the animosity they both felt for the Custer clan.[16]

The acrimony between these three officers—Custer, Reno, and Benteen—was a key factor in the events that began unfolding during the march of the Dakota Column. Less important from a command viewpoint, but worthy of mention because of circumstances of time and place, was one of Custer's junior officers, Lt. James G. (Jack) Sturgis. A year out of West Point, he was the son of Col. Samuel Sturgis, the Seventh Cavalry's nominal commanding officer.

The progress of the expedition was unendurably slow. The animals provided for the contract wagons were inferior, and some of the government mules were young and unbroken. Weather also slowed the column. In one of his early dispatches to the St. Paul newspaper, Captain Smith, the adjutant, wrote:

> The expedition started in the midst of the rainy season, when even good soil is unfit to support the wheels of heavily laden vehicles, when every little slough is a bottomless quagmire, and when the alkaline tracts are only less treacherous than a "quaking bog. . . ."[17]

Streams and ravines were impassable, and Terry was often forced to halt, sometimes overnight, while Lt. Edward Maguire, his field engineer, supervised construction of bridges. Thirteen spans were required on one fourteen-mile stretch before reaching the Little Missouri. During the first two weeks, a day's march of ten miles was more or less the norm.[18] Much of the problem was the route. Terry had hoped to use the trail established in Colonel Stanley's railroad survey of 1873. Rain, however, had obscured the path, forcing the general to send out scouts in search of landmarks, and confusing the guides, who sometimes led the column astray.[19]

On May 29, the troops arrived at the Little Missouri, having marched 166 miles in thirteen days, less than half the distance Crook normally covered in the same time. Since the earliest alarming reports of Indians leaving the reservations, rumor held that they intended to make their stand along the Little Missouri. To ascertain the truth, Terry sent Custer up the river valley with several companies of cavalry and Ree scouts to look for signs of the hostiles.[20]

Among the Rees was Custer's favorite, Bloody Knife, son of a Hunkpapa father and Ree mother. The first fifteen or sixteen years of this Indian's life were miserable, for they were spent among his father's people, who treated the mixed-blooded boy as a pariah. Thereafter, he lived among the Rees, with whom he identified, and was quick to join any military expedition against the Lakotas. Although he had formally enlisted several times, he was now between hitches, and accompanied the Dakota Column as a civilian employee. Bloody Knife liked Custer, and Custer repaid his loyalty with more respect than he appeared to give most people, Indian or white.[21]

Officially, Custer *claimed* to have marched his men an exhausting fifty miles in eleven hours. Returning to camp, he reported there had been no Indians in the area for six months, "not even a small hunting party." While it is unlikely there were hostiles in the area, some question exists as to how much effort Custer actually spent looking for them. His account to Libbie described a picnic more than a scouting expedition. Horses bogged down in the mud of the Little Missouri, and it became a game to see who would get thrown.[22]

Amusing though it may have been to the Custer clan, the situation was embarrassing to General Terry, who had assured Sheridan that he would encounter and make quick work of the Indians. He also was beginning to see through Custer's games. As the command crossed the Little Missouri on May 31, Terry noted, "Custer [was] behind playing Wagon Master." The same day left the column "without any authority whatever."[23]

The unauthorized departure from the column was another day of frolic among the Custers, which the colonel and Tom occupied with pranks on younger brother Boston. Terry, however, was less amused, for with the Custer boys cavorting about the countryside, and Charlie Reynolds off trophy hunting for bighorn sheep, the command got lost again. "We were not on Stanley's trail," the general noted in his diary, "turned back & examined ground. . . ." Part of the sentence is illegible, but Terry's mood is evident.

Reprimanded by the general, Custer tried to excuse himself by saying that he thought he would be more useful riding in advance. Nevertheless, Terry's rebuke had the desired effect. Custer, who realized that his very presence on the expedition was due solely to Terry's intercession on his behalf, began paying closer attention to the business at hand.[24]

After crossing the Little Missouri, the column marched eleven miles and went into camp among the badlands beyond the river valley. Although it was the last night of May, the temperature plunged, and about midnight, snow began falling. The snowfall continued the next day, but melted as it hit the ground, churning up thick mud and forcing Terry to remain in camp for thirty-six hours.[25]

Late in the bitterly cold day of June 3, scouts arrived with a message from Colonel Gibbon, who was on the north branch of the Yellowstone opposite the mouth of the Rosebud. There he was waiting for supplies from Fort Ellis before continuing eastward to meet Terry. He had encountered no Indians on the north side of the Yellowstone, but he reported those who shadowed him on the south bank. There was no mention of the giant village that Bradley had seen twice.

The news from Gibbon—or lack of it—combined with the failure to locate Indians on the Little Missouri, convinced Terry that they were farther south than anticipated. Changing plans, he decided to bypass Major Moore's depot at Glendive, and head directly for the Powder River. Gibbon, meanwhile, would continue scouting the north bank of the Yellowstone, to keep the Indians from crossing. "It is hoped," Captain Smith wrote to the *St. Paul Pioneer-Press*, "that by this arrangement the Indians will be caught between this column and Gibbon's."[26]

Pushing southwest, the Dakota Column found its first sign of Indians, "three 'Wickey-ups' with leaves still green," according to Terry. Four days later, the troops finally reached the Powder, about twenty-five miles from its confluence with the Yellowstone. Terry took two companies of cavalry down to the mouth of the Powder at the Yellowstone, where the steamer *Far West* waited. The next morning, the boat carried him up the Yellowstone to meet Gibbon. More than four months after the government declared hostilities, two of Sheridan's three columns had finally linked. They had not, however, caught any Indians between them.

PART III

THE INDIANS ASCENDENT

11

Crook Tries Again

IN THE PLATTE, THE EXPERIENCE OF WINTER—SO DIFFERENT FROM that season in Arizona—convinced Crook he could not mount a prolonged campaign until late spring, when there was ample grass for the horses and the ground had dried from the early thaws. Besides being better from a logistical standpoint, a spring campaign would give Terry's forces time to get into the field for a coordinated offensive. The delay also provided an opportunity to pressure the wavering agency Indians to side with the government.

Crook, however, could not wait too long. The Reynolds debacle had damaged morale. A large number of enlisted men deserted from Fort D. A. Russell, claiming they would not serve under officers who abandoned their dead and wounded to the Indians. Captain Noyes had already been tried for his mistake in the fight, but his sentence was only an administrative reprimand. Although timely court-martials for Reynolds and Moore would have helped restore confidence, their trials were delayed because the serious nature of the charges against them required extensive preparation, and the immediate demands of war took priority.[1]

In early May, Crook learned between 800 and 1,000 warriors had left the Red Cloud Agency, heading north beyond the Powder River. Most of their families had also deserted. Some fifty lodges

(about 350 individuals) were also missing from the Spotted Tail
Agency. A week later, a prominent chief named No Water, and
Crazy Horse's protégé, Little Big Man, led another ten lodges from
Red Cloud, taking government horses and mules, "right in the face
of the agent, and in spite of his remonstrances."[2]

Exasperated, Crook telegraphed Sheridan: "Can't you do something about this[?] Indications are that we shall have the whole
fighting force of the Sioux nation to contend with. . . ."[3]

Crook's frustrations were compounded because even with anticipated delays, his expedition was behind schedule. Arriving in
Cheyenne May 10, after an overnight train ride from departmental
headquarters in Omaha, he told a reporter from the Cheyenne
Leader that he initially had planned to take the field from Fort Fetterman in five days. But because government funds had not been
forwarded to purchase fresh horses for the cavalry, and delivery of
supplies was slow, he was now unable to fix an exact starting date.[4]

The next day, accompanied by Bourke, Grouard, and the indefatigable correspondent Robert Strahorn, Crook left for the Red
Cloud Agency looking for scouts. Although the government authorized pay and allowances for only 50 Indians, he wanted at
least 300, promising plunder and government rations in lieu of
cash. While he doubted the agency Lakotas would cooperate, he
wanted the scouts enough that he convinced himself it was worth
the 200-mile trip from Cheyenne.

Despite his misgivings, Crook almost succeeded in his mission.
Agent Hastings, who had no use for the army, was away at the
Spotted Tail Agency, and in his absence the general's first meeting
with the chiefs appeared promising. When Hastings returned,
however, he advised the Indians not to cooperate. As a result, in
their second meeting with Crook, the mood of the chiefs was defiant. Disgusted, Crook berated them with the fact that the Crows,
Bannocks, and Shoshones—all hereditary enemies of the Lakotas—had offered to send scouts. If the agency Lakotas refused to
serve, he would accept the offer from these other nations.[5]

Crook went on to Fort Laramie, and from there sent a telegram
to divisional headquarters in Chicago, asking Sheridan to notify
the Crows that he wanted 200 to 300 warriors to meet him at Fort
Reno on May 30. He also reported the defiant attitude encouraged

by Agent Hastings. This prompted the lieutenant general to transfer Lt. Col. Eugene Carr and eight companies of the Fifth Cavalry from Gen. John Pope's Department of the Missouri to Wyoming. Carr would straddle the trail from Red Cloud to the war zone, blocking any agency Indians who might try and join the hostiles.

Initially, Sheridan planned to send these new troops to police the Red Cloud and Spotted Tail Agencies, but decided to wait until he could "examine the condition of affairs myself." While he did not question that Indians were leaving the reservation to join the hostiles, the estimated numbers reaching Chicago had become so large that he was beginning to wonder whether the reports were overly alarmist.[6]

Because of commitments in the East, Sheridan's inspection tour of the agencies was weeks in the future. It was not necessary for Crook to wait and personally escort the lieutenant general, nor did he intend to. Preparations continued for the new expedition. At the same time, Crook also was refining his notions of warfare on the northern plains. The Sioux and Cheyennes, he believed, were "a brave and bold people," but could never stand the punishment of a prolonged military campaign as had the Apaches of Arizona. The difference was that the Apaches had little in the way of material goods, and were fighting to preserve their independent way of life. The Plains Indians, however, had acquired extensive wealth in ponies, buffalo hides and robes, food stores, and trade articles, "and the loss of that would be felt most deeply." Thus Crook hoped to hammer away at the Indians, harassing them, destroying their villages and pony herds, and denying them the ability to hunt and acquire food, hides, and robes. He would wreck their economy and thus their ability to wage war.[7]

As Crook labored to get his expedition into the field, public opinion was beginning to divide about the war. Although the expansionist *New York Herald* continued to thunder against the Indians, as did many of the western newspapers, opposition was building, not only against the war, but against the entire government Indian policy. In the face of economic hardship wrought by the ongoing financial panic, the program appeared to be an expensive failure, particularly in view of mounting evidence of corruption throughout the system.[8]

Even the *Omaha Herald*, close to the frontier and at the administrative seat of Crook's department, felt things had gone too far:

> Our latest Indian war was as needless as it is proving to be cruel and damaging. The movement of Gen. Crook in the winter has driven the Indians upon the war path. The failure of the campaign resulted in the failure to awe the red men and renewed their confidence in their ability to resist the lawless spirit of encroachment in which this whole Black Hills occupation originated.[9]

Indifferent to such criticism, Crook left Fort Laramie for Fort Fetterman on May 17, to complete preparations for his new advance northward toward Terry and Gibbon. He completed the now familiar eighty-one-mile trip the next day, and was followed five days later by three companies of the Ninth Infantry. Last to move out was the Third Cavalry, which departed for Fort Fetterman May 27 under Lt. Col. William B. Royall.

The new campaign, now officially designated the Big Horn and Yellowstone Expedition, began moving north from Fort Fetterman at 1:00 P.M., May 29. "The long black line of mounted men stretched for more than a mile with nothing to break the sombreness [sic] of color save the flashing of the sun's rays back from the carbines and bridles," Bourke wrote. "A long, running streak of white told us our wagons were already well underway and a puff of dirt just in front indicated the line of march of the Infantry Battalion."

The expedition's combat strength included ten companies of the Third Cavalry and five companies of Second Cavalry, all under command of Colonel Royall; and three companies of Ninth Infantry and two companies of Fourth Infantry, under Maj. Alex Chambers—a total of 992 officers and enlisted men.[10]

Royall was perhaps the most experienced soldier on the campaign, having enlisted thirty years earlier as a volunteer lieutenant. Cited for gallantry in the Mexican War, he was transferred to the Midwest, where he had his first Indian fight in 1848. In 1855, he accepted a commission as first lieutenant in the cavalry, and served on the Texas frontier where he was again cited for gallantry. Royall distinguished himself in the Civil War, and on the Indian frontier after the war ended.[11]

One of the most innovative and talented cavalry officers under Royall was Capt. Anson Mills, who had distinguished himself in the Reynolds fight. Mills was nominally a company commander in the Third Cavalry but in combat was often placed in charge of an entire battalion.

A native of Thorntown, Indiana, Mills entered West Point in 1855, resigning in his second year after being found deficient in mathematics. He then went to Texas, which he henceforth considered home. Despite his loyalty to his adopted state, Mills remained a Unionist, and when Texas seceded, traveled to Washington where he secured an appointment as a lieutenant of the infantry. After the Confederate surrender, he was part of the contingent of regulars sent to relieve volunteer troops who had protected the western frontier during the war. In 1876, he had been stationed in Dakota and Wyoming for ten years, and was nearing his forty-second birthday.[12]

Crook's column also included the usual civilian personnel, such as guides, scouts, packers, and wagon drivers. Among them was a woman, Martha Jane Cannary, who passed herself as a man and inadvertently was hired as a driver by the wagonmaster at Fort Fetterman. Though few had heard of her at that time, she later gained notoriety and entered legend as Calamity Jane.[13]

With the war gaining momentum, the number of professional news correspondents had grown. Besides Strahorn, there was Joe Wasson, representing the *New York Tribune* and San Francisco *Alta California,* who had accompanied Crook's Apache Campaign in Arizona; Thomas C. MacMillan, a twenty-five-year-old Scotsman of the Chicago *Inter-Ocean;* Reuben Briggs Davenport, who went so far as to stencil "New York Herald" on virtually everything but his horse; and John F. Finerty of the *Chicago Times,* a tough, twenty-nine-year-old Irishman who was probably Strahorn's chief rival in determination and daring. Ironically, Finerty had hoped to cover Custer, with whom he was acquainted. But Wilbur F. Storey, owner and editor of the *Chicago Times,* assigned him to Crook instead, a decision that probably saved the correspondent's life.[14]

The day of Crook's departure from Fort Fetterman, a Lakota named Yellow Robe arrived at the Red Cloud Agency from the hostile camp, which he said now contained 1,806 lodges, and 3,000 warriors who were determined to fight. The camp was then on the Rosebud about 250 miles northwest of Fetterman, but Yellow Robe believed it would soon move to the Powder.[15]

YELLOW ROBE WAS WRONG ABOUT THE PROJECTED MOVE. THE Sioux nations and their allies were still along the Rosebud, and planned to remain there. Hunting was good. They had followed the buffalo into the Rosebud country, moving slowly since the summer wanderers, only recently departed from the reservation, still needed time for their ponies to strengthen from the winter deprivation.

Each day, the great file of people grew longer. Among them was a thirteen-year-old Oglala boy named Black Elk who, many years later, would provide a graphic account of these last days of Lakota freedom. His family had spent the winter at the Red Cloud Agency. In May, his father decided they would join Crazy Horse, since he said the agency Indians were betraying their people to the whites.[16]

Not everyone was going for the purpose of making war. It was almost time for the annual Lakota council, and many were interested in the social activities this always entailed. Friends and relatives would exchange gifts. Young men would meet girls. Hunts would be organized. One of the most compelling reasons was collective security. Many of the agency Indians fled to Sitting Bull and Crazy Horse because they feared retribution at the hands of a government that traditionally did not distinguish friend or neutral from foe.[17]

Sitting Bull's band arrived at the Rosebud on May 19, going into camp about seven or eight miles up from the juncture with the Elk River. It is a narrow, grassy valley, with meadows sloping up to tablelands and finally to bluffs. Wild roses grow in profusion, giving the river and valley their name, and at this time of year the first fragrant, pink blooms would have begun to appear.

There were six camp circles on the east side of the river, with the Hunkpapas at one end and the Cheyennes at the other, about a mile and a half apart, with the other tribes in between. This was the vast village Leforge and Bradley had seen and reported to Gibbon on May 27. Strangely enough, no one in the village appears to have seen the whites. Among the Cheyennes, a rumor did spread that Crows were sighted in the vicinity, but most discounted it and remained unaware they had been discovered. They were busy hunting among the nearby buffalo herds, and apparently it never occurred to them that soldiers might be in the area.

In the Cheyenne camp, there was rejoicing. Charcoal Bear, their chief medicine man, had arrived with the medicine lodge and various sacred objects. "It put good thoughts and good feelings into the hearts of all Cheyennes," the young warrior Wooden Leg recalled.[18]

By this time, Sitting Bull not only held an unprecedented position of power among the Lakotas but had immense prestige among the Cheyennes and affiliated bands as well. Wooden Leg remembered Sitting Bull's unique stature.

> [He] had now come into admiration by all Indians as a man whose medicine was good—that is, as a man having a kind heart and good judgment as to the best course of conduct. He was considered as being altogether brave, but peaceable. He was strong in religion— the Indian religion. He made medicine many times. He prayed and fasted and whipped his flesh into submission to the will of the Great Medicine. So, in attaching ourselves to the Uncpapas [sic] we other tribes were not moved by a desire to fight. They had not invited us. They simply welcomed us. We supposed that the combined camps would frighten off the soldiers. We hoped thus to be freed from their annoyance. Then we could separate again into the tribal bands and resume our quiet wandering and hunting.[19]

Security and—hopefully—a moral victory by a massed show of strength had now become the strategy of the Indian leaders. The initial war fever over the Reynolds attack had cooled, and the chiefs were beginning to ponder the long-term effects of such a conflict. Many young warriors still wanted to look for a fight, but their elders held them in check. They would fight only if attacked. Even as they planned for war, the Indians waited, hoping to intimidate the soldiers by the sheer immensity of their numbers.[20] If that failed—if the soldiers attacked—there would be a stand, the one decisive battle to break the white will.

Sitting Bull, meanwhile, began to go alone to the top of a butte to commune with the *Wakan' tanka,* the Great Mystery that controlled all events. During one of these meditations, he saw a vision of soldiers riding out of the east under the cover of a great dust storm. The dust storm crashed into a white cloud representing the Indian village. When the storm beat itself out, the white cloud remained. This meant the soldiers from the east would attack the village, but would fail, and the Indians would win a great victory. In response, the chiefs sent scouts eastward to watch for any unusual activities by the military.

Once, Sitting Bull summoned three relatives to accompany him to a hilltop to pray. As the others listened, he beseeched the *Wakan' tanka* for plentiful game to feed his people through the next winter, for power among men of virtue, and for unity among the Sioux nations. If the Great Mystery granted his prayer, Sitting Bull promised to perform the Sun Dance for two days and nights, and give a whole buffalo as an offering.[21]

DOWN IN WYOMING, CROOK'S TROOPS WERE HEADING NORTH for the depot at Fort Reno, where he planned to meet the Crows, then push farther into the Bighorn country, up toward Montana and the Yellowstone. The same cold, bleak weather that had hindered Terry struck Crook on May 31. A bitter wind blew down from the Bighorns, and the company water buckets had crusts of ice. The next morning was overcast with heavy rainclouds. Thick snow and sleet fell, and the men built fires to keep warm.

A day later, the command marched into Reno, to learn the Crows had not yet arrived. Grouard, Big Bat Pourier, and Louis Richaud were sent out to look for them.[22] There was a momentary break in routine when Calamity Jane's true gender was discovered, she was arrested, and "placed in improvised female attire under guard."[23]

The column marched out of Reno at 4:00 A.M., June 3, turning northwest toward Cloud Peak, the highest mountain in the

Bighorns, near what is now Sheridan, Wyoming. Fresh pony tracks were found close to the road, and smoke signals and a few Indians were seen in the distance. The sky was clearing, breezes were balmy, and the soldiers began to think summer had actually arrived.[24]

On the night of June 4, two miners came into the camp. They were from a party of sixty-five that was camped on the Crazy Woman River. They had not actually seen any Indians, but plenty of sign was about, so they had secured their animal herd, erected a makeshift palisade around their camp, and dug rifle pits. The soldiers followed suit, with mounted outriders surrounding their own bivouac. Entire companies were placed a mile or two outside of camp to intercept any Indian forays against the horse herd. In each company, a platoon was kept mounted and ready for instantaneous response. The others were allowed only to loosen the cinches on their saddles.

The rest of the mining party now joined the command, and proved anything but a burden. Watching them, Bourke said, "It always seemed to me that that little party of Montana miners displayed more true grit, more common sense, and more intelligence in their desperate march through a scarcely known country filled with hostile Indians than almost any similar party which I can now recall. . . ."[25]

The troops continued northwest, camping near the ruins of Fort Phil Kearny, and visiting the mass grave of Fetterman and his troops. The road beyond here was grown up with grass and weeds, which made for hard marching. Several rattlesnakes were killed on the road, and more were found in camp.[26] With bitter cold still an immediate memory, heat and mosquitoes now became almost unbearable.

On June 7, Pvt. Francis Tierney, who served in Company B of the Third Cavalry under the alias of Doyle, died of an accidental gunshot wound inflicted on himself several days earlier. Everyone not on duty turned out for the funeral.[27]

Finerty wrote, "It was, indeed, a sad destiny that led this young man to die, accidentally, it is true, by his own hand, the first of Crook's brigade to lay his bones in the terra incognita of Wyoming."[28]

12

The March to the Rosebud

ON JUNE 5, WHILE CROOK HEADED UP TOWARD MONTANA, GEN-
eral Sherman met in Washington with Interior Secretary Chandler
and newly appointed Secretary of War J. D. Cameron. A bill had
been introduced into Congress that Chandler believed would pass,
appointing a commission to confer with Red Cloud and Spotted
Tail. The goal was to force a new treaty on the Indians, requiring
them to cede the Black Hills to the government and emigrate to
other reservations.

Sherman then informed Sheridan that if the commission was appointed, the Fifth Cavalry would escort the commissioners, and
would supervise the agencies while Crook and Terry dealt with the
hostiles. "In the meantime," he said, "the old treaty [is] to be respected & no intrusion on the reservation to be encouraged or permitted."[1] It is doubtful Sherman seriously expected Sheridan to
abide by the old treaty. The Black Hills were rapidly being settled,
with towns now established, and the most the army could do
would be to protect them. It was no longer in a position to evict the
settlers.

Even as Sherman was discussing the Black Hills problem with
the cabinet members and Sheridan, Lt. Col. Wesley Merritt of
Sheridan's staff was inspecting the Red Cloud Agency, in advance

of the lieutenant general's visit. This was Merritt's second inspection. He had been there in March, and his report on shortages at that time had led to the emergency appropriation for rations at Red Cloud and Spotted Tail.[2]

Now, in June, Merritt discovered that food was still scarce, and calculated that 1,500 to 2,000 Indians, a large number of whom were warriors, had left since May 10. He believed Agent Hastings tended to "underestimate" the number who were missing. He concluded the agent was being duped by his charges, and reported to Sheridan, "The Indians here are not friendly in their feelings; in fact they are generally hostile." Merritt then headed to Cheyenne, to await Sheridan, who was en route.[3]

The lieutenant general arrived in Omaha on June 12, where he noted Colonel Carr had departed the previous day for Cheyenne with six companies of the Fifth Cavalry. Sheridan himself arrived in Cheyenne on June 13, and immediately left for the agencies. Three days later, he reached Red Cloud where he found the situation less serious than had been reported. The agent proved cooperative, and simple mathematics told Sheridan that the number of Indians reported leaving the reservation was exaggerated. Correspondence with Ben Clarke, his old friend and guide in the Indian Territory of Oklahoma, indicated many of the Cheyennes were actually heading south, away from the war zone.[4]

Still Sheridan realized that the agency Indians, while now relatively quiet, remained a potential source of trouble, and he continued to lobby for military control over the agencies, as well as for additional forts. For the time being, however, the agencies could be handled by troops already assigned to them, so Sheridan ordered Carr to take the Fifth north to block the Powder River Trail, a favorite Indian route between the agencies and the Powder and Yellowstone Rivers.

"I think this will stir things up," he wrote to Crook, "and prove advantageous in the settlement of the Indian question. Carr's means of transportation will not keep him out longer than six weeks; but in that time, with Terry operating probably up Powder River and you down that River and Carr from this side, [I believe] that good results must follow."[5]

Crook, meanwhile, was still bivouacked along the Tongue, waiting for Grouard, Big Bat, and Louis Richaud with the Crow and Shoshone scouts. The expedition had assumed the nature of a wilderness excursion. Although mounted pickets were posted in the hills about a mile from camp, those not on duty were idle much of the time. Soldiers cleaned up and washed their clothing in the clear, cold water. Some officers "pass the day in reading, some in writing journals of the trip," Bourke wrote in his own journal. Rank having its privileges, the officers gathered in the evenings around company headquarters tents for a drink.[6]

ELSEWHERE, THE INDIANS WERE ALSO RELAXING AND ENJOYING themselves. After weeks of travel and avoiding soldiers, they had joined together in the single, gigantic camp along the Rosebud, and more people were coming in all the time. Recalling his own band's arrival, Black Elk said:

> We could see the valley full of tepees, and the ponies could not be counted. Many, many people were there—Oglalas, Hunkpapas, Minneconjous [sic], Sans Arcs, Black Feet, Brulés, Santees, and Yanktonais; also many Shyelas and Blue Clouds [Cheyennes and Arapahos]. The village was long, and you could not see all the camps with one look. . . . Great men were there with all those people and horses.[7]

"The grass grew high and our ponies became strong," a Cheyenne woman known as Kate Bighead remembered more than fifty years later. "Our men killed many buffalo, and we women tanned many skins and stored up much meat."[8]

The camp periodically shifted, to allow fresh grazing for the ponies and to follow the buffalo herds, but always it remained in the Rosebud Valley.[9]

The tranquillity was disrupted when a group of reservation Cheyennes arrived with sobering news: "Lots of soldiers are being sent to fight the Indians." Little Hawk led ten Cheyennes with pack horses out to hunt buffalo, and perhaps, get a glimpse of these soldiers if they were, in fact, coming.

The party rode southeast from the Rosebud to the Tongue, and then to the Powder River, where they spotted Crook's camp from the top of a hill. Concealing themselves among the hills and gullies, they waited until night for a raid on the horses. But it was late when the Indians moved toward the camp, and the soldiers were gone. They gathered up some scraps of meat, cooked it on the still smoldering campfires, and sampled a box of rain-soaked hardtack, then moved on to look for the troops.

The Cheyennes found them again late the next afternoon. Watching the enormous camp, however, they decided that even a raid on the horse herd was entirely too risky. Six started back toward their own camp on the Rosebud, while the others remained to shadow Crook.[10]

By June 8, Crook had shifted westward to the Tongue. About 11:00 P.M. the troops were awakened by the yapping of coyotes, a cry often imitated by inbound Indians to determine whether a camp was friendly. Soon, an Indian voice was heard shouting at the soldiers from a bluff overlooking the river. With Grouard and the others gone, Ben Arnold, a half-breed scout, was the only person in camp who could speak the Indian languages. Half-asleep, Arnold recognized a Crow dialect, but thought the accent sounded unusual, as if the Indian were accustomed to speaking another language.

"Any half-breeds there, any Crows?" the Indian asked.

Still groggy, Arnold gave a reply that the Indian apparently did not understand, for he asked more loudly, "Have the Crows come yet?"

This time Arnold answered in Lakota. The stranger immediately broke off discussions, and was neither seen nor heard from again that night. Crook was furious, for the Indian's reaction to hearing Lakota only confirmed that he was an advance courier for the Crow allies, and Arnold's mistake further delayed their arrival.[11]

If the Crows were hesitant about coming in, the hostiles were not, for at 6:30 P.M. the next day—broad daylight—they fired into the camp, their bullets riddling tents, breaking ridgepoles, and knocking pipes loose from the Sibley stoves that warmed the tents.

Three companies of infantry crossed the river and ascended the bluffs where the Indians were concealed. Unwilling to face the long-range Springfield infantry rifles, the Indians withdrew. While the infantry secured the bluffs, another group of hostiles rushed the horse herd, but was driven back by covering fire from the Second Cavalry. Several companies of Third Cavalry caught the Indians above the bluffs by the river, chasing them across an open plain to a second line of bluffs where, concealed among the rocks and ravines, they regained the advantage and the cavalry broke off pursuit. Despite the damage in camp and the loss of several horses and mules, the only casualties were two men slightly wounded by ricocheting bullets.[12]

It was now impossible for Crook to surprise any Indian camp, since they knew exactly where he was. He had heard nothing of the Crows or Shoshones since Arnold's mishandling of the initial night contact. Grouard, Big Bat, and Richaud had been gone for ten days looking for the Indian allies, and there was no word from them. Furthermore, he had received no news of Gibbon or Terry, did not know where they were, or where he was supposed to meet them and close the ring against the hostiles.

On the other hand, Crook now believed the main Indian camp must be somewhere farther along the Tongue or the Rosebud, and that the attack on his own camp had been designed to draw attention away from it.[13]

By June 11, the expedition's herd of almost 1,900 horses and mules had exhausted the grass around the bivouac on the Tongue, so camp was moved seventeen miles south to a confluence of the two forks of Goose Creek. Here, the soldiers found good pasturage in the foothills of the Bighorns, pure water, and plentiful firewood. Aside from the weather, which was now rainy, everyone enjoyed the change, and the daily routine resumed its relaxed atmosphere. Men fished and hunted. Crook, an avid whist player, generally had a group of officers in his tent for a game.[14]

Up on the Rosebud, the Hunkpapas were preparing for the Sun Dance, which was essentially their affair, although throngs of Indians from other tribes came to watch. The time was propitious, for the sun in June was at its zenith, and its power over the earth greatest.

The entire ceremony lasted twelve days. The first four were spent preparing the site, which was on the flat bottomland right by the river.[15] The dance circle was a large arbor, facing east, from which the sun came. Scouts guarded this sacred place, while a solitary holy man prowled the woods to locate a suitable dance pole, a forked cottonwood. Young maidens, whose virtue was beyond question, ceremoniously cut down and trimmed the tree. When they had finished, hereditary chiefs carried it to the dance circle, stopping four times en route to give thanks for the four seasons.

The following day, the pole was erected in the center of the sacred dance circle. Nursing mothers lay their babies at its base so the boys would grow up to be brave warriors and the girls, mothers of brave warriors. Then the people abandoned themselves to two days of dancing and celebration around the pole. Men and women publicly joked in a risqué fashion that normally never would have been tolerated. "We smaller boys had a good time during the two days of dancing," Black Elk said, "for we were allowed to do almost anything to tease the people, and they had to stand it." At the end of those two days, however, virtue and discipline reasserted itself when a warrior symbolically killed the spirits associated with evil, thus purifying the ritual.[16]

Now, the actual Sun Dance began. Young men who would participate in the ordeal had fasted and purified themselves in sweat lodges. Then their bodies were painted by the holy men, and they lay down at the base of the dance pole, which was hung with long strips of rawhide. The holy men made incisions in the backs or chests of the participants, pushed the rawhide through, and tied it, tethering the flesh to the dance pole. Then the young men would get up and perform the Sun Dance to the beat of the drums, straining away from the pole, their flesh pulled by the strips, until they could no longer stand the pain or until the flesh tore loose.[17]

The Sun Dance climaxed toward the end, when Sitting Bull prepared to fulfill his vows to the *Wakan' tanka*. After purifying himself in a sweat lodge, he entered the dance circle. He sat with his back against the dance pole, legs extended, arms hanging down, while his adopted brother, Jumping Bull, inserted an awl into his left arm, starting from the bottom and working up, until he had removed fifty small pieces of flesh. Then, he did the same to the right arm. Blood flowed as Sitting Bull invoked the Great Mystery.

After the flesh was removed, Sitting Bull danced around the pole. He was not tied by rawhide, but danced freely, his face toward the sun. Hours passed in unbroken motion when, suddenly, he stopped and went into a trance. The other participants eased him to the ground and sprinkled water on his face. When he recovered, he related a vision he had seen in the trance.

Soldiers and horses were falling headfirst, from the sky into the village. Some Indians were also upside down. The significance was that the soldiers were coming to attack the village, but would be massacred. Indians would also die, as indicated by their own people upside down; nevertheless, it would be a great victory. But the spirit of the vision also told him the bodies of the soldiers must not be plundered in the usual Indian fashion.[18]

ON JUNE 14, GROUARD, BIG BAT, AND RICHAUD FINALLY ARRIVED and confirmed it was a Crow who had spoken with Arnold that night on the Tongue. As Crook had guessed, the packer's response in Lakota had alarmed the Crows, who retreated. They were further irritated by Crook's move from the Tongue to Goose Creek, which they said was away from hostile camps, and questioned whether the soldiers actually intended to fight. There were 175 Crows camped nearby, and Capt. Andrew Burt, whom they knew and trusted, led a detail to escort them to camp.[19]

Bourke recorded the troops' reaction when they entered:

A curious crowd of lookers—officers, soldiers, and teamsters—congregated around the little squads of Crows watching with eager attention their every movement. The Indians seemed proud of the distinguished positions they occupied in popular estimation, and were soon on terms of easy familiarity with our soldiers, some of whom can talk a few words of Crow and others a little of the "sign language."

With the warriors came a group of boys, none over fifteen, to hold horses and run errands during scouting. As was customary among Indian scouts, they also brought their women.[20]

From Grouard and the Crows, Crook learned that Gibbon's Montana Column was camped on the Yellowstone opposite the mouth of the Rosebud, but could not cross because of high water. The hostiles, likewise stranded, watched the Montana troops from the opposite shore. The Crows also erroneously reported that Sitting Bull was camped at the confluence of the Tongue and Yellowstone.[21]

After retreat, Crook held officers' call in open space in front of his tent. In two days, he said, they would cut loose from wagons and pack trains, with four days' rations and a hundred rounds of ammunition in each man's saddlebags. Each officer and enlisted man was allowed one blanket, either his bedding blanket or a saddle blanket. No extra clothing would be permitted. Lariats and sidelines would be carried for the horses, but no extra shoes or picket ropes. All men who could be mounted and equipped would accompany the march, including three companies of infantry under Maj. Alex Chambers, and volunteers from the teamsters and packers. Mules for the infantry would be drawn from the pack train, and saddles from the extra equipment brought by the cavalry. One hundred soldiers would remain behind to guard the camp. Wagons would be parked, and mules corralled in a defensible position.[22] Although they were not mentioned in any military reports, since they were not connected with the expedition in any official capacity, the Black Hills miners encountered earlier on the march also joined the fighting force.

Just as the conference ended, there was one final addition to the attacking force. The Crows began pointing south and saying "Shoshone." Looking out toward the bluffs in that direction, the soldiers saw "a line of horsemen, brilliantly attired, riding at whirlwind speed," their highly polished lances and firearms glittering in the setting sun. There were eighty-six warriors, under their feared and renowned chief, Washakie.

With the Shoshones were three Texans, Tom Cosgrove, Bob Eckles, and a man named Yarnell, and a French-Canadian half-breed named Luisant. Cosgrove had been a captain in a Texas cavalry regiment of the Confederate Army, and his influence was evident as the Indians rode into camp. Finerty recorded that the Shoshones

> crossed the creek in columns of twos, like a company of regular cavalry, [and] rode in among us. They carried two beautiful American flags and each warrior bore a pennon. They looked like Cossacks of the Don, but were splendidly armed with government rifles and revolvers. Nearly all wore magnificent war bonnets and scarlet mantles.[23]

With the Shoshones settled in, Crook called a general council with his officers and the chiefs. The Shoshones said very little. Most of the talking for the Indians was done by Old Crow, the paramount chief of the Crows, who told the group:

> These are our lands by inheritance. The Great Spirit gave them to our fathers, but the Sioux stole them from us. They hunt upon our mountains. They fish in our streams. They have stolen our horses. They have murdered our squaws, our children. What white man has done these things to us? The face of the Sioux is red, but his heart is black. But the heart of the pale face has ever been red to the Crow. . . . The scalp of no white man hangs in our lodges. They are thick as grass in the wigwams of the Sioux. . . . The great white chief [General Crook] will lead us against no other tribe of red men. Our war is with the Sioux and only them. We want back our lands. We want their women for our slaves, to work for us as our women have had to work for them. We want their horses for our young men, and their mules for our squaws. The Sioux have trampled upon our hearts. We shall spit upon their scalps.

Crook and Old Crow shook hands, amid shouts of approval by the Crows and Shoshones. By the time the council adjourned, it was agreed the Indians would scout by their own methods, without interference from the whites. According to the general plan, if a village was discovered, the Crows and Shoshones would hit first, running off the horses, and leaving the dismounted hostiles to face the soldiers.[24]

The council ended at 10:20 P.M., and the Indians had ridden hard all day. But instead of going to bed, they began feasting and dancing. The drums, chants, and incantations, strange to white ears, attracted every soldier not on duty, and they watched their allies in both fascination and revulsion. Nickerson noted the ceremonies "with all their hideous grotesqueness [lasted] until the following morning."[25]

No one doubted that a battle was near, and many soldiers' thoughts turned toward home and family. In his diary, Lt. Thaddeus Capron wrote:

> I should be so much pleased if I could hear from the dear absent wife and little ones before starting on the trip, but cannot and will trust that a kind and over ruling Providence has taken good care of them, and may God in his kindness return me to them ere long, to find all in the enjoyment of life and health.[26]

Crook prepared a final dispatch to Sheridan outlining his proposed march against the hostiles. Noting that each person would carry four days' rations, he wrote, "If we can strike them at all, we shall probably do it inside that time."[27]

Capron would return to his family, and Crook would get his fight. But for one soldier, there would be no more thoughts of home or war. Amid the chanting of the Indian allies, and preparations for battle, Pvt. William Nelson, Third Cavalry, died in the field hospital from causes not recorded.[28]

13

Crook Defeated

Azor Nickerson was awakened the next morning "by a series of groans and cries as though the author was enduring excru-
tiating [sic] torture." Looking out from his tent, he saw an old
Crow warrior riding through camp, waving his rifle in the air like
a drum major's baton. "His wild eyes appeared to be fixed on objects, invisible to the outer world, and which he seemed to think
were hovering around him; great tears rolled down his cheeks, as
he pleaded, prayed and exhorted—the empty air."

The warrior was crying to the spirits for scalps, asking that in
the coming fight, he be allowed to take many.[1]

In their own way, the whites were also preparing for the march.
The most difficult task was trying to mount 175 infantrymen on an
equal number of cantankerous mules. "The majority of the men
did not know how to saddle properly," Capt. Gerhard Luhn
wrote. "As soon as a man would get his mule saddled he would
mount and probably would [not] be many minutes when he would
be sprawling on the ground."

The Crows and Shoshones roared with laughter and, from time
to time, some young warrior would chase down, mount, and ride
a seemingly intractable mule to show how easily it could be done.

By late afternoon, the infantrymen were finally mounted and ready for the field.[2]

Compared with the infantry, the civilian packers and Black Hills miners experienced no trouble at all with their animals. Chief Packer Tom Moore had selected twenty volunteers, "every one a fine rider, and as near being a dead-shot as men get to be on the frontier," according to Bourke.[3]

Crook intended to move swiftly against what he hoped would be the main body of hostiles. The wagons were packed and corralled so they could be easily defended by the troops, teamsters, and packers designated to remain in camp. The mule train would likewise be left behind. Aside from the infantry mounts, only one extra mule, for surgical instruments, would be taken. The soldiers drew rations and ammunition, slipping a little extra in their packs as a precaution against any unforeseen emergency.[4]

The march began at 5:00 A.M. the next day, June 16, with the Indians in the lead. "It was easy to see they had come for war to the death upon the Sioux," Bourke observed. Finerty, too, was impressed: "I felt a respect for the American Indian that day."

After the Indians came fifteen companies of cavalry, followed by the packers, with the mounted infantry battalion bringing up the rear. The infantrymen had done better than expected; not one was thrown upon mounting. Morale was high. Most of the men on sick list had been left behind under protest. "The great mass of the soldiers were young men," Finerty noted, "careless, courageous and eminently light-hearted."[5]

Anson Mills was not so confident. "I did not think that General Crook knew where [the hostiles] were, and I did not think our friendly Indians knew where they were, and no one conceived we would find them in the great force we did," he recalled.[6]

Crook moved rapidly, allowing only short halts to graze the animals. The first leg of the march was twenty-five miles, first along Goose Creek, then across the Tongue and north before ordering a two-hour halt to unsaddle and rest the cavalry horses, and have coffee. Large herds of buffalo were everywhere. Presently, the buffalo began to run, which, according to the Indian scouts, meant the animals were being chased by a hostile hunting party.[7]

The command mounted again shortly after noon, and crossed over to the headwaters of the Rosebud, where Crook bivouacked, after marching a total of forty-two miles. Men and animals were tired. In the distance, the soldiers could hear constant rifle fire, indicating the Lakotas and Cheyennes were killing buffalo not far away. To guard against a night raid on the horses and mules, camp was formed in a hollow square, with the animals inside. Pickets were posted on the surrounding hills.[8]

Crook had ordered no fires, to avoid betraying his position to any hostiles lurking about, but the Indian scouts lit them anyway, and dined on roasted buffalo meat while the soldiers had a cold supper. And as if that weren't enough, when they were finished, they began a long war chant that penetrated the night. Crook was exasperated, but needed the Crows and Shoshones too badly to complain.

Rain began falling, and the night turned cold. Each soldier shivered in his single wet blanket, trying to sleep with a saddle for a pillow and weapons by his side, as the Indian chanting continued. Capt. Alexander Sutorius, of Company E, Third Cavalry, was rolled up next to Finerty. Just before they fell asleep, Sutorius whispered, "We will have a fight tomorrow, mark my words—I feel it in the air."[9]

There was more reason than that for his anxiety. Earlier in the evening, Crook had sent out Tom Cosgrove, Frank Grouard, and a group of Crows to reconnoiter. As the troops were drifting off to sleep, this party returned, reporting it had found the remains of a partially cooked meal left by a Lakota hunting party in a small gulch. Apparently, in their haste the hostiles had abandoned not only their meat on the fire, but their rubber-treated blankets as well.

"We are now right in among the hostiles and may strike or be struck at any hour," Bourke predicted.[10]

What Grouard, Cosgrove, and the scouts had discovered did not belong to the Lakotas, however, but to five Cheyennes, who were likewise responsible for at least some of the gunfire heard as the soldiers went into camp. The group, composed of the warriors Little Hawk, Yellow Eagle, Crooked Nose, Little Shield, and White Bird, had left the main Cheyenne camp the night of June 15. The next day, they found a herd of buffalo and killed a bull.

They were cooking the meat when they discovered a herd of buffalo cows not far away. Crooked Nose agreed to stay by the cooking fire while the others went out to kill a cow, whose meat was fatter and more tender than a bull's. As they rode toward the cows, however, they looked back and saw Crooked Nose motioning them to return. Crooked Nose said they had been discovered. He indicated a hill and said, "I saw two men looking over, and after looking a little while, they rode up in plain sight, each one leading a horse. They rode out of sight [among the bluffs] coming toward us. I think they are coming in our direction—right toward us."

Assuming the strangers were Lakotas, Little Hawk suggested giving them a scare. They would slip around, and pretend to attack. The Cheyennes rode up the gully to the bottom of a hill. Little Hawk dismounted, crept to the top, and peered over. He saw masses of troops. Indeed, it seemed "as if the whole earth were black with soldiers." The Cheyennes retreated hastily.

In the meantime, the Indian village complex had moved away from the Rosebud, having exhausted the game, grazing, and firewood in that vicinity. It was now located about twenty miles to the northwest, on a creek that flowed into the Little Bighorn River. Little Hawk's group found the new site late in the night of June 16–17, and reported their discovery. The news was sent to the Lakotas. Warriors immediately began rounding up their horses and painting themselves for battle.[11]

The camps were in turmoil. Everyone expected a hard fight. Some of the chiefs urged they only defend themselves: "Young men, leave the soldiers alone unless they attack us." The young warriors, however, were too agitated. They had to fight. The Lakota-Cheyenne war machine, already in motion, could not be halted. Women began taking down tipis and packing anything not immediately needed; they were to move farther west, closer to the Little Bighorn and out of harm's way. The chiefs knew after the Reynolds fight, that the soldiers would try to hit the pony herds, and sent extra guards for the animals during the move.[12]

*   *   *

THE COLD MADE SLEEP DIFFICULT AND CROOK'S TROOPS BEGAN stirring about 3:00 A.M., June 17. A heavy fog had set in, obscuring fires so that everyone was allowed to brew one cup of coffee. Every horse and mule was saddled and loaded with its equipment.

The Crow and Shoshone scouts were just beginning breakfast when Crook sent the white scouts to hurry them out. They were all quiet now, with none of the singing or joking that had characterized them before. "It is evident that both tribes had a very wholesome respect for Sioux prowess," Finerty remarked. Despite some reluctance among the Crows, the Indians were eventually ready, and in the first dim light, rode out of camp and disappeared over the bluffs.[13]

The soldiers laughed and joked quietly while waiting for the order to march. Some chewed tobacco to pass the time, while others threw their arms over their saddles and, leaning against their horses, grabbed a little extra sleep. At 6:00 A.M. the order came to march. The infantry moved out first, followed by the cavalry. The government Indians were already somewhere far ahead, scouting for signs of hostiles.

As the column moved northeast along the Rosebud, the valley narrowed and the trail became twisted and rugged. At times, the turns were so sharp that the soldiers were unable to see fifty feet ahead. After about four miles, the path opened out onto a wide bottomland along the river. Away from the stream on either side, the ground began to roll until it reached a series of low bluffs, 200 to 300 feet high, where the ground was broken and rocky. On top of the bluffs was open country continuing on to a second line of bluffs. At the far end of the valley, the bluffs closed in on the river, to form another blind canyon.

Because of the narrow trail from the campsite to the valley, and the large number of men and animals riding single or double file according to terrain, the command was strung out along the entire four miles. Crook ordered a halt along the wide bottomland to allow the tail of the column to catch up, and to rest the horses and mules. Colonel Royall and the Third Cavalry were sent across the river, while the general remained on the left bank with the Second Cavalry and mounted infantry. This would shorten the line when the march resumed and, hopefully, allow the soldiers to stay closer together. Animals were unsaddled and allowed to graze, and pickets were sent to the tops of the bluffs.[14]

Not far away, the hostiles, who had ridden almost twenty miles over rough terrain since leaving their camp in the middle of the night, likewise stopped and unsaddled to rest their ponies. Altogether, there were almost a thousand warriors, including Cheyennes, Oglalas, Miniconjous, Sans Arcs, Brulés, and Hunkpapas. Scouts were sent ahead, and at dawn, the whole fighting party saddled and began moving slowly up the Rosebud toward the army column, staying among the hills away from the river itself.[15]

In those same hills, the army's Indian scouts were now moving toward the top of a rise, unaware that the Lakota and Cheyenne scouts were approaching from the other side. Reaching the crest, the government Indians saw the hostiles and opened fire. The Lakota-Cheyenne scouting party whipped their ponies and charged to the top, driving the government Indians back toward Crook's bivouac.[16]

In the valley below, the troops on the left bank with Crook could see nothing beyond the bluffs immediately behind them. They heard gunfire in the distance and, at first, thought it was an attack. Then the shooting stopped as suddenly as it began. Captain Sutorius, a Swiss who had been smoking and chatting with Lt. Adolphus von Luettwitz, a German, remarked in English, "They are shooting buffaloes over there," then resumed his conversation with Luettwitz. Some soldiers were stretched out on the grass, dozing. Crook was playing whist with Bourke and some of the other officers.[17]

On the right bank, where distance gave a less obstructed view, Anson Mills saw the hostiles riding down toward the soldiers on the left. He immediately ordered his battalion to saddle and prepare to mount, then called across the river to Crook. Almost simultaneously, a couple of Crow scouts came riding at full speed into Crook's bivouac, shouting, "Sioux! Sioux!" There was more shooting in the hills to the left as the pickets opened fire on the hostiles. Skirmishers went out to reinforce the pickets and cover the companies as they saddled.

Crook ordered Mills to bring his men across the river and report to him. Upon doing so, Mills told the general that they "were about to be attacked by a large force, and that the Indians were coming from due north. He told me to march rapidly and as soon as I got to higher ground to take the bluffs and hold them."[18]

Capt. Frederick van Vliet of Company C, Third Cavalry, was ordered to take and hold the ridge south of the river overlooking the right bank, to protect Crook's rear. He rushed his company into position, arriving and securing the ridge just before a party of hostiles got there.[19]

Now a long Lakota-Cheyenne line could be seen on the crest of the north ridges, moving toward the bivouac. One group separated and headed toward the soldiers' horses and mules. The pickets held them off until Crook's troopers could counterattack.[20]

Mills, meanwhile, was pushing the Lakota-Cheyenne vanguard back up the hill. A Hunkpapa named Iron Hawk, fourteen at the time, recalled nothing but confusion and terror in this part of the fight. "I don't know whether I killed anybody or not," he said, "but I guess I did, for I was scared and fought hard, and the way it was you couldn't keep from killing somebody if you didn't get killed, and I am still alive."

When a Crow pulled a nearby Lakota off his horse, Iron Hawk and several others began running, with the Crows hard on their heels. Suddenly, about thirty cavalrymen loomed ahead. Somebody shouted in Lakota, "Take courage! This is a good day to die! Think of the children and the helpless at home!" Heartened, Iron Hawk's group charged through the soldiers and reached their own people.[21]

Mills had dismounted his men, and on foot the troopers crowded the Indian vanguard back into the hills. Several Lakotas were cut off, surrounded, and killed. At that moment, the main force of Lakotas and Cheyennes charged the soldiers from the right and, with this new support, the vanguard turned and moved back down again. But Mills stood his ground and pushed them back over the top and onto the next ridge, fighting his way slowly toward the narrow canyon at the far end of the valley.[22]

Ignoring their own safety three Cheyennes—White Shield, Comes-in-Sight, and White Bird—and the Lakotas, Jack Red Cloud and Low Dog, rode back and forth in front of the soldiers, drawing fire to cover the movements of the others. Comes-in-Sight had just made a pass when his pony was hit, somersaulting forward, and pitching him off. A group of government Indians closed in for the kill. As Comes-in-Sight stood waiting for death, his sister, Buffalo Calf Robe Woman, broke through on a fast horse. He jumped up behind her and was carried off to safety. In tribute to her bravery, the Cheyenne name for the battle became "Where the Girl Saved Her Brother."[23]

Jack Red Cloud also came through alive but well may have wished himself dead. This eighteen-year-old son and namesake of the famed Oglala chief rode into battle wearing an elaborate war bonnet. Like Comes-in-Sight, his pony was shot out from under him and, according to plains custom, he was supposed to prove his valor under fire by removing the bridle before seeking safety. Instead, Jack hit the ground running, and was chased down by three Crows, who lashed him with their riding crops, shouting that he was only a boy and had no right to the war bonnet. Jack was reportedly begging for his life when one of the Crows snatched the war bonnet from his head. A group of Lakotas rode in to rescue him, and the Crows retreated, satisfied with humiliating the boy.[24]

A Cheyenne decked out in war bonnet and red leggings charged past the Hunkpapa warrior White Bull, a nephew of Sitting Bull. White Bull tried to get ahead of him, but the Cheyenne had a faster pony. Suddenly they were faced with a line of Indian scouts and soldiers, and the Cheyenne retreated. A Shoshone charged straight at White Bull, firing twice from his repeating rifle. He missed, and White Bull fired two shots of his own into the shoulder of the Shoshone's horse. The scout went down, and White Bull shot him in the right leg, then retreated back toward the other Lakotas and Cheyennes.[25]

The battle had begun so suddenly, and was developing so rapidly that despite the fight raging among the ridges and hills, Crook's main force was still not organized.

Colonel Royall, having crossed the river, was now on the extreme left of Crook's line. With Capt. Guy V. Henry's cavalry battalion and an additional company under Capt. William H. Andrews, he pushed on toward the retreating Indians.

Lt. Henry R. Lemly, Royall's adjutant, wrote:

Our entire line was now under fire from the Sioux, who occupied the highest ridge in our front, but shot rather wildly. As we advanced, they retired successively to ridges in their rear and, throwing themselves prone upon the ground, reopened fire while their well-trained ponies grazed or stood fast at the extremity of their lariats, upon the reverse of the slope. . . .[26]

The fight was following Indian battle tactics only slightly modified from those used against Fetterman in 1866. As Nickerson astutely noted:

Our efforts were directed toward closing in with the enemy by a series of charges, and theirs to avoiding close contact until, by the nature of the ground, our forces began to get scattered, and then their tactics changed from the defensive to an offensive. Each separate detachment was made the objective of terrific onslaughts. . . .[27]

The assault came just as Royall received orders from Crook to begin moving toward the right to connect with the main body of troops, and then to withdraw back toward the valley where the various military units could consolidate. Royall sent the horse holders ahead, leading their horses under the protection of the skirmish lines. The rough ground disrupted the movement, forcing the units to spread out. The Indians "began to close in upon us in large numbers . . . we were now subjected to a severe direct flank and rear fire."

From the hill the soldiers had just abandoned, the Indians had a commanding position over Henry's battalion, which came under a withering fire from three points along the crest, and the Lakotas and Cheyennes attempted to turn his rear and capture his horses. The battalion made up the bulk of Royall's force, and now he was in real danger. With one more defile to cross before regaining Crook's main unit, he sent Lemly to the general requesting assistance. The mass of Indians were on him, however, so he directed the company commanders to move independently, and regain the command as rapidly as possible. Capt. Peter Vroom was ordered to take his company from Henry's battalion and occupy a crest covering the retreat, "but by this time," Royall admitted, "the position assigned was too exposed to be even temporarily occupied."

Royall was completely surrounded, and it appeared the cavalrymen might have to cut their way through. Several young Lakotas managed to lash the troopers with their riding crops before shots from army carbines brought them down.

"I must say that I never saw so great a body of Indians in one place as I saw at that time, and I have seen a great many Indians in my time," Trooper Phineas Towne recalled. "It seemed that if one Indian was shot five were there to take his place."

An isolated group from the Third Cavalry's Company F, under Sgt. David Marshall, fought until their ammunition was exhausted. They then used their carbines as clubs but were overwhelmed and killed. A panic-stricken recruit tried to surrender, handing his carbine to a warrior, who beat him senseless with it.

Trooper Towne, who appears to have been the only one to escape from Marshall's group, was caught alone in a ravine, surrounded by Indians. His carbine was taken from him, and a lariat thrown around his feet. As he struggled, he was knocked unconscious. The shock of a bullet striking his body brought him back to his senses, for he was aware of being dragged behind a horse. The sudden appearance of a group of cavalry prompted the Indians to cut him loose and he was recovered, badly wounded, but alive.[28]

One soldier's horse started to buck as he tried to mount. The Cheyenne White Shield rode between the man and the horse, knocking the trooper down. As the soldier rose up again, a second Cheyenne, Scabby, jumped off his horse and threw the man down. The soldier, however, managed to shoot Scabby, mortally wounding him.[29]

Finally, two infantry companies arrived, charging the Indians and allowing Royall to complete his withdrawal. As he neared safety, Captain Henry took a bullet through his face, which pierced both cheeks near the joint of the jawbone and fractured the pallet. Two Crows helped him back on his horse and he reached Crook's line.

Last off the field was Colonel Royall himself, who calmly trotted his horse back to the line as Indian bullets tore up the ground all around him.[30]

*   *   *

CROOK'S ORDER FOR ROYALL TO WITHDRAW AND REINFORCE THE
main column was based on the general's erroneous assumption
that the Indian village was still downriver, beyond the lower
canyon. Believing the battle would accomplish nothing unless the
village was taken and destroyed, he tried to get the command assembled and organized to push toward it.

Royall was still fighting his way down from the ridges when
Crook decided not to wait any longer, but to strike immediately at
the imagined village. The fight on the ridges was generating so
much chaos and diverting so many Indians that the general believed Mills could move up the canyon with relatively little opposition.

Having leapfrogged from ridge to ridge, Mills already controlled
the heights overlooking the mouth of the canyon, and now Tom
Moore was ordered to form his packers and Black Hills miners
into line among a group of sandstone rocks in the ravines leading
to the canyon itself to keep the hostiles from edging closer. The Indians rushed the position, but the frontiersmen drove them back,
killing and wounding several.[31]

With the entrance to the canyon secure, Crook ordered Mills
and nine companies of cavalry to locate and capture the supposed
village, holding it until Crook arrived with the rest of the command.

Mills led his companies some six miles until the canyon opened
out into another valley. At that point, Nickerson arrived with orders to rejoin the command immediately, since Crook was unable
to provide support. Rather than return through the canyon, Mills
came out into the valley, doubling back around along the bluffs.
His arrival on the battlefield prompted the Lakotas and Cheyennes
to break off the action and withdraw.[32]

CROOK'S HANDLING OF THE BATTLE WAS HAPHAZARD AT BEST AND
hinted, in the words of a Helena, Montana, editorial writer, that
despite his record in Arizona, "General Crook was not the man to

be intrusted with the conduct of the military expeditions in the Powder River country."[33]

"In one word," Bourke later said, "the battle of the Rosebud was a trap. . . ."[34] Crook first fell into it by sending his men to chase the Indians from ridge to ridge, scattering the soldiers into increasingly smaller units, and making them vulnerable to counterattack. Instead of consolidating by moving his entire force up to the ridges, he ordered those on the ridges to withdraw into the valley, putting them on the defensive where the broken terrain clearly favored the Indians. The hasty decision to send Mills up the canyon to attack a nonexistent village, while Royall was still fighting on the ridges, freed a large group of hostiles from covering Mills, and allowed them to concentrate on the already beleaguered Royall.

The only thing that could be said for Crook, as he went into camp on the battlefield, was that he made certain all his dead and wounded were accounted for. "There was no leaving of dead and dying . . . this trip," Bourke observed.[35]

14

The "Unknown Quantity"

THE BATTLE OF THE ROSEBUD LASTED ABOUT SIX HOURS. YOUNG Iron Hawk, who spent most of the time trying to keep out of the way, remembered it as "a pitiful, long-stretched-out battle." The Indians had tried to lure the soldiers into the hills and overwhelm them piecemeal as they had done with Fetterman. After initially falling into the trap, however, the troops had pulled back and re-grouped. The fight then turned into a protracted, seesawing affair, which the Indians hated because it ran up their casualties.

Crook had no idea how many Lakotas were killed, but thirteen bodies were found close to government lines. The mortally wounded Scabby became the only Cheyenne death. Nine soldiers were killed during Royall's withdrawal from the ridges, where thirteen were wounded of a total of twenty-one. Among the gov-ernment Indians, one Shoshone was killed.[1]

At dusk, Crook held a council with the Crows and Shoshones. Still believing the hostile camp was beyond the lower canyon, he proposed a night march and dawn attack. The Indians, however, were understandably against it. The lower canyon was a death trap. The bluffs were covered with timber, perfect for concealing warriors above a government column moving through the canyon.

The government Indians had also been slightly unnerved by the inability of the soldiers to distinguish friend from foe during the fight. When Crook and Gibbon had decided that government Indians would wear red, they were unaware of the popularity of that color among all the tribes of the region, including the hostiles. Apparently no one had consulted the Crows who, when told to wear red, had readily complied. Captain Lemly commented, "Its unfortunate adoption only added to the confusion [of the battle]."[2]

Crook had just enough rations to get back to his base camp at Goose Creek. The fight had reduced his ammunition to fifty rounds per man. No doubt he initially believed he could take the hostile camp in a dawn attack and resupply from Indian stocks, but the objections from his own Indian scouts ended that idea; it was just as well—the camp was nowhere within miles of Crook's estimate. Given the extent of his food and ammunition shortage, he had no option but to return to Goose Creek.[3]

About midnight, the dead soldiers were wrapped in blankets and laid out in a long trench on the banks of the Rosebud, near a clump of wild rose bushes by the water's edge. The grave was filled with stones and mud, the earth packed down, and a bonfire built on top, which was allowed to burn all night.[4]

The command turned out at three o'clock the following morning for breakfast of coffee, hardtack, and bacon. There was a heavy frost on the ground. The surgeon reported that the condition of the wounded "was all that could be hoped for" and they had passed a good night. The tired animals had recuperated to some extent from the good pasturage and cool weather. Travois were made for the severely wounded, and each was attended by a detail of six enlisted men.

The Shoshones buried their dead comrade at sunrise, at a point in the streambed that was frequently crossed by horses, and warriors rode back and forth over the fresh grave to obliterate any traces. The entire column then marched over the mass grave of the soldiers. It was hoped that the Lakotas would not find it and desecrate the bodies.[5]

They made twenty miles the first day, keeping south of the earlier trail, on higher ground so the wounded would not be dragged through water at the crossings. On steep grades, the enlisted attendants unhitched the travois with the wounded, and carried them as litters. Despite the precautions, the wounded were badly jolted. In a particularly rough area, one of Captain Henry's travois poles broke, pitching the badly wounded officer twenty feet down a draw into some rocks. When his face was wiped clean and he had been given water, Henry was able to stammer that he felt "bully," and said, "Everybody is so kind," comments that startled the other officers, for he was normally a chronic complainer.[6]

In camp that night, the Crows departed for home. Customarily Indians left when no more fighting was imminent, but they promised they would be back within fifteen days, when coincidentally Crook expected fresh troops to arrive.[7]

The next day, the troops reached the Goose Creek camp, bivouacking about two miles beyond the wagon corral to take advantage of better grazing. Crook sent a courier to Fort Fetterman with a preliminary report on the fight to be telegraphed to Sheridan. After a brief description of the action, he said, "The command finally drove the Indians back in great confusion, following them several miles, the Scouts killing a good many during the retreat."[8]

The bragging was that of a general who had won a victory. There was no reference to the fact that he had barely escaped annihilation, or that the Lakota and Cheyenne forces were intact when they left the field.

Among the officers, Capron was more cautious, noting in his diary, "The result of [the] fight is in our favor but we did not do as much as could have been done." Mills, however, was more candid and later recalled, "All of us made very brief reports of the battle, having little pride in our achievement."[9] The enlisted men knew they had been beaten, and began calling Crook "Rosebud George."

Since Crook intended to remain in the Goose Creek camp, the wounded were placed in wagons and sent to Fort Fetterman, amid the cheers and good wishes of their comrades. Captain Nickerson and Tom MacMillan of the Chicago Inter-Ocean, both in failing health, accompanied the wounded. The train was escorted by two infantry companies, commanded by Capron and Luhn.[10] Later that day, the Shoshones also left for their home in western Wyoming, leaving four of their warriors as a pledge that they would return.

Crook estimated that within fifteen days he would be reinforced with five additional companies of infantry armed with long-range Springfield rifles, one new company of cavalry, a large body of civilian scouts, sixty days' supplies and rations, 300 to 400 extra rounds of ammunition per man, and 300 to 500 Crows, Shoshones, and Nez Percés, and possibly Pawnees as well. By that time, he also expected to be in communication with Terry and Gibbon, who were pushing toward him from the north.

"The Sioux must divide up to hunt the buffalo and thus place themselves in our power, remain in one body and be hacked to pieces, or go in upon the Reservations, whipped," Bourke remarked.[11]

Viewed in the long term, Bourke's assessment was correct. For the time being, however, the army was the weaker of the two antagonists and, as the Rosebud had shown, could not "hack to pieces" a large body of hostile Indians. Although Crook was left in possession of the battlefield, tactically and strategically he had been defeated. The *New York Herald* editorial writers saw this very plainly:

> The retreat of Crook southward after the battle left Sitting Bull free to choose the future seat of his operations, making him a very "unknown quantity" indeed.[12]

The editorial infuriated Crook, who charged the *Herald*'s coverage of the fight consisted of "most villainous falsehoods." In fact, Crook was deluding himself with falsehoods; the *Herald*'s coverage of the campaign was factual. Correspondent Davenport, whose truthful dispatches to New York served as the basis for the editorial, was treated with "contempt hard to be borne," and the *Herald* retaliated with a three-month campaign against Crook.[13] Yet the editorial assessed the situation as well as any military analyst could have done. The Lakotas and Cheyennes controlled an entire region and freely moved about large sections of three federal territories. No one knew where they were or what they were doing.

The soldiers credited Crazy Horse with leading the hostile forces at the Rosebud. Although he participated in the fight, reliable Indian accounts do not tell of an overall command structure centering on one person; their concept of warfare was too individualized to accept such control. But faced with justifying the defeat of a large military force, it suited the generals to believe they were up against an Indian Napoleon and, increasingly, Crazy Horse was promoted in white imagination to fit the image. As a result he became the most important adversary, a symbolic "boogie man" responsible for every army setback, and whose own defeat would mean the defeat of the Plains Indians.[14]

AFTER THE BATTLE, THE TIRED BUT PROUD LAKOTAS AND CHEYennes returned to their village, now located about five miles east of the Little Bighorn River. Some families tended their wounded or mourned their dead, but most stayed up all night celebrating and listening to warriors recount their deeds. Many warriors had not participated in the fight, but listened eagerly to those who had.

The next morning as Crook withdrew, about twenty young men went back to the battlefield. It took no time at all to find the large area of freshly disturbed earth, over which a fire had burned. They did not realize it was the mass grave, but suspected the whites had hidden something valuable. They began digging with their hands.

Soon they uncovered the bodies. They stripped off the burial blankets, which, as far as they were concerned, were more useful to the living than the dead. They also took jewelry from the bodies, and at least one soldier was scalped. When the Indians had plundered the grave, they straggled up to the top of the ridge, where they could see Crook's troops in the distance, retreating south toward his base in Wyoming.[15]

In the Indian camp, the women were taking down the tipis, preparing to move a short distance westward to the banks of the Little Bighorn. Scabby, the lone Cheyenne fatality, was buried according to their custom, in a cave in the hillside. The Lakotas left their dead in their lodges. It was bad fortune to occupy a lodge where someone had died, so these were left standing, consecrated as sepulchres for their owners, and abandoned.[16]

The valley of the Little Bighorn is a narrow, grassy plain. Looking north, the river meanders along the right, and in 1876 was lined with clumps of cottonwood trees. Across the river to the east,

the banks slope up to a series of steep ridges. The countryside beyond the ridges is hilly, rolling plains. On the left or western side,
the floor of the valley gives way to gently sloping hills, broken here
and there by ravines.

Satisfied that Crook had retreated far to the south, and that no
other danger threatened, the people spent their time in the new village grazing their horses, hunting, and providing for their families.
The chiefs held their councils. At night, there was feasting and
dancing.

"There were more Indians in those six camps than I ever saw together anywhere else," the woman known as Kate Bighead recalled.[17]

The council sessions rotated from camp to camp. Heralds would
go through the entire village announcing the location. The individual camps continued to operate under the internal government
of its particular tribe. When the chiefs convened, they met as
equals but as host, Sitting Bull was recognized as paramount chief
of the entire village.

Not all the Lakota chiefs were present; the leaders of the Red
Cloud and Spotted Tail factions remained at the agencies. The
Cheyenne representatives, however, included nearly all of their
forty governing chiefs, as well as two of the four "old man" or senior chiefs.[18]

Among the warriors still bedridden from wounds suffered in the
Rosebud fight was a Lakota named Rattling Hawk, who had been
shot through the hip, and whose recovery was doubtful. But a
medicine man, Hairy Chin, who drew his power from the bear
spirit, would not give up.

First, Hairy Chin summoned Black Elk and five other boys to act
the part of bears. He painted Black Elk's body and face yellow,
with a black stripe down either side of his nose. Then he tied up his
hair to look like a bear's ears, and put eagle feathers on his head.
The other boys were all painted red and had real bears' ears on
their heads. Hairy Chin himself donned a bearskin, and began
chanting. Two girls entered the tipi, one with a cup of water and
the other with herbs, which were offered to the wounded Rattling
Hawk. Then he was handed a red walking cane; he stood up and
hobbled out of the tipi behind the girls. The boys meanwhile

bounded around him and made growling noises like bears. Finally, Hairy Chin emerged from the tipi on all fours, dressed in the bearskin—Rattling Hawk, incredibly, began to improve.[19]

Black Elk remembered this ceremony as occurring on June 24. The same day, the chiefs decided to move the camp from the rugged east bank of the Little Bighorn, to the flatland across the river, to give the hunters easier access to large herds of antelope that had been seen there.[20]

En route to the new location, a scout brought word of a new danger—soldiers were approaching from the northeast along the Rosebud. The chiefs decided to remain in this spot only one night, and move the camp farther down the valley the next day to put more distance between themselves and the troops. Meanwhile, the scouts would watch the soldiers. If they turned toward the Little Bighorn and approached the camp peacefully, the Indians would parley. Their attitude was recorded by Cheyenne tribal historian John Stands in Timber:

> It may be something else they want us to do now, other than go back to the reservation. We will talk to them. But if they want to fight we will let them have it, so everybody be prepared.[21]

The new camp was established near the bank of the river. The village had by now grown to the point that it stretched more than three miles along the river, and at its widest point extended about two miles out onto the plain.

PART IV

CUSTER'S WAR

15

Terry Changes Plans

THE TROOPS WHO NOW CAUSED SO MUCH CONCERN IN THE INDIAN camp belonged to Custer. They were part of a two-pronged movement consisting of Custer, east of where the Indians were believed to be, and Gibbon to the west. Finally adhering to Sheridan's pincer strategy, General Terry hoped to trap the Indians between these two columns and either finish them or drive them south against Crook.

It had taken Terry almost two weeks to gather enough information to send these forces into the field, and the effort had often been frustrating. For despite Lieutenant Bradley's remarkable scouting for Gibbon, very little of the information was passed on to the general, and he knew almost nothing of where the Indians might be. Accordingly, on June 10 he ordered Major Reno to take six companies of the Seventh Cavalry—half the regiment—together with a Gatling gun and make a reconnaissance. Reno was to follow the Powder south from the Yellowstone for some seventy miles or so, then swing west to the Tongue. Turning north again, he would descend the Tongue to its juncture with the Yellowstone. Reno's total march would cover some 200 miles or so, and he was supplied subsistence rations and forage for twelve days. Mitch Boyer, the half-

Sioux, was detached from Gibbon to guide Reno, who was also assigned eight Indians.[1]

The second day out, the troopers found a campsite of some thirty families or lodges, which was about a week old. Five days later, on June 16, they reached the banks of the Tongue, where Dr. DeWolf recorded in his diary, "Now boil water for camp & poor grass." This was a major campsite. The water and grass had been ruined by the vast Indian pony herds muddying up the river while drinking, and trampling and overgrazing the grass.

Boyer estimated the size at 400 lodges, and correctly surmised this was the site of the village that Bradley and the Crows first saw a month earlier, during Gibbon's march. Having accompanied Gibbon's column, Boyer also knew that when Bradley found the village a second time, it had moved over to the Rosebud.

Boyer's conclusions placed Reno in a difficult situation. He could obey his orders, stay on the route Terry had given him, and head back down the Tongue with month-old information. Or he could strike west for the Rosebud in an effort to find the village. He opted for the Rosebud, marching to within a short distance of that river, then going into camp while the scouts checked out the valley ahead.

A few hours later, they returned with word of an immense southbound trail about a week old. Reno ordered the column to resume moving at 8:30 P.M., and followed the trail for another three hours. Trooper Peter Thompson remembered:

> The trail was so wide and so torn up by teepee poles that we found it difficult to secure a good camping place for the night. This was especially so around watering places which were so necessary to us.[2]

By the time the soldiers finally did find a good campsite, they had pushed so far that Boyer predicted the Indians were only about a day's march ahead. Double pickets were placed around the camp. No bugles were allowed, and the soldiers were cautioned against any loud noises. They could have relaxed, because the Indians were much farther south than Boyer estimated; this was the eve of their victory over Crook, some sixty miles away.

The following morning, Reno followed the trail along the Rosebud another six and a half miles, ordering the soldiers into camp at ten o'clock, while the scouts investigated the surrounding countryside. As they waited, the soldiers speculated about what Reno would do. They were, of course, unaware that Crook and the Indians were south of them on the same river and, at that moment, desperately engaged.

The scouts returned that afternoon, after finding that much of the ground on the giant trail was newly disturbed. Not realizing the fresh sign was made by various small, independent bands and family groups traveling to the great Indian council, they presumed they were close behind the main village. Accordingly, they reported that if they continued along the trail they risked discovery and annihilation by a far superior force. Having learned all he could, and with the horses wearing out, Reno decided to follow the Rosebud back to the Yellowstone. At 4:00 P.M., he turned north, rejoining Terry's main force on June 20, after an absence of ten days.[3]

While Reno was following the trail with half the Seventh Cavalry, Terry's Dakota Column had marched up the Yellowstone to the mouth of the Rosebud, where it united with Gibbon's Montana Column. Terry now had access to Bradley's scouting reports and, on June 15 ordered Custer to take the other half of the Seventh down the south bank of the Yellowstone and investigate along the Tongue where it was presumed he would link up with Reno (Terry was still unaware that Reno had cut over to the Rosebud).

Bradley's reports should have enabled Custer to accomplish at least as much as Reno. But Custer's reputation as an Indian fighter was far greater than his actual experience, and he failed to grasp important clues to what the Indians were doing. Although he found nothing to indicate their current whereabouts, he did locate a campsite from the previous winter. Among the remains were the skull and bones of what appeared to be a cavalryman. Custer took the nearby "dead embers of a large fire" as evidence the man had been tortured to death.

The remains were of more emotional interest than tactical value. Custer should have paid closer attention to a more recent Lakota body, found on a burial scaffold decorated to denote the remains of a brave man. Inspecting the body on Custer's orders, interpreter

Isaiah Dorman found a partly healed wound just below the right shoulder, indicating a recent fight. In writing a dispatch to the *New York Herald,* Custer did not even mention the dead Indian although he dwelt at length on the bones of the soldier.

Having found nothing else of interest, Custer rode back to the Yellowstone where he met the returning Reno.[4] Terry was waiting at his headquarters on the steamer *Far West* when the two halves of the Seventh Cavalry linked up.

Custer and Terry were both furious with Reno for deviating from his assigned route, although for different reasons. No doubt Custer remembered that when he was in trouble with Grant, Reno had tried to take over the Seventh. Seizing the opportunity to get even, Custer criticized Reno and described Terry's reaction to what he had done in a dispatch to the *Herald.*

> Reno took up the trail and followed it about twenty miles, but faint heart never won fair lady, neither did it ever pursue and overtake an Indian village. Had Reno, after first violating his orders [to stay on the Tongue], pursued and overtaken the Indians, his original disobedience of orders would have been overlooked, but his determination forsook him at this point, and instead of continuing the pursuit and at least bringing the Indians to bay, he gave the order to countermarch . . . and reported the details of his gross and inexcusable blunder to General Terry, his commanding officer, who informed Reno in unmistakable language that the latter's conduct [in following the Rosebud instead of the Tongue] amounted to positive disobedience of orders, the sad consequences of which could not yet be fully determined.[5]

Such a public attack, unthinkable in our time, was common enough in the nineteenth century, when rival officers frequently slandered each other in print. Custer also wrote from wounded vanity since he had accomplished nothing while Reno, in disobeying orders, had provided the most useful intelligence Terry had received so far.

Terry's anger was equally unreasonable—Reno's information forced him to change his plans. He had intended to keep Gibbon on patrol north of the Yellowstone, while Custer searched the area to the south. Now it became necessary to send Gibbon south, on a parallel column with Custer, hoping to catch the Indians in the middle.[6] A desk soldier for eleven years since the end of the Civil War, Terry preferred things neat and orderly. He resented having to alter any program that in his mind was already final, even when military necessity dictated otherwise.

Officially, Terry was more restrained, noting only that Reno had discovered "traces of a large and recent camp" on the Rosebud. Based on that information, Custer would throw a dragnet around the entire region where the Indians were thought to be. He would follow the Rosebud south, then turn west to the upper reaches of the Little Bighorn, following it north to its juncture with the Bighorn. Gibbon, meanwhile, would move up the Yellowstone to the mouth of the Bighorn, then follow the Bighorn south to the Little Bighorn and link up with Custer. Terry, who did not wish to remain idle on the Yellowstone, would accompany Gibbon.[7]

Terry outlined his new plan during a conference with Custer and Gibbon, held in *Far West* about noon June 21. From scouting reports, the general suspected the Indian trail might lead to the hostile camp "at some point on the Little Big Horn." If so, Custer was not to follow it, but keep to the south, allowing Gibbon time to press the Indians from the north. Terry believed that by utilizing the scouts and guides to their greatest capabilities, the columns would come close enough together so that if one engaged, the other could reinforce it quickly. "At the same time," Terry wrote, "it was thought that a double attack would very much diminish the chances of a successful retreat by the Sioux, should they be disinclined to fight."[8]

Custer would take fifteen days' rations on pack mules, traveling lightly, without tents. "In this manner," he wrote in the third person, in his last dispatch to the *Herald*, "his command will be able to go wherever the Indians can." After the conference ended, he advised his officers to carry an extra supply of salt, in case the march extended beyond fifteen days and they were forced to live off game.[9]

Terry's written instructions to Custer, transmitted according to protocol through Capt. Edward Smith, the adjutant, were delivered the following day:

Headquarters Department of Dakota
(In the Field)
Camp at Mouth of Rosebud River,
Montana, June 22nd, 1876

Lieut. Col. G. A. Custer, 7th Cavalry
Colonel:

The Brigadier-General Commanding directs that, as soon as your regiment can be made ready for the march, you will proceed up the Rosebud in pursuit of the Indians whose trail was discovered by Major Reno a few days since. It is, of course, impossible to give you any definite instructions in regard to this movement, and were it not impossible to do so, the Department Commander places too much confidence in your zeal, energy, and ability to wish to impose upon you precise orders which might hamper your action when nearly in contact with the enemy. He will, however, indicate to you his own views of what your action should be, and he desires that you should conform to them unless you shall see sufficient reason for departing from them. He thinks that you should proceed up the Rosebud until you ascertain definitely the direction in which the trail above spoken of leads. Should it be found (as it appears almost certain that it will be found) to turn towards the Little Horn, he thinks that you should still proceed southward, perhaps as far as headwaters of the Tongue [about twenty miles south of the Rosebud], and then turn [northwest] towards the Little Horn, feeling constantly, however, to your left, so as to preclude the possibility of the escape of the Indians to the south or southeast by passing around your left flank.

The column of Colonel Gibbon is now in motion for the mouth of the Big Horn. As soon as it reaches that point it will cross the Yellowstone and move up at least as far as the forks of the Big and Little Horns. Of course its further movement must be controlled by circumstances as they arise, but it is hoped that the Indians, if upon the Little Horn, may be so nearly inclosed by the two columns that their escape will be impossible. The Department Commander desires that on your way up the Rosebud you should thoroughly examine the upper part of Tullock's Creek, and that you should endeavor to send a scout through to Colonel Gibbon's Column, with information of the results of your examination. The lower part of the creek will be examined by a detachment from Colonel Gibbon's command.

The supply steamer will be pushed up the Big Horn as far as the forks if the river is found to be navigable for that distance, and the Department Commander, who will accompany the Column of Colonel Gibbon, desires you to report to him there not later than the expiration of the time for which your troops are rationed, unless in the meantime you receive further orders.

Very Respectfully,
Your Obedient Servant,
Ed. W. Smith, Captain, 18th Infantry
Acting Assistant Adjutant General[10]

Much has been made of the statement that Terry did not "wish to impose . . . precise orders which might hamper" Custer. The contention is he gave Custer freedom to act at his own discretion. The key sentence, however, is the one in which Terry declared his intention "to indicate to you his own views," and "desires that you should conform to them. . . ." As any soldier knows, a brigadier general's "views" and "desires" carry the weight of orders and, barring a *very* "sufficient reason," a lieutenant colonel goes against those views and desires at his peril.

Although Custer was authorized to use his own judgment "when nearly in contact with the enemy," the wording indicates he was to avoid such contact if at all possible, until Terry and Gibbon were close enough for support. Meanwhile, he was to scout the area, ascertain the approximate location of the hostile bands, and communicate this information to Gibbon.

Terry's writings show he envisioned a decisive engagement once Custer and Gibbon were close enough to coordinate their moves. Custer's command now consisted exclusively of cavalry—all twelve companies of the Seventh, as well as the offer of a company of the Second Cavalry, which he declined. As Gibbon later noted, cavalry was best suited to locating and striking the enemy, while his own troops, mainly infantry and Gatling guns, were most useful in blocking.[11]

The assignment of scouts is also significant. Custer's Rees were unfamiliar with the country, while Gibbon's Crows knew it thoroughly. Six of the most competent Crows were transferred to Custer, as was Mitch Boyer.[12]

Terry obviously intended for Custer to locate the hostiles and notify Gibbon. Then Custer would attack from the east, driving the Indians west into the infantry and Gatlings, which would block their retreat and destroy them.

Failing that, Terry at least must have hoped the two columns would force the Indians south toward Crook.[13] No one on the Yellowstone knew that Crook had been defeated and had retreated back into Wyoming, or that the Indians, more unified than at any time in their history, were neither afraid of nor impressed by the army.

Shortly after noon, Thursday, June 22, 1876, the Seventh United States Cavalry marched out of camp, leaving the Yellowstone behind. The twelve companies included almost 700 officers and enlisted men. There were twenty-four scouts and guides, among whom were the Rees and their interpreter Fred Girard, Charlie Reynolds, and the six Crows, Mitch Boyer, and George Herendeen, loaned by Gibbon.[14] Custer also carried a number of civilian packers and, in violation of Sherman's previous injunction, correspondent Mark Kellogg.

Custer was in a good mood and, as Gibbon recalled, "chatted freely with us, and was evidently proud of the appearance of his command." Gibbon cautioned, "Now, Custer, don't be greedy, but wait for us."

"No, I will not," Custer said, in a cryptic reply that could mean anything. Then, with a wave of his hand, he spurred his horse, Old Vic, forward to the head of the column.[15]

16

The Trail to Disaster

As HE HAD PREDICTED BACK IN ST. PAUL, CUSTER HAD NOW "CUT loose" from Terry. "All knew that General Custer, if left to his own devices, would soon end the campaign one way or another," Private Thompson wrote. The cheerfulness of the departure from the Yellowstone was gone. Faced with the probability of a fight, the troops became solemn as they marched.[1]

Custer was especially moody. Noticing Pvt. John Burkman with the mule train instead of with his company, he summoned the man and demanded to know why he wasn't in his proper place. Burkman, who moonlighted as Custer's servant and rarely allowed abuse from the colonel to go unanswered, saluted and replied curtly that he had been assigned to the train by the officer of the day. Without another word, he wheeled about and resumed his place with the train. Presently, Custer rode back and said, "Everything's all right, John. It was my mistake. I'm sorry."[2]

At officer's call that evening, Custer opened by complaining that some officers had criticized him to members of Terry's staff. Henceforth, he insisted that all criticism and suggestions be sent to him through channels according to army regulations.

To Benteen, this appeared to be the resumption of an old feud, going back to the massacre of Major Elliott's troops during the

Washita Campaign of 1868–69. When the campaign ended, Benteen had publicly criticized Custer for failing to send a search party that might have saved Elliott. Custer never forgave Benteen for the criticism, and occasionally mentioned it. Now, it appeared Custer was bringing it up again, and Benteen demanded he be more specific.

"Colonel Benteen," Custer replied, "I am not here to be catechised [sic] by you, but for your own information, will state that none of my remarks have been directed towards you."

The answer satisfied Benteen, and Custer moved on to other matters.³ He told the group that he had declined Terry's offer of the Second Cavalry, "confident that the Seventh could handle the matter alone." He had declined the Gatling battery for the very sound reason that the clumsy, top-heavy weapons would hamper movements in the rough terrain.

Judging from the number of lodge fires that Reno had discovered in the abandoned camp on his scout, Custer estimated they could expect to meet at least a thousand warriors, and "there might be enough young men from the agencies, visiting their hostile friends, to make a total of fifteen hundred."

He advised the officers to conserve their rations, and not to overtax the horses and mules, as they might be out longer than the period for which they had been provided. He said he intended "to follow the trail until we could get the Indians, even if it took us to the Indian agencies on the Missouri River or in Nebraska."

Then came the most unsettling part of the meeting—Custer asked for suggestions from officers, henceforth, at any time. Accustomed to their commander's domineering self-reliance, the officers left the conference with what Lt. Francis Gibson later remembered as "a queer sort of depression."

As they walked back to their makeshift tents, Lt. George D. Wallace remarked, "I believe General Custer is going to be killed."

"Why?" Lt. Edward S. Godfrey asked.

"Because I never heard him talk in that way before—that is, asking the advice of anyone."⁴

With the gallows humor that often accompanies military expeditions, many officers made half-joking bequests in case they were killed. Gibson had a standing arrangement with Lt. Algernon

Smith, concerning Smith's watch fob, which Gibson admired. Around the campfires, Smith would sometimes remark, "Gib, if I'm killed first, I will the fob to you, and if you go first, I get your bloodstone ring."

Given Custer's unusual behavior, these conversations now took on a new sense of urgency. Lt. William W. Cooke, regimental adjutant, asked Gibson to witness his will, saying, "I have a feeling that the next fight will be my last."[5]

As the evening passed, some of the officers began to relax, and several gathered at Lt. Winfield Edgerly's tent where they spent an hour singing. Interestingly, the group included Reno, who rarely socialized.[6]

A sense of impending doom still hung over the regiment the next day. Everyone felt it. Instead of the usual horseplay with Tom, Boston, and Autie Reed, Custer was quiet. The soldiers, riding four abreast, were likewise silent. The column was spread out into small units so the dust would not give it away. The steady movement through the hills, silent except for the jangle of gear strapped to the saddles, was unnerving.[7]

Riding parallel to the Rosebud, they were now following the southbound trail Reno had discovered. Indian sign was everywhere. "Find large deserted camps," Dr. DeWolf wrote. "The valley completely barren. [There] has been an enormous number of horses passed about 10 to 20 days ago."[8] Lieutenant Varnum and his scouts rode well ahead of the column, watching for branching trails that might indicate the hostiles were dividing. The column crossed the river and finished the march of June 23 after thirty-three miles.

The next morning the southward march resumed on the opposite bank, and the troops came to the great circle where, earlier in the month, the Hunkpapas had held their Sun Dance. All signs pointed to a confident enemy.[9] The Ree scouts were nervous. They thoroughly understood the power of the people they had come to fight. It took courage for these Indians to stay with the soldiers who, they were beginning to realize, were little more than marching dead men.

The column was now beyond the farthest extent of Reno's scout. The track was growing confused, with various branching trails.

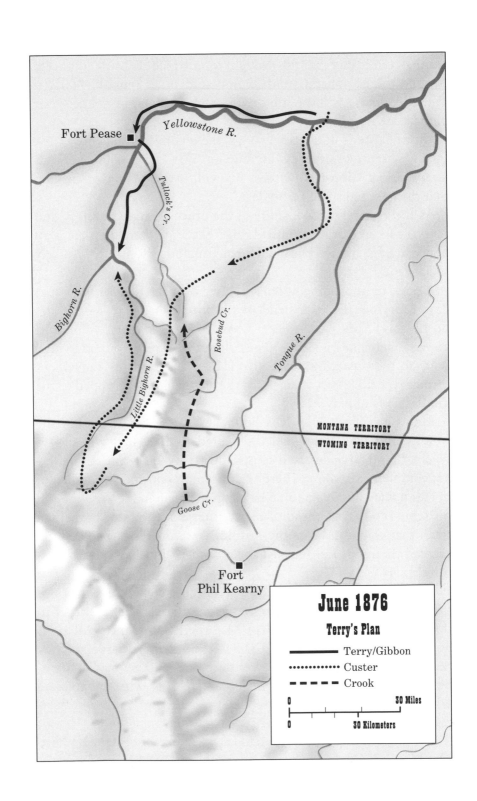

Fort Pease

Yellowstone R.

Tullock's Cr.

Bighorn R.

Little Bighorn R.

Rosebud Cr.

Tongue R.

MONTANA TERRITORY

WYOMING TERRITORY

Goose Cr.

Fort
Phil Kearny

June 1876

Terry's Plan

———— Terry/Gibbon

·············· Custer

— — — Crook

0   30 Miles

0   30 Kilometers

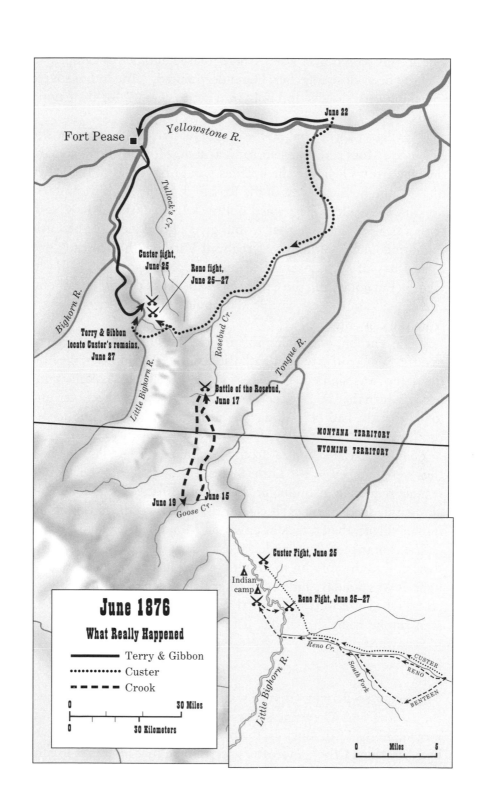

Fort Pease

Yellowstone R.

June 22

Tullock's Cr.

Custer fight,
June 25

Reno fight,
June 25–27

Bighorn R.

Terry & Gibbon
locate Custer's remains,
June 27

Little Bighorn R.

Rosebud Cr.

Tongue R.

Battle of the Rosebud,
June 17

MONTANA TERRITORY

WYOMING TERRITORY

June 19 June 15
Goose Cr.

June 1876

What Really Happened

—————— Terry & Gibbon

•••••••••• Custer

– – – – – Crook

0 ———————— 30 Miles

0 ———————— 30 Kilometers

Custer Fight, June 25

Indian
camp

Reno Fight, June 25–27

Little Bighorn R.

Reno Cr.

South Fork

CUSTER

RENO

BENTEEN

0 ———— Miles ———— 5

The troops passed over areas where a large number of camps had recently been close together. Herendeen noted, "The Indians were travelling very slowly, and only moving for grass" for their pony herds.[10]

At twilight, Custer halted for coffee just below the present site of Busby, Montana, and sent for Varnum. He told the lieutenant that the Crows believed the hostiles would be found in the valley of the Little Bighorn, west of the Rosebud. In the Wolf Mountains dividing two valleys there was a hollow known as the Crow's Nest, with a peak to one side that would give a good view of the Little Bighorn country. Although he realized Varnum "had already had a hard day of it," Custer asked him to accompany Mitch Boyer, Charlie Reynolds, and the Crows to the peak, so that if the Lakota-Cheyenne camps were visible, he could estimate their strength from the campfires.[11]

While Varnum was riding toward the Crow's Nest, Custer visited the Ree bivouac to chat with the scouts. He said when the hostile camp was sighted, the Rees would attack the Lakota pony herds, which they could keep as plunder. He was more relaxed and jovial than he had been in days, and he and Bloody Knife teased brother Tom.[12]

About 9:00 P.M. a courier from Varnum confirmed that the hostiles were camped in the Little Bighorn Valley. Custer decided to resume marching at midnight. He planned to take the command across the divide, conceal it, spend the following day scouting the Indian village, then attack at dawn on Monday, the twenty-sixth.

The cantankerous mules delayed his start until about 1:00 A.M., then slowed the column so that it covered just eight miles by daylight. It was Sunday, June 25. Custer had ordered another halt for coffee when a second courier arrived with a note that Varnum had seen smoke from the village. The colonel mounted a horse and rode toward the Crow's Nest.[13]

THE FIRST TO NOTICE CUSTER'S SOLDIERS APPEAR TO HAVE BEEN the Lakota and Cheyenne scouts who arrived as the village was moving to the Little Bighorn the previous day. These warriors had been watching Crook and, after ascertaining that he was marching back south, they were returning to their people when they saw Custer's men on the Rosebud. Soon after they brought this news, several lodges of Oglalas arrived. They where heading toward the Red Cloud Agency when they had seen the soldiers and, frightened, decided to go back to the village. Initially, the people were alarmed, but their leaders counseled a wait-and-see position.

The chiefs realized some of the young warriors might ride out to provoke an incident, following the ancient tradition of being first to meet the enemy. This, they decided, was no time for tradition— none of the responsible leaders wanted a fight, and steps were taken to prevent it. The heads of both the Lakota and Cheyenne military societies summoned their warriors and sent them out to patrol the hills. Toward sundown, while the Seventh Cavalry was having coffee just over the mountains and Custer was joking with the Rees, groups of warriors rode out to some ten or fifteen stations among the hills on both sides of the river, cordoning off the camps.[14]

Wooden Leg was skeptical of the reports. Only a week had passed since they had defeated Crook, and he did not believe the soldiers would dare fight the Indians for a long time to come. Each camp was holding dances that night, and the great gathering meant an opportunity to expand his social contacts.

"My mind was occupied mostly by such thoughts as regularly are uppermost in the minds of young men," he said, adding by way of explanation, "I was eighteen years old, and I liked girls."[15]

Wooden Leg remembered the dance in the Cheyenne camp as a strictly social event for the young people, with no military or ceremonial significance. The women and girls cleared and leveled a broad area in the middle of the camp circle to serve as a dance floor. Charcoal Bear, the medicine chief, brought a buffalo skin, which normally hung from the top of the sacred tipi, and tied it to the end of a long pole. The young warriors raised the pole in the center of the dancing ground. A bonfire was built, and musicians began beating drums and singing Cheyenne dance songs.

"It seemed that peace and happiness was prevailing all over the world, that nowhere was any man planning to lift his hand against his fellow man," Wooden Leg recalled.

Many of the young Indians went from one camp to another.

They had a wide selection for amusement. Stretching out along the Little Bighorn River from southwest to northeast were the camps of the Hunkpapas, Miniconjous, Sans Arcs, and Cheyennes. West of that first line of camps, again running from southwest to northeast were the Oglalas, Yanktons, and Santees. The Sans Arcs appear to have shared their camp with the Blackfeet, Brulés, and Two Kettles, since none of these four tribes were represented in sufficient numbers to have their own camp circles.[16] When all the tribes were taken together, however, thousands of people were congregated on that little course of river in southeastern Montana.

Black Elk and some of his friends worked the dance circuit until they were too sleepy to continue, and went to bed. In the Oglala camp, Crazy Horse's bachelor brother-in-law, Red Feather, stayed up late dancing, later admitting he "was after the girls." When he finally turned in, he slept soundly. Growing tired of the dancing in the Cheyenne camp, Wooden Leg and three friends went to visit the Sans Arcs where, according to Indian custom, the girls asked them to dance. The Sans Arc women kept the Cheyenne boys well fed and happy, and they stayed the rest of the night.[17]

In some of the Lakota camps, the dancing began to take on a new, serious tone. Several boys had announced they would take a suicide vow, to fight to the death in the next battle. Their people were putting on a Dying Dance to formalize the oath. An extreme ritual rarely practiced at any time, the suicide vow had originated with the Cheyennes, from whom the Lakotas learned it; some Cheyenne boys said they would also take the oath.[18]

A large area was cleared, and the boys were brought in with such loud song and commotion that they could not hear each other talk. The crowd completely surrounded them, men and women singing their praises. No more than twenty took the vow, and no one seemed to believe they would have to fulfill it. They made the pledge as a precaution, in case there was a fight.

The dances ended at dawn with a parade in honor of the boys who had taken the suicide vow. They marched in front, with an old man on either side calling on the rest to look at them well, since they would not come back from the next fight. They marched through the various camps, and then around each camp perimeter before returning to their own lodges.[19]

Wooden Leg, who was not interested in fighting or dying, wandered wearily back to the Cheyenne camp and, hesitating to go into his family's lodge at that hour, dropped down on the ground beside it and went to sleep. A few hours later, he awoke and went inside, where his mother fixed him breakfast, then sent him and his brother, Yellow Hair, down to the river to bathe. When they got there, Indians of all ages and both sexes were splashing around in the cool water. When the two Cheyenne brothers finished, they lay down under the trees on the riverbank, talked about the dances, and drifted off to sleep.[20]

A Hunkpapa woman, Pte-San-Waste-Win, awoke about dawn when her brother, White Eyebrows, drifted in from the dance and asked for breakfast. She stewed some buffalo meat with turnips, and as he ate, the camp began stirring. Since the chiefs had decided to move again that day, some of the early risers among the women began packing. Across the river, an old man shot a buffalo, and some went out to skin and dress it, while others dug wild turnips nearby.[21]

EIGHTEEN MILES EASTWARD ON THE PEAK ABOVE THE CROW'S Nest, Varnum was straining to see through the early morning haze. The origin of the name "Crow's Nest" is obscure. Varnum understood the Crows used to hide in the hollow during horse-stealing expeditions against the Lakotas.[22] Some local residents, however, maintain that the broken, irregular ridges surrounding the hollow follow the same, general, uneven pattern a crow uses in building a nest. The ridges mark a high point in the Wolf Mountains.

Arriving about 2:00 A.M., Varnum and the scouts rested in the hollow until daylight, then ascended the peak, a near-perpendicular climb of over 1,000 feet, and found a rocky outcropping that offered a wide view of the broken country leading toward the Little Bighorn River. Off in the distance, barely a smudge in the center of the horizon, was the stand of trees marking the river and the edge of the Lakota-Cheyenne camp.

The Crows pointed, saying there was a large pony herd on a hillside beyond the village. Varnum strained, but could not see it.

"No look for horses," the Crows insisted, "look for worms,"

since that's how the herd appeared at that great distance. Varnum still could not see it, but closer to his position he noticed one lone tipi standing, and another partly wrecked. He sent the courier to bring Custer.

While Varnum and the scouts waited, they saw two Indian riders, about a mile in front, one of whom was leading a pony. They were riding toward a gap where the trail crossed the divide, and no doubt would discover the troops. Varnum, Reynolds, Mitch Boyer, and two Crows started down to kill them, but had not gone far when the other Crows called them back, saying they had changed their course. "But they changed it again and did cross on the trail," Varnum recalled, "and we watched them discover our column. . . ."[23] As Varnum rode out to meet Custer, another group of Indians appeared, and he could tell they were watching the approaching Seventh Cavalry.

On the peak, the Indians tried to show Custer the distant horse herd, but he could see nothing either. Boyer commented, "If you don't find more Indians in that valley than you ever saw together before, you can hang me."

"It would do a damned sight of good to hang you, wouldn't it?" Custer replied. The uncharacteristic profanity stuck in Varnum's mind; it had been three years since he last heard Custer swear.[24]

When Custer descended from the peak, Tom met him with some disconcerting news. During the night march, Capt. George Yates's Company F had lost a pack containing several boxes of hardtack, and Yates had sent Sgt. William Curtis with a detail to recover it. When the detail returned, Curtis reported that as they approached the missing pack, they saw an Indian trying to open one of the boxes with his hatchet. The Indian immediately fled out of range of the troopers' carbines.

Custer issued an officers' call, and related this information, together with the fact that Varnum's scouts had also seen Indians, making it obvious the column had been discovered. This made it imperative that the Seventh attack the village at once, instead of waiting until the next morning. The companies fell into line with Benteen in the lead, and began moving out.[25]

Shortly after resuming the march, Custer formed the column into three battalions, personally assuming command of one battalion, composed of Companies C, E, F, I, and L, about 225 men. Reno was in charge of Companies A, G, and M, about 112 men; and Benteen, Companies D, H, and K, approximately 125 men.[26] Capt. Thomas McDougall's Company B, which had dallied falling into line, was assigned the ignoble task of guarding the pack trains. Although McDougall's troopers probably resented it at the time, it was a duty that saved most of their lives.

Once across the divide, Custer came to the creek on which the Indians had camped during the Rosebud fight, and followed it into a narrow valley with hills on either side. This valley led northwest to the larger valley of the Little Bighorn, where the creek flowed into the Little Bighorn River. After several miles, he ordered Benteen to take his unit to the left, through broken terrain, to a line of high bluffs three or four miles distant. If Benteen saw nothing there, he would move to the next line of bluffs, and continue moving until he saw the valley of the Little Bighorn. If he ran across the hostiles, he was to send word to Custer, then "pitch in" on them.

Custer never revealed any sort of plan beyond simply attacking the village. From his deployment of troops, however, it may be surmised that he decided to hit with his and Reno's battalions. He probably believed the Indians would not fight, but would try to flee with their families and possessions. With Benteen on the left, near the head of the valley, the fleeing Indians would be intercepted and forced back toward Custer and Reno.[27]

After Benteen moved out, Custer sent Reno's battalion across the creek, with instructions to move down the left bank toward the Little Bighorn River, while he continued parallel on the right bank with the remaining troops.[28] Soon the Rees came across the tipis that Varnum had seen from the peak by the Crow's Nest. Breaking into the lodge that was still standing, they found the body of a warrior, little realizing he had died of wounds received in the fight with Crook. As they were examining the remains, Custer rode up together with Girard, who upbraided the Rees, saying, "You were supposed to go right on in to the Sioux village [and steal the ponies]."

The Rees continued to rummage through the tipi, prompting the exasperated Custer to exclaim, "I told you to dash on and stop for nothing. You have disobeyed me. Move on to one side and let the soldiers pass you in the charge. If any man of you is not brave, I will take away his weapons and make a woman of him."

The scouts resented this, and one snapped at Girard, "Tell him if he does the same to all his white soldiers who are not so brave as we are, it will take him a very long time indeed."

The other Rees laughed.[29]

Custer ordered the tipi burned, then, looking ahead, saw dust rising about two miles away, near the mouth of the creek where it flowed into the river. Summoning Half-Yellow-Face, chief of the Crow scouts, Custer asked him what it might be.

"The Sioux must be running away," Half-Yellow-Face replied.

"I am through with the scouts," Custer said, "you have brought me to the Sioux. I will throw my left wing [Reno] South in case the Sioux should go south."[30]

A short time later, Girard rode up to the top of a knoll, where he saw a group of Indians galloping away. Waving his hat to attract Custer's attention, he shouted, "Here are your Indians running like devils."

Custer waved across the creek to Reno, and sent Cooke to advise him that the village was only two miles away, and appeared to be preparing to flee. Reno was to continue down the left bank of the creek to the Little Bighorn, ford the river, and, as he later recalled, "move forward at as rapid a gait as prudent and to charge afterwards, and that the whole outfit would support me."

As Reno started down the creek, Girard told the Rees, "We are going to go with this party; fall in."

The clear, thin air of the Montana mountains plays tricks, often making things seem closer than they are. As it turned out, the village was more than four miles away. Accompanied by Cooke and Capt. Myles Keogh, commander of Company I in Custer's battalion, Reno moved at a fast trot, only to find it was two miles to the mouth of the creek at the Little Bighorn, and another two and a half miles downriver to the village. At the ford of the river, Cooke and Keogh returned to Custer, and Reno took his men across. Here he halted for about ten minutes to consolidate and regroup, then sent word to Custer "that I had everything in front of me and that they [the hostiles] were strong."[31]

The Indians in camp had first noticed soldiers, likewise plainly visible, when they were still some six or eight miles away, on the divide between the Little Bighorn and the Rosebud. Their weapons glinted in the sun as they came toward the village. Over the next hour or so, the women and children went about their business, while some of the men kept an eye on the troops working down the ridges from the divide. In the Hunkpapa camp, some of the men hurried the women about their chores. They were not ready for a fight, and believed the soldiers would realize this and ride on, leaving them unmolested. They continued to watch the soldiers on the ridge, paying no attention to the flat valley before them where Reno was forming his battalion into line.[32]

Two miles to the southwest, Reno placed the Rees to his left, then charged down the valley toward the Hunkpapa camp. Meeting no resistance, and not realizing the village extended some three miles beyond the first circle of tipis, the three companies of cavalry, scouts, and civilian auxiliaries dashed across the valley floor. The galloping horses scattered Indians who were out in the fields above the camp.[33]

Lieutenant Varnum saw Indians rushing madly about and running away from the cavalry. Advancing rapidly, his company pulled ahead of the others. Then he looked back and saw the other companies dismounting. His scouts had disappeared, so he took his company back to the line of soldiers.[34]

Reno had dismounted his men on an open plain some 700 yards short of the village because the horses were becoming unmanageable. The animals had been on the trail all night, and covered the eighteen miles from the Crow's Nest in three hours. They had come the last two miles down the creek at a trot, then charged across two miles of valley at full gallop. They could do no more. Even before everyone could dismount, several of the exhausted, frightened horses bolted, carrying their helpless riders straight to their deaths in the Indian camp.

Reno's men formed into a skirmish line and opened fire. The fight had begun.[35]

17

The Little Bighorn

No one knows the exact time Reno's charge opened the two-day series of fights collectively known as the Battle of the Little Bighorn and popularly as Custer's Last Stand. Based on the distance and type of terrain covered by the Seventh Cavalry since it had halted for coffee shortly after sunrise, the best one can say is Reno attacked sometime close to 3:00 P.M.

Having celebrated until after daylight, many Indians were still asleep in their lodges, and camp routine started unusually late. Barely awake, Crazy Horse's brother-in-law, Red Feather, was dimly aware of the stirring in the Oglala camp. First someone ordered the young men to take the horses to pasture. Then another person noticed a cloud of dust in the distance and shouted, "Go get the horses—buffaloes are stampeding!" Almost immediately someone else came dashing in with the horses, yelling, "Get away as fast as you can, don't wait for anything, the white men are charging!"[1]

Down by the river, Wooden Leg dreamed a crowd of people was making a racket. It startled him awake and he realized it was no dream. There was a great commotion, punctuated by gunfire. The noise also woke his brother, Yellow Hair, and together they ran out of the trees to have a look. The gunfire came from the Hunkpapa camp, at the southwest end of the village, about two miles away. People were dashing about, women screaming and men shouting war cries. The old men were yelling, "Soldiers are here! Young men, go out and fight them."[2]

Black Elk, who was supposed to be taking the family ponies to graze, had joined some friends for a swim. In the distance, he saw women digging wild turnips. Black Elk's cousin brought the ponies down to get a drink and cool off. Suddenly, they heard the crier in the Hunkpapa camp yelling, "The chargers are coming! They are charging! The chargers are coming!" The cry was taken up in the Oglala camp, and spread north from camp to camp.[3]

"We had no time to consult one another as to what action we should take," the Miniconjou chief, Red Horse, recalled. "We gave directions immediately for every Indian to take his horse and arms; for the women and children to mount their horses and get out of the way, and for the young men to go and meet the troops."[4]

Mothers and children were searching desperately for each other. Herders were running to catch ponies for the warriors. Warriors from the various camps were rushing to help the Hunkpapas fight off the attack. Black Elk hurried back to the Oglala camp, where his father told him, "Your brother has gone to the Hunkpapas without his gun. Catch him and give it to him. Then come right back to me." Black Elk jumped on his pony and caught up with his brother. He had his own revolver as well and, instead of returning immediately as his father had ordered, he continued on toward the Hunkpapas. Ahead he could see a large cloud of dust beyond the camp. No one had any idea of what was happening or why. Many had never heard of Custer or Reno, and presumed Crook had returned to even the score for the Rosebud.[5]

The Hunkpapas, whose camp was in Reno's direct line, were thrown into total confusion. Terrified and not knowing what else to do, many were running around aimlessly and yelling. Others, still wet from bathing in the river, were running toward the camp. Some warriors hid in the timber, and Black Elk and his brother joined them.[6] Men and women alike were trying to flee from the Hunkpapa camp. Black Elk watched as the soldiers on their heavy government horses emerged from the dust cloud. The Rees, and two Crows who accompanied the column, peeled off from the soldiers and headed toward the pony herd.[7]

Then the Indians saw a second column of troops—Custer's—on the ridges across the river. The men did not seem to know what to do or who to fight. Pte-San-Waste-Win remembered:

> We women wailed over the children, for we believed that the Great Father had sent all his men for the destruction of the Sioux. Some of the women put loads on travois and would have left, but that their husbands and sons were in the fight. Others tore their hair and wept for the fate that they thought was to be the portion of the Sioux, through the anger of the Great Father. . . .[8]

Reno's men, now on foot and formed in line, were firing into the camp. The two wives and three children of the Hunkpapa war chief Gall were killed.[9] Enraged, he began rallying the warriors and turning them back to fight. Someone shouted, "Take courage! Don't be a woman! The helpless are out of breath!" The women and children were sent downstream toward the Cheyennes at the far end of the village, away from the fighting.[10]

In the adjacent Oglala camp, Crazy Horse felt no sense of urgency. Instead, he consulted a medicine man and invoked spirits, spending so much time at it that many of the young warriors became impatient.[11]

In dismounting, Reno had lost the momentum of his charge. As soon as the Indians began fighting back, the soldiers were reduced from attackers to defenders. To those in the skirmish line, however, Reno had done the right thing. "Good for you," Lt. Charles DeRudio remarked when he heard the order to dismount. The Indians were already recovering from the shock of the attack, and DeRudio was certain that if the command had ridden 500 yards farther, it would have been butchered.[12] As the dust settled, the soldiers saw the Indians circling around toward their rear. Troopers began falling. Pvt. William C. Slaper saw his sergeant and several others go down. After an initial moment of terror, Slaper recovered and "had no further thought of fear, although conscious that I was in great peril and standing a mighty good chance of never getting out alive."[13]

From his place on the line, Varnum glanced across the river, saw the Gray Horse Company E in column with Custer, and took comfort in the knowledge that they were following the bluffs to hit the village from the other end. As it was, the situation on Reno's skirmish line was serious enough. Varnum could not determine the size or extent of the village, and didn't even try to guess the number of warriors. He only knew that during his entire life, he had never seen so many Indians in one place.[14]

The Indians were gathering strength and concentrating on Reno. More were pouring out onto the field and working back behind the soldiers' line, while others were pushing the Rees and Crows away from the ponies. With Custer still riding along the ridges and well beyond the range of this fight, some Indians crossed the river and moved up the opposite bank, then crossed again in the rear, working into position for a rush on Reno's horses.

All along the line, ammunition was running low. Capt. Thomas W. French's Company M was pinned down among a group of prairie dog burrows, and the troopers flattened themselves, using the low mounds as breastworks—an effort that would have been comical had it not been so desperate. It was the best they could do, and their lieutenant, Benjamin H. Hodgson, walked up and down the line encouraging them.[15]

The skirmish line was becoming untenable. Lieutenant Wallace tried to convince the half-Blackfoot scout William Jackson to take a message to Custer, asking for help. Noting the ever increasing number of Indians coming into the fight, Jackson waved him off with the comment, "No man could get through that alive."[16] Sgt. Ferdinand A. Culbertson believed if they stayed in place three minutes longer, no one would get out alive.[17]

Reno reportedly rode up to Captain French and asked, "Well, Tom, what do you think of this?"

"I think we had better get out of here," French is said to have replied. Reno agreed and ordered the command to fall back to several hundred yards to the left, toward a small stand of timber along the river.

Many soldiers never heard the order or any bugle call, but somehow word circulated among the troops to mount and move out. The firing from the skirmish line died down as the soldiers fell back to their horses, and the Indians took advantage of it to crowd in with a galling fire. A shot through the stomach knocked Pvt. Henry Koltzbucher off his horse. Pvt. Francis Neely went over to help, but could not get him back into his saddle. Neely saw the wound was probably mortal, and he and Private Slaper dragged Koltzbucher to some brush, concealing him there and giving him a canteen before riding off to join the others. When Koltzbucher's body was recovered after the fight, it was not mutilated. Almost certainly he had died without being discovered by the Indians.[18]

Some of the horses broke away from the handlers, leaving soldiers to run for safety as best they could. Scout George Herendeen was on foot and one of the last to reach the timber, turning to fire a few parting shots at some Indians who were trying to infiltrate the trees from the river and the rear. He found his horse and joined the command, which was mounted in a clearing and formed in line of battle. Bloody Knife was next to Reno, who had lost his hat and was wearing a red handkerchief around his head. Suddenly, a volley rang out. A soldier cried, "Oh! my God! I have got it!" and fell from his saddle. A bullet from the same volley shattered Bloody Knife's head, splattering his brains all over Reno's face and tunic.

Sgt. John Ryan looked to the rear and saw Indians, lying flat on their ponies, slipping into the brush from behind. He reported it to Captain French, who disagreed, "Oh, no: those are General Custer's men." As he said that, one of the Indians fired. The bullet struck Pvt. George Lorentz in the back of the neck, coming out of his mouth; he fell forward in his saddle and slipped to the ground. Shooting opened up from all sides.[19]

Reno now ordered a dismount, and the troopers hit the dirt, lying prone and fighting as best they could. They were surrounded, however, with the Indians on higher ground. The widely spaced trees did not offer adequate protection for an entire battalion, and the Indians used what cover there was to infiltrate the line. Increasingly, officers and men alike were beginning to wonder, where was Custer? The promised support had not come. They were alone.

The veteran Sergeant Ryan, who was probably more competent than many of the officers, had had enough. Turning to Captain French, he said, "The best thing we can do is to cut right through them."²⁰ Officers shouted their ideas back and forth from their positions on the line, in what Sergeant O'Neill called a "brisk consultation"; consensus was to get out. Reno gave the order to remount, then rode along the line shouting, "Any of you men who wish to make your escape, follow me." A scouting detail under the half-Sioux Lt. Donald McIntosh determined the path to the river was momentarily clear, and the command prepared to move out.

Pinned down at the edge of the woods, Varnum was sharing a drink with Lonesome Charlie Reynolds and Fred Girard, out of Girard's pocket flask. The situation looked hopeless, and Varnum was more interested in his drink than in what the Indians were doing. They were still at it when Varnum realized everybody else was already mounted and moving out. He grabbed his horse and started through the woods to avoid being left behind. Soon the fast Kentucky thoroughbred overtook the head of the column, and Varnum, not seeing any other officer, tried to rally the men to go back and attack. A voice sharply reminded Varnum that he was not in command. He looked over and saw Reno.²¹

Almost without exception, the survivors agreed the move began without panic. The command, however, was strung out too thin. About this time, according to Indian accounts, Crazy Horse arrived, leading the Oglalas straight into the line of soldiers. Inspired by this, the warriors of the other tribes "advanced furiously with great yelling, coming down on the flank," according to the young Hunkpapa warrior Iron Hawk.

> The soldiers broke and ran in retreat, the Indians using war clubs as the principal weapon, a few using bows and arrows, most of the execution being by knocking troopers from their horses, the Indians moving right in among them.²²

The Indians closed in on those in the center and rear, dividing Reno's men into small groups. Warriors rode alongside the soldiers, resting their new Winchester rifles across the pommels of their saddles, which put the muzzles level with the troopers' abdomens. All they had to do was pull the triggers and the troopers fell. When the soldiers tried to return fire, the Indians swung down behind their ponies.²³

"I ran the gauntlet . . . and they didn't touch me or my horse," Lt. Luther Hare wrote to his father, a judge in Sherman, Texas. "To kill a man's horse was certain death to him. My first sergeant was killed about two yards from me on one side, and one of the men was killed in about a foot of me on the other side."[24]

Pvt. Roman Rutten rode past the black interpreter, Isaiah Dorman, whose horse had been shot. Dorman was down on one knee, firing his sporting rifle into the Indians crowding around. As Rutten passed, Dorman looked up and called, "Goodbye, Rutten." Farther on, Rutten saw Lieutenant McIntosh, separated from the others and trying to ride through twenty or thirty Indians who surrounded him. He never saw McIntosh again. The lieutenant died at the hands of his mother's people.[25]

Reaching the riverbank, Reno's men found a six-foot drop into the water. Many of the terrified, exhausted horses refused to jump until pressure from those behind forced them in. The retreat turned into a rout, and it was here that Reno's command suffered the worst butchery—of the 112 officers and men in the battalion, 29 were killed crossing the Little Bighorn.[26]

The valiant Lieutenant Hodgson was knocked off his horse and wounded at the edge of the river. Trumpeter Henry Fisher rode up, kicked out his stirrup, and Hodgson held on to it while Fisher towed him across. As they struggled up the steep embankment on the other side, the Indians began firing at them and Hodgson, so close to safety, was killed.[27] Also among the dead were Charlie Reynolds, Dr. DeWolf, and Isaiah Dorman.

As the remnants of Reno's command crossed and retreated up the bluff to a hill overlooking their erstwhile battleground, the Indians fell to stripping the dead soldiers. One soldier was still kicking, and a Lakota rode up to Black Elk and said, "Boy, get off and scalp him." Black Elk dismounted and set to work. "He had short hair and my knife was not very sharp. He ground his teeth. Then I shot him in the forehead and got his scalp."[28]

Chance had brought Reno to a semicircular ridge that formed a saucer-shaped depression. The depression sloped down away from the river and onto the plains. The ridge itself curved up to form two summits, one at either end. On each of these summits, rifle pits were dug to cover the depression where it sloped down to the plains, creating a cross fire against any Indians who might try to come up that way. In short, except for nagging fire from Indian sharpshooters on adjacent heights, or a full assault by all able-bodied warriors, the position was impregnable. As the Brulé warrior Two Eagles recalled, years later, Reno "was too well fortified."[29]

Incredibly, some whites were still alive across the river in the timber. Among them were Lieutenant DeRudio and Sergeant O'Neill, both of whom had lost their horses. O'Neill and DeRudio found each other, then discovered Fred Girard and William Jackson, who were still mounted. DeRudio said the horses might give them away, and suggested Girard and Jackson drive them off. When they refused, the lieutenant crawled off to hide himself. He found a dry creek bed covered with underbrush, and slipped down to the bottom. He had not been there more than ten minutes when he heard shots, followed by the "silvery, but to me diabolical" voices of several Indian women. Peering out, he watched as they began mutilating the body of a trooper.[30]

On their hill, Reno's exhausted troopers heard gunfire off in the distance, and knew Custer was engaged somewhere to the north. But, even though their height commanded a considerable area, the view to the north was blocked by a high ridge. Most of the Indians had departed in that direction, leaving enough of their comrades to keep Reno pinned down on the ridge and pick off any troopers who went down to the river for water.[31] It had been about forty-five minutes since Reno's men began shooting. The first phase of the Battle of the Little Bighorn was over.

18

Catastrophe on the Ridges

AFTER SEPARATING FROM RENO, CUSTER CONTINUED DOWN THE north side of the creek at a slow pace, pausing briefly to water the thirsty horses.[1] He was still on the creek when Girard caught up with Cooke and Keogh, told them Reno had opened the fight, then turned about and headed back to the field. As Custer was nearing the juncture with the Little Bighorn, he turned north among the ridges along the east side of the river.

The ridges do not form a solid line, but rather a series of steep hills broken by ravines, some of which slope down almost level with the riverbank. It is five miles from where Reno had found his hilltop refuge to Custer Ridge, where the so-called Last Stand occurred. From Reno's position the trail between the two climbs a peak now known as Weir Point, then descends into a deep depression called Medicine Tail Coulee, finally ascending the ridges leading to Custer Ridge. These ridges are broken by a second large, wide depression, Deep Ravine, which runs east from the river and forks into a Y. On the north side, the main fork of the Y continues as Deep Ravine, while the tributary fork on the south is called Calhoun Coulee. Instead of marching at a consistent level, where they could see everything across the river, Custer's men would cover a roller-coaster pattern, sometimes seeing across the river, and sometimes with the view completely obstructed.

While Reno was still fighting in the open field in front of the village, Sgt. Daniel Kanipe of Custer's battalion saw Indians on top of the same hill to which Reno later retreated. Kanipe's sighting, together with Cooke's report that Reno had now engaged, prompted Custer to send four of his five companies up the hill, but by the time they arrived, the Indians were gone. From the top, however, the soldiers could see several hundred tipis.

Custer joined them, and watched the village for several minutes. There were a few women and children moving about, and some dogs and ponies, but no warriors could be seen. No one realized that this was only a fraction of the village. Nor did they understand that the warriors, fully armed, were running toward the Reno fight.

The colonel waved his hat and shouted, "Hurrah, boys, we've got them. We'll finish them up and then go home to our station."

Tom Custer, commanding Sergeant Kanipe's company, told the sergeant to find Captain McDougall with the pack train, which had fallen behind. "Tell McDougall to bring the pack train straight across to high ground," Tom ordered. "If the packs get loose don't stop to fix them, cut them off. Come quick. Big Indian camp." After that, Kanipe was to find Benteen and tell him to rejoin Custer.

As Kanipe rode off, he glanced back to see the men start down the other side of the hill. Some of the excited troopers were riding past Custer, who shouted, "Boys, hold your horses, there are plenty of them down there for us all."[2]

Mitch Boyer and four of the Crows stayed behind on the hilltop and watched the village for a while. When one of the Crows remarked there weren't many warriors, Mitch replied they were probably "out campaigning somewhere," and suggested they hurry and rejoin the column.[3]

Custer, meanwhile, had ridden at a fast pace for about a mile, until he reached Medicine Tail Coulee, which led down to a convenient ford across the river. Summoning trumpeter John Martin, who had immigrated from Italy three years earlier as Giovanni Martini, Custer said, "Orderly, I want you to take a message to Colonel Benteen. Ride as fast as you can and tell him to hurry. Tell him it's a big village and I want him to be quick, and to bring the ammunition packs."

When Martin turned his horse to obey, Cooke said, "Wait, orderly, I'll give you a message." Then he scribbled:

Benteen.
Come on. Big village. Be quick. Bring pack[s].
W.W. Cooke
P.[S.] Bring pac[k]s

Handing him the message, Cooke said, "Now, orderly, ride as fast as you can to Colonel Benteen. Take the same trail we came down. If you have time, and there is no danger, come back; but otherwise stay with your company."⁴

Martin turned about and rode back down the trail, the last surviving white to see Custer or Cooke alive.

Why Cooke felt it necessary to write the message, when all previous orders that day had been verbal, is a mystery. Although an immigrant, Martin's position as trumpeter was comparable to the radioman of the twentieth-century army, making him responsible for all types of communications; to qualify for his post, he had to demonstrate the ability to repeat a twenty-word message verbatim. Once already that day he had chased down Benteen, given him a verbal order from Cooke, then returned to Custer's side. With a fight imminent, however, perhaps Custer and Cooke saw this as an opportunity to rid themselves of Benteen by sending a written order. Then, if he failed to comply in a timely manner, they could bring him up on charges.⁵

The last thing Martin saw as he left Custer to look for Benteen was part of the column descending at a gallop into Medicine Tail Coulee, heading toward the river. By now, the battalion had divided into two wings: the right, composed of Companies C, I, and L, with Keogh commanding as senior captain; and the left, Companies E and F, under Capt. George W. Yates, and accompanied by Custer and his staff.

Still trailing behind, Mitch Boyer and the Crows were now on the summit of Weir Point, where they could see everything. They watched the hostile warriors shift positions as soon as Custer came to the river. Looking back, they saw Reno's men fighting their way across the river and up onto the hill they themselves had left only a few minutes earlier. Mitch said he was going to join Custer, and ordered the Crows to return to the pack train. Then he rode down toward Medicine Tail Coulee. The Crows never saw him again.[6]

BENTEEN WAS NOW WORKING HIS WAY BACK NORTH TO CUSTER, having traveled perhaps seven miles without seeing anything. Although the countryside appears at a distance to be rolling hills, close inspection shows it to be rugged, and many of the slopes are steep and broken. The horses were worn out by the constant climbing and descending, and some of the men were starting to fall behind. Far in the distance, the soldiers could see Custer's battalion, which they recognized by the gray horses of Company E, and two or three times, they heard loud cheering and a few shots, probably from Reno's charge.

The slow-moving pack train was just coming up the trail when Benteen's troopers returned from their pointless mission. Pulling ahead of the mules, Benteen came to a morass where one of the region's many water courses bubbled out of the ground, and paused to water the horses, which, like Custer's, had not been given a drink since the previous afternoon. Hearing more gunfire in the distance, Capt. Thomas Weir, commander of Company D and a member of the Custer faction, became impatient with the delay and started moving ahead.

As the battalion finished watering, the mules arrived. "Many of them had been poorly packed, and they had sore backs and were pretty tired," Pvt. Charles Windolph said. "They had gone close to twenty-four hours without water." Despite the efforts of the packers and muleskinners to control them, several broke loose and plunged forward, becoming mired in the boggy ground. Getting them out took time, and Benteen moved on, leaving the mules to follow.[7]

As they rode past the still burning burial lodge, Sergeant Kanipe arrived, having delivered Tom Custer's message to Captain McDougall at the pack train. Delivering it once again to Benteen, he attached himself to that battalion until he could return to his own.[8]

Trumpeter Martin was not far behind. Reading the message he brought from Cooke, Benteen opted against waiting for the packs, and pushed toward Reno's original ford of the Little Bighorn. His battalion arrived in time to see the tail of Reno's column, dismounted and trapped downriver in the second ford, and the remainder fleeing across the river and up the hill. He realized something had gone terribly wrong. Moving to the left, he encountered three or four Crows, who told him there were "heaps" of Sioux just ahead.

"From long experience in the cavalry," Benteen wrote in his report, "I judged there were 900 veteran Indians right there at that time, against which the large element of recruits in my battalion would stand no earthly chance as mounted men. I then moved up the bluffs and reported my command to Maj. M. A. Reno."[9]

ARCHAEOLOGISTS BELIEVE THAT ONE OF CUSTER'S TWO WINGS AT Medicine Tail Coulee went as far as the river, while the other stayed on the ridge. The Indians remembered seeing the soldiers split into groups, and at least one recalled the gray horses of Company E at the ford. Thus it may be more or less surmised that Custer and Yates took Companies E and F to the river, while Keogh waited above with C, I, and L.

At the ford, some shots were exchanged and, although the Indians claim they drove the soldiers back, there is no evidence of any real fighting.[10] Assuming, then, that the withdrawal from the river was voluntary and not forced on Custer, either of two explanations is possible:

1. Coming to the ford, he saw the women and children had fled, and this part of the village was virtually empty. Then, as archaeologist Richard Allan Fox, Jr., contends, Custer decided to go around the village and capture the fleeing families as hostages, forcing the warriors to surrender.[11] Mackenzie had done this successfully in Texas.
2. Or, he realized the village was larger than he had anticipated, that he was not at the end of it, but at the middle, and turned north to find the end and sweep through it.

In any event, archaeological studies and Indian narratives indicate that after this first attempted crossing, Keogh's wing remained on the ridge separating the forks of Deep Ravine and Calhoun Coulee, while Custer and Yates continued northward at least two more miles, following the ridges as they began to slope gently down to the plains. They probably intended to scout the river crossing by the Cheyenne camp and determine where a strike might be most effective.

The Cheyenne camp was occupied. Warriors were still moving down toward the Hunkpapas to fight Reno, when some of the men came galloping back. Kate Bighead, who was in the camp, said at first she thought they had been beaten and were running away. Then she heard an old man shouting, "Other soldiers are coming! Warriors, go and fight them!" Looking across the river, they could see Custer's men coming down the slope toward the crossing. A few warriors had already gone to meet them, and sporadic shooting broke out. This resistance seemed to convince Custer he could not cross the river with only two companies, because he backtracked about a mile up onto the ridges again. He halted on top of a high bluff, apparently to await Keogh, who was still on his ridge another mile behind on the opposite side of Deep Ravine.[12]

Keogh, meanwhile, was beginning to feel pressure from the Indians. He had one company in a skirmish line along the hill and the other two in reserve. Some idle sniping appears to have broken out between the skirmishers and the Indians below.

"We were lying down in gullies and behind sagebrush hillocks," Wooden Leg remembered. "The shooting at first was at a distance, but we kept creeping in closer all around the ridge." Keogh responded by sending Calhoun with one of the reserve companies, which scattered them. The Indians fled down Calhoun Coulee while the company dismounted and occupied a low ridge commanding the depression. Calhoun's company was the only unit in Custer's entire battalion that left evidence of any real attempt to deploy and fight in an organized manner.

Disgusted at the display of Indian timidity in the face of Calhoun's skirmish line, Lame White Man, a Cheyenne war chief, rode around on his pony calling out, "Come. We can kill all of them."[13] The Oglala chiefs also began calling to their people, who were fighting alongside the Cheyennes.

The Indians began working up the coulee, making short dashes, diving for cover and waiting, then moving up again. The braver ones stayed on their horses, exposing themselves to the gunfire. Standing Bear, a sixteen-year-old Miniconjou, was riding up the hill when he met a Lakota named Long Elk. Blood was pouring from Long Elk's mouth and splashing down on the shoulders of his pony. Farther up, he saw another Lakota, on foot, bleeding and dizzy, who would walk a few steps, fall, then get up and try to walk again. Wooden Leg saw him, too, and got a close look at the Lakota's face as he staggered past. The entire lower jaw was shot away. The sight of the horribly disfigured face was too much for Wooden Leg, who vomited.

On the hill, the army horses, exhausted by two days of continuous marching and frightened by the gunfire, were beginning to struggle and circle about their handlers. Several broke loose.

Shouting "*Hoka hey!* [It is a good day to die!] Hurry! Hurry!" one group of Indians made a dash for the animals. Hand-to-hand fighting broke out between the Indians and the horse handlers, while the frightened horses began running toward the river. Seeing their means of withdrawal threatened, Keogh's troops panicked. "Right away, all of the white men went crazy," Wooden Leg observed.[14]

"We had them surrounded," Two Moons said, "and first the Sioux and then the Cheyennes would charge them. In our first big charge, when all swept in together, nearly one whole band [of Keogh's soldiers] was killed."

No one could call the soldiers cowards for, as Fox points out, cowardice is a conscious decision to avoid battle. These men had accepted battle on that bare ridge. But the constant marching without sleep, the hordes of Indians, and the stampede of the horses were simply too much. They were tired and they were scared. Keogh's line crumbled. A few soldiers may have stood and fought, but most were cut to pieces as they ran. Jimmi Calhoun and his second lieutenant, John J. Crittenden, probably died trying to hold their skirmish line together, for their bodies were later found on the line.[15]

U.S. commissioners meet with Indians to negotiate the Fort Laramie Treaty in 1868. General W. T. Sherman of Civil War fame is second to the right of the center post.
LITTLE BIGHORN BATTLEFIELD NATIONAL MONUMENT

The Oglala leader Red Cloud, who humbled the government in 1866–68, was restrained by his people from joining the hostiles in 1876.
U.S. MILITARY ACADEMY LIBRARY

The Hunkpapa chief
Sitting Bull, pictured
here in 1884, was the
living symbol of Indian
traditionalism and
resistance. PHOTO BY
PALMQUIST AND JURGENS,
AUTHOR'S COLLECTION

Lieutenant General Philip
H. Sheridan commanded
the Military Division
of the Missouri, in which
the war was fought.
KANSAS STATE HISTORICAL
SOCIETY, TOPEKA

Lieutenant John Gregory Bourke, Crook's aide-de-camp, kept a diary, which was the most detailed account of the war and the actions of the generals.

Always conscious of his public image, Brigadier General George Crook is posing here as he wished to be seen, the avid outdoorsman with canvas suit and pith helmet.

Colonel Joseph J. Reynolds, shown in a contemporary engraving as a Union Army general, earned the hatred of his officers and men by leaving his dead and wounded to fall into Indian hands. AUTHOR'S COLLECTION

Frank Grouard, Crook's chief scout, exhibits the polyglot features that created so much speculation about his origin. FROM JOE DEBARTHE, *THE LIFE AND ADVENTURES OF FRANK GROUARD*

Captain Anson Mills's calculated risks saved Crook's men during the Reynolds fight and at the Rosebud, but got Mills into trouble at Slim Buttes. FROM JOE DEBARTHE, *THE LIFE AND ADVENTURES OF FRANK GROUARD*

The Cheyenne warrior Wooden Leg, photographed here in 1927, participated in virtually every major action of the war. LITTLE BIGHORN BATTLEFIELD NATIONAL MONUMENT

Colonel John Gibbon's excessive caution cost him a chance to suppress the tribes before they had finished consolidating.
LITTLE BIGHORN BATTLEFIELD NATIONAL MONUMENT

Lieutenant James H. Bradley located the main Indian camp twice, only to see his efforts wasted when Gibbon failed to act on his reports.
LITTLE BIGHORN BATTLEFIELD NATIONAL MONUMENT

The mild, scholarly Brigadier General Alfred H. Terry had not commanded troops in the field for eleven years when ordered to lead the Dakota troops into Montana. LITTLE BIGHORN BATTLEFIELD NATIONAL MONUMENT

One of the last photos of Lieutenant Colonel George Armstrong Custer, taken a few months before his death at the Little Bighorn. PHOTO BY JOSÉ MARIA MORA, AUTHOR'S COLLECTION

Black Elk *(left)*, posing with the warrior Elk while touring Europe with Buffalo Bill, was too young to participate in most of the fighting, but left a vivid account of how the war affected the Indian way of life.

Major Marcus A. Reno was unfairly accused of failing to support Custer at the Little Bighorn. By the time Custer engaged the Indians, Reno was desperately trying to save his own command.

LITTLE BIGHORN BATTLEFIELD NATIONAL MONUMENT

In December 1876, only a few months after the Little Bighorn, Frederick Whittaker published a fanciful biography that gave birth to the Custer legend. This engraving from the book was one of the first efforts to depict the so-called "Last Stand." The scene is totally imaginary, prompting one writer to call it the "Indian Austerlitz."

FROM FREDERICK WHITTAKER, *A COMPLETE LIFE OF GEN. GEORGE A. CUSTER*

A relaxed group portrait shows four officers of the Great Sioux War. The three seated *(from left)*, Charles A. Varnum, Frederick W. Benteen, and Benjamin Hodgson were at the Little Bighorn, where Hodgson was killed during Reno's retreat. Their companion, Nelson Bronson *(standing)*, served with the infantry protecting the supply steamers.

LITTLE BIGHORN BATTLEFIELD NATIONAL MONUMENT

During General Crook's starvation march through Montana and the Dakotas, a soldier dispatches an exhausted horse . . .

. . . which the hungry troopers cut up for food.

Near the end of their exhausting ordeal, two troopers demonstrate how the wounded from Slim Buttes were carried on travois. These photographs were made by Stanley J. Morrow, a member of the relief expedition that carried supplies to Crook.

Beset with bouts of insanity and suspicious to the point of paranoia, Colonel Ranald S. Mackenzie nevertheless won the government's first decisive victory, six months to the day after the Custer disaster at the Little Bighorn. AUTHOR'S COLLECTION

Older and more experienced than General Crook, Lieutenant Colonel Richard Irving Dodge was unimpressed with Crook's reputation, bluntly calling him "a humbug." FROM RICHARD IRVING DODGE, *OUR WILD INDIANS*

Dull Knife, one of the senior chiefs of the Cheyenne Nation.
Mackenzie's destruction of Dull Knife's village on the Red Fork of the
Powder River broke Cheyenne military power forever. NATIONAL
ANTHROPOLOGICAL ARCHIVES, SMITHSONIAN INSTITUTION

A self-made soldier, Colonel Nelson Miles was the
most successful independent commander of the war.
LITTLE BIGHORN BATTLEFIELD NATIONAL MONUMENT

Dressed in his trademark bearskin coat and wearing a beard to protect
his face from the cold, Miles *(center)* poses with his officers (including
Frank Baldwin, *fifth from left*) in January 1877, as they prepare for the
final thrust against Crazy Horse at Wolf Mountain. LITTLE BIGHORN
BATTLEFIELD NATIONAL MONUMENT

A Miniconjou whose name, Mahpiyah Luwa Isaye, has been loosely translated as "Lights," could not remember any effort at a stand. "If there was a stand made, it was short," he said in an interview much later. A Brulé named Two Eagles remembered about ten or twelve troopers running down a ravine toward the river. "Most of the soldiers killed were dismounted and moving," he commented.

Keogh's body later was found among a large group of soldiers behind Calhoun's line. Perhaps he was trying to make a stand, but it is just as likely that the troopers simply bunched together in a panicky and futile effort at mob security.

The men of Company C were spread over a wide area of the ridge. First Sgt. Edwin Bobo may have been trying to lead a large party toward Custer when it was overwhelmed. Some distance to the south, Sgts. Jeremiah Finley and August Finckle were found among bodies of Company C troopers scattered out along the ridge, suggesting a rout.

Sgt. James Butler of Company L somehow was separated from the rest and died alone, far from his unit. His total isolation is a mystery that has never been solved.

Now worked up to a frenzy, the Indians began acting irrationally. One saw a warrior lying on his face and shouted, "Scalp that Ree!" The Indian was scalped. Then the body was turned over and they realized they had scalped a Cheyenne.

Many of the army horses, having broken free, were standing quietly in the river, drinking, resting, and cooling off. The women and old men began rounding them up and driving them into the camps.[16]

One of Keogh's soldiers managed to get hold of a strong horse, broke loose from the melee, and dashed south. Several Indians chased him, but the trooper's mount was too fast, and one by one they gave up. Just as the last Indian was preparing to turn back, the panicky soldier put his pistol to his head and committed suicide— less than a mile from Reno's position and safety.[17]

Kate Bighead sat on her pony near the edge of the fighting, watching as the warriors finished off Keogh's men, stripped the carbines and cartridges from the dead troopers, and began moving toward Custer a mile away. She sang battle songs, hoping that somehow they would reach her nephew, Noisy Walking, who had taken a suicide vow.[18]

Five miles to the south, Reno's shattered battalion was regrouping on the hill. Arriving with Benteen, Private Windolph remembered:

> Here were a little group of men in blue, forming a skirmish line, while their beaten comrades, disorganized and terror stricken, were making their way on foot and on horseback up the narrow coulee that led from the river, 150 feet below.[19]

Benteen showed Reno the order to come with packs, and asked, "Where's Custer?"

"I don't know," Reno replied. "He went off downstream and I haven't seen or heard anything of him since."

Then Benteen noticed that Weir's company was missing, and Reno told him Weir had, without orders, ridden on down the river. Benteen took his battalion and started after him, while Reno mounted his men to follow. Reaching the peak now called Weir Point, they saw Weir's company hurrying back toward them, pursued by "hordes" of Indians. Benteen and Reno deployed their troops on the slopes to cover the retreat.[20] They attempted to hold the point but, finding the position untenable, ordered a withdrawal back to Reno Hill.

The sortie having failed, the troopers dug in again on Reno Hill. Reno was physically and emotionally exhausted. As Windolph noted, "Major Reno had just come through a terrible experience, and at the moment was glad to have Benteen, his junior, take over."

Benteen formed the troopers into skirmish lines. Since Reno's men had expended most of their cartridges, they shared Benteen's until, finally, the lumbering pack train arrived, and they were able to draw more ammunition. The train with its escorting company raised the strength on Reno Hill to more than 400 men—seven of the twelve companies that made up the regiment. The question in everyone's mind was: Where was Custer with the other five?[21]

*   *   *

ON THE RIDGES AROUND CALHOUN COULEE, KEOGH'S THREE companies had been annihilated. A mile to the north, beyond Deep Ravine, Custer had only his immediate staff, Yates's two companies, and, possibly, a handful of survivors from Keogh. Less than a hundred frightened men faced at least seven times their number. There is little evidence of organized resistance; nothing remained but to die. Besides the large supply of weapons and ammunition just acquired from the bodies of Keogh's men, many Indians were armed with Winchester and Henry rifles, whose multiround magazines made them better at close quarters than the single-shot army Springfields.[22]

Now, the Lakota heralds arrived, shouting for the warriors to stand aside and watch the suicide boys, who were down by the river preparing for their assault on Custer's position. The suicide boys would plunge in among the troops, engaging them in hand-to-hand fighting, and distracting them. Then, the rest would move in and finish off the soldiers.

The suicide boys charged. Some went among the army horses, stampeding the grays. The rest rode straight into the mass of soldiers. While the troops concentrated their fire on these youthful warriors, swarms of Indians swept in from all directions.

Indians and troopers fought in a big tangle. Everyone fired wildly. No one stopped to see who was who. They were so densely packed that the Indians were shooting each other. The Indians were too close for carbines, forcing Custer's men to empty their pistols; there was no time to reload. Many of the Indians threw down their guns, hacking away with clubs or hatchets. Soldiers died, but the Indians were paying a terrible price—every one of the young suicide warriors was either killed outright or mortally wounded.

It was every man for himself. Some troopers managed to mount whatever horses they could find. Others, on foot, went among the horses, trying to use them for cover. At first, soldiers on foot trotted alongside their mounted comrades, but as the horses gained speed, the mounted soldiers pulled ahead, leaving the others behind. The foot soldiers stopped long enough to get off some shots before being cut down. The horsemen didn't try to fight, but scattered into the surrounding countryside, where they were chased down and killed, or died of privation.

Disoriented in the smoke, dust, and confusion, many of Custer's remaining men sought refuge in Deep Ravine. Groups of soldiers ran down the depression toward the river where the Hunkpapas waited. With a shout, the Hunkpapas dashed out on their ponies and cut them down.

Correspondent Mark Kellogg was living the biggest story of his life, but he probably thought only of survival. A civilian, he did not belong in this desperate fight and took off alone, getting as far as the edge of the ridges. Before him, the terrain sloped down into a quiet little valley. That was as far as he got. His mutilated, decomposing body was found on the slope four days later.

On the ridge, Custer's remaining soldiers ran toward the highest available ground, a knoll at the head of Deep Ravine. Gathered with their backs to the knoll and facing the onslaught coming up the ravine, the officers may have briefly restored some semblance of order. But the soldiers were now bunched into a single group, and this made the killing much easier. If there was a last stand, it was here, and today the knoll is known as Last Stand Hill. Within minutes the bodies of the Custer family—the colonel, Tom, Boston, and Autie Reed—and Lts. Cooke, Algy Smith, and William Reily were strewn down the side of the hill and along the upper reaches of Deep Ravine.[23]

A few remaining soldiers tried to use their horses as breastworks. One small group broke away and ran down one of the coulees toward the river. Mitch Boyer died about midway down the coulee, and Dr. George Edwin Lord, the regimental surgeon, almost made it to the river. Finally, the field grew quiet. After waiting a few minutes, some Indians went among the fallen troops, and called out that everyone was dead.

Not quite.

A wounded captain (the Indians remembered his shoulder straps) raised up on his left elbow. His right hand held a revolver. A Lakota stepped forward, grabbed the revolver, and shot him through the head. Others beat him and stabbed him.[24]

Custer's fight was over.

19

Valley of the Dead

IT WAS LATE AFTERNOON. THE DUST CREATED BY THE CUSTER fight was settling, and the women and children came across the river to loot the dead. Some had remained in the village through the fight, but Sitting Bull had taken most into a ravine in the hills across the valley where, guarded by a handful of warriors, they watched fearfully, ready to flee if their people were beaten.[1] Now, their terror of the soldiers was gone, and they were laughing and singing.

Violating Sitting Bull's injunction against plundering, the women removed jewelry from the corpses, and if a ring proved difficult to take off, they severed the entire finger. The young warrior Iron Hawk noticed two fat old women stripping a soldier, who was only wounded and feigning death. When he was completely naked, they started to cut something off of him—Iron Hawk did not say what. The soldier jumped up, grappled with one of the women and started swinging her around, while the other tried to stab him. Finally, a third woman ran up and shoved her knife into the soldier. Iron Hawk found the entire scene amusing.[2]

Whenever the body of a relative was found among the fallen Indians, the women would begin wailing.[3] These enraged women were responsible for many of the mutilated white bodies. Although some of the work had been done by warriors late in the fight and immediately afterward, the women went to it with a vengeance, slashing and hacking away with sheath knives and hatchets. Hands and feet were cut off; limbs, torsos, and heads were repeatedly stabbed and slashed. The women were getting even not only for this fight, but for past losses. Two Eagles, a Brulé warrior, remembered the viciousness of a Cheyenne woman whose hair was cut short in mourning for a son lost eight days earlier on the Rosebud. She wandered across the Custer battlefield with an ax. A wounded soldier tried to escape, but was grabbed and held by two warriors while the woman hacked him to death. The three Rees killed during the Custer and Reno fights were severely mutilated.[4]

Kate Bighead rode across the field looking for Noisy Walking. She found him in Deep Ravine. He had been shot and stabbed several times, and she stayed with him while one of the warriors went for his mother.[5]

The Cheyenne children were also on the field. A seven-year-old boy named Spotted Hawk and some of his friends began cutting the waistbands of the trousers to remove them from the bodies. As they did, green paper spilled out. They thought the decorated paper was pretty and found virtually every soldier had some. They didn't understand paper money—the accumulated pay issued on the march—but since it was so carefully concealed inside the clothing, the children thought it might be valuable, so they took it back to their camp. Later, as they made clay figures for play, they would make a horse, fold the money up for a saddle blanket, and then mount a clay rider.[6]

Wandering over the field, Wooden Leg was struck by one corpse. It had been stripped and the head was battered to pieces, but there were tattoos on the chest and arms. Other Indians later told Wooden Leg the soldier had been wearing a buckskin jacket, making it almost certain that the victim was the tattooed Tom Custer.

Wooden Leg found another body that also fascinated him. The soldier had long dundreary whiskers hanging down from each cheek. This was undoubtedly Lieutenant Cooke. "Here is a new kind of scalp," Wooden Leg said to a companion, and skinned one side of the face, tying the whiskers to an arrow.

Farther on, Wooden Leg found the scalped body of an Indian. At first he thought the dead warrior might have been a Crow or Shoshone scout, but something didn't look right. He went to find Yellow Hair, and they returned and rolled the body over for close examination.

"It is Lame White Man," Yellow Hair remarked. They called other Cheyennes who confirmed it was the body of their favorite chief, whom the Lakotas had mistakenly scalped for a Ree. Yellow Hair took the blanket from his own horse, and covered the body. Another warrior went to tell the family, and about an hour later Lame White Man's widow and some other women came with a horse and travois. The warriors carefully wrapped the body in the blanket, and laid it on the travois. Although the Cheyennes said nothing to the Lakotas, they took grim satisfaction that a dead Hunkpapa, mixed with a group of fallen soldiers, had likewise been mistaken for a government Indian and repeatedly lanced before the error was discovered.[7]

Indian losses had been heavy, particularly among the Lakotas. Although the exact total will never be known, most witnesses place the Lakota death toll at thirty to forty,[8] high figures for a tribal society that could not replace a slain warrior until a new generation reached fighting age.

By the time the Oglala youth Black Elk arrived from the Reno fight, Custer's men were all down, although many were still breathing. Black Elk and the other boys rode among the fallen soldiers, shooting arrows into them. One trooper was crawling helplessly around with arrows sticking out of his body. Black Elk took the dying soldier's watch, although he did not know what it was, or why it made the ticking sound.

Black Elk came to the spot where Company E had been cut down, and saw the dead gray horses. A trooper raised his arm and groaned. Black Elk shot an arrow into his forehead and watched as the arms and legs quivered. He then wandered over to a group of Oglalas who were trying to support one of their comrades, and recognized the wounded man as one of his cousins. "His father and my father were so angry over this, that they went and butchered a Wasichu [white] and cut him open," Black Elk recalled.

In the distance, Reno and Benteen had been driven back from

Weir Point to their original position on Reno Hill. Most of the warriors were returning to camp. Black Elk was tired, and beginning to feel sick from the sight and smell of so much blood. He, too, went back to the village.[9]

ACROSS THE RIVER FROM RENO HILL, THE INDIANS SET FIRE TO the timber, forcing Lieutenant DeRudio out of his hiding place in the creek bed. He slipped down the bed and was crawling up the bank when he heard someone call, "Lieutenant. Lieutenant." He moved toward the voice and found Girard, O'Neill, and Jackson, who had tied the horses and followed him down into the creek bed. Now, they all had to get away from the fire. Fortunately, the wind subsided and a light rain began to fall, arresting the blaze. Indians were everywhere. The whites could hear them talking. Expecting to be discovered and overrun, they lay on their stomachs, each man's eyes level with the top of the bank, watching in different directions. DeRudio cautioned them not to fire their weapons unless actually discovered.[10]

O'Neill was doubtful of their chances, particularly when a group of women came so close he feared they would see them. The women were gathering up their own dead with anguished wails, and furiously mutilating the corpses of the soldiers. O'Neill felt sick with the thought that they soon might be cutting up his body.[11]

Darkness came. The firing from Custer's position had long since stopped, and now they noticed it tapering off from Reno's command as well. All four were terribly thirsty. They had had nothing to drink since before the fighting started. The moon rose, providing only dim light, and they decided to make a break for it. The scouts recovered their horses, and the two soldiers grabbed their tails to keep up and trotted behind. Girard said if they were discovered, the soldiers should hide while the scouts would run for Reno's position and notify the major that there were still survivors in the timber.

Clearing the trees, they came out onto the plain. Mutilated bodies were scattered about. Indians were still wandering through, on their way back to the village, but nobody noticed the four whites.

They found a ford in the river, where O'Neill filled his hat with water and passed it around. "We all declared it was the sweetest water we had ever tasted," he said.

While crossing the river they saw eight or ten Indians off to the right, their lances gleaming in the dim light. DeRudio and O'Neill ducked behind the horses and started moving toward cover, while Girard and Jackson began to pull away. One of the Indians, whom the scouts could understand, called out, "Are you afraid? We are not white troops." Then they rode off in the opposite direction.

Girard and Jackson tried to make a dash for Reno, but their horses slipped in the river and threw them. Remounting but disoriented, they returned to the timber they had just left, leaving the two soldiers behind. DeRudio, crouching in the water with his revolver cocked, eased toward the bank where he met up with O'Neill. Off in the distance, they could hear the yelling and whooping of the Indians, and see the fires blazing in the village.[12]

ON THE HILL, RENO'S MEN WELCOMED THE DARKNESS BUT FEARED what dawn might bring. "We felt terribly alone on that dangerous hilltop," Private Windolph said. "We were a million miles from nowhere. And death was all around us." The sound of the Indian drumming, the flicker of the fires, and the wailing of the grieving women frightened them. At least a dozen men had been killed by Indian snipers during the last three hours of daylight, and dozens more were wounded and crying for water. Some of the hungry soldiers gnawed on hardtack and raw bacon, but without water it was "like hay scratchin' down our dry throats," according to Private Burkman. The line was spread too thin, and someone, most likely Reno, ordered the various companies to draw in to better positions. Most soldiers worked on rifle pits, digging with mess kits, knives and forks, tin cups, or their fingers. A light rain began to fall, a chill came over the windswept hilltop, and some of the men unstrapped their greatcoats from their saddles and put them on.[13]

The men were worried because there had been absolutely no news of their commander. They knew that Custer had been engaged, and the fight had been bad. But then what? Had he managed to link up with Gibbon and Terry? Why had they been left on their own? Several scouts went out to look for him, but soon reported back that the country was full of hostiles.

Benteen expressed a general belief among the officers that Custer "had found more indians [sic] than he could conveniently handle with his battalion . . . and that he had fallen back to connect with General Terry & Gibbon." Like the men, the officers felt they had been deserted; they had no idea Custer had been dead for hours.[14]

The command began to settle in. Horses were unsaddled and mules unpacked. The animals were picketed in a hollow square around the field hospital at the head of the depression.

Exhausted after three days with little or no sleep and the terror of the afternoon, some of the men began to hallucinate. They thought they saw a column of troops on the ridges, and heard the horses, the commands of the officers, or the bugle calls. So real were these images that some of the men fired their carbines, and the buglers began sounding calls to alert the oncoming troops. Someone mounted a horse and galloped along the line, shouting, "Don't be discouraged, boys, Crook is coming." Then reality set in, and the men resumed digging rifle pits. Finally, those on the line began drifting off to sleep. Benteen and Lieutenant Gibson walked among them, trying to keep them stirred, but found even kicking had no effect. They did manage to keep a couple of sentries awake.[15]

BECAUSE PLAINS CUSTOM REQUIRED THE REMOVAL OF CAMP WHEN any death occurred, as soon as the dead were brought in, the Indian village was relocated slightly down the valley and farther back from the river. Most of the tipis and lodgepoles remained packed for a quick escape, the women erecting wickiups of bent willows.[16] The tipis still standing in the old camp were consecrated for burial or mourning.

In the Cheyenne camp that night, Wooden Leg went to see Noisy Walking. The wounded man had been placed on a bed of buffalo robes, inside a domed lodge of bent willows. His father, the medicine man White Bull,[17] tended him while his mother sat just outside the entrance.

"How are you?" Wooden Leg asked.

"Good, only I want water."

Wooden Leg did not know what else to say, so he sat down by the dying suicide boy. Finally, he said, "You were very brave."

Noisy Walking was growing weaker and his hands were trembling. Finally, he looked up at his father and said, "I wish I could have some water—just a little of it."

"No," White Bull replied. "Water will kill you."

Wooden Leg saw that White Bull "almost choked" when he refused his son's request. But with his medicine man's knowledge of anatomy, White Bull knew the boy could not drink.

Noisy Walking died during the night, bringing the Cheyenne death toll to six, with a seventh who was mortally wounded. Others had crippling wounds. All the camps were in mourning. Women slashed their arms and legs in grief. Most people were praying. Occasionally, a fire flared up as a grieving family burned its lodge and all possessions. In the Sioux camps, scaffolds were being prepared for their dead. The Cheyenne bodies would be placed in crevices in the ravines and covered with rocks. Warriors were coming and going all the time, patrolling the surrounding countryside and spelling those watching Reno's position. Knowing the fight was not over, heralds went about the camps singing battle songs and shouting, "Young men, be brave."[18]

TWO ISOLATED SHOTS INAUGURATED THE SECOND DAY'S FIGHTING on the hill, and soon the air was filled with lead. The noise stirred the sleeping soldiers to action, and Benteen, who had been without sleep for three days, decided he could catch a nap. He stretched out on the hillside and was dozing off when one bullet hit the heel of his boot, and another threw dust under his armpit. Then a sergeant came and told him Gibson's men were "having a regular monkey & parrot time of it," so Benteen gathered up some soldiers and packers, and had them carry over sacks of bacon, boxes of hardtack, pack saddles, and other equipment for breastworks.[19]

The Indians pushed so close that a warrior was able to shoot one of Gibson's men, then dash up and touch him with his coup stick before himself getting killed. Benteen saw a large group of Indians gathering at the base of the hill and, after consulting with Reno, organized four companies for a charge.

"All ready now, men," he called. "Now's the time. Give them hell. Hip, hip, here we go!"

Keyed up by this chance to hit back, the cheering troopers rushed down the hill, scattering the Indian line until Reno recalled them.

As the sun rose higher, the thirst on the hilltop became unbearable. The wounded, in particular, were suffering. Seventeen men volunteered for the near suicidal mission of bringing water from the river. Four of them—all Germans—took an exposed position on the crest of the hill, to draw fire and pump as much lead as they could into the bushes along the river where the Indians were hiding. The rest worked their way through the brush to the bottom of the hill, then dashed across the last few yards of open space for the river, filling kettles and canteens. Some were severely wounded, but the detail returned with water. Most of it was given to the wounded, so that some soldiers did without. Still, the fact that water had been obtained boosted morale throughout the command.[20]

In the village, the Indians were beginning to sort out what had happened. Until now, most assumed these soldiers were Crook's men. But the Cheyenne old man chief Little Wolf, whose band had arrived just as the Custer fight ended, said these troopers had come from a different direction, away from the Rosebud. Once it was determined the majority of the dead government scouts were Rees, rather than Crook's Crows or Shoshones, it dawned on the Indians that more soldiers were in the area. Then, during the afternoon, they learned Terry and Gibbon were coming up the Little Bighorn Valley. Full of confidence, the young warriors wanted to fight them as well. The chiefs, however, held a council and ordered the village to break camp and move. They would not fight unless there was no other alternative. To cover their movements, they set the grass on fire.[21]

Looking out from their hilltop perch as the gunfire tapered off,

Reno's troopers could sometimes see the retreating Indians through breaks in the smoke. It reminded Windolph of "some Biblical exodus . . . a mighty tribe on the march."[22]

Some warriors remained behind to snipe at Reno's men until dark, after which they caught up with their bands. The Hunkpapas, bringing up the rear as usual, posted scouts to keep an eye on Terry while the village retreated. On the hill, the troopers began burying their dead in the rifle pits. The smell of dead men and animals in the June heat was unbearable, and Reno ordered a withdrawal to a new position by the river. With plenty of water now, the company cooks prepared hot coffee and the first real meal in thirty-six hours. That night, DeRudio, O'Neill, Girard, and Jackson rejoined the command, ending their terrifying ordeal in the timber.

The Battle of the Little Bighorn was over. But the question still nagged in everyone's mind: Where was Custer?[23]

20

"So Different from the Outcome We Had Hoped For"

DURING THE PAST FIVE DAYS, TERRY'S FORCES HAD BEEN WORK-ing toward the rendezvous with Custer. Gibbon was ill and unable to ride. He traveled on the *Far West* from the Yellowstone up the Bighorn River to its confluence with the Little Bighorn, while Terry took direct command of the column marching overland. Lieutenant Bradley's detachment scouted ahead of the column. On the morning of June 25, some of Bradley's Crows were reconnoitering the Little Bighorn and saw smoke far up the river. Reporting back to the column, they said the smoke indicated a large village. Terry ordered the infantry to remain in camp, while he took the cavalry and Gatling battery toward the Little Bighorn, to get as close as possible to the supposed village. The infantry would catch up the next day.

Terry marched into the night, darkness and rain making the rough terrain all the more difficult. First the Gatling battery, then the cavalry went astray. Eventually, however, they reached a valley where Terry called a halt at midnight to rest men and animals.

At daylight, Bradley sent his Crows out, joining them half an hour later. After a three-mile ride, they came onto the fresh trail of four ponies. A large column of smoke was visible about fifteen or twenty miles ahead, and they surmised it was the camp to which these four ponies and their riders belonged. Bradley sent a message back to Terry, then he and the scouts followed the trail another two miles to the Little Bighorn River. There they found an abandoned pony and personal gear, indicating the Indians had crossed in a hurry. Inspecting the equipment, Bradley was dismayed to find it belonged to some of the Crows he had loaned to Custer.

To the south, Bradley saw three Indians watching them from a safe distance on the opposite side of the river. After an exchange of signals with the Crows, the three strangers moved closer until they were directly across the river. The Crow leader, Little Face, went down to talk, and returned wailing "with a bitterness of anguish such as I have rarely seen," Bradley wrote in his journal.

As Little Face told the story, the rest of Bradley's Crows went off to the side and sat, rocking back and forth as they joined in the mourning song. The soldiers listened in terrified fascination as Little Face explained these strangers were three of the six Crows furnished to the Seventh Cavalry. The previous day, Custer had struck a large hostile village on the Little Bighorn, was overwhelmed, and killed with most of his men. When the three Crows last saw them, the battered survivors were pinned down on a hill. The bodies of Custer's men were "strewn all over the country," and the trio estimated that by now everyone would be dead, since they did not see how the men on the hill could hold out much longer. Two of their own people, White Swan and Half-Yellow-Face, were dead. A third, Curly, was missing and presumed dead.

"It was a terrible, terrible story, so different from the outcome we had hoped for this campaign, and I no longer wondered at the demonstrative sorrow of the Crows," Bradley wrote. He hoped that the three frightened Crows from Custer had exaggerated the extent of the fight, but deep inside he knew "that there had been a disaster—a terrible disaster. . . ."[1]

About that time, Terry's column appeared over the ridge, and Bradley rode back to report to the general in person. Terry was surrounded by his staff, and accompanied by Gibbon, who had recovered enough to rejoin the march. At first they listened in silence, but soon the officers began to scoff at the story. There was no question that Custer was victorious. The column of smoke, which everyone saw, meant he was burning the village. The three scouts had obviously fled in panic early in the fight and had fabricated the story to cover themselves. Through it all, General Terry sat on his horse, biting his lower lip, saying nothing. After a long silence, he shouted, "Forward!" and the march resumed.[2]

The infantry caught up with the cavalry on the Little Bighorn at noon. During an afternoon break, Bradley sent Henry Bostwick and Muggins Taylor, the civilian scouts, to reconnoiter the supposed village and make contact with Custer. Shortly after 5:00 P.M., Bostwick returned at a full gallop, saying the way was blocked by Indians.

Bradley had already spotted several warriors a few miles ahead, and deployed his men as skirmishers. More Indians were seen up the valley and on the surrounding hills. Bradley took part of the detachment up the valley, while a detail under Lt. Charles Roe moved along the bluffs overlooking the Little Bighorn. From that position, Roe could see a long line of "moving dark objects defiling across the prairie from the Little Big Horn toward the Big Horn, as if the village were in motion retreating before us." Immediately ahead of Roe's detail were some 300 men, some in blue uniforms, carrying guidons, and appearing to move in formation. Three soldiers, sent to establish contact, hurried back and reported they had been fired on by Indians wearing army uniforms. Later, Muggins Taylor rode in, exclaiming indignantly that he had been fired on by Custer's Indian scouts, and swearing he would kill them when the two columns met.[3]

On the distant hills to the east, one officer saw what appeared to be buffalo lying down in the grass. "Night comes on before anything definite can be determined," Lt. Edward McClernand wrote in his journal, "but it is evident that General Custer has not been entirely successful. . . . Whatever the result of the fight has been, every one anticipates another one tomorrow."[4]

No fires were allowed in camp, and each man slept with weapons. The officers gathered in small groups to discuss the situation. Most of the infantrymen believed the Crows' massacre story. The majority of the cavalrymen, however, refused to accept anything but a Custer victory. Some even insisted there were no Indians, and that the riders they had seen during the day belonged to

Custer. Others acknowledged there had been Indians, and said Terry should have sent the cavalry charging in to cut them to pieces and finish the impasse. Bradley, who had an immense respect for Indian fighting ability, was glad Terry had discovered them too late in the day to start a fight.[5]

The following morning, Tuesday, June 27, Bradley began scouting to the east, across the Little Bighorn in the direction of the hills where the officer had seen the forms that resembled buffalo. McClernand, meanwhile, took a party to reconnoiter the timber by the river. Advancing beyond the trees, the group soon came upon two tipis, then farther on discovered the remains of a huge village. It was obvious the Indians had left in a hurry, since lodgepoles, buffalo robes, blankets, camp utensils, dried meat, and about fifty or sixty ponies had been left behind. They also found an officer's buckskin jacket, with bloodstains, two bullet holes, and the name "Sturgis" written on it. Several burial lodges were noted. McClernand found a grazing government horse, which was wounded and unserviceable. Some of the soldiers recognized the animal as Comanche, issued to Myles Keogh.[6]

Bradley's detachment meanwhile had seen the body of another government horse in the distance and on investigating was appalled to find the ridges and ravines beyond covered with dead soldiers. What had been taken for buffalo the night before was the carcasses of their horses. A quick count showed 197 bodies in groups on the ridges and scattered along the ravines leading to the Little Bighorn River. A rider was sent to inform General Terry, who was now in the village across the river with McClernand.[7]

"The situation, gloomy as it had been, was made immensely more so by Bradley's report," McClernand commented. They were still pondering this development when Lts. George Wallace and Luther Hare arrived from Reno, reporting his plight and giving the location of his command.

"Where is Custer?" someone asked.

Waving his hand, Wallace replied, "The last we saw of him he was going along that high bluff toward the lower end of the village. He took off his hat and waved to us. We do not know where he is now."

"We have found him," Terry said, certain that the bodies among the ridges and ravines belonged to Custer's battalion. The general's eyes were full of tears.

Wallace and Hare were aghast at the news, unable to comprehend that their terrible ordeal had been only part of a much larger action.[8] They led the command back to Reno's position, where Benteen asked Terry if he knew Custer's whereabouts.

"To the best of my knowledge and belief he lies on this ridge about four miles below here with all his command killed," the general said.

"I can hardly believe it," Benteen remarked. "I think he is somewhere down the Big Horn grazing his horses. At the Battle of the Washita he went off and left part of his command, and I think he would do it again."

"I think you are mistaken," Terry said, "and you will take your company and go down where the dead are lying and investigate for yourself."

Bradley escorted Benteen and Weir to the battlefield, where they and another officer of the Seventh officially identified Custer's body. Returning, Benteen was pale and shaken. "We found them," he told the others, "but I did not expect we would."[9]

The corpses had been out in the hot Montana sun for two days, when the survivors of the Seventh and the members of the Terry-Gibbon column began the grisly task of identification and burial. Searching Algy Smith's body, someone found his watch fob, and sent it to his widow. Aware of the campfire bequest, she later gave it to Lieutenant Gibson.[10]

Terry composed the following message:

> Headquarters Department of Dakota,
> Camp on Little Big Horn River, Montana,
> June 27, 1876.

To the Adjutant General of
the Military Division of the Missouri,
Chicago, Ill., via Fort Ellis:

It is my painful duty to report that day before yesterday, the 25th instant, a great disaster overtook General Custer and the troops under his command. At 12 o'clock of the 22d he started with his whole regiment and a strong detachment of scouts and guides from the mouth of the Rosebud. Proceeding up that river about twenty miles, he struck a very heavy Indian trail which had previously been discovered, and, pursuing it, found that it led, as it was supposed it would lead, to the Little Big Horn River. Here he found a village of almost unexampled extent, and at once attacked it with that portion of his force which was immediately at hand.

Terry then described the Reno fight, and the movements of Benteen and McDougall.

Of the movements of General Custer and the five companies under his immediate command scarcely anything is known from those who witnessed them, for no officer or soldier who accompanied him has yet been found alive. His trail, from the point where Reno crossed the stream, passes along and in the rear of the crest of the bluffs on the right bank for nearly or quite three miles. Then it comes down to the bank of the river, but at once diverges from it as if he had unsuccessfully attempted to cross; then turns upon itself, almost completes a circle, and ceases. It is marked by the remains of his officers and men and the bodies of his horses, some of them dotted along the path, others heaped in ravines and upon knolls, where halts appear to have been made. There is abundant evidence that a gallant resistance was offered by the troops, but that they were beset on all sides by overpowering numbers.

Just what that evidence was, Terry did not specify. Surely the position of the bodies, vaguely approximated by the government markers today, indicated a complete collapse. Yet the statement has been accepted at face value for more than a century, despite contradictory statements from Indians and recent archaeological evidence to the contrary. Not yet certain about the total losses to Custer's command, Terry listed some of the officers then known to be killed or missing, and continued:

It is impossible as yet to obtain a nominal list of the enlisted men who were killed and wounded; but the number of killed, including officers, must reach 250; the number of wounded [with Reno] is 51.

Terry then went on to describe his last conversation with Custer, his own movements from the time of separation, the way in which the command learned of the disaster, and estimates of Indian strength from Reno and Benteen. The message was given to Muggins Taylor, who left for the nearest telegraph office, at Fort Ellis, on July 1.[11]

While the soldiers buried their comrades, the *Far West* was still miles away at the mouth of the Little Bighorn, those aboard oblivious to what had happened. About noon, June 28, Curly, the missing Crow scout from Custer's command, appeared on the riverbank. He was visibly shaken, but since there was no interpreter, the most anyone could determine was there had been a fight. The following day, however, three scouts arrived from Terry with news of the disaster. The steamer was barricaded and prepared to receive wounded, who arrived about 1:00 A.M., June 30. Among them was the horse Comanche, officially the only survivor of Custer's command, who limped aboard with multiple gunshot wounds.[12]

The first sketchy reports reached the east on July 5. Taylor had arrived at Fort Ellis on the evening of July 3. A *Helena Herald* correspondent, who happened to be at the post, picked up the story and telegraphed it south to Salt Lake City, where the Associated Press sent it to New York. The following day, the *New York Times* announced the disaster, filling the gaps with editorial conjecture.[13]

In a country caught up in patriotic euphoria over the Centennial Exposition in Philadelphia, the news was met with disbelief. Incredibly neither Sherman nor Sheridan, both in Philadelphia for the celebration, knew anything about it yet. A break in the telegraph line east of Bozeman had temporarily disrupted direct communication between Fort Ellis and Chicago, and Terry's message had not arrived. When confronted with the story from Salt Lake City via New York, the generals labeled it preposterous, and pointed out such rumors were common on the frontier. Nevertheless, Sheridan wired his adjutant in Chicago:

Send any news that you receive from Terry's Command without delay. Newspaper[s] report from Helena information . . . that Custer & some three hundred men were killed in fight on the little horn.[14]

The following day a confidential message arrived from General Terry who, unaware that his initial report had not been delivered, gave a personal assessment of the Custer fight in a telegram transmitted through Fort Abraham Lincoln.

I think I owe it to myself to put you more fully in possession of the fact of the late operations. While at the mouth of the Rosebud I submitted my plan to Genl. Gibbon and General Custer. They approved it heartily. It was that Custer with his whole regiment should move up the Rosebud till he should meet a trail which Reno had discovered a few days before but that he should send scouts over it and keep his main force further to the south so as to prevent the Indians from slipping in between himself and the mountains. He was also to examine the headwaters of Tullock's creek as he passed it and send me word of what he found there. A scout was furnished him for the purpose of crossing the country to me. We calculated it would take Gibbon's column until the twenty-sixth to reach the mouth of the Little Big Horn and that the wide sweep which I had proposed Custer should make would require so much time that Gibbon would be able to cooperate with him in attacking any Indians that might be found on that stream. I asked Custer how long his marches would be. He said that they would be at first about thirty miles a day. Measurements were made and calculation based on that rate of progress. . . . The plan adopted was the only one that promised to bring the Infantry into action and I desired to make sure of things by getting up every available man. . . . The movements proposed for Genl. Gibbon's column were carried out to the letter and had the attack been deferred until it was up I cannot doubt that we should have been successful.

As it turned out, however, Custer had covered the territory at a breakneck pace that appeared calculated to bring him into contact with the Indians before Gibbon arrived. He did not follow the assigned route but kept to the Indian trail, completely bypassing Tullock's Creek.

> I do not tell you this to cast any reflection upon Custer. For whatever errors he may have committed he has paid the penalty and you cannot regret his loss more than I do, but I feel that our plan must have been successful had it been carried out, and I desire you to know the facts. In the action itself, so far as I can make out, Custer acted under a misapprehension. He thought, I am confident, that the Indians were running. For fear that they might get away he attacked without getting all his men up and divided his command so that they were beaten in detail.

Terry said he planned to continue his pursuit, though he doubted much could be accomplished because of his column's diminished strength in the wake of the disaster.[15]

This message inferring blame for the disaster infuriated Sheridan. Not having received Terry's initial report, it was his first official notification through army channels that Custer had been defeated and was dead. To make matters worse, General Sherman mistook a reporter from the *Philadelphia Inquirer* for a government messenger, and handed him Terry's confidential evaluation, which the *Inquirer* published. Then a report from Reno, which not only blamed Custer but questioned the government Indian policy as well, appeared in newspapers before Sheridan had a chance to see it.[16]

THE RECRIMINATIONS BEGAN ALMOST IMMEDIATELY. WHILE SOME blamed Custer, most of the accusations fell on Major Reno. John Burkman was vitriolic.

> The men caught the skeer from the coward Reno and acted accordin'. . . . [They] was brave men, nat'ral, good soldiers, but the skirmish they'd been through down below with Reno, plumb out of his head with skeer yellin' orders they couldn't hear, and the panicky retreat up the hill kinda made 'em crazy for the time bein'.[17]

Burkman was hardly an impartial source. As Custer's servant, he was closer to the colonel than most soldiers, and the position had ensured him an easier life. Yet many shared his opinion, and spread the blame to Benteen as well. Within a few months of the fight, an extensive biography of Custer appeared, written by Frederick Whittaker. Whittaker, who served under Custer during the Civil War and knew him well, asserted, "Had Reno fought as Custer fought, and had Benteen obeyed Custer's orders, the battle of the Little Horn might have proved Custer's last and greatest victory." He was especially hard on Benteen, who he said "stopped and let his chief perish."[18]

Whittaker was one of those armchair tacticians still fighting Confederates. He did not know the terrain or Indian fighting. In accusing Benteen and Reno of failure, he underestimated the ground Benteen had to cover and the number of Indians Reno had to fight. He also assumed that Custer had a detailed plan of battle and that the Indians fought according to the West Point manual. Nevertheless, Whittaker continued his slanderous attacks, aided by Libbie Custer, until Reno finally demanded an inquiry, which exonerated him.[19]

Reno was also ready to assess blame. In a letter to Gen. Stephen Vincent Benét, chief of ordnance, he complained that 6 of the 380 Springfield carbines in his sector were defective and, when fired, caused the extractors to malfunction so that the cartridge casings jammed in the chambers.[20] Six malfunctioning carbines out of 380 is hardly enough to change the course of battle. On the Custer battlefield itself, only 3.4 percent of the cartridge cases recovered in modern archaeological investigations showed evidence of extractor failure. The problem was a common complaint among military units throughout the Great Sioux War, yet it did not materially affect the outcome. Nevertheless, cartridge-extractor failure has entered the mythology of the Little Bighorn as a major factor in the disaster, and is likely to remain so as long as the fight is remembered.[21]

Ultimately, the blame for the defeat must fall on happenstance. It was simply a day when the predictable suddenly became the unpredictable—where everything went wrong; where the established

military system simply broke down; where the Indians took extraordinary measures to defend their homes and families; where an
entire battalion, terrified beyond the limits of endurance, fell apart.

For the men who ran the army, however, the Battle of the Little
Bighorn had a distinctly positive result. Despite his faults, Custer
had been popular with the public. The disaster galvanized many
who had previously been indifferent or opposed to the war, and
threw them solidly behind the generals. Congress would have to
give the army whatever it needed to punish what the *New York
Times* was now calling "the red devils."[22] Custer was performing
greater service dead than he had ever done alive.

PART V

THE TURNING POINT

21

"Congress Is . . . Willing to Give Us All We Want"

EVEN BEFORE HE KNEW ALL THE DETAILS OF THE CUSTER DIS-aster, there was no question in Sheridan's mind that new measures were necessary. From a local campaign, the war had assumed the character of a major insurrection, and the ominous reports from Montana showed that the military forces originally assigned were unequal to the task. Simply stated, the Indians were winning. They moved freely through hundreds of square miles and, with their present forces, there was nothing Crook or Terry could do about it.

On July 7, Sheridan notified Brig. Gen. John Pope, commanding the Department of the Missouri, to send six companies of infantry "fully equipped for the field and without delay via railroad to Yankton, to be there shipped by steamboat to General Terry on the Yellowstone." Pope responded by sending part of the Fifth Infantry under Col. Nelson Miles. This not only augmented the troops assigned to Terry, it also brought officers and men whose experience on the southern plains made them seasoned campaigners.[1]

The most able commander, however, was Mackenzie, who had built the Fourth Cavalry into the army's best mobile assault force. Presently, he was at Fort Sill, where he commanded the Western

District of the Indian Territory, guarding the tribes recently involved in the Red River War. Pope, realizing the seriousness of the
situation in the north, suggested Sheridan send four companies of
artillery to Fort Sill "so that Mackenzie can be foot loose in case of
emergency." But Sherman, knowing the fear Mackenzie inspired
among the Kiowas and Comanches near Sill, had already advised
Sheridan to leave the Fourth there, and instead send a battalion of
the Tenth Cavalry from Texas to Wyoming. To reinforce Terry,
Sherman tapped the Military Division of the Atlantic, transferring
six fully equipped companies of the Twenty-second Infantry from
as far away as New York, to Sheridan's division.[2]

Crook, meanwhile, remained in camp at Goose Creek, in
Wyoming, where he had retreated after the Rosebud fight. For a
man who had recently lost a major battle, Crook was remarkably
placid, and was beginning to convince himself the fight was a victory. The camp itself had a safari air. With selected officers, Crook
spent almost every day hunting and fishing in the mountains. Even
the enlisted men had an easy life. "Within the picket lines, squads
of men are devoting their leisure hours to bathing and trout-catch-
ing," Bourke wrote in his diary.[3]

On June 25, he noted:

> Colonel Mills brought in this afternoon, one hundred trout caught
> by himself and assistants. Other parties were equally successful.
> What was lately a luxury, is now become a component of the daily
> ration.[4]

At that moment, less than sixty miles north of Crook's camp, the
Seventh Cavalry was being cut to pieces.

During his fishing trip (which correspondent Finerty politely
called "an informal reconnaissance"), Mills noticed a great column of smoke to the north, toward the Little Bighorn and speculated that it must have been "a prairie fire or something of that
kind." By their own means of communication, which defied all
white comprehension, Crook's remaining Indian scouts knew better, and began talking about a massacre in which many soldiers
had died. The whites, however, paid no real attention at the time.
Yet the stories persisted. On June 30, some half-breeds came into

camp saying there had been a fight in which every soldier had died. The officers believed it was the story of their own fight at the Rosebud, which had now made the complete circle, embellished by the Indians as it passed from camp to camp.[5]

The following day, Big Bat and Frank Grouard left for the Crow Agency to prod the scouts into returning, and Crook organized a group of selected officers and correspondents to explore the Bighorns and, of course, get in a little hunting and fishing. Returning July 4, he learned Big Bat and Grouard had ridden only twenty miles before deciding there were too many hostile Indians in the vicinity, and doubled back to camp. Grouard believed the Indians were concentrated somewhere along the Bighorn River, and recommended scouting that area instead of going to the Crow Agency. Crook ordered Lt. Frederick W. Sibley, Second Cavalry, with a sergeant and twenty-four enlisted men, to escort Grouard on a reconnaissance toward the Little Bighorn.

Sibley's detail left camp at noon July 7, each man carrying a hundred rounds of ammunition and several days' rations.[6] The following morning, near the headwaters of the Little Bighorn, some fifty miles from Crook's camp, the soldiers ran into a party of more than 400 Cheyenne warriors, which chased them deep into the Bighorn Mountains. The Indians trapped the soldiers in a small valley, pinning them down until nightfall, when Sibley ordered the horses abandoned and led his men up through the mountains to safety.

About 6:30 A.M., July 9, Sibley's hungry, footsore men encountered a Second Cavalry detail bound for the Tongue River area on a hunting trip. Warning them that they were riding toward an area controlled by the Indians, Sibley sent them back to camp for hot food and horses for his men. About midmorning, Sibley and his men rode into camp looking, according to Bourke, "more like dead men than soldiers of the army; their clothes were torn into rags, their strength completely gone, and they faint with hunger and worn out with anxiety and distress."[7]

Crook was pleased with Sibley, not only for saving his command but also for carrying out his mission and locating the Indians. There were, however, more important considerations. The next day, Louis Richaud and Ben Arnold came into camp with dispatches from Sheridan reporting the disaster that had befallen Custer. "The shock was so great that men and officers could hardly speak when the tale slowly circulated from lip to lip," Bourke wrote. The same night, the hostiles set fire to the grass around Crook's camp, "and for the next two weeks paid us their respects every night in some manner, trying to stampede stock, burn grass, annoy pickets, and devil the command generally." The harassment continued until heavy rains saturated the ground and impeded rapid movement around the camp, making the tactic unfeasible.

In the meantime, the Shoshone chief Washakie had rejoined the command with 213 warriors. A few days later, Washakie took a large scouting party to the site of Sibley's fight, where they found a Cheyenne grave. Opening it, they identified the body of the war chief White Antelope, who had been shot through the head.[8]

Three tattered soldiers of the Seventh Infantry arrived in Crook's camp on July 13, sent by Terry with dispatches sewn in their clothes describing the massacre of Custer. Something had to be done and already Sheridan had set a plan in motion. The next day, Colonel Chambers arrived from Fort Fetterman with seven companies of infantry and a wagon train of supplies. He brought dispatches from Sheridan advising that Wesley Merritt had been appointed colonel of the Fifth Cavalry, and was en route to the Goose Creek camp from the Red Cloud Agency with ten of the regiment's twelve companies. Crook was to remain in camp until Merritt arrived, then resume his campaign.

Because the grass was giving out, Crook broke camp on July 16, moving along the foothills of the Bighorns farther down Goose Creek. He wrote Terry advising him of the safe arrival of his three infantrymen, and the shift in his position. Once Merritt arrived, he proposed to move against the Indians immediately, which would probably mean linking with Terry's troops.

I am rationed up to the end of September and will share with you and your command everything I have as long as it lasts. Should the two commands come together, whether the Indians shall be found in this or your Department, if you think the interests of the service will be advanced by the combination, I will most cheerfully serve under you.[9]

The message was given to a miner named Kelly, who made two attempts to reach Terry but was driven back by Indians each time before the third attempt succeeded.[10]

WHILE CROOK WAITED FOR MERRITT AND TERRY REORGANIZED his shattered command, support for the war gained momentum in the East. In his report the previous November, which had led directly to the conflict, Indian Inspector Watkins had predicted that a thousand troops would be sufficient to subjugate the Indians. Instead, the Indians had defeated a larger force under Crook, and had annihilated Custer.[11] It was obvious that the government's policy of limiting the army's size to little better than a national police force, while economical, was not practical, particularly when the government provoked a war.

On July 7, as the full impact of the Custer disaster reached the East, Congress called on Secretary of War Cameron to report on the origins of the war and the government's objectives, including all relevant correspondence. The government had anticipated this, and already had prepared its case so thoroughly that Cameron was able to respond within twenty-four hours.

The report blamed the conflict on a small group of non-treaty bands that roamed the unceded lands at will, attacking settlers, murdering citizens, and unduly influencing those Indians who were peacefully inclined. Ignored was the fact that the Indians had a legal right to roam the unceded lands, and that the "victims" had been trespassers on lands guaranteed the Indians by treaty. Incredibly, the Black Hills gold strike was not listed as a contributing factor, but a convenient by-product. One paragraph in particular shows a carefully contrived deception that would become all too familiar over the next century:

> The present military operations are not against the Sioux Nation at all, but against certain portions of it, which defy the Government, and are undertaken at the special request of that bureau of the Government [i.e., the Indian Bureau] charged with their supervision, and wholly to make the civilization of the remainder possible. No part of these operations is on or near the Sioux reservation. *The ac-*

cidental discovery of gold on the western border of the Sioux reser-
vation, and the intrusion of our people thereon, have not caused the
war, and have only complicated it by the uncertainty of numbers to
be encountered. . . . The object of these military expeditions was in
the interest of the peaceful parts of the Sioux Nation, supposed to
embrace nine-tenths of the whole, and not one of these peaceful or
treaty Indians has been molested by the military authorities.[12] [ital-
ics added]

Sheridan, personally, was no longer interested in justifications.
The army had been humiliated twice in June, and one of its most
colorful commanders killed with almost half his regiment. The
eastern press was clamoring for vengeance, and the lieutenant general was willing to provide it. He wanted three things: an increase
in the size of the army, two forts on the Yellowstone (for which he
had been lobbying since assuming command of the division), and
direct military rule over the Indian agencies.

Congress was ready to comply. Sen. Algernon S. Paddock of Nebraska introduced a bill authorizing the president to call for volunteer troops from the western states and territories, to work in
conjunction with the Regular Army. Support for this bill was remarkable, considering the disdain easterners normally felt for
western volunteer forces. Now, however, the situation was different; the orderly progress of civilization was in danger and drastic
action was needed to save it. Volunteers who had something to defend would know how to defend it.

Sherman blocked the move, believing that the general excitement might lead to a vicious, bloody Indian hunt beyond the
army's ability to control. Instead, he sought redistribution of regular troops, who were disciplined and could be directed toward the
specific goals of the government.[13]

On July 14, he notified Sheridan that the Senate had approved
money for the two forts on the Yellowstone, effectively negating
the 1868 Fort Laramie Treaty by replacing those posts abandoned
under the terms of the treaty. He also told Sheridan to send the remaining companies of the Fifth Infantry to join Miles, concentrating the regiment to full strength.[14]

Eight days later, Sheridan learned President Grant had signed the bill for the new military posts, and site selection could begin. More important, Sherman told him that Secretary of War Cameron and Secretary of the Interior Chandler had approved military control of all the agencies in the war zone. According to Sherman, Chandler

> wants for good reasons both of the agents at Red Cloud and Spotted Tail removed and their duties to be performed by the Commanding officers of the Garrisons. Also that no issues [of food or equipment] to be made at any of the agencies unless the indians [sic] be actually present, that all who are now or may hereafter go outside of the reservation are to be treated, as you propose, as enemies, disarmed and their ponies and guns taken away, you can do this by the present troops or by such others as you may send there. . . . We must not have another massacre like Custer[']s and Congress is now in session willing to give us all we want.[15]

Sheridan now had virtually absolute power over all Indians in the war zone—friendly or hostile—regardless of treaty or law. He intended to make full use of this power.

22

"First Scalp for Custer"

WHILE SHERIDAN TIGHTENED HIS GRIP ON THE RESERVATIONS, Crook was becoming increasingly nervous about his position. Sibley's scouting expedition, and the Indian efforts to burn him out convinced him they were still gathered together in a large force, and could strike at any time. He was coming to terms with his narrow escape at the Rosebud. That, together with Custer's annihilation, left him shaken, perhaps even frightened. He wanted a link with Terry but, more urgently, he wanted Merritt and the Fifth Cavalry.[1]

In a telegram to Sheridan, Crook said:

> I find myself inmeasurably [sic] embarrassed by the delay of Merritt[']s Column as the extreme hot weather of the last few days has so completely parched the grass excepting that on the mountain tops that it burns like tinder. . . . On the powder, tongue & rosebud rivers the whole country is on fire and filled with smoke[.] I am in constant dread of an attack[.] In their last [attempt] they set fire to the grass and as much of it was still green we extinguished [it] without difficulty but should it be fired now I don't see how we could stay in the country[.] I am at a loss what to do[.] I can prevent their attack by assuming the aggressive[,] but as my effective strength is

less than (1200) twelve hundred exclusive of indian allies I could do but little to subdue them until cold weather narrowed their limits & in the meantime they could do an incalculable amount of damage to the settlements.[2]

UNTIL MERRITT BECAME ITS COLONEL, THE FIFTH CAVALRY'S OPERA-tional structure closely resembled that of the Seventh. Just as Lieutenant Colonel Custer had commanded the Seventh in the field, while its nominal commander, Colonel Sturgis, was on detached duty, so had Lieutenant Colonel Carr commanded the Fifth in the field since 1868, and the nominal commander, Col. William H. Emory, served elsewhere. When Emory retired in the summer of 1876, many in the regiment assumed that Carr would be promoted, since he was largely responsible for the "Dandy Fifth's" fighting reputation. Merritt's appointment was a surprise, particularly since he had not led troops in combat for eleven years since the end of the Civil War.

Carr did not quarrel with Merritt's promotion, which followed army seniority rules, but did resent his taking actual field command instead of remaining on detached duty as Emory had done. "It seems curious," he wrote to his wife, "that the Government should find it necessary to spend large amounts of money and some blood to teach Terry, Crook and Merritt how to fight these Prairie Indians when there are others who know better how to do it." Publicly, however, he kept his hard feelings to himself, and prepared to work in a subordinate role with the new colonel.[3]

Despite his lack of experience fighting Plains Indians, Wesley Merritt was an able soldier who knew the frontier. A native of New York, he graduated from West Point in 1860, and was sent to Utah. With the outbreak of the Civil War, he went east, distinguishing himself in action and ultimately becoming a brevet major general. Reduced in rank after the war ended, he was appointed lieutenant colonel of the Ninth Cavalry in 1866, serving in an administrative capacity in western Texas for several years before joining Sheridan's staff.[4] Although a month past his forty-second birthday, he had a boyish face, which a mustache failed to age significantly.

Merritt joined the Fifth on July 1, at its camp northwest of the Red Cloud Agency in Nebraska, where the regiment was still covering the trail between the agency and the Powder River country. Two days later, one of the companies unsuccessfully chased a small group of Cheyennes, riding two horses to death and exhausting at least a dozen others. This prompted Merritt to move the camp closer to the trail and send out scouting details. During the march to the new camp, the troops found rifle pits and the bodies of two men, probably Black Hills miners who had been jumped by the Indians.[5]

On June 12, Merritt received orders to refit at Fort Laramie, then join Crook at Goose Creek in northern Wyoming. The command marched sixteen miles, and was going into camp when a message arrived from Capt. William Jordan, commanding Camp Robinson, three miles from Red Cloud. Jordan advised that hundreds of Cheyennes planned to leave the agency, presumably to join the hostiles.

Merritt was determined to intercept the Indians and force them back to the agency. During the next two days, he backtracked fifty-one miles until, on July 14, he camped in northwestern Nebraska, on the road between Fort Laramie and Red Cloud. He hesitated, however, to move closer to the agency itself, since he considered it unnecessary and believed it might force the Indians out before he was ready to fight them. Instead, he sent one company under Maj. Thaddeus Stanton to investigate the situation at the agency. Shortly before noon the next day, Stanton and Jordan sent Merritt a note that some 800 Cheyennes "and a lot of Sioux" planned to leave the agency either later that day or the next.[6]

In fact, the reports were exaggerated; only about 200 Cheyennes were leaving the agency. Merritt, however, had to rely on the information he was given, and prepared his new command for the first of the "lightning marches" that would become his hallmark as an Indian fighter.

Within an hour of receiving the dispatch from Stanton and Jordan, Merritt was pushing seven companies of cavalry north. He proposed to cut in front of the Cheyennes, meet them head-on, and throw them back toward the agency. This meant retracing the same trail he had just covered, then turning east across the path he presumed the Indians would use. He left a small detail to guard his wagon train, whose commander was told to follow along and catch up when the cavalry halted or went into camp.[7]

Merritt's scouts were Little Bat Garnier, Jonathan White, sometimes called Charley White and more often "Buffalo Chips," and, greatest and most colorful of all, William F. Cody, better known as Buffalo Bill. At thirty-one, Buffalo Bill Cody was already a semi-legendary figure. Large and handsome, with flowing locks and well-groomed mustache and imperial, "he realized to perfection the bold hunter and gallant sportsman of the plains," according to one admirer.[8]

A native of Iowa, Cody was seven years old when his family moved to Kansas. At fifteen, he obtained work as a freight driver and over the next several years worked as a freighter, Pony Express rider, stagecoach driver, and at other jobs until experienced enough to find employment as a government scout for the Fifth Cavalry. When not scouting, Cody contracted to provide buffalo meat for Kansas Pacific Railroad construction crews, and was so successful that he came to be called Buffalo Bill. His broad experience, conviviality, and natural flair for showmanship brought him Sheridan's unofficial patronage. He rapidly became the lieutenant general's favorite scout, and through the influence of Sheridan's New York friends, had recently gone into show business.

Despite the flamboyance, Cody had substance; the soldiers trusted him as they trusted no other scout. He was performing with his theatrical group in the East when Anson Mills notified him that Crook wanted him as a scout. Arriving in Chicago, however, he learned that Carr had telegraphed division headquarters requesting his services, and the sentimental attachment to the Fifth proved too strong. Now, he rode with Merritt, glad to be out on the plains again, looking for excitement and for experiences that could be worked into his theater performances.[9]

Cody was perhaps the most famous chronicler of Merritt's march, but there were others, among them, Lt. Charles King, a prolific writer who not only recorded events but also would become one of the originators of the western novel. Others were Sgt. John Powers, and Pvts. Daniel Brown and Alfred McMackin, who served as correspondents for the Ellis County *Star,* at Hays,

Kansas, and Pvt. James Frew, a letter writer who also kept a diary on scraps of paper.

Merritt had taken his men about thirty-five miles by 10:00 P.M., when he ordered a bivouac to rest the horses and graze them on what slight nourishment the local buffalo grass could provide. The soldiers were little better off. "Very hungry—no supper," Frew remarked.

The march began again before 5:00 A.M. About midmorning, the cavalrymen halted at the pallisaded camp of a Twenty-third Infantry company commanded by Lt. George M. Taylor, which guarded the springs that fed Sage Creek, a local watercourse. The troopers were allowed a quick lunch, and when the wagon train caught up, were told to break open ammunition cases and stuff their pockets and belts with cartridges.

Merritt had decided to leave the heavy supply wagons under guard at the infantry camp, taking only the light company wagons with three days' rations. He also commandeered Lieutenant Taylor's company of infantry, loading them into the wagons with one company of Ninth Infantry, which was already guarding the train. Less than an hour after stopping, the Fifth was on the march again. The objective was a crossing over War Bonnet Creek, sometimes called Hat Creek, which the Indians were known to use on their way to Wyoming.[10]

"The day is hot," King wrote, "we are following the Black Hills road, and the dust rises in heavy clouds above us. But 'tis a long, long way to the Indian crossing and we *must* be the first to reach it."

At sunset, they saw the "winding belt of green in a distant depression," marking the trees that lined the War Bonnet Creek, and by 8:00 P.M. they were entering the timber where they bivouacked on a little plateau against a line of bluffs. "We have marched eighty-five miles in thirty-one hours," King wrote, "and here we are, square in their front, ready and eager to dispute with the Cheyennes their crossing on the morrow." They had completely outrun the wagon train, which was miles to the rear.[11]

In camp, only a few fires were allowed, and these in deep holes where the flames could not be seen. Company K, commanded by

Capt. Julius Mason with King as his lieutenant, was assigned to guard duty. The men were posted in hollows and ravines where they could see objects silhouetted against the sky. Since this precluded their walking about, and as they had held the same duty the previous night, they were sleepy, and King and Mason continually walked about, trying to keep them awake. The night passed slowly and toward morning grew cold. Merritt had left orders to be awakened at 3:30 A.M., and was up immediately when King called him.

Returning to his position in the growing light, King saw two conical hills, which blocked the view beyond. He sent a detail to the northernmost hill closest to the camp while he took two troopers and a corporal to the southern hill, about a hundred yards farther out. Lying prone on the top of the hill, King swept the horizon with his binoculars. About 4:30 A.M., the corporal pointed to a distant ridge to the front and said, "Look, Lieutenant—there are the Indians!"

About a minute after this first group was spotted, they saw more warriors, about two miles from their position on the hill. Within ten minutes at least six groups had come in and out of view. By 5:00 A.M., their line was drawn up about three miles away, all along the front, but there they remained, obviously watching something. Looking off to the southwest, King's group saw the wagon train four miles away, moving slowly and steadily toward camp. This caused more interest than concern among the soldiers, for the train was guarded by two companies of infantry, which the quartermaster had apparently concealed in the wagons. King observed the quartermaster "is probably only afraid that the Indians *won't* attack him."

Merritt and his staff joined the group on the hill and watched for a while. Finally Merritt asked the adjutant, "Have the men had coffee?" Told they had, he said to Carr, "Then let them saddle up and close in mass under the bluffs."

By that time, Buffalo Bill, Little Bat, and Buffalo Chips White had joined the group on the hill. Now, in full daylight, they noticed that the southern slope had eroded almost to a sheer drop into a ravine that came down from the distant ridge where the Indians were. Although the trail and the ravine intersected to form a V, the terrain was such that neither could be seen from the other. They saw a party of thirty or forty Indians moving excitedly about the head of the ravine, about a mile and a half away.

"What in thunder are those vagabonds fooling about?" Cody wondered.

Then they saw two couriers had overtaken the train, and were heading toward Merritt's camp with dispatches. The Cheyennes lashed their ponies and started down the ravine toward the dispatch riders. They would have to pass under the soldiers on the hill.

"By Jove! General," Cody said. "Now's our chance. Let our party mount here out of sight and we'll cut those fellows off!"

"Up with you, then!" Merritt replied, and to King, he said, "Stay where you are. . . . Watch them till they are close under you; then give the word. Come down, every other man of you!" They slipped down the hill, mounted, and concealed themselves to catch the Cheyennes in the ravine.[12]

The soldiers with the wagon train had seen the Indians on the distant ridge, and presumed them to be Merritt's men. When they were recognized as Indians, the infantry tumbled out of the wagons and formed up. By now, the smaller group of Cheyennes was riding hard toward the couriers. As they approached the hill, King shouted, "*Now*, lads, in with you!"

The scouting party rode out and opened fire, while Merritt and the corporal returned to the hilltop to observe. The startled Cheyennes reined back and returned fire, one bullet barely missing Merritt's face. Somebody shouted, "Look to the front! Look! Look!" The remaining Indians had started down from the ridge to rescue their trapped comrades.

"Send up the first company!" Merritt shouted to the concealed soldiers of the Fifth, then mounted his horse and went down to join the fight.[13]

Down in the ravine, Buffalo Bill picked the leader of the first group, a warrior named Yellow Hair.[14] In his autobiography, Cody intimated that he and Yellow Hair knew each other, and claimed a grudge duel ensued, starting with rifles and finishing with knives. He said on killing the warrior, he scalped him and, waving the scalp lock and war bonnet in the air, shouted, "First scalp for Custer!"[15] This was the version in his Wild West shows, in dime novels, and finally immortalized on film by Joel McCrea and Anthony Quinn.

Witnesses tell a story that while no less valiant is different. Yellow Hair fired and missed, although Cody's startled horse bucked and threw him. Jumping to his feet, Buffalo Bill sent a bullet through the warrior's leg and killed his pony, tumbling horse and rider into a confused heap. Recovering, Yellow Hair was raising his rifle for another shot when a second bullet from Cody hit him in the brain. Several Cheyennes tried to retrieve the body, but were forced back by the cavalrymen, and Cody took the scalp.[16]

The Cheyennes were now on the run. Merritt's troops chased them three miles back toward the agency, killing between three and six, and wounding perhaps five, before halting to regroup. The only soldier injured was a Private Jeffers, whose horse fell down the embankment. Merritt spent the rest of the day following the Cheyennes forty miles back to the Red Cloud Agency.[17] Reporting the action to Sheridan, Merritt said:

> I will move without delay to Fort Laramie and as soon as possible move to join Crook. My men and horses are very tired but a few days reasonable marching with full forage will make them all right.[18]

Tactically, the skirmish on War Bonnet Creek was a minor affair, hardly worth noting. Strategically and psychologically, however, it was the best news Sheridan had heard all summer. So far there had been nothing but defeat and humiliation. Now Merritt had responded to an urgent report that agency Indians were bolting, had made a forced march, intercepted those Indians, beaten a large vanguard, and sent the whole band back to the agency—with no losses to himself. The fight, and the ensuing show business hype about Buffalo Bill's "duel" (little different from the "guts and glory" productions of Hollywood from 1942 to 1945) boosted morale for a disillusioned public. At the moment, it was just what the country needed.[19]

23

The Long, Terrible Summer

DESPITE THE VICTORIES OVER CROOK AND CUSTER, THE GREAT congregation of Indians in the north was suffering. The convergence of soldiers in the area forced them to travel rapidly, and hunting parties dared not venture too far from the main band. There was not enough food, and many went hungry. Buffalo were scarce, so most game consisted of elk, antelope, and deer. Some Cheyenne hunters managed to kill several buffalo, and were loading the meat onto their packhorses when someone thought he saw soldiers. They scattered and hid until night, then retrieved the meat.

To boost morale, the Cheyenne encampment held a dance on the Rosebud near the site of the fight with Crook. The warriors bragged about their feats at the Little Bighorn. Each told his story, and called on friends to verify it. Wooden Leg's grandmother showed Lieutenant Cooke's skinned whiskers as proof that her grandson had been in the fight, then, apparently nervous about the unusual scalp, she threw it away.[1]

The Hunkpapa band to which White Bull belonged had separated from the main group after the Custer fight and at the end of July was camped far to the east on Beaver Creek between the Yellowstone and the Little Missouri. White Bull and a warrior named Iron Claw left the camp and headed south for the Black Hills, where they hoped to steal some horses from the whites. Along the way, they met Crazy Horse and a band from the main camp, who were returning from their own raid into the Black Hills. The two groups camped together overnight, after which Crazy Horse's band headed northwest, while White Bull and Iron Claw continued south to the hills. A few nights later, they came upon a camp of white teamsters with a wagon and two horses. The teamsters were sound asleep, and the two Indians managed to steal the horses without being detected, then rode back to their people.[2]

SHERIDAN WAS BUILDING UP HIS FORCES IN THE WAR ZONE. UNITS of the Twenty-second Infantry, borrowed from the Division of the Atlantic, were coming from as far as New York. In Sheridan's own division, Miles's infantry was heading north from Oklahoma, and a battalion of Eleventh Infantry had even been ordered up from Fort Brown, on the southern tip of Texas. Despite Sherman's misgivings about leaving the southern plains—Kansas, Oklahoma, and Texas—unprotected, Sheridan also wanted Mackenzie's Fourth Cavalry. The southern tribes were defeated and disorganized; other units could guard that frontier, and Sheridan needed the combat-seasoned troops where they would be most useful.

In Fort Leavenworth, General Pope consulted Mackenzie and determined six companies of the Fourth could be sent north. The other six companies could patrol the reservations in western Oklahoma, provided the forts were garrisoned with infantry and artillery units.[3] Pope, however, had begun to balk at sending Mackenzie himself, since it was obvious that the Kiowas and Comanches were more awed by the man than by his soldiers.

"Mackenzie is worth here a good deal more than the six companies sent off," Pope wired Sheridan. "Indeed, his presence at [Fort] Sill justifies sending away half his regiment. If you consider him absolutely necessary[,] of course he must go."[4]

Sheridan did consider Mackenzie absolutely necessary, and Pope reluctantly sent him north with the six companies of his regiment.

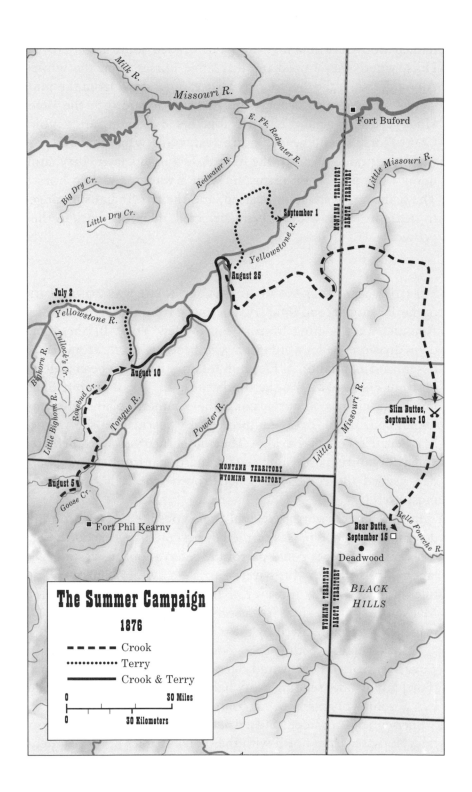

Milk R.

Missouri R.

Fort Buford

E. Fk. Redwater R.

Little Missouri R.

Big Dry Cr.

Redwater R.

Little Dry Cr.

September 1

MONTANA TERRITORY

DAKOTA TERRITORY

Yellowstone R.

August 25

July 2

Yellowstone R.

Bighorn R.

Tullock's Cr.

August 10

Little Missouri R.

Little Bighorn R.

Rosebud Cr.

Tongue R.

Powder R.

Slim Buttes,
September 10

August 5

Goose Cr.

MONTANA TERRITORY

WYOMING TERRITORY

Little Missouri R.

Fort Phil Kearny

Bear Butte,
September 15

Belle Fourche R.

Deadwood

WYOMING TERRITORY

DAKOTA TERRITORY

BLACK
HILLS

The Summer Campaign

1876

- - - - Crook

········· Terry

———— Crook & Terry

0   30 Miles

0   30 Kilometers

He would assume command of the District of the Black Hills, with headquarters at Camp Robinson.[5]

On July 25, Sherman advised Sheridan that the agents at Red Cloud and Spotted Tail had been formally notified of their discharge. The military authorities at Camp Robinson would assume control of the Red Cloud Agency, and Spotted Tail would be under the jurisdiction of Camp Sheridan. While army officers were prohibited by law from serving as agents, they could function on an interim basis until new agents subservient to the military were appointed.

Sherman also said the secretary of war had received authorization to build the cavalry up to the full strength of 100 men per company, provided the size of the army did not exceed the legal limit of 25,000. "We propose to send all Recruits to the Reg[imen]ts. of Cavalry & infantry now in the Sioux Country as fast as they are made [ready] leaving other Companies to fall below the minimum," he wrote. Meanwhile, Secretary Cameron was pushing a congressional resolution expanding the army to 27,500 for the duration of the war.[6]

With the uproar over the Custer fight, and the country still in the throes of a depression, the army had very little trouble finding recruits, who began calling themselves "Custer's Avengers." They were not necessarily ideal soldiers, however. Lt. Hugh Scott, fresh out of West Point and assigned to the Seventh Cavalry in the wake of the Little Bighorn, and now responsible for training the regiment's recruits noted, "Many of them were criminals that were got rid of by court martial from time to time. . . ."[7]

AT GOOSE CREEK, CROOK WAS JOINED BY THIRTY-FIVE UTES. HE had been pressuring for their services and they had been trying to join for over a month. Their agent, however, had blocked their enlistment until Interior Secretary Chandler bluntly ordered him not to interfere. Merritt finally arrived on August 3, bringing the expedition to about 2,000 men and 160 wagons. Crook still hoped to trap the Indians between himself and Terry, but this would be impossible if the pace were set by the wagons. Consequently, on August 4, he ordered:

All tents, camp equipage, bedding, and baggage, except articles hereinafter specified, [are] to be stored in the wagons, and wagons turned over to the care of the chief quartermaster by sunrise tomorrow. Each company to have their coffee roasted and ground and turned over to the chief commissary at sunset tonight. Wagons will be left here at camp. A pack-train of mules will accompany each battalion on the march, for the protection of which the battalion will be held responsible. The regiment will march at seven A.M. tomorrow, 'prepared for action,' and company commanders will see to it that each man carried with him on his person one hundred rounds of ammunition and four days' rations, overcoat and one blanket on the saddle. Fifty rounds additional per man will be packed on mules. Four extra horses, not to be packed will be led with each company. Currycombs and brushes will be left in wagons. *Special instructions for action:* All officers and noncommissioned officers to take constant pains to prevent wastage of ammunition.[8]

Crook broke camp August 5, moving northward along the Tongue in weather that Finerty estimated at 105 degrees in the shade. Not finding an Indian trail, Crook cut westward to the Rosebud, halting frequently to give men and animals a break from the heat and dust. They reached the Rosebud about six miles north of the battlefield where Crook had narrowly averted disaster in June, and continued northward down the valley. At night, the camp was lighted by fires in the timbered hills. On the third day of the march, the heat and drought broke. Rain fell, blown by a cold north wind, but now Crook's trail turned into heavy mud. The men suffered, having only an overcoat and blanket, with no tents or ponchos.[9]

On August 10, Crook was about thirty miles south of the Rosebud's confluence with the Yellowstone. The weather once again was hot and dry. Ahead, the troops saw what Finerty called "a mighty column of dust, indicating a large body of men and animals in motion. . . ." Buffalo Bill rode ahead to investigate, while Finerty asked one of the Shoshones about the dust cloud. The Indian squinted and replied, "Heap pony-soldier. No Sioux—Sioux far off—run when pony soldier and good Indian come strong—heap strong now."

A few minutes later, Cody returned and reported it was Terry with "enough wagons to do an army corps."[10]

The sight of Crook's men startled Terry's, who were deploying into a skirmish line when Cody rode toward them waving his hat. Crook, meanwhile, established an impromptu headquarters under a tree, and sent Lt. Walter Schuyler to welcome Terry and his staff and escort them over.[11]

Describing the feeling of both commands, King wrote, "The question is asked, in comical perplexity, 'Why, where on earth are the Indians?' Except for our allies, none are in sight. They have slipped away between us."[12]

Crook's men used the meeting to clean up and draw rations from Terry's well-stocked train. However, the deficiencies of both sides were soon evident. As usual, Terry packed his supplies on poorly trained wagon mules that, according to Bourke, lost or damaged more in one day than Crook's mules had during the entire campaign so far. The bulk of Terry's cavalry strength was the badly mauled Seventh, which needed a complete reorganization after the Little Bighorn.

But Terry's men were comfortably equipped and well fed compared with Crook's soldiers. Having left most of their equipment behind, they had only the clothes on their backs and were living on subsistence rations. Already dirty and hungry, Crook's troops now faced the erratic weather that precedes the onset of winter on the northern plains. The day had been unbearably hot, but that night cold rain fell in sheets on the unprotected soldiers.

"We built Indian 'wickyups' of saplings and elastic twigs, threw ponchos and blankets over them, and crawled under; but 'twas no use," King wrote. "Presently the whole country was flooded, and we built huge fires, huddled around them in the squashy mud, and envied our horses, who really seemed pleased at the change."[13]

Shortly before meeting Terry, Crook had located the Indian trail that led east from the Rosebud back toward the Tongue. For the next two days, the two columns plodded through the mud, parallel to each other. The march was especially hard on Terry's infantrymen, many of whom became so exhausted by the weight of the mud on their feet that they collapsed and had to be carried on mules or travois.

By now, the generals had lost all hope of catching the hostiles. The trail, such as still existed after the rain, split three ways, with one group of Indians fleeing south along the river, another north, and a third continuing east, cross-country toward the Powder.[14]

Miserable as the soldiers were, they were better off than the Lakotas and Cheyennes. The combined forces of Crook and Terry had kept constant pressure on the main band, forcing it to flee eastward. As Wooden Leg recalled, "There was no stopping for special hunting. I believe we remained only one sleep at each of the camps."

Although Indians often recovered from virtually any injury except a bullet in the brain, heart, or spine, some of those wounded at the Little Bighorn were beginning to die. Wooden Leg believed they would have recovered had they been allowed to rest quietly in a lodge instead of being carried from place to place on travois since the fight.

The meat supplies were gone, and the captured army horses were giving out. Every day, the chiefs held a council, finally deciding to break up into smaller bands. This would hinder pursuit, as well as give them time to hunt and prepare for the coming winter. Dull Knife, who had arrived since the Custer fight, doubled back to the southwest, taking his Cheyennes into the Bighorn Mountains of Wyoming. Small parties of Lakotas started for the agencies. The remaining Lakotas turned east, pushing to remain ahead of the soldiers. This separation was marked by the three trails that Crook and Terry had encountered.[15]

By this time, Dull Knife was probably disturbed about a new development. There were stories from the southern tribes about a soldier chief with a mutilated hand called Bad Hand or Three Fingers, whom the whites called Mackenzie. This soldier pursued Indians relentlessly and was always victorious. Now, there were rumors that the Bad Hand was coming north, and Dull Knife later admitted the possibility worried him.[16]

*   *   *

CROOK'S SHOSHONE SCOUTS, WHO HAD NEVER TRAVELED SO FAR from their villages, began to get homesick and to question the fidelity of their wives during their absence. The grain-fed government horses, unable to subsist on grass alone, were starting to weaken. "Our whole line of march from the Rosebud to the Powder and Yellowstone rivers was dotted with dead or abandoned horses," Finerty noted. Even had they been able to subsist on grass, there was little available since the retreating Lakotas had burned it in order to starve the government animals.[17]

Having determined that the main body of Indians had moved east toward the Powder River, Crook decided to follow that trail. On reaching the Powder, the command then marched north to its juncture with the Yellowstone, where it was replenished from Terry's steamboats. At that point, the Shoshones and Utes decided they had had enough. The Crows were also growing restless and said they did not want their young warriors to venture out of their home territory with so many Lakotas and Cheyennes about. Twenty-one of Crook's men, in failing health because of the privations of the march (one was completely insane), were loaded on steamers and sent back East. Buffalo Bill also departed, asking to be released from duty because of the coming theatrical season.[18]

On August 20, a bad storm broke. Rain mixed with hail pelted Crook's men, who had no cover. "No stringing together of words can complete a description of what we saw, suffered, and feared during that awful tempest," Bourke wrote. "The stoutest hearts, the oldest soldiers, quailed. . . . The exposure began to tell upon the officers, men and animals . . . no one who followed Crook during those terrible days was benefited in any way."[19] Three nights later, an even worse storm hit.

The soldiers complained as soldiers always do. One blamed his enlistment on whiskey. Another said he would desert or get a discharge before going on any more Indian campaigns. One of the column's inevitable Irish soldiers remarked that if he had listened to his mother and stayed home in Cashel, "it isn't like a drowned rat I'd be this night."[20]

The soldiers were not alone in their misery; the rain also fell on the Lakotas, who were in scattered encampments in the extreme northwestern corner of what is now South Dakota, near a spur of the Black Hills called Slim Buttes. Their own ponies were wearing out in the deep mud, and they thought how much worse it was for the starving government horses.

Sitting Bull's small son had been killed by a kick from a pony. The chief spent several days mourning, then he and Gall took their Hunkpapas and started on a long, circuitous journey whose eventual destination was Canada. Others were breaking away all the time. Crazy Horse was adamant, however, that he would not leave a country he considered his own.[21]

THE ARMY COLUMNS BEGAN MARCHING BACK SOUTH ALONG THE Powder on August 24, mostly on foot, leading the worn-out horses. They managed to cover ten miles before bivouacking for the night. The sky cleared but it was bitterly cold. The joint expedition continued for one more day. Then, at 7:50 A.M., August 26, Crook struck out on his own, while Terry started back north toward the Yellowstone.

Crook now moved east, along the old Stanley Trail, backtracking the route taken by Custer and Terry earlier in the summer. Fuel was becoming scarce. As the command started up a bluff, some of the men found wood at the base and strapped it to the exhausted horses. Merritt saw them and shouted loud enough for "some eighty acres of hillside" to hear, that the soldiers had less than five seconds to drop the wood. Later that day, he composed a general order pointing out that a cavalryman's first duty was to protect his animals.[22]

The column went into camp at a spring overlooking Cabin Creek in extreme eastern Montana, and remained there August 29 and 30. The only food was bacon, coffee, and hardtack. Hunting detachments were sent out to get food for the growing number of sick men. Neuralgia, rheumatism, malaria, and diarrhea were common complaints. When the march resumed, one lieutenant could barely sit on his horse. Another had to be carried on a travois. A rainy norther blew in on the night of August 31, the temperature plunged, and the wet, summer-clad soldiers suffered terribly.

Eventually the command reached the Little Missouri in North

Dakota and ran across one of Terry's old campsites, where his horses had scattered corn from their feed. A crop had since sprung up, and the young ears were fed to the famished horses. The troops also found an abundance of bullberries and half-ripened plums, which they ate as a precaution against scurvy. They gathered and ate the fruit of the prickly pear cactus, and even tried the pads, after burning off the spines and boiling them.[23]

Crook continued on toward the Heart River, thirty miles east of the Little Missouri. The soldiers felt the Indians were near, since fresh sign was evident all along the trail. As the column reached the Heart, they heard shots ahead, and the troops grew excited at the thought of a fight. The scouts had caught up with the Indian rear guard and there was some shooting, but the fresh Indian ponies soon outdistanced the jaded army mounts.[24]

The general was convinced the Indians planned to attack the unprotected settlements of the Black Hills, which began some 200 miles to the south. Fort Abraham Lincoln, only five days' march to the east, was closer than the Black Hills settlements. But if he went to the fort to reprovision, he estimated he would lose half his horses while accomplishing nothing. On the other hand, he felt there was much to gain by heading straight to the Black Hills, where he could protect the settlements and perhaps catch the Indians. Either way, there would not be enough food. On half-rations, the men could eat for another two and a half days. Crook decided to try for the Black Hills.

The short rations, the general told correspondent Finerty, must last for at least seven days. "The Indians have gone to the Hills and to the agencies," he continued. "The miners must be protected and we must punish the Sioux on our way to the south or leave this campaign entirely unfinished."

Finerty could hardly believe it. "You will march 200 miles in the wilderness with used-up horses and tired infantry and two and one-half days rations!"

"I know it looks hard," Crook replied, "but we've got to do it, and it shall be done. I have sent a telegram for supplies to General Sheridan. The wagons will meet us at Crook City or Deadwood. If not, the settlements must supply our wants. Nobody knows much about this region, but it looks fair. We'll kill some game, too, perhaps, to make up for short rations. Half-rations will be issued after tonight. All will be glad of the movement after the march has been made. If necessary, we can eat our horses."[25]

After a long march the following day, the command camped by an alkaline pond without enough wood or sagebrush even to make a fire for coffee. Most of the soldiers went to bed on completely empty stomachs, but Lieutenant Schuyler and several others managed to get together enough grass to boil coffee in their cups. The next night they managed to build a fire after soaking some soggy wood in alcohol obtained from the surgeon. That was the extent of their enterprise for, as Schuyler commented the following morning, "breakfast—water and tightened belts."[26]

They were passing through a grassy country now. Bourke noted the wild onions "which we dug up and saved to boil with the horse-meat which was now appearing as our food. . . ." The new diet was particularly hard on the cavalrymen. "To us who have to depend on them so much, it seems like murder to kill horses," Schuyler commented. Even so, when a horse gave out, it was shot and butchered, and the men often got into fights over the meat. Crook was as ragged and filthy as the rest, existing on hardtack, boiled horse, and such coffee as he could brew in his cup.[27]

Describing the march in a letter to his father, Schuyler said:

I had told you what I experienced on this march, but you can gather from that no realization of the suffering of the men, particularly the Infantry. I have seen men become so exhausted that they were actually insane, but there was no way of carrying them, except for some mounted officer or man to give them his own horse, which was done constantly. I saw men who were very plucky, sit down and cry like children because they could not hold out. When there came a chance to fight however, everyone was mad enough to fight well.[28]

24

Bloody Retribution at Slim Buttes

By the end of the first week of September, Crook realized he had overextended himself and needed help. On September 7, near the head of the Grand River in the northwest corner of South Dakota, he ordered Lt. John W. Bubb, his commissary officer, to try and reach Deadwood or Crook City, settlements about a hundred miles to the south, to purchase supplies and quinine. Capt. Anson Mills was assigned to provide an escort of 150 men from the Third Cavalry, while Tom Moore would have charge of fifteen packers and sixty-one mules. Assisting Mills with the escort would be Lt. Frederick Schwatka, adjutant, with Lt. Emmet Crawford and Lt. Adolphus von Luettwitz each commanding seventy-five soldiers. Grouard was designated as scout, assisted by Jack Crawford.[1]

Bubb recalled Crook specifically telling Mills to avoid a fight if at all possible, and detour around any villages he might find; his first duty was to procure the supplies. Meanwhile, Crook intended to rest his men in bivouac all day September 8, a clear indication that Mills could not expect immediate support in case of a fight. Mills, however, claimed that as his command departed on the night of September 7, Crook gave him verbal orders to attack and hold any Indian village he might encounter.[2]

Mills led his men out about 7:00 P.M., riding some eighteen miles in total darkness, the surrounding terrain completely invisible in the night. About midnight, Grouard lit a match and saw fresh pony tracks by the edge of a little pond. Knowing the Indians were close but unable to see anything, Mills ordered a halt, and the men tried to get some sleep.[3]

The tracks could have belonged to any of several Lakota-Cheyenne groups, many of which used this area for their fall camp. One group was to the east by Antelope Buttes, building up their ponies on the rich grazing lands and hoping to trade with the nearby Rees for corn and other supplies. Crazy Horse was less than twenty miles to the southeast, en route south to Bear Butte, which he planned to use as a base for the winter.

Near Crazy Horse's camp, and directly in Mills's path was a camp of perhaps thirty-five to forty lodges of Miniconjous, Oglalas, Brulés, and Sans Arcs, led by an Oglala, Roman Nose, and a minor Miniconjou chief, Iron Plume, known to the whites as American Horse (not to be confused with the Cheyenne Roman Nose, killed at Beecher's Island in 1868, or the great Oglala American Horse). Like Crazy Horse, they were heading south toward Bear Butte, although from there, they planned to work their way southeast around the Black Hills avoiding the soldiers until they reached the Spotted Tail Agency. Many of the warriors were away; some were trading for ammunition to hunt while others, unaware of the military takeover of the agencies, had gone ahead to Spotted Tail to arrange for the arrival of the main group.[4]

This Indian camp was located on both sides of Gap Creek north of its confluence with the Moreau River in South Dakota, about fifty-five miles east of the Montana line. Seen from the north, the camp was in a wooded depression in front of a series of bluffs, which were broken by ravines—the northernmost edge of Slim Buttes. The woods concealed the camp, and the adjacent plains and nearby water provided good hunting, allowing the Indians to lay in a supply of food before making the almost 200-mile trek southward to the agency.

AFTER SPENDING A RAINY NIGHT LYING IN THE MUD AND HOLDING their horses by their lariats, Mills's troopers moved out again at daylight, September 8. It was still raining, but they could see the distant slopes of the Slim Buttes and knew they were approaching the Black Hills. After a while, the rain let up, but now a dense fog settled in, obscuring vision. Early that afternoon, the fog lifted, and Grouard spotted several Indian hunters in the distance, their ponies packed with game. He signaled a halt and reported to Mills they were near the Indian village. About 3:00 P.M., they saw some forty ponies grazing about three miles distant. Mills consulted with the guides and decided it would be impossible to approach closer without being seen. He moved back about a mile, and ordered the soldiers to conceal themselves in a deep ravine.[5]

After dark, Mills moved ahead with a small reconnaissance detail. Grouard later claimed that he went into the village disguised as an Indian, and determined "we had sufficient force to capture the entire village." Mills, however, said Grouard was afraid of approaching the village too closely, and had actually advised against attack. He did admit that Grouard managed to steal a pony from the Indian herd, since his own pony was worn out, but added, "He was acting so cowardly and hesitatingly, that I at once suspected he was getting himself in shape to get away should we get into a hot fight."[6] Mills was probably expressing a personal dislike for Grouard, for the scout probably exaggerated his story, but his previous record and subsequent actions leave no reason to doubt his bravery.

Although Grouard apparently brought Mills almost no information about the village, the captain had already made up his mind to attack. The soldiers waited until 2:00 A.M. before moving out, and Mills commented, "The night was one of the ugliest I ever passed—dark, cold, rainy, and muddy in the extreme." Approaching to within a mile of the village, he left the pack train under command of Lieutenant Bubb, with twenty-five soldiers, and 125 horses. The rest moved ahead, Emmet Crawford and Luettwitz each commanding fifty dismounted soldiers, and Schwatka with twenty-five mounted men. The plan was for Crawford and Luettwitz to hit the village from each end, while Schwatka took the pony herd. This assault on a village of unknown size or strength bore an uncomfortable resemblance to Custer's disastrous attack in June, and some of the officers hesitated. Mills, however, was adamant that Crook had ordered him to attack any village, and argued that if they were discovered before they could hit the camp, they might end up in a defensive fight, since their horses were in no condition for a quick escape.[7]

The move through water and mud took about an hour. As the command came within a hundred yards of the end of the village, however, a small herd of loose ponies smelled the government horses and stampeded through the camp. Grouard told Mills that all opportunity for surprise was lost, and without waiting further the captain signaled Schwatka to charge after the ponies and drive them as far as he could. Schwatka's men rode through, firing their pistols left and right at the tipis, while the dismounted troopers poured a heavy carbine fire into the south end of the village.

The Indians found themselves trapped in their elk hide tipis, because rain had soaked the leather lacings, swelling them and making them hard to unfasten. They cut their way out with knives. The warriors attempted to return fire, while the women carried the dead, wounded, and children, and fled into rocks and ravines among the bluffs. Almost immediately, Luettwitz took a bullet, which shattered his right kneecap, and apparently severed an artery. He grabbed Mills's arm and fell toward him. The scout Jack Crawford rushed over, untying his own neckerchief and twisting it around Luettwitz's thigh to stop the flow of blood. One of the sergeants carried the wounded lieutenant to safety behind a low ridge. By now, however, the soldiers controlled most of the camp and seeing resistance hopeless, the Indian warriors fled as soon as they were certain the women were safe, "leaving everything but their limited night-clothes in our possession, Schwatka having rounded up the principal part of the herd," Mills reported.[8]

On hearing the gunfire in the distance, Lieutenant Bubb had started ahead with the pack train. Grouard, meanwhile, was convinced there were other villages in the area, and when Bubb arrived, Mills ordered him to send two couriers back to General Crook for reinforcements.

Once their families were safely hidden in one of the ravines, some Indian warriors moved up to the bluffs and began firing into the camp. They made several rushes toward the ponies, but were thrown back by Lieutenant Crawford's men. Mills positioned his soldiers to defend the camp and dig trenches facing the ravine where many of the Indians were hidden. From their hiding place, the Indians shouted defiance, confirming Grouard's belief that more of their people were nearby and would come to the rescue. Mills was worried, since to the best of his knowledge Crook was still in camp some thirty-five miles to the northwest. He sent a third courier to explain the urgency of his situation and hurry the general along.[9]

Fortunately for Mills, Crook was closer than he thought. The day in camp had done much to restore Crook's men, and taking a calculated risk with his almost depleted food supply, the general had ordered the last of the hardtack to be issued in full, along with a substantial amount of horse meat. There was enough wood to build large fires, and the remaining coffee was brewed. On the morning of September 9, as Mills was attacking the village, the march resumed and, according to Bourke, "Our men were much more cheerful to-day, having had the exhilarating influence of good warm fires and good, invigorating coffee last night and this morning."

They marched quickly and steadily and, by the time the couriers arrived from Mills, the vanguard was only ten miles away.

Crook directed Dr. Bennett A. Clements, the chief surgeon, to prepare for wounded, and sent Merritt ahead with such cavalry as still had serviceable horses. The infantrymen, finally offered a chance to fight, "pressed on through the drizzling mist, determined not to be passed by the mounted troops," Bourke said, adding, "So well did they succeed that in the long stretch of (10) ten miles intervening, they marched fully as quickly as the Cavalry. . . ."[10]

Crook arrived between 11:00 A.M. and noon, to find most of the Indians had withdrawn into the ravine, and the area had grown quiet. A cordon was thrown up to cover the ravine, and the general ordered the village searched. The Indians had a large supply of game, berries, and dried fruit, and the hungry soldiers were soon rummaging through the tipis looking for something to eat. In one lodge, Pvt. William J. McClinton came across a guidon or company banner belonging to the Seventh Cavalry, lost at the Little Bighorn. The troopers also found clothing issued to the Seventh, Myles Keogh's gauntlets, equipment, and a large amount of paper money. There were army saddles, and several horses were branded "US" and "7C," showing they had been issued to Custer's regiment. The enraged soldiers were further incensed to find provisions issued by the Indian Bureau, as well as safe conduct passes given to individual warriors at the agencies.

Investigating a tipi, the soldiers found a little girl, about three or four years old, who screamed and tried to run away until she was caught and taken to Mills, who had young children of his own. He stroked her hair and gave her food, attempting to assure her that she would not be hurt, and eventually she calmed down.[11]

While the soldiers scattered through the village in what Lieutenant Schuyler called "orderless confusion," the Indians were digging shelters in the sides of the ravine, with their knives and other implements. Some worked so hard that they managed to scrape out a small cave, large enough to hide several people. The ravine itself extended south from a dry creek, and was about 200 yards long. The bank on the east side was perhaps twenty-five or thirty higher than the west. The bottom was covered with thick brush, providing ample concealment and obstructed the view from outside. Thus sheltered, the warriors began sniping into the camp again. The soldiers moved up to clear them out and were met by a hail of gunfire, which left one trooper killed and several wounded.[12]

The troops saturated the Indian position with bullets. Through the din, Big Bat Pourier heard a child crying, and shouted that women and children were in the ravine. Crook ordered a cease-fire and told Big Bat and Grouard to parley. Big Bat jumped down into the gully, where an Indian woman, shivering with fright, grabbed hold of him and said she wanted to live. He replied if that was the case, she should come out and surrender. At that point a young warrior pulled out a revolver, but Pourier jerked it away and threw it to an officer on top of the bank. He took the first woman up the bank, then brought up a wounded woman, along with the disarmed young warrior and a girl about ten years old. Going back into the ravine with his weapon cocked, Bat saw a man on his knees with a gun. Aiming at him, Bat ordered him to drop the gun, get up, and accompany him to the top. The man obeyed.[13]

As soon as the prisoners were taken out of the line of fire, the still-hidden warriors began shooting at the now exposed soldiers, and Crook decided the time had come to dislodge them. The soldiers were sent up to the top of the embankment to fire down into the ravine. Big Bat, Buffalo Chips White, Little Bat Garnier, and a scout named Richard Stirk were on a high, tree-covered point along the east bank. Determined to get an Indian, Chips borrowed a Sharps rifle from an officer. Someone raised a hat on a stick to draw the Indians out from cover and allow White to get a good shot with the heavy rifle. The Indians quickly caught on to the ruse, forcing Chips to raise up higher. Stirk and Big Bat both warned him to get down, but he ignored them, easing higher until his upper body was exposed. A shot rang out. Chips grunted, and said, "Oh! God!" then rolled down the bank with a bullet in his heart.[14]

His casualties rising, Crook sent twenty volunteers under Lt. Philo Clark to storm the Indian position. At first they advanced as a group, fired, then withdrew as the Indians returned fire. When this had been repeated a few times, Clark realized nothing was being accomplished, and so formed the men into three ranks. The first rank fired, then lay down while the second rank advanced and fired, then finally, the rear rank fired. By that time, the first rank was reloaded and ready to move forward again.

Bullets tore into the Indian pits as the troopers approached. With Crook's entire command now on the scene, there were more than 2,000 soldiers, and the noise attracted many spectators. Bourke wondered that soldiers weren't killed in the confusion. Finally, the throng of ragged bluecoats—enraged by their own losses, by the privations of the summer, and by the recovery of Custer's equipment in the camp—charged in behind Clark's men, raining bullets into the Indian position. "The oaths and yells of the surging soldiers, pressing in behind us made the scene truly infernal," Bourke wrote. Hearing the screams of women, Crook shouted for a cease-fire, but the order was lost—or ignored—in the din. Eventually, some semblance of discipline was restored. Bourke noted a pile of women and children "covered with dirt and blood and screaming in a perfect agony of terror" and saw "three or four dead bodies . . . weltering in their own gore."

Big Bat and Grouard meanwhile were again parleying with the Indians who, this time, had had enough. The remaining warriors and their women and children began coming out, and were led down the ravine where Crook waited. The prisoners understood immediately that the general was chief of this band of soldiers and, grateful to be alive, grasped his hand as they passed, some women placing their children's hands in his, or turning so he could touch the babies in their cradleboards.[15]

Learning that one of the chiefs, American Horse, was still in his pit in the ravine, Crook sent one of the women back to reassure him that he could safely surrender. She returned with a young warrior, who met with Crook then accompanied Big Bat back. They found American Horse with a bad abdominal wound. As he stood, they saw he was trying to contain his intestines with his hands. Big Bat and the young warrior assisted him back to Crook, who ordered him taken to the surgeon.[16]

Mills wandered down to see the captives and the dead, accompanied by his orderly, who carried the little girl found that morning in the tipi. The soldiers were removing the dead Indians from the pits, among them the bodies of two women. The girl screamed and struggled until the orderly put her down, and she ran over and threw her arms around one of the dead women, who was her mother. They pulled the girl away and returned to camp, where Mills told Lt. Henry Lemly that he planned to adopt her, since he was responsible for her mother's death.

A short time later, Crook ordered Mills to leave at daybreak and continue on to Deadwood according to the original plan. Lemly asked if he planned to take the girl along. When Mills answered affirmatively, Lemly asked, "Well, how do you think Mrs. Mills will like it?" Mills realized he was unable to consult his wife, and decided to leave the girl among her own people.[17]

With the fight over, the men set about burning the lodges and destroying all supplies that could not be carried. About 4:00 P.M., however, large groups of Indians started moving down from the bluffs—reinforcements led by Crazy Horse. The warriors went for the pony herd, but were held off as 1,600 soldiers deployed in a skirmish line.

The sight of so many troopers disturbed the chiefs. The requests for assistance from the Slim Buttes camp had reached them when the fight only involved Mills's 150 troopers, and they had arrived to find a much larger force. They retreated up into the bluffs, where they and the troops sniped at each other. The cavalry attempted to chase them out, but the worn-out government horses were not up to it.

One of the larger tipis was converted into a hospital, where American Horse died during the night. The surgeons were forced to amputate Lieutenant Luettwitz's leg. Two soldiers and Buffalo Chips were dead, and a large number were seriously wounded.

The command moved out at 6:30 A.M. the next day. As in past fights, the dead were buried in unmarked graves and the troops marched over them, although the Indians later claimed to have opened them and taken the scalps. The First Battalion of the Fifth Cavalry remained behind to finish the destruction of the village and, on moving out to catch up with the rest of the column, was attacked by a group of Indians but drove them off, killing five. "Our rations are not sufficient to follow the Indians," Lieutenant Capron noted, "and the first thing to do is to get food and clothing."[18]

Indeed, food and clothing—not the recent fight—were foremost in the minds of most. The day after the fight, Captain Luhn reckoned that the dried meat taken in the village was enough to sustain 2,000 men for two days, adding, "I think I can hold out three days longer."[19]

Many of the soldiers were thoroughly disgusted with Crook, and the name "Rosebud George" was cropping up with increasing frequency. Trooper McMackin, the freelance journalist, wrote his paper:

> So far the result of this expedition has been nothing but disaster, and a depletion of the public purse. Custer and his 300 brave soldiers still remain unavenged, and the Indian Question is further from solution than ever.

He even suggested that Crook was suffering "from slight attacks of abberration [sic] of the mind."[20]

The column continued southward. Despite the bloody release of Slim Buttes, the officers and men were more miserable than ever.

PART VI

CLOSING THE RING

25

Showdown at the Agencies

WHILE CROOK'S STARVING, RAGGED SOLDIERS MARCHED TOWARD the Black Hills settlements, Mackenzie arrived at Camp Robinson some 140 miles to the south, and was asserting his authority over the Nebraska agencies.

At thirty-six, Ranald Slidell Mackenzie was one of the few senior officers who thoroughly understood Indian warfare, turning their own hit-and-run tactics against them in swift, destructive raids. Not only was his combat record impressive, newspaper correspondents found him personally interesting. Finerty called him "a noble specimen of the beau sabreur, tall, well built and with a frank, handsome face."[1] He was five feet, nine inches tall, a respectable height for his time, and his lean, spare frame gave the impression of being taller. He was clean-shaven except for a large mustache, and with a face that bore a certain resemblance to twentieth-century Canadian actor Michael J. Fox. His most outstanding feature, however, was his light gray eyes—sometimes soft, sometimes piercing, always dominating.

A native of New York City, Mackenzie came from a prominent family. He graduated first in his class at West Point in 1862, entered the Union Army, and won Sheridan's praise for bravery and leadership during the Shenandoah Campaign. He was breveted to brigadier general and held a command position during the Appomattox Campaign. General Grant called Mackenzie "the most promising young officer in the army."[2]

After the war, Mackenzie was posted to the Texas frontier where, on February 24, 1871, he assumed command of the Fourth Cavalry. His subsequent Indian campaigns culminated in 1874, with a victory at Palo Duro Canyon that broke the Kiowas and Comanches.

Mackenzie's success had a price. He suffered seven major combat wounds to his arms, legs, and back. He lost part of his right hand during the siege at Petersburg in 1864. Walking and riding were extremely painful. His campaigns were spartan to the extreme, and the constant stress and deprivation of the field undermined his health. After a severe head injury in 1875, he showed symptoms of cerebral subdural hematoma, an excessive accumulation of blood pressing against the brain tissue.

By the time he was assigned to Camp Robinson, Mackenzie was mentally unstable. Foul-tempered and occasionally irrational, he was convinced his advancement was hindered by plots in the army command. He believed himself infallible, and did not hesitate to lecture Sherman himself on military matters. Sherman disliked him, and Sheridan was often ambivalent. At his best, however, Mackenzie was a brilliant commander who in many ways was indispensable. So the generals tolerated him in times of peace, and made maximum use of his many talents in war.[3]

It was typical of Mackenzie that as soon as he was ordered to Camp Robinson, he sent Sheridan a series of near-demands, which, despite their high-handed tone, showed the extent of his planning. Among other things, Mackenzie specified that Company M should be included among the six units of the Fourth going north "on account of [the] great number of old soldiers." He insisted the horses be shipped in easy stages so the long railroad trip would not tire them. Experience with the seven-shot Spencer carbine on the Texas plains had convinced him that a repeating weapon was preferable to the Springfield. On learning the Spencer was no longer available, he requested the Fourth be armed with Winchesters, and rifle boots on the saddles altered accordingly.

"The Ordnance Dept. can do it if they will not stop at trifles," he remarked.[4]

This last request infuriated Lt. Colonel J. B. Benton, commander of the Springfield Arsenal, already smarting under Reno's allegations that jamming Springfields had contributed to the disaster at the Little Bighorn. Tests proved the Springfield superior in range and penetration to both the Model 1873 .44-40 Winchester and the Model 1866 Spencer carbine, and Benton reported these results to General Benét, chief of ordnance. Benét, who no doubt resented Mackenzie's comments about his department's concern with "trifles," supported Colonel Benton with a memorandum for general circulation, which Mackenzie took as a personal attack.[5]

This misunderstanding, minor enough on its own, was typical of how situations could be blown out of proportion once Mackenzie was involved. The army command solved the problem by ignoring both sides.

ALTHOUGH IT WOULD SOON BE UPGRADED TO A FORT AND SUB-stantially expanded, Camp Robinson in 1876 was a small quadrangle that still exists in a corner of the present Fort Robinson State Park, about twenty miles southwest of Chadron, Nebraska. One side of the parade ground is lined with the original officers' quarters built of plastered adobe, and fronted with wooden porches. Facing them across the parade are log structures for barracks, sergeants' quarters, the adjutant's office, and the guardhouse. The former military reservation is on a rolling plain about a mile south of a line of buttes, with the Red Cloud Agency about three miles to the east.

One of Mackenzie's first acts on arrival was to conduct a census of Indians then drawing rations at the agency. The tally showed 4,760, of whom 1,080 were adult males. Another thousand enrolled at Red Cloud were staying less than twenty miles away at the Spotted Tail Agency. This meant there were 5,760 Indians enrolled at Red Cloud, whereas the agent's paperwork showed 11,000.

Reporting the discrepancy, Mackenzie noted, "The Interior Department has been for months issuing [food] to a great number of people who were not here." He immediately curtailed the issue, remarking, "The Indians are of course very much dissatisfied at drawing one Beef where they have been drawing two."[6]

Now that the army controlled the agencies, similar discrepancies between agents' counts and military censuses were appearing throughout the system. The generals were quick to charge corruption in the Indian Bureau, specifically that the agents were lining their pockets by selling off the excess annuity goods and rations.

This was hardly fair to the agents. During the previous year, many of the corrupt ones had been replaced by honest men, yet the inflated counts had continued. Part of the reason, as reports throughout late 1875 and the first half of 1876 showed, was that government rations simply were not sufficient if each Indian family was given its official allotment. The agents knew that hungry Indians were dangerous, and an agent's life often depended on keeping them adequately fed. Even if the agent were not concerned for his own safety, simple humanity dictated he inflate his figures to avoid suffering among his charges.

Deliberate inflation aside, the 1875 count had been distorted by abnormal Indian activity. During the great council that year, when the government had tried to purchase the Black Hills, many wandering Indians—not attached to any agency—checked in at several en route to and from the council, and each agent entered them on his rolls. Consequently, the figures for 1875 were particularly high, especially compared with 1876 when the winter wanderers stayed away from the agencies, the summer wanderers left before the army census, and many agency Indians also fled in desperation.[7]

At the Red Cloud Agency, Mackenzie believed "at least half and probably much more than half of the men who belong at this Agency have been away fighting Generals Crook and Terry, indeed that half are still away." He realized that, despite the personal animosity between Sitting Bull and Red Cloud, Red Cloud himself was entirely sympathetic to the hostiles, and was "involved in the troubles of the past year." In fact, most of the missing warriors were from bands under Red Cloud's direct control.[8]

*   *   *

WHILE MACKENZIE WRESTLED WITH THE ADMINISTRATION OF THE agencies, Congress decided to resolve permanently the Black Hills question. On August 15, it approved an ultimatum that the Indians receive no further rations until they relinquished all claim to the unceded lands of Wyoming and Montana, as well as all of the Great Sioux Reservation west of the 103rd meridian, which included the hills. President Grant appointed a treaty commission consisting of George W. Manypenny, former commissioner of Indian affairs; former Dakota Territorial Governor Newton Edmunds; Bishop Henry Whipple, one of the cadre of Christian reformers who had created so much grief in the name of civilization; Albert G. Boone and Jared W. Daniels, former Indian agents; Assistant Attorney General A. S. Gaylord; and Henry C. Bulis.[9]

The commissioners did not go west to negotiate but to dictate, and the terms they presented amounted to an American Versailles.

According to the new terms, an additional million dollars would be attached to the Sioux appropriation bill for rations alone. None of the appropriation could be used to supply any band engaged in hostilities, and no future appropriations would be released until the Sioux Nation first relinquished the territory specified by Congress, granted right-of-way for three roads across the reservation, agreed to receive supplies at the Missouri River, and agreed to a plan to make themselves totally self-supporting.

Apart from these terms, the commissioners demanded a triangle of reservation land east of the 103rd meridian between the forks of the Cheyenne River. In exchange for compliance, the government agreed to provide schools, distribute land to heads of households, construct houses, and provide subsidies for those who farmed.[10]

Moreover, rations would be withheld from those who did not "labor" by white definition of the word, or whose children were not in school.

When stripped of all its finery, the message to the Indians was surrender their lands and adapt to white standards—or starve.

President Grant had misgivings about anyone's ability to farm the Dakota plains. Indeed, it was almost impossible with the technology of the period. Grant believed farming would be more successful in the western Indian Territory of Oklahoma, and instructed the commissioners to offer the unoccupied lands of western Oklahoma to the Sioux tribes in exchange for their Dakota reservation.[11]

The Indians were understandably appalled at the terms. Even the notion of being supplied along the Missouri was unthinkable. They remembered their previous experience with Missouri River agencies from 1868 to 1870, when they had been weakened by the climate, and corrupted by liquor from nearby white settlements. This had been the reason for the relocation of the Spotted Tail Agency to western Nebraska.

As firm a hand as Mackenzie usually was, he also was uneasy about the proposed relocations. While commanding the western Indian Territory during the previous year, he had established that part of Oklahoma was no better suited for farming than the Dakotas. He also believed the timing of the proposal was "very unfortunate in my judgement." He was certain that while the commissioners "seem as a rule very excellent people . . . it unsettles the minds of these Indians."[12]

ELSEWHERE, CROOK'S COMMAND WAS ON THE LAST—AND WORST —leg of its three-month ordeal, heading south toward the Belle Fourche River, where he planned to meet the supply trains from nearby Deadwood and Custer City. The trek was so brutal that within the next fifteen years, scores of its veterans—relatively young men—were either dead or permanently disabled.[13]

They slogged through heavy gumbo clay, softened by merciless rain. Every time a soldier took a step, several pounds of muck stuck to his foot. The mud pulled the shoes off the horses and mules, and balled around their hooves. Mules stumbled and fell, throwing the wounded out of their litters. Lieutenant Luettwitz's amputation kept him in agony. The mood of the men was growing ugly. Dr. Valentine McGillycuddy, one of the surgeons, noticed one "mob of dismounted cavalry, wet to the skin . . . ready for trouble." Only exhaustion prevented a mutiny.

The atmosphere was especially foul among the soldiers of the Fifth Cavalry, who had served with Crook when he won his general's star, and believed he did it with their blood. A popular music hall song was amended on the march by an Irish trooper.

But 'twas out upon the Yellowstone we had the damnedest time.
Faix, we made the trip wid Rosebud George, six months without a
   dime.
Some eighteen hundred miles we went through hunger, mud, and rain.
Wid backs all bare, and rations rare, no chance for grass or grain;
Wid 'bunkies shtarvin' by our side, no rations was the rule;
Shure 'twas ate your boots and saddles, you brutes, but feed the
   packer and the mule.
But you know full well that in your fights no soldier lad was slow.
And it wasn't the packer that won ye a star in the Regular Army, O.[14]

Crazy Horse's warriors still stalked the column, and a rear guard
was deployed to pick up any stragglers. Falling behind meant
death. The guard was almost always busy, for many soldiers were
so worn out they were willing to risk the Indians just for a chance
to rest and would hide behind rocks or bushes, praying they would
be safe. Most were found by the guard, and pushed ahead with
kicks and oaths or, if necessary, bayonets. Despite these efforts, the
Indians killed one soldier who wandered off without permission.[15]

Throughout the march, Crook had sent couriers with dispatches
advising Sheridan of his situation. On September 9, the day of the
Slim Buttes fight, the lieutenant general had ordered Mackenzie to
ship 50,000 pounds of grain and ten days' rations north to Custer
City, "in the shortest time practicable" using any transportation
that became available. Mackenzie responded by sending his entire
transportation department.[16]

The troops reached the Belle Fourche on the afternoon of September 13, and not long after rations began coming in from Deadwood. "The cheer that went up when the herd of beef cattle came
in sight was magnificent," Schuyler wrote. Wagons loaded with
flour and vegetables arrived shortly after, "accompanied by delegation from the towns in the Hills, who came out to welcome the
army that had come through so much hardship to save them from
massacre."[17]

The Indians would have found this statement incredible, for if
anything their situation was worse than that of the soldiers. Although Crook had caught only one small band, his constant
marching kept them on the move, denying them time to lay in their

own supply of provisions for the winter, and driving them deeper and deeper into the rugged mountains. Having themselves burned the grass to deprive the army horses of forage, they now doubled back across the wasteland, and their own ponies began to starve. The people were also growing hungry, for the fires had driven off buffalo and other game. They called it the Black Road, because of the fire-blackened land.

As an early winter set in, the rains gave way to snow, and the ponies, unable to find what little grass was left, began dying. As they died, the Indians ate them. "Wherever we went, the soldiers came to kill us," Black Elk remembered, adding, "and it was all our own country." Many gave up and started toward the agencies to surrender.[18]

BACK AT THE RED CLOUD AGENCY, THE SPECTER OF MILITARY power had finally broken the resistance of the chiefs. Most agreed to cede the Black Hills, although it is doubtful they fully understood the implications of the document to which they affixed their marks. They did, however, understand the meaning of the Missouri River and the Indian Territory and—for the moment at least—flatly refused to give up the remaining part of the Dakota reservation for either place.[19]

Even on federal terms, however, Sheridan was unwilling to accept a negotiated settlement. The army had suffered too much during the past year, and he blamed the civilian arm of the government. In his mind, the only solution was permanent military conquest. For the moment, his primary concern was Red Cloud, who, with his followers, had finally left the vicinity of the agency, and was camped on Chadron Creek about twenty miles northeast of Camp Robinson. On September 21, Crook, Sheridan, and Mackenzie met at Fort Laramie and began drafting plans to make an example of Red Cloud, seize total control of the agencies, and disarm and unhorse all Indians, friendly and otherwise.

First, Mackenzie would demand that Red Cloud return to the immediate jurisdiction of the agencies, an order the three officers knew would be refused. The formalities out of the way, Mackenzie would then draft a letter recommending the Red Cloud and

Spotted Tail Agencies be sealed off, outlying bands (i.e., Red Cloud's) returned by force, and all horses and arms seized. This letter would be favorably endorsed by Crook and Sheridan, thus strengthening the army's hold on the agencies. Elsewhere, the newly rebuilt Seventh Cavalry would carry through the same policy among the Missouri River agencies in General Terry's jurisdiction. The plan was implemented with the desired effect, and Mackenzie prepared to move against Red Cloud.[20]

Eight companies of Fourth and Fifth Cavalry under Mackenzie left Camp Robinson at sundown October 22. About midnight, they met a company of Pawnee scouts under Maj. Frank North just arriving from the Indian Territory, then rode northeast at a steady trot until about 4:00 A.M., when they neared Chadron Creek. There were two camps, one under Red Cloud and the other under the Brulé chiefs, Red Leaf and Swift Bear. Mackenzie encircled Red Cloud's camp, while Maj. George A. Gordon secured the Brulé camp.

At dawn, the Indians were notified that they were surrounded and must surrender immediately. The women and children tried to escape, but were forced back by the line of troops. Other soldiers went through and disarmed the warriors. The women were ordered to pick a sufficient number of ponies to pack their gear, take down and pack the tipis, and prepare to return to the agency. At first they refused, but when the soldiers set fire to several tipis, they hurried to comply.[21]

Mackenzie's confrontation with Red Cloud was recounted by Capt. Frederick Mears to correspondent Joe Wasson, who published it in the *Alta California:*

> For the first time in the life of Red Cloud, he heard in plain and firm language, from General Mackenzie . . . what was expected of him in the matter of turning over the hostiles to the General, if any of them attempted to come in to the Agency and be peaceful for the Winter. . . . Never in Red Cloud's life had he ever been talked to by a white man, as he was in this interview, and never in his life was he ever lifted from his lofty breech-clouted pedestal and made to feel that he stood in the presence of his superior. . . .[22]

This was a chauvinistic account, but after a summer of humiliation and defeat an army officer had faced down the man who planned the destruction of Fetterman in 1866, forced the government to his terms in 1868, and, more than any other Lakota for a longer period of time, had symbolized Indian resistance. The soldiers believed they had a right to crow. As the Cheyenne *Leader* commented, "This will put a new phase on affairs here, and we shall know hereafter who are friendly and who are hostile."[23]

That night, Red Cloud and Red Leaf's bands were disarmed. Crook, however, disobeyed Sheridan's order to disarm all agency Indians, allowing the remainder to keep their weapons and ponies. He explained:

> The other bands . . . here have been loyal to us, and to have disarmed them with the others, would simply have arrayed the white man against the Indian and placed the loyal and disloyal on the same footing.

Allowing the loyal bands to remain armed was an act of faith that Crook believed did more to ensure their support than any government pledges. "This good effect was at once manifested in the desire of warriors from these bands to enlist, and enlistments have since been going on . . . in large numbers." Crook felt part of the summer campaign's failure was lack of Indian scouts who thoroughly knew the country in which the troops would operate. By enlisting agency Lakotas, he would have an edge in the winter campaign that he was now planning.

Sheridan, who distrusted all Indians, was furious, and wrote across the bottom of Crook's report that the action was "disapproved." But Chicago was a long way from the agencies and, presented with a fait accompli, there was little he could do but fume.[24]

The roundup and disarmament of the two bands was witnessed by several members of the peace commission, who had returned intent on taking a delegation to inspect the Indian Territory; Sheridan had insisted, despite the opposition of the chiefs. Because of Red Cloud's influence, the commissioners expected him to accompany the delegation but were curtly told by the military authorities they could not communicate with the chief at the present time.

The rapidly developing events placed Spotted Tail in an uncomfortable position. General Crook, now at the Red Cloud Agency, called a council of chiefs, and rudely and unequivocally told them what the government expected. Red Cloud was deposed as head chief of the two agencies, and replaced by Spotted Tail, who no doubt enjoyed that part of the talk since the two chiefs intensely disliked each other. On the other hand, Spotted Tail now had to lead the delegation visiting the Indian Territory. This was one of the hardest tasks of his life, since the mere mention of the Territory had angered him in the initial negotiations. Bowing to the inevitable, however, and prepared to do whatever necessary to ease the military heel on his people, Spotted Tail gathered up the other chiefs and prepared for the trip south, although he stipulated he would say or do nothing that might be construed as agreeing to resettlement.[25]

26

"The Beginning of the End"

THE HOSTILE INDIANS WERE STILL ON THE MOVE IN THE DEPART-
ment of Dakota where, despite the severe climate, Nelson Miles
was determined to march against them. Field operations had de-
volved on Miles because Terry, returning to his camp on Glendive
Creek in eastern Montana, had disbanded the Montana and
Dakota Columns on September 5, ordering Gibbon's troops back
to their posts. Terry himself departed for St. Paul.[1]

Viewing efforts so far as a failure, Miles wrote his wife:

> Terry means well enough . . . but he has had little experience and is
> too much under the influence of those slow inefficient men like Gib-
> bon to reap good results. This business to be successful should be
> conducted on sound military principles first, and then with great en-
> ergy and persistency.[2]

Miles had energy and persistency. Called "Bear Coat" by the Indians because of his winter dress, Nelson Appleton Miles was one
of the most controversial soldiers ever produced by the United
States Army. At his best, he was a brilliant, aggressive field commander; at worst, he was a martinet. Married to Sherman's niece,
he used this connection shamelessly, though not always success-

fully. Despite the family tie, however, Miles was essentially self-made and resented West Pointers. He and Mackenzie loathed each other, and in the race for promotion in the very limited ranks of the nineteenth-century army, an intense rivalry developed that Sherman often manipulated to get maximum performance from both men.

Born in 1839 on a farm near Westminster, Massachusetts, Miles was a clerk in Boston when the Civil War broke out. Using borrowed money, he outfitted a company of volunteer infantry and was commissioned a second lieutenant. At the end of the war, he was brevet major general. In 1869, he was named colonel of the Fifth Infantry and sent to Kansas, distinguishing himself in the Red River War. That conflict demonstrated Miles's considerable abilities as an Indian fighter and led to his transfer to Terry's department.[3]

Miles's forces, designated the Yellowstone Command, included the entire Fifth Infantry, along with six companies of the Twenty-second Infantry under Lt. Col. Elwell S. Otis—almost 800 men. His mission was to occupy the Yellowstone Valley for the winter, establishing military posts at the junction of the Tongue and Yellowstone Rivers, and in the country west of the Black Hills. These guarded all crossings on the 210-mile stretch of the Yellowstone between the Powder and the Tongue, while steamers patrolled the river itself, blocking possible Indian movement toward the north.[4]

Not content, however, with building forts and blocking routes to the north, Miles intended to force the issue with the Indians.

> My opinion was that the only way to make the country tenable for us was to render it untenable for the Indians. . . . I was satisfied that if the Indians could live in that country in skin tents in winter, even though sheltered by favorable bluffs and locations and not required to move, that we, with all our better appliances could be so equipped as to not only exist in tents, but also to move under all circumstances.

After the abortive Crook-Reynolds expedition the previous March, Terry had misgivings about Miles's plan for a winter campaign. Bypassing him as well as Sheridan, Miles pressured Sherman directly for Sibley tents, artillery, and cavalry.[5]

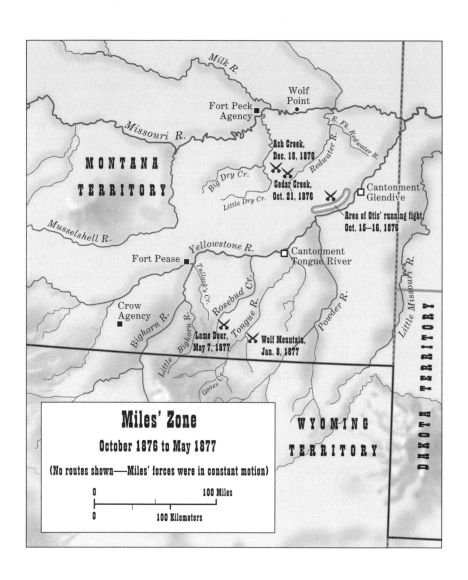

Milk R.

Wolf
Point

Fort Peck
Agency

E. Fk. Redwater R.

Ash Creek,
Dec. 18, 1876

MONTANA

Big Dry Cr.

Redwater R.

TERRITORY

Little Dry Cr.

Cedar Creek,
Oct. 21, 1876

Cantonment
Glendive

Missouri R.

Area of Otis' running fight,
Oct. 15–16, 1876

Musselshell R.

Yellowstone R.

Fort Pease

Cantonment
Tongue River

Tullock's Cr.

Crow
Agency

Bighorn R.

Rosebud Cr.

Tongue R.

Powder R.

Little Missouri R.

Little Bighorn R.

Lame Deer,
May 7, 1877

Wolf Mountain,
Jan. 8, 1877

DAKOTA TERRITORY

Goose Cr.

Miles' Zone

October 1876 to May 1877

(No routes shown—Miles' forces were in constant motion)

WYOMING
TERRITORY

0   100 Miles

0   100 Kilometers

The water level in the Yellowstone, meanwhile, had fallen, ending steamer traffic west of Terry's depot at Glendive Creek until spring. As head of navigation and the nearest depot to the new cantonment on the Tongue River, Glendive was developed into a major post, with a garrison of about 16 officers and 220 enlisted men under Colonel Otis. These troops provided escort for about three supply trains per month for the Tongue River Cantonment, to the southwest along a twisting 140-mile road.[6]

IN SITTING BULL'S CAMP, NOW NEAR THE YELLOWSTONE IN EASTern Montana, there was a curious newcomer, a half-breed named Johnny Bruguier, whom the Indians called "Big Leggins" because of the large cowboy chaps he wore. Bruguier was born in 1849 to Theophile Bruguier, a prosperous merchant and one of the first settlers of Sioux City, Iowa. Johnny was one of thirteen children from the elder Bruguier's polygamous marriage to two Santee sisters. The seven boys of the group were educated in the College of the Christian Brothers in St. Louis. After their mothers died, however, Theophile Bruguier married a white woman who apparently did not get along with her stepchildren, and they eventually went to live with their Indian relatives.[7]

Johnny served as an army scout and interpreter, and once escorted a delegation of chiefs to Washington. But by the time he rode into Sitting Bull's camp, in the autumn of 1876, he was fleeing a murder charge at the Standing Rock Agency. Billy Bruguier, Johnny's younger brother, had gotten into a drunken brawl with an agency employee named William McGee; Johnny intervened, clubbing McGee so hard that he died the next day.

Despite Johnny Bruguier's Indian features, self-assurance, and ability to speak a Siouan dialect, his white clothes and manner prompted Sitting Bull's people to suspect he was an army spy. Nevertheless, Sitting Bull welcomed him, and he became a sort of clerk, making himself useful in dealings with the soldiers during the coming weeks.[8]

*   *   *

MILES HAD SPIES AMONG AGENCY INDIANS WHO DEALT WITH THE hostiles, and therefore was kept aware of their activities. He was en route from Camp Glendive to Tongue River Cantonment with a thirty-man escort October 10, when he was overtaken by a courier who said the hostile bands had separated and Sitting Bull was heading north with a large band of Hunkpapas, Sans Arcs, and Miniconjous. They were expected to reach the Yellowstone between the mouth of the Tongue and Glendive Creek in about three days.[9]

The information, however, was older than Miles realized, for despite his patrols the Hunkpapas had forded the Yellowstone the same day, putting themselves directly in his path. At midnight, a party of about twenty or thirty young warriors raided his camp for horses, but were driven off by the guards. Ordering a forced march, Miles arrived safely at the Tongue River Cantonment.

Early the next morning, the Indians attacked the camp of a west-bound train of ninety-four wagons from Glendive, bound for the Tongue Cantonment, under command of Capt. C. W. Miner. They captured forty-seven mules, forcing the train back to Glendive.[10] On October 14, the train started out again. It now comprised eighty-six wagons driven by soldiers because the frightened civilian teamsters refused to go. Together with the military escort, there were 11 officers and 185 infantrymen armed with long-range rifles and Gatling guns, and commanded by Colonel Otis.

Otis camped twelve miles out from Glendive the first night, during which sentries exchanged shots with Indian snipers. The next morning he formed the wagons into four lines surrounded by infantry. The train traveled three miles to Spring Creek, where Indians jumped two advance riders, chasing them back to the wagons. Otis sent one company ahead to drive off the warriors while the train crossed the creek and ascended a plateau.

As the wagons traversed the plateau, more Indians arrived but stayed well ahead until the troops reached the deep ravine of Clear Creek. Entering the ravine, Otis saw more than 200 warriors on a bluff to the left, and sent two companies up the heights to drive them away, while he took on water for soldiers and livestock at Clear Creek. After the train crossed the creek, it began moving up the ravine on the opposite side to the bluffs beyond.

Here the Indians tried to block the train again, but after heavy fighting the infantrymen pushed out a thousand yards and forced the Lakotas to back away so the wagons could keep moving.[11]

The Hunkpapa White Bull rode toward the wagons, trusting in the luck that had carried him unscathed through so many fights this year, and hoping to count coups before retreating. Suddenly, a bullet struck him in the upper left arm, breaking the bone. The impact of the heavy .45-caliber rifle slug knocked him senseless and he swayed on his horse. Two friends took hold of him and carried him back to camp.

The withdrawing Indians set fire to the grass. The line of wagons closed into a tight formation, surrounded by infantry, and passed through the flames, halting from time to time while the soldiers forced the Indians away from the road ahead.[12]

By now it was late afternoon and, after gaining several more miles, Otis ordered a halt on high ground where he could see in all directions. The wagons were corralled and surrounded by rifle pits. After a couple of hours of sniping, the Indians broke off for the night.

The Indians continued their sniping the next morning but made no further effort to attack the wagons. A short time after the march got under way, the soldiers saw a lone Indian ahead, waving a piece of white cloth. He put it on a stake in the ground, then rode off. Scout Robert Jackson retrieved the cloth, which proved to be a note written by Johnny Bruguier on behalf of Sitting Bull. It stated:

> YELLOWSTONE
> I want to know what you are doing travelling on this road. You scare all the buffalo away. I want to hunt in this place. I want you to turn back from here. If you don't I will fight you again. I want you to leave what you have got here, and turn back from here.
> I am your friend,
> Sitting Bull
> [P.S.] I mean [leave] all the rations you have and some powder. Wish you would write as soon as you can.[13]

Otis sent Jackson with a reply that he would take the train through despite all the Indians on earth, and that if Sitting Bull wanted a fight, Otis "would be glad to accommodate him at any time and on any terms."[14]

Sitting Bull was now in an embarrassing position. His chiefs were tired of fighting and were ready to parley. They were encouraged by Bear's Face and Long Feather, couriers from the Standing Rock Agency, who brought a message from Lt. Col. William Carlin, commanding officer of the agency, urging surrender. While the chiefs argued, the warriors opened fire once more on the wagon train, but were held off by skirmishers. When the shooting died down, Bear's Face and Long Feather rode toward the train under a flag of truce and, on behalf of the chiefs, asked for a parley. Otis agreed to see them inside the army lines.

The chiefs admitted to Otis that they did not want war, but repeated Sitting Bull's assertion that the military presence was driving off the buffalo. They again demanded the rations and ammunition sought in the note.

Otis replied he did not have the authority to agree to anything. On the other hand, if they would withdraw southwest to the Tongue, he would vouch for their safety there. As a pledge of good faith, he ordered 150 pounds of hardtack and two sides of bacon left on the road for the Indians to collect. They then allowed him to proceed unmolested.[15]

THE MEETING WITH THE CHIEFS OCCURRED ON OCTOBER 16, THE day the original train was supposed to arrive at the Tongue River Cantonment. But the initial attack against Miner, the reorganization at Camp Glendive, and the subsequent fighting under Otis put it substantially behind schedule. Concerned, Colonel Miles started east up the Glendive road to see what was wrong. His command, which left Tongue River on the afternoon of October 17, consisted of 449 officers and soldiers, 10 civilians, and 2 Indian scouts; it was the first time in eighteen years that the Fifth Infantry had operated as a complete unit.

Among the civilians was Luther "Yellowstone" Kelly, one of the most experienced frontiersmen in the region. Now aware that the Hunkpapas were north of the Yellowstone, Miles hoped to intercept them as well as ascertain the whereabouts of the train, and sent Kelly with five other scouts to look for the Indian camps.[16]

The troops, meanwhile, "marched all day through . . . dust and sand," Trumpeter Edwin M. Brown recalled. "We stopped at night, made a cup of coffee and once more resumed the march; marched all night long."[17]

The next afternoon, Miles's exhausted troopers met the train some forty-four miles from Tongue River. The two groups camped together that night, and the next morning Miles started his foot-sore infantrymen after the Indians. About 11:00 A.M., October 21, he overtook them, and was met by Bear's Face and Long Feather, the two couriers from Standing Rock, who asked for parley. Agreeing to meet Sitting Bull between the lines, Miles said he would be escorted by one officer and five troopers, and Sitting Bull could bring the same number of warriors.[18]

Sitting Bull left his camp at the head of 200 warriors. When they saw the troops, they halted. Long Feather unfurled a white flag and galloped over to Miles's line, while a soldier rode over to the Indians. The trooper shook hands with the chief and said, "Sitting Bull, the soldier chief wants to talk to you."

"All right," Sitting Bull replied. "Tell him to come ahead and talk to me if he wants to."[19]

The trooper returned with the message and the two leaders, each with six of his own men, met between the two lines, dismounted, and arranged themselves on a buffalo robe provided by the Indians. Bruguier stood by to translate.

Studying Sitting Bull, Miles noted:

He was a man of few words and cautious in his expressions, evidently thinking twice before speaking. He was very deliberate in his movements and somewhat reserved in his manner. At first he was courteous, but evidently void of any genuine respect for the white race. Although the feeling was disguised, his manner indicated his animosity toward those whom he had to meet. During the conversation his manner was civil and to some extent one of calm repose.[20]

According to Miles, Sitting Bull said he wanted "to hunt buffalo, to trade, (particularly for ammunition) and agreed that the Indians would not fire on the soldiers if they were not disturbed."[21]

Miles replied

that we were out to bring him and his Indians in, and that we did
not wish to continue the war against them, but that if they forced
the war it would end, as all Indian wars had ended and must end,
by their putting themselves under the authorities at Washington. He
was told that he could not be allowed to roam over the country,
sending out war parties to devastate the settlements. He claimed
that the country belonged to the Indians and not to the white men,
and declared that he had nothing to do with the white men and
wanted them to leave that country entirely to the Indians. He said
that the white man never lived who loved an Indian, and that no
true Indian ever lived that did not hate the white man. He declared
that God Almighty made him an Indian and did not make him an
agency Indian either, and he did not intend to be one.

To shake Sitting Bull's confidence, Miles told him he knew the
chief's plans.

"Where am I going?" Sitting Bull asked.

"You intend to remain here three days, and then move to the Big
Dry and hunt buffaloes."

The accuracy of the colonel's information alarmed Sitting Bull,
and Miles remembered, "His jaws were closed tightly; his lips were
compressed, and you could see his eyes glistening with the fire of
savage hatred."[22]

Nothing was accomplished, but each man returned to his own
lines with a tacit agreement to meet again the next day. Miles's
troops withdrew eight miles to Cedar Creek, where they could intercept any attempt by the Indians to break for the north. In the Indian camp that night, it was decided to abide by whatever
agreement emerged between Miles and Sitting Bull.

Experience had taught Miles that the Indians would probably
use the time to move their families out. He posted soldiers to watch
the camp, and resolved to advance on them early the next morning.[23]

His prediction was confirmed when, arriving back at the parley
ground, the soldiers could see the Indian noncombatants abandoning their camp and moving off in the distance. On the bluffs di-

rectly in front was Sitting Bull with a line of warriors. The two leaders met again, and Sitting Bull, now accompanied by a group of Sans Arc and Miniconjou leaders, told Miles he would accept nothing less than a complete white withdrawal from the entire region, excepting only trading posts. The colonel replied that all Indians were required to submit to the government and laws of the United States. If they refused, he said the war would continue until one side or the other was beaten. Both men grew angry, but Miles, the more sophisticated of the two, orchestrated his anger toward Sitting Bull alone. The Miniconjou and Sans Arc chiefs were wavering, and he wanted to give the impression that the dispute was a personal matter between him and Sitting Bull. Finally, he informed them the truce would remain in force until Sitting Bull returned to his camp, but if the Indians had not accepted the terms within fifteen minutes, the soldiers would open fire. The Indians withdrew, accompanied by Johnny Bruguier, whose presence had by now aroused Miles's interest.[24]

As the warriors moved back, some of them set fire to the prairie grass. Miles sent one of the scouts out to stop them. The scout exchanged shots with the Indians, and the soldiers started forward while the Indians retreated through the burning grass. "The opera had commenced," Brown wrote, "bullets whistled lively overhead, without doing much material damage."[25]

Still weak from his wound, White Bull nevertheless shouted, "Come on, let's go and rub them out." Sitting Bull grabbed his bridle, saying, "It is only six days since your arm was broken. You are not fit to fight." He sent White Bull back to the rear, with orders for his father to keep an eye on him.[26]

The ground in front of the soldiers was a plain, leading up to a succession of hills and ridges, broken by the usual ravines. The Indians moved back into the ravines, hoping to catch the soldiers there, but instead, the infantrymen fanned out across the plain, cutting around the edge of the broken ground to outflank the warriors.

Unable to lure the soldiers into the ravines, the Indians counterattacked and forced the troops into a square. Now, in the classic infantry formation, they moved ahead, five paces at a time, and there was nothing the Indians could do to break them. A Rodman rifled cannon was brought up to a knoll, which gave it a commanding position, and the gunners opened fire, scattering the Indians as much by its noise as by its projectiles. The soldiers pressed the warriors along the broad plain, which offered few places to hide.[27]

"All that day we fought them through fire and smoke which nearly suffocated us," Brown wrote. Yellowstone Kelly and his men, arriving from their scout in the middle of the fight, were almost shot by their own people who mistook them for Indians through the smoke. Finally the hostiles fell back, and the soldiers went into camp in the abandoned village, although in the distance the troops could see the dancing and shouting warriors silhouetted by the burning grass, and sniping between individual Indians and sentries continued all night.[28]

In camp, Miles questioned Kelly extensively about the terrain, distances, and probable route of the fleeing Indians. Kelly was impressed that "while all around the ground was covered with sleeping bodies the commander was awake and taking measures for the coming day's work."[29]

The pursuit continued the next day. The Miniconjous and Sans Arcs were growing disillusioned, and Sitting Bull, realizing he no longer had unanimous support among the chiefs, broke away. With Gall, Pretty Bear, and several other leading Hunkpapas, he took about 400 people and headed north toward the Missouri, hoping ultimately to take refuge in Canada. Since they would probably have to fight their way north, Sitting Bull discouraged his wounded nephew, White Bull, from coming along. White Bull stayed with the main band, which retreated south toward the Yellowstone.

Although Miles pursued the main band southeast some forty-two miles, there was little his infantry could do to force another fight. He was frustrated by lack of cavalry, which he blamed on the wastage of horses and men during Crook's summer campaign. The foot soldiers could stay on the heels of the Indians, but could not move fast enough to maneuver into position for battle.[30]

Nevertheless, the fight and ensuing chase wore down the Indians. According to Miles, they lost "a few of their warriors and a large amount of property both in their camp and on their retreat, including their horses, mules and ponies, which fell into our hands."[31]

Miles reached the Yellowstone late October 23 to find the Indians had already forded and were camped on the south side, leaving a trail of lodgepoles and dead and crippled ponies. Kelly found a good ford, and had reported back to the command when an Indian appeared on the other side with a flag of truce and asked for a parley.[32] In the ensuing conference, four chiefs and one leading warrior turned themselves in as hostages against the surrender of their people. These five represented over 2,000 Miniconjous and Sans Arcs attached to Sitting Bull's band. Miles told them their people could continue unmolested to the Cheyenne Agency where they would surrender, "there to remain at peace subject to the orders of the government."

Miles believed that magnanimous treatment of these Indians might even prompt Sitting Bull to surrender. Writing Terry, he said:

> What is to be accomplished will depend upon the manner in which these chiefs are treated, and the reception their people receive on their arrival. . . . They are very suspicious and of course afraid that some terrible punishment will be inflicted upon them. . . . I believe Sitting Bull would be glad to make peace, at least for a time; but he is afraid he has committed an unpardonable offense.

Regardless of what Sitting Bull did, however, Miles considered the surrender of the Miniconjous and Sans Arcs "the beginning of the end."[33]

For White Bull, who was part of the surrendered band, it was indeed the end. Bracing himself to endure the unendurable, he prepared to face life as an agency Indian.[34]

27

The Noose Tightens

DESPITE HIS PERSONAL ANIMOSITY TOWARD MILES, SHERMAN WAS pleased with the outcome so far. He wired Sheridan:

> I congratulate you and all concerned on the prospect of closing this Sioux war at this critical period. Genl. Miles has displayed his usual earnestness & energy and I hope he will crown his success by capturing or killing Sitting Bull and his remnant of outlaws.[1]

Sherman had every reason to believe that the war was entering its final stages. For more than three months, bands of Indians from throughout the region had been moving to the agencies. Already the population at the Standing Rock Agency had doubled, from 2,000 to 4,000. Trying to assess the increase, Colonel Carlin, military commander at the agency, wrote:

> While it is extremely difficult to decide where the additional two thousand have been, it is safe to say that half the number were with the hostiles till recently. . . .
>
> It is my intention to visit the Blackfeet and Uncpapa [sic] camp in a short time and arrest all that cannot satisfactorily account for their absence.[2]

Carlin also reported that the chiefs Kill Eagle and Little Wound surrendered with 140 people, all arms and ammunition, and about a hundred ponies. Passing this information on to army headquarters in Washington, Sheridan pointed out this group included twenty-nine men "all of whom were in the fight on the Little Big Horn."[3]

AFTER BREAKING AWAY FROM THE MAIN GROUP THAT HAD FOUGHT Miles, Sitting Bull sent runners to the Fort Peck Agency about eighty miles to the northwest, saying he planned to come in for food and ammunition, and did not intend to make trouble. Agent Thomas J. Mitchell replied that no ammunition would be issued. Nevertheless, Sitting Bull continued on toward Fort Peck, eventually setting up his camp of about thirty lodges on Big Dry Creek, twenty-five miles south of the agency.

On October 31, another 125 lodges of Hunkpapas affiliated with Sitting Bull's band reported to Fort Peck, telling Mitchell their supplies of food and ammunition were exhausted and they wanted peace. Sitting Bull, they said, was awaiting word of the outcome of their council with the agent. Mitchell ordered them to surrender all arms and government property taken in battle with the troops, and await further instructions from his superiors. Grudgingly, the Indians agreed. That evening, however, when a runner brought word that a steamer loaded with troops was coming up the Missouri River toward the agency, many of the newly surrendered Hunkpapas panicked and fled to the Big Dry, swelling Sitting Bull's meager camp to more than a hundred lodges.[4]

The steamer, which docked at Fort Peck the next morning, carried Col. William B. Hazen and 140 troops from Fort Buford, Dakota Territory, with rations and forage for Miles, who was en route from the Tongue River Cantonment. After sending the hostage chiefs with an escort to the Cheyenne Agency, Miles had returned to Tongue River, where he reorganized his command and headed north with 435 infantrymen in pursuit of Sitting Bull. He was following the trail toward the Big Dry when a blizzard obliterated all traces. Forced now to guess at the direction the Indians might take, he continued north until he crossed the Missouri, then turned west, reconnoitering nearly a hundred miles to the mouth of the Musselshell River, known to be a favorite hunting ground.

Sitting Bull, however, had kept a close eye on Miles and, as the troops approached the Big Dry, moved his camp east toward the forks of the Red Water River, south of its confluence with the Missouri. Thus, after losing the trail in the snow, Miles had struck out in the opposite direction from his quarry. The problem was compounded when a freakish spell of warmer weather thawed the Missouri, trapping the soldiers on the north bank, while Sitting Bull remained south on the mouth of the Red Water. Finally, Miles gave up his pursuit and turned east toward Fort Peck, to rendezvous with Hazen and make new plans.[5]

WHILE MILES WAS TRYING TO DEAL WITH SITTING BULL, CROOK prepared for a new expedition against Crazy Horse, who he believed was camped in northern Wyoming. After Miles's initial success in obtaining the surrender of the Sans Arcs and Miniconjous, Sherman had high hopes, telling Sheridan:

> Should Gen. Crook be as successful with Crazy Horse & if we could collect all the Sioux on the Missouri River as near Fort Randall [eastern South Dakota] as possible, disarmed and dismounted, it would reduce itself to a simple question of feeding them till they learn to raise some food for themselves. Meantime miners and settlers will fill up [the country] north of [Fort] Laramie and [illegible] the Black Hills so that these troublesome Indians would gradually become [peaceful] like those in Minnesota.[6]

Informants at the Red Cloud Agency advised Crook "that many of the Indians from that Agency had been led to leave there by the reported appearance of large herds of buffalo on the Rosebud and Powder Rivers," and were with Sitting Bull and Crazy Horse in that country. Unaware that Sitting Bull was already on the Missouri, Crook began assembling his forces at Forts Laramie and Fetterman, hoping to attack both chiefs.[7]

Mackenzie arrived at Fort Laramie on November 4, at the head of twenty companies of cavalry, infantry, and artillery and almost

160 Indian scouts from the agencies. He was at the peak of his powers and Bourke noted he "was looked upon by the whole army as the embodiment of courage, skill and dash in an eminent degree," although he added Mackenzie also was "impetuous, headstrong, perhaps a trifle rash. . . ."[8]

The same day, Crook organized the Powder River Expedition, naming Mackenzie as commander of the cavalry, consisting of one company from the Second Cavalry, two from the Third, six from the Fourth, and two from the Fifth. Lt. Col. Richard Irving Dodge, Twenty-third Infantry, was placed in charge of the infantry and artillery battalions, with four companies of Fourth Artillery, five companies of Ninth Infantry, two companies of Fourteenth Infantry, and three companies of Twenty-third Infantry.[9]

Dodge was fifty, with almost thirty years of experience on the western frontier. Since the close of the Civil War, most of his career had been spent in command positions. Like Bourke, he was a keen observer of people and events, and was especially fascinated by the Indians. But his interests went beyond anthropology into natural history, and his scientific paper on the buffalo is still a definitive work. Although he wrote several books about the West, his greatest literary contribution to the Powder River Expedition was his diary. Unawed by Crook's rank or Mackenzie's reputation, he candidly recorded events as they occurred and people as he saw them.

On November 5, Crook left Fort Laramie for Fort Fetterman, arriving two days later. At Fetterman, he called a council with the Indian scouts to settle the conditions of their participation. Most of the discussion dealt with Indian scouting methods, and assurances that they would get their fair share of horses and ammunition. The Lakota scouts, however, were also concerned about postwar annuities and an invitation to Washington to negotiate reservations and compensation.

Crook bluntly told the Indians their traditional way of life was rapidly disappearing, and white rule and white civilization were inevitable. He added the government would continue to back the authority of the scouts when the army discharged them and they returned to their reservations. Nevertheless, Crook advised them not to depend on government annuities, but become self-supporting stockmen. Then, he said, they would not have to wait for an invitation to Washington, but would have the financial resources to travel wherever they pleased.[10]

Mackenzie arrived at Fetterman on November 9, and Dodge brought the last of the infantry a day later. Bourke commented:

> The present expedition impresses me as the best equipped and best officered of any with which I have ever served; the experience of the past summer has opened the eyes of the National Legislature to the urgency of the situation and consequently appropriations for supplies have been awarded on a scale of unusual liberality. The Cavalry companies are stronger than they have been since the [Civil] War, and the personnel of all recruits of a superior standard.[11]

Determined not to repeat the privations of the past, Crook procured heavy winter gear for the troops. "We are so well fitted out that cold weather will be rather welcome than otherwise, as it makes the chances of success much greater," Bourke commented. "We begin to fear that Crazy Horse may surrender without a blow; a fight is desirable to atone and compensate for our trials, hardships and dangers for more than eight months."[12]

The anticipation was dampened by news from the East. Taking advantage of the scandals in the Republican administration, the Democrats mounted a hard-fought campaign to put Samuel Tilden in the White House, against Republican nominee Rutherford Hayes. With Reconstruction in the South drawing to a close, both sides claimed the swing states of Louisiana, North and South Carolina, and Florida. Florida appeared on the verge of bloodshed, and Gen. Christopher C. Augur, commanding the Department of the South, had been sent there with troops. Reports reaching Fort Fetterman caused apprehension among the officers that the army might be drawn away from the West to once again fight in the South.[13]

ON NOVEMBER 14, CROOK STARTED HIS COMMAND NORTH. ALL together, the expedition consisted of 61 officers, 1,436 enlisted men, 367 Indian scouts, 400 pack mules attended by 65 packers,

168 wagons, and 7 ambulances. As Sheridan intended one of his new posts to be in the Department of the Platte, Crook had abandoned his depot at old Fort Reno, opting instead to establish it some forty miles to the northwest, by the present site of Buffalo, Wyoming. From this point, which he designated Cantonment Reno (later Fort McKinney), he could strike in any of several directions, following the broad north-south valley between the Bighorn Mountains and the Black Hills.

Dodge enjoyed the march.

> It was a beautiful and exhilarating sight—the long lines of Cavalry, Artillery, Infantry, Indians, pack mules and wagons. . . . The Command is now extended for three miles along the valley—and makes a brave show. I have never seen so large and well fitted a Command in Indian Warfare.[14]

He was, however, beginning to take an intense disliking to Crook.

> General Crook passes for a Sybarite—who utterly condemns anything like luxury or even comfort—yet he has the most luxurious surroundings considering the necessity for short allowance that I have ever seen taken to the field by a general officer.[15]

A far more serious morale problem was what both officers and men felt was undue consideration for Indian scouts and mules. The Horse Meat March of September had made a profound psychological impression on Crook. Never again would he allow himself to run so short on supplies. Yet it now seemed he spent too much time and attention on the civilian packers and mules, and not enough on the soldiers who would do the actual fighting.

"The Cavalry and Infantry are nobodies," Dodge complained. "The Indians and pack mules have all the good places. He scarcely treats McKenzie [sic] and I decently, but he will spend hours chatting pleasantly with an Indian or a dirty scout."

Dodge sympathized with the ostracized correspondent Davenport of the *New York Herald*. "He stated what he saw and is cordially hated for it," Dodge wrote.[16]

A snowstorm blew in on November 17, with a north wind hitting the soldiers in the faces until midmorning. But, "as we marched along, it grew quite fine," James McClellan, a Third Cavalry sergeant, noted in his diary. "As we reached the top of the divide[,] the Powder River Valley and the Big Horn Mountains then burst on our view in all their splendor. The mountains all clad in snow."

They marched twenty miles that day, going into camp only fifteen miles short of Cantonment Reno. The Texans Tom Cosgrove and Bob Eckles arrived with three Shoshones from the hundred assembled at Reno, and told Crook almost all the hostile trails were running up toward the sources of the Crazy Woman and Tongue, and Clear Creek, a tributary of the Powder. The next day, the command reached Reno after a four-hour march.[17]

Over the next few days, Crook held another council with the Indian scouts, to coordinate activities among the various tribes enlisted, many of whom had only recently fought each other. The soldiers spent the time drilling and preparing for the coming expedition. Somehow, whiskey became available, and both soldiers and Indians got drunk. One intoxicated recruit wandered off into the cold night. He was found the next morning, suffering from exposure and died shortly after being taken to the post hospital. Bourke, always ready to cover for General Crook, said the whiskey was sold by "a citizen" whose cart and trade goods were confiscated, and whose liquor barrels were destroyed. Dodge, on the other hand, said the whiskey was sold by the post trader.

> I asked General Crook to shut up the Trading Store, but he being a personal friend (it is said they are partners in a sheep ranch in Oregon) of the trader, refused, and said I could regulate it.

Since Dodge could only regulate infantry and artillery, but had no authority over cavalry, teamsters, Indians, or miscellaneous citizens and personnel, he finally complained to Capt. Edwin Pollock, commander of Cantonment Reno, who shut the trader's store.[18]

Based on reports of miners and other civilians arriving at Cantonment Reno, Crook telegraphed Sheridan:

> Indications are that there has been a considerable body of the hostiles concentrating on the West side of the Big Horn Mountains

during the past month; [Lakota and Arapaho] scouts are expected back to-day or to-morrow with definite information [and] as soon as that arrives we shall move with all possible dispatch.[19]

On November 21, the scouts returned to camp with a prisoner, a young Cheyenne named Beaver Dam. Leaving their military trappings at Reno, they had ridden some fifty miles west to Clear Creek and were setting up camp when Beaver Dam happened along and asked where they were going. They told him they were a war party on their way to fight the Shoshones. Beaver Dam was in a chatty mood, and the scouts encouraged him to talk. According to Bourke:

> They readily deluded the young hostile who gave them all the news of the day, where the different villages were and how many in each. By the time he had finished, half a dozen revolvers were cocked and pointed and he [was] told to surrender his guns. This he did without a word, but showed much amazement when the strangers told him they were . . . soldiers.[20]

After interrogating Beaver Dam, Crook wired Sheridan:

> Cheyennes have crossed over to the other side of the Big Horn Mountains . . . Crazy Horse and his band are encamped on the Rosebud near where we had the fight with them last summer. We start out after his band tomorrow morning.[21]

The command broke camp and marched out of Reno at 6:20 A.M., November 22, cutting across country and marching more than twenty-five miles north to the banks of the Crazy Woman. Crazy Horse's village was estimated to be a hundred miles beyond, and Crook decided to take the wagons no farther. Pack mules would carry ten days' rations. Realizing the implications of his talk, Beaver Dam was now contradicting himself, saying he had lied about the location of Crazy Horse's camp. "If he did," Dodge remarked, "Crook will hang him."

Early the next morning, as tents were being struck and the camp prepared to move, the pickets spotted an Indian waving a white flag from the top of a hill. He proved to be Sitting Bear, a Cheyenne whom Mackenzie had sent from the Red Cloud Agency to deliver a surrender ultimatum to the hostiles.

Sitting Bear related Miles's fight with Sitting Bull, and reported Crazy Horse was on the Rosebud, exactly where Beaver Dam had said he was. Then came the bad news. Sitting Bear had also encountered Beaver Dam's people, a camp of five lodges. Alarmed when he failed to return, they had investigated, discovered the soldiers, and were now en route to warn Crazy Horse.[22]

"This then changed my plan," Crook wrote, "and I determined to attack the Cheyenne village first and with this view sent out Col. MacKenzie's [sic] 4th Cavalry, with the cavalry of the command and the Indian allies."[23]

The Cheyenne village was southwest, on the Red Fork of the Powder River. Mackenzie started for it at noon November 23, with the Indian scouts, the Cheyenne prisoner Beaver Dam, and all but one company of the cavalry. The infantrymen were delighted at the thought of remaining in camp while the cavalry made a forced march through the snow and fought Indians. The camp was warm, since a vein of coal had been found nearby, although Dodge commented it looked "like Pittsburg [sic]."[24]

Meanwhile, the cavalry pushed twelve miles south through the valley of the Crazy Woman along the eastern base of the Bighorn Mountains, before going into camp in a concealed spot among the bluffs, with water and abundant grass, which the terrain had sheltered from the snow. Nevertheless the night was cold, and the men had no tents. "The ground was very wet and uncomfortable for all hands and not much wood for to make fires," Sergeant McClellan remarked.[25]

The column continued in the same general direction the next morning, cutting southwest diagonally toward the mountains. One detachment spent almost an hour with picks and shovels to construct a causeway over a stream because, Bourke explained, "In the wintery season, the banks of these creeks acted upon by the stem frost offer grave obstacles to cavalry, especially with smoothly shod animals." Several men were thrown, and one trooper nearly drowned when his horse slid down the bank into the water.

After marching ten miles, the Indian scouts rode in, reporting the

Cheyenne village was about fifteen miles to the south. They did not know how many lodges or ponies, but their earnest manner prompted Mackenzie to order a halt until dark. The command bivouacked under a projecting spur of the mountains. Fires were forbidden; smoke might betray their presence. Lunch consisted of raw fat pork and hardtack. No one was allowed outside of camp. While the soldiers rested, the Indians rode their war ponies hard around the bivouac, which Frank Grouard explained was to build up their wind for the coming fight.[26]

About sunset, Mackenzie ordered the troopers to saddle up and strap everything down tight. Mules would remain behind. Then, a few minutes before dark, the cavalry started around the spur and up a narrow ravine about a mile long, then over a series of red clay knolls littered with broken fragments of limestone that hindered the horses.[27] They were entering the mountains now, on what Capt. Luther North of the Pawnee scouts called, "the hardest march we ever had."

> We climbed up and up, it seemed for miles, then over a ridge, and down again. In many places the trail was so narrow along the side of the mountain that we could march only in single file, and the command was strung out for perhaps a couple of miles; then if the valley or canyon spread out, we would trot our horses and close up the ranks.[28]

Watching the north star, the cavalrymen and their Indian allies maintained a steady course south-southwest, climbing all the while. Some defiles were so narrow that Pvt. William Earl Smith, Mackenzie's semiliterate orderly, remarked, "If the hostils had of [known] we were a comming they could of [killed] every man of us in some of these places." Horses began to give out because of the elevation. Many of the soldiers, and even some of the Pawnees, were nauseated from the continuous exertion in the cold, thin air. Others were exhausted and dozing in their saddles. "I was so sleepy and tired I could not keep awake," Sergeant McClellan wrote. Some troopers fell out of ranks to rest and sneak a smoke, which had been forbidden by the officers.[29]

Nearing the Cheyenne camp, the Indian scouts halted, shifting their saddles from their riding ponies to their war ponies, changing to battle dress, and painting themselves. Mackenzie ordered a rest for a few minutes to allow them to finish. As Lt. Homer Wheeler dismounted to remove his overcoat, the strap of his binoculars broke and they fell to the ground. Reaching over to pick them up, he found a second pair of binoculars right at his feet. Inquiries among the officers determined no one had lost theirs, and Wheeler thought this curious.

Suddenly a shot rang out in the rear, where a trooper dispatched his exhausted horse. Mackenzie lost his temper. "You had [ought] to hear the Genrall curse," Smith noted. "He was to mad for any [use]." He soon regained his composure, however, and ordered the column ahead.[30] Bourke wrote:

> General Mackenzie's natural impatience was aggravated by the so-licitudes of our Indian guides, who kept coming back every few minutes to urge the column forward, saying in a low tone to the interpreters that the hostile village was at hand. True enough, we even heard in a vague but awe-inspiring sort of indistinctness the thump! thump! thump! of war drums, and the jingling of their rattles sounding the measure of a war dance. Only a mile of distance intervened, but the light had broken in the East. The hostile drums ceased beating, a sign the Cheyenne village had finished its dance and retired to rest.[31]

The column stopped one last time under an immense rock shelter, and Mackenzie sent the entire detachment of Indian scouts forward. McClellan wrote:

> The Indian warriors came by us on the run in all their war rig and we could see there was something up and in a few minutes the three companies ahead of us moved forward at the run.[32]

Bourke's thought was, "Now or never!"[33]

28

The End for the Cheyennes

THE CHEYENNE VILLAGE HAD MORE THAN 200 LODGES, EACH lodge sheltering as many as eight men, women, and children. It was in a stand of willows along the Red Fork of the Powder River, which here is about thirty feet wide. The river runs through the middle of a sheltered valley about a mile wide, surrounded by steep, broken slopes leading up to sheer mountains. The valley is scarred by small ravines running into the river. The landscape is red, powdery clay, turning to gray rock as it moves up the mountainsides. Only on the south do the mountains lead down to gentle slopes. There are two passes through the mountains, on the south and east, and a third entrance, following the river, on the north. The north entrance is sheltered by a slab of rock, more than an acre in size, which eons ago sloughed off the side of the mountain. Here, under this rock, Mackenzie's troops paused before moving in.

Dull Knife and Wild Hog were principal chiefs of the village. Among the more than 1,600 people camped here were two great medicine chiefs of the Cheyenne Nation, Black Hairy Dog and Coal Bear, and the war chief Two Moons. Also present was Last Bull, powerful leader of the Fox Soldier Warrior Society, whose

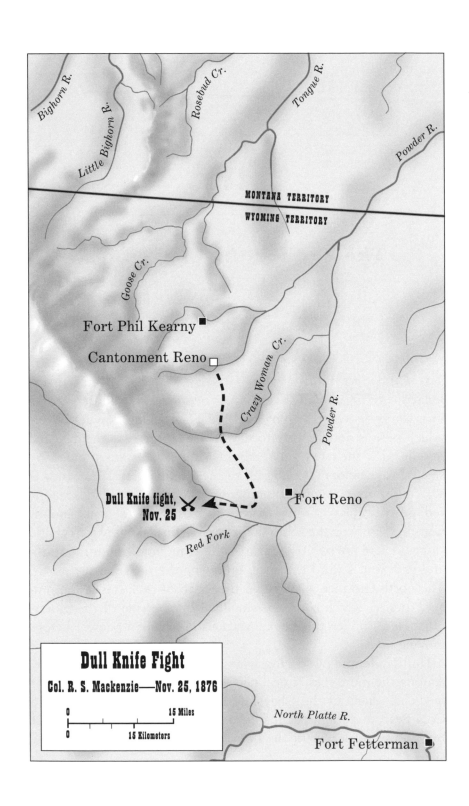

Bighorn R.

Little Bighorn R.

Rosebud Cr.

Tongue R.

Powder R.

MONTANA TERRITORY

WYOMING TERRITORY

Goose Cr.

Fort Phil Kearny ■

Cantonment Reno ▫

Crazy Woman Cr.

Powder R.

Dull Knife fight, ✕
Nov. 25

■ Fort Reno

Red Fork

North Platte R.

Fort Fetterman ■

Dull Knife Fight

Col. R. S. Mackenzie—Nov. 25, 1876

0   15 Miles

0   15 Kilometers

stubborn determination to stand and fight contributed to the disaster that followed—the Cheyennes had known for days that the soldiers were coming.

The events on the Indian side were collected from the survivors by the great explorer and naturalist George Bird Grinnell, and Cheyenne historian John Stands in Timber. According to Grinnell, the Indians learned of the approaching troops when some young warriors reported seeing the tracks of many horses heading north along the Powder, obviously the trail of Crook's main force as it marched from Fort Fetterman to Cantonment Reno.

The next morning, the chiefs decided to send four young warriors, Hail, Crow Necklace, Young Two Moons, a nephew of the chief, and High Wolf, to follow the trail and find out what it meant. The four scouts departed, riding some distance from each other to make sure the ground was thoroughly covered, each looking for trails and carefully watching the countryside. On the third night, they reached the wagon road leading north toward Reno, and followed it until they came to a hill. It was dark and snowing, so they decided to wait until daylight before they climbed the hill and examined the country beyond.

At first light, the four Cheyennes ascended and saw smoke rising in a bend of the river. As the light grew brighter, the long rows of tents of Cantonment Reno stretched out before them. The soldiers and government scouts had turned their horses loose near the hill, and two of the herd guards rode within 200 yards of the young Cheyennes, who flattened themselves on the ground until the soldiers had passed.

Since they could not leave their hilltop perch without being seen, they remained there until dark. By then, the horse herd had been driven back into camp, and the young Cheyennes could finally move down and investigate further.

They rode to within half a mile of the camp before dismounting. The army horses were tied in a long picket line, and Young Two Moons and Crow Necklace decided to slip in to steal some. Believing boldness would attract less attention than stealth, they simply walked into the camp, hoping they would be mistaken for government scouts. Passing an Indian campfire, they noticed

Shoshones and Arapahos playing a game, and recognized two Cheyennes who were singing by the fire. Farther on was the Pawnee camp.

Young Two Moons and Crow Necklace stayed among the Indians until most had settled down for the night. Then they stole three ponies from the Pawnees, and were leading them out when they noticed an Arapaho frying cakes.

"We had better go in there and get something to eat," Young Two Moons suggested. They turned the ponies loose and went over to the Arapaho camp, where the scouts were singing. Someone shouted, "Stop singing, and keep a good lookout," and the Arapahos broke up and returned to their lodges. The two Cheyennes were nervous about remaining any longer. They stole three ponies from the Arapahos to replace the Pawnee ponies they had freed, then returned to their companions.

The Cheyenne village had moved to the valley of the Red Fork during their absence, but they found it and reported what they had seen, including the large number of Indian scouts that, from the languages they heard, they presumed to be Pawnees, Shoshones, Arapahos, and Cheyennes. "If they reach this camp," Young Two Moons said, "I think there will be a fight."

The medicine chief Black Hairy Dog wanted to move immediately, working along the base of the mountains until they reached Crazy Horse. But Last Bull, the Fox Soldier chief said, "No, we will stay here and fight."

Four days later, November 24, word spread through the camp that Mackenzie was approaching their valley. According to Cheyenne tradition recorded by Stands in Timber, a herald came through the camp, repeating the words of Box Elder, a blind medicine man with the gift of prophecy. "Many, many soldiers are coming, and many Indians with them," the herald called. "They are on the way to kill all the Cheyennes. But I am going to ask the Great Spirit to prevent them."

Box Elder had a second vision, and again sent the herald through camp, this time crying that the village should be evacuated except for fighting men. The soldiers would charge the abandoned tipis, not realizing they would find armed resistance.

Meeting in council that evening, the chiefs wanted to move up the slopes to the south and throw up breastworks to protect the women and children. "There are so many of them that we cannot carry them all away if we are attacked," one chief pointed out.

"No," Last Bull replied. "We will stay here. We will dance here all night." To emphasize the point, he and Wrapped Hair, another leader of the Fox Soldiers, went through camp, cutting the pack saddle cinches of those preparing to leave.

Shortly before sundown, they built a large dance pyre and after dark set it on fire and began dancing. Some of the warriors, however, were uneasy and kept glancing toward the valley's north entrance, its most vulnerable point. Occasionally, they slipped past the Fox Soldier pickets and rode up to the ridges, trying to get a view of the whole valley.

As time passed, a man named Sits in the Night went down to check on his ponies, which had been turned out to graze near the rock shelter to the north. Approaching the animals, he saw someone driving them away. He ran back with the news, which a herald spread through the camp. As the people gathered, Sits in the Night said:

> I reached my horses in time to see people driving them off, and whipping them. I was so near that I could hear the blows as they struck them. I think the soldiers are there, for farther down the stream I heard a rumbling noise.[1]

With that, a herald went through camp, shouting, "They have already taken Sits in the Night's ponies; we had better look about the place to build breastworks."

Crow Split Nose, chief of the Crooked Lance Warrior Society, told his herald to advise the women and children to take down their lodges, move up the south slope, and begin building breastworks. Those whose ponies were grazing close to camp brought them in, began packing them, and started toward the slope. They were turned back by the Fox Soldiers who, under orders from Last Bull, had surrounded the camp and permitted no one to leave. Those who had struck their lodges were told to reerect them and unpack.

"We will stay up all night and dance," Last Bull said.[2]

Neither Last Bull's assumption of dictatorial powers nor the camp's almost blind obedience has ever been satisfactorily explained. Although leaders of Cheyenne warrior societies had more arbitrary authority than most chiefs, Crow Split Nose was Last Bull's equal and his Crooked Lance Society was not bound to obey the Fox Soldiers. Last Bull's apparent desire for a Wagnerian last stand also defied the time-honored Indian war code, which dictated that under no circumstances would families be exposed to danger. In every major fight so far during this war, the warriors had either been protecting their families from direct assault, as at Slim Buttes and the Little Bighorn, or been standing in the way of the army and their homes, as at the Rosebud. Now, a single chief wanted to risk a village with hundreds of noncombatants, and amazingly the people allowed him to do it.[3]

Perhaps they were overconfident. As historian Cyrus Townsend Brady wrote, "They fondly believed the place impregnable—as, indeed, with careful guarding it would have been."[4] Or perhaps they were simply tired of war and privation, and no longer cared how it ended.

The Cheyennes danced until almost daylight. With the coming dawn, however, Young Two Moons had a premonition that something would happen with the rising sun. Hurrying to his lodge, he woke his father, and his father's two wives, who dressed and began to pack, despite Last Bull's dictum.

They were not alone. The father of Brave Wolf, a Southern Cheyenne whose family lived with the Northern tribe, told him to sleep wearing his clothes and moccasins, in case the soldiers attacked.[5]

As Mackenzie's forces moved in, the Arapaho scouts magnanimously gave the prisoner Beaver Dam a fast horse and told him to get out. Taking advantage of the confusion, the young Cheyenne rode around the eastern edge of the valley to rejoin his people.[6] Behind him, the soldiers charged.

Bourke remembered the sound of the cavalry as "the thundering roar of a waterfall." To Private Smith, sent to the rear to hurry the column along, "It seemed as if the horses had [got] new life. When

I [got] to the last Company I turned back and I never hird such a thunder of horses in all my life, for it was all rocks where we were."[7]

The Indian scouts rode in the lead, the Lakotas, Arapahos, and Cheyennes under Lt. Hayden Delaney, the Shoshones under Lt. Walter Schuyler and Tom Cosgrove, and the Pawnees under Maj. Frank North. More than 500 professional soldiers, civilian auxiliaries, and government Indians were attacking 1,600 warriors, old men, women, and children.

In the Cheyenne camp, the medicine chief Black Hairy Dog had untied his ponies and was driving them up one of the hills to graze. The young warrior Little Hawk had just gone to bed after the all-night dance, and was lying half asleep, watching growing light through the smoke hole in the peak of the tipi. He was dimly aware of a voice—it was Black Hairy Dog's—crying, "Get your guns. The camp is charged. They are coming." The Southern Cheyenne Brave Wolf was just drifting off to sleep when he was disturbed by the sound of gunfire. Off in the distance, at the north end of the valley, people could see the muzzle flashes of carbines.[8]

The first shot was fired by a Cheyenne sentinel, who mounted his pony and rode hard for the camp. That raised the blood of the government Indians,[9] and Bourke recalled:

> The screeching and jubilant singing of our allies, the yells of the incoming battalions, the sharp words of command as the apparently inextricable entanglement of men and animals, deployed rapidly into line of battle met with no response from the foe, but the sharp crack of their rifles and the 'sipping' of bullets about our ears.

In the dim winter dawn, the soldiers saw shapeless forms dashing about. Bourke's horse balked at an object on the ground—the body of "an almost naked Cheyenne youth, shot as he was running out to save their herds."[10]

The government Indians turned up the steep slopes on the east side, drawing the fire of the Cheyennes. This left a clear field for the soldiers, who cut off and seized the pony herd. The Cheyenne warriors maintained a steady fire as the screaming women and children fled to the heights in the south, then counterattacked trying to recover their ponies. Lt. John A. McKinney charged across a small plain to head them off but found his way blocked by one of the ravines, where Little Hawk and his friends, Yellow Eagle, Two Bull, and Bull Hump were hiding, together with several other warriors. Just as McKinney's company was turning, the Cheyennes opened fire, hitting the lieutenant six times.

The company, composed largely of fresh recruits, began to fall apart. Taking advantage of the confusion, Yellow Eagle dashed out, counted the first coup on McKinney's body, and took his carbine. Two Bull and Bull Hump also counted coups, then rejoined the others in the ravine.

Mackenzie, meanwhile, ordered two companies to support McKinney's panicky troops. The two units dismounted and charged the ravine on foot, fighting the Cheyennes hand-to-hand. More Cheyennes began closing around but were cut to pieces by heavy fire from Schuyler's Shoshones on a crag overhead. "Scarcely one of the Cheyennes escaped alive from that particular ravine, eight bodies falling into our hands, and the soldiers claiming to have killed ten more," Bourke wrote.[11]

Young Two Moons was trying to find his friend, Crow Necklace, who had been with him on the scout to Cantonment Reno. Riding his pony along the north side, he saw Crow Necklace on the south. He rode through the village, dashing in and out among the fighting soldiers and Cheyennes, but just as he reached the south, he saw Crow Necklace fall.

Fighting his way from one position to the next, Young Two Moons ran into the former prisoner, Beaver Dam. The bad luck that had dogged him for days was running true to form; the Arapahos had given him one of the horses taken from Sits in the Night's herd as the fight was beginning. Two other warriors, recognizing the horse, charged down, ready to kill him as a government scout.

"I am not a scout for the soldiers," Beaver Dam protested. "I left Sitting Bull's camp to come home, and on my way was captured by the Arapahoes [sic] and taken into their camp. I was in the soldier camp the night you took those three horses."

Among the challenging warriors was Gypsum, who had lost all his sons in the ravine and was ready to kill Beaver Dam despite his protestations of innocence. As the Cheyennes held Gypsum back, the warrior Left Handed Wolf pointed out Beaver Dam had not been gone long enough to have served as a government scout. "Let him alone," he said.

"No," Gypsum cried. "I shall kill him. My sons are dead."

"This man did not kill your sons," Left Handed Wolf replied angrily and, pointing toward the village, continued, "You hear those people shooting. They have not ceased since we have been here. They killed your sons. Fight them. If you do not let this man alone, I will lay my whip on you," and to show he meant it, he lashed Gypsum once across the head.

They sent Beaver Dam up to join the women in the rocks above, then moved back down to the foothills where the other Cheyenne warriors were slowly retreating under the pressure of the soldiers.[12]

By now, Mackenzie had total control of the village. Those Cheyennes still alive had been driven to the rocks above, and could only snipe at the soldiers as they inventoried the village. Just over 600 ponies had been captured, which Bourke said was "of slight consequence compared with the utter destruction of a village of 200 lodges, in the inclemency of a Wyoming winter and not less than ten days' march from the band of Crazy Horse[,] the only one capable of relief."[13]

On Mackenzie's order, the village was put to the torch. As the tipis burned, thousands of rounds of ammunition that the Cheyennes had carefully hoarded exploded. Large quantities of buffalo meat were fed to the flames, along with buffalo robes and hides.

Thirty bodies had been found, although Mackenzie believed many more had been carried off by the Cheyennes. His own losses were Lieutenant McKinney and five troopers dead, and twenty-six wounded. The death toll rose to six troopers, when one was killed by Cheyenne snipers that afternoon. By then, however, the pack mules had arrived with rations for the troops and 30,000 extra cartridges, which would be sufficient—if necessary—to storm the rocks and drive out the Cheyennes. Mackenzie, however, preferred to avoid that and sent a message to Crook asking for infantry with long-range rifles.[14]

In their search of the village, the soldiers found grim trophies of Cheyenne battle prowess. Among them were the scalps of a white girl and a Shoshone girl, both about ten years old, and a necklace made of human fingers. More significant to the soldiers, however, were relics of the Custer fight: a pillow case made from a silk guidon; the guard roster of Company G, Seventh Cavalry; memorandum books of the first sergeants; military hardware marked with the letters of the various companies of the Seventh; personal clothing, parts of uniforms, and other equipment. This also explained the binoculars Lieutenant Wheeler had found on the trail the night before. Ironically, it was November 25, exactly five months after the Custer fight.[15]

The Shoshones and Pawnees had captured the Cheyenne war drums, and were now pounding them, singing victory songs and taunting their enemies in the rocks. Finally, Dull Knife asked for a parley, and an interpreter was sent to the base of the rocks.

Dull Knife shouted down that he had lost his three sons that morning. Although he was prepared to surrender, the other chiefs refused. To the Lakotas and Cheyennes in the government forces, he shouted, "Go home. You have no business here. We can whip the white soldiers alone, but can't fight you too."

Several of the other Cheyenne chiefs shouted that there was a big Lakota village nearby and they were going for help. They would come back and annihilate the soldiers. But this was a bluff, and everyone knew it. Finally, they offered to surrender if their ponies were returned. Told this was impossible, one chief called out, "You have killed and burned a heap of our people. You may as well stay now and kill the rest of us."[16] By now, however, the soldiers had been deployed and the Cheyennes beaten to such an extent that they no longer represented a serious threat, and were left alone, without food or cover, in the barren rocks.

The soldiers camped in the burning village that night. A field hospital had been set up on a hill on the west side, and Mackenzie's headquarters was nearby. The night was bitterly cold. A heavy snow fell, and the cries of the wounded visibly upset Mackenzie. His lightning-fast, hit-and-run raids were generally accomplished with minimal losses, and he was not accustomed to such heavy casualties.

The loss of Lieutenant McKinney was especially bitter. McKinney had joined the Fourth Cavalry upon graduating from West Point in 1871. At the time, he had a tendency toward going into debt and the beginnings of a drinking problem. Mackenzie, however, had recognized potential in the young lieutenant, guided him along, and ultimately came to consider McKinney "one of the most gallant officers and honorable men that I have ever known." Now McKinney was dead, and Private Smith, the orderly, saw Mackenzie pacing back and forth. "I don't believe he slept a bit that night," Smith commented. The next morning, the colonel and his orderly had coffee together, and Mackenzie talked at length about the casualties.[17]

The destruction of the camp was finished about 11:00 A.M. Satisfied that the Cheyennes were no longer a threat, Mackenzie moved out to meet Crook whom he expected to find coming with reinforcements. Many of the horses were now weak from forced marches and exposure, and were shot along the trail.[18]

THE CHEYENNES WERE ALSO MOVING. THEY HAD NO FOOD, NO lodges, and very few robes to protect themselves from the cold. They were heading north to the only help they knew—Crazy Horse's Oglalas. Scouting ahead, Young Two Moons and two other warriors found three Pawnees driving a large herd of Cheyenne ponies, their share of the plunder from the camp. The three Cheyennes rushed the Pawnees and managed to recover about seventy-five or eighty ponies.

The main band, meanwhile, had traveled about six miles from the valley when they were spotted by some of Mackenzie's Indian scouts. The Cheyennes also saw the scouts, but neither side moved toward the other. The government Indians could tell the Cheyennes were already starting to suffer, for they found the remains of six ponies butchered for food.[19]

Although Wooden Leg belonged to this band, he was not present for the fight. He and nine other warriors had gone north to raid against the Crows before Mackenzie attacked the camp. Not finding any Crows, they came to the Little Bighorn battlefield, where they reminisced about their great victory of the previous summer.

Some of the soldiers' bodies were partly exposed in their shallow graves. Military equipment and decaying carcasses of horses were scattered about. Since Wooden Leg had a military carbine, he picked up unused cartridges.

Leaving the Little Bighorn, the ten Cheyennes headed south toward their own people. After four days, they saw a large band of Indians coming toward them on foot. Soon, they recognized the members of their village, fleeing Mackenzie's devastation.

"They had but little food," Wooden Leg remembered. "Many of them had no blankets nor robes. They had no lodges. Only here and there was one wearing moccasins. The others had their feet wrapped in loose pieces of skin or of cloth. Women, children, and old people were straggling along over the snow-covered trail down the valley. The Cheyennes were very poor."[20]

"That was a hard winter for us," Kate Bighead commented.[21]

CROOK, WHO WAS MOVING UP THE INFANTRY TO REINFORCE Mackenzie, met him on the trail shortly before noon November 29. The next day, Thanksgiving, a funeral was held for the enlisted men killed in the fight. Two generals—Crook and Mackenzie—led the procession.[22] Mackenzie's depression had deepened and, with the terrible grandeur of the military burial, he snapped. The fight, he insisted, was a failure. The blame was his. He ought to kill himself. Alone in his tent with Dodge,

> Mac opened his heart to me. . . . He said he had often done better with a third of the forces at his command here—that he believed he degenerated as a soldier as he got older—that he was a fool and ought to have captured every Indian—that he regarded the whole thing as an utter failure. He even stated that he was sensitive lest some one might attributed cowardice to him—and much more of the same kind. He was so worked up that he could hardly talk and had often to stop and collect himself.

Dodge calmed him down, then reported his condition to General Crook. "The General was greatly worried and soon left my tent, I think to send for Mac and get him to play whist or something."[23]

Despite Mackenzie's outburst—a sign of his growing insanity—
the Dull Knife fight was the government's first real strategic victory. The military power of the Northern Cheyennes was forever
broken. No one was more aware of this than General Sherman,
who telegraphed the War Department:

> I can't commend too highly [Mackenzie's] brilliant achievements
> and the gallantry of the troops of his command. This will be a ter-
> rible blow to the hostiles, as those Cheyennes were not only their
> bravest warriors but have been the head and front of most all the
> raids and deviltry committed in this country.

Sheridan passed Sherman's praise on to Crook and Mackenzie,
adding his own congratulations.[24] Between Mackenzie in the south
and Miles in the north, at last the end seemed to be in sight.

29

Opportunity Lost

THE DEVASTATED CHEYENNES MARCHED NORTH THROUGH THE bitter cold. They moved in stages, an advance group of young men building large fires so that the others could stop and warm themselves, while the young men went ahead again to build more fires. A few buffalo were killed, but not enough for the large number of people, and without cooking utensils the best they could do was lay the meat across the open flames. Thus they traveled several days from one fire to the next, weakening from hunger and the elements, north to the Tongue River.[1]

Eventually, they reached the Oglala camp. What happened then becomes vague. In later years, perhaps with grievances dimmed by time, some Cheyenne survivors said they were received with the same kind-hearted openness that had characterized their reception after they had lost everything in the Reynolds fight.[2] This, however, does not correspond with statements of the Cheyennes who surrendered in the ensuing months. They claimed Crazy Horse, his own resources strained, aided them only briefly before sending them on their way.[3]

Black Elk, who belonged to Crazy Horse's camp, described the Cheyennes as destitute. Many of their babies had already died from exposure before reaching the camp. The Oglalas shared their clothing, but had very little food to spare because by then they themselves were eating ponies. Eventually, he said, the Cheyennes departed for Camp Robinson to surrender.[4]

There can be little doubt that, bound by the rules of Plains Indian hospitality, Crazy Horse provided for the Cheyennes as best he could, but urged them to leave as soon as possible—so soon that their ancient alliance was ruptured forever. Departing, the Cheyennes wandered until they crossed Crook's trail, then followed his line of march, scavenging among the abandoned army campsites.[5]

Back in the Oglala camp, people were noticing a change in Crazy Horse. "He was always a queer man, but that winter he was queerer than ever," Black Elk remarked. He spent most of his time away from camp, alone in the cold wilderness. No one saw him eat. Sometimes, if a person went out to encourage him to come into camp, he would issue instructions for the people. Once he told Black Elk's father not to worry, that he found shelter in caves and holes, and was making plans for his people. Black Elk later wondered if Crazy Horse had foreseen his own death, and was pondering their welfare after he was gone.[6]

CROOK'S EXPEDITION SEEMED TO LOSE ITS SENSE OF PURPOSE after Mackenzie's fight. The troops returned to Cantonment Reno on December 2, but the post lacked adequate forage or supplies for such a large number of men, and the animals were almost worn out. The following morning, the weary soldiers and animals moved out again, marching twenty-eight miles to Buffalo Springs on the Dry Fork of the Powder River, where they went into camp several days.[7]

"I was disgusted," Dodge complained in his diary, "but there is no use in being so with Crook's orders. He really does not know what he intends to do. Makes up his mind at the last moment, and then acts at once—expecting everybody else to do the same."[8]

Over the next three weeks, Crook marched his men back and forth over much of northeastern Wyoming, missing rendezvous with supplies, wearing down his men and animals, and accomplishing nothing. The stress was aggravated by political news from the East; Republican Rutherford Hayes had been declared president-elect, but there was still a strong possibility of insurrection. One officer at Fort Peck wrote a friend: "Troops are slowly and quietly being concentrated at Washington, with what object, no one seems to know." The possibility of a new civil war worried the already exhausted officers on Crook's expedition.[9]

The lack of information from scouting parties convinced Crook that if any large hostile camps still existed, they were too far away to attack, given the present condition of his men and horses. There were only enough provisions for two more weeks. He therefore decided to end the expedition and return to Fort Fetterman. Calling a council of the remaining Indian scouts, he thanked them for their service and released them to return to their reservations. Then he turned south toward Fetterman. When the expedition reached the fort, Mackenzie departed for Washington where he had been summoned to command the troops who might have to defend the capital in the election crisis.[10]

IN MONTANA, MILES WAS IMPATIENT TO FINISH THE WAR. ARRIVing at Fort Peck, he met with Johnny Bruguier, who had impressed him during the council with Sitting Bull. Bruguier had come in with the group that had initially surrendered on October 31, but remained at the fort when the Indians bolted and joined Sitting Bull. On November 17, he and Miles worked out a deal—Bruguier would serve as an emissary to persuade the hostile bands to surrender, and the colonel would intercede on his behalf in the murder charge at Standing Rock.[11]

The following day, Miles met with agency Indians in an effort to determine the situation among the hostiles. Among other things, he received the erroneous impression that Sitting Bull was camped southwest of Fort Peck, among the Black Buttes about forty miles below the Missouri. Writing directly to Sherman, he said:

> I believe we have divided Sitting Bull's people and that his strength & influence is fast breaking down. I think he as well as they are satisfied that we can whip him every time and that has a very discouraging effect upon his people.

Miles claimed he could have already captured Sitting Bull's entire band with his existing force, but was hindered by "broken down mules" and an inadequate number of scouts.

> If you expect me to be successful see that I am supported or give me command of this whole region and I will soon end this Sioux war, and I would be very glad to govern them afterward for the more I see of them the more respect I have for them and believe their affairs can be governed to their entire satisfaction as well as for the interests of the govt.[12]

Before governing the tribes, however, Miles had to subdue them, with or without additional support. On November 19, he divided his command "in order to more fully reconnoitre the country." He retained personal command of six companies, placing the rest under Capt. Simon Snyder. Miles would move directly toward the Black Buttes, while Snyder scouted south and west, meeting Miles at the buttes in some eight to ten days.

Miles spent the next week marching through a trackless wilderness. "A more desolate . . . country I never saw," one lieutenant wrote, calling it "as barren as a barn floor." One day, the fog was so thick the troops navigated by compass alone.

On November 25, the day Mackenzie attacked Dull Knife's camp, Miles attempted to cross the Missouri near its confluence with the Musselshell River, where the current was swift with large ice floes. Some of the soldiers detached a wagon box, covering it with canvas to create a boat, while Lt. Frank Baldwin supervised construction of a large raft. The following morning the raft was launched with Miles, Baldwin, Lt. James W. Pope, and a dozen soldiers on board. It was quickly swept downriver by the current, until it caught on a snag. The men ashore launched the wagon box, then sent out a second box, trying to secure ropes to draw the raft between the two banks. After eight hours of fruitless maneuvering with the ever increasing danger of losing both the wagon boxes and the raft, a soldier swam out with a rope, perhaps by riding the current, and the raft with its "shipwrecked colonel" was hauled back to the north bank.

On November 27, Baldwin managed to get a line across the

river, and began drawing men across to the south side. For the next three days, the men fought the rising river and its ice floes until finally, on Thanksgiving Day, Miles learned the Missouri was frozen solid eighteen miles farther up. He decided to march up to the frozen section and complete the crossing there.[13]

The aborted crossing was only one of Miles's frustrations. The delay at the river had extended Snyder's battalion beyond its rationing period, forcing him to the Tongue River Cantonment without making his rendezvous. And, on November 29, Miles learned that Sitting Bull was nowhere near Black Buttes, but was still camped far to the east on the Red Water. Johnny Bruguier found him there, and obtained substantial information about his plans. About the time Bruguier left on December 3, the Missouri froze again, and Sitting Bull led his people to the north side, hoping to obtain ammunition from traders. He camped on the Milk River above Fort Peck, his following now reduced to about 250 people in three lodges and ninety-two shelter tents.[14]

Aware now that Sitting Bull was north of the Missouri, Miles detached Baldwin with three companies to go after him. The lieutenant's objective was to keep Sitting Bull moving more or less in circles, cutting him off from the Yellowstone and Crazy Horse in the south, and keeping him from fleeing north into Canada.[15]

The thirty-four-year-old Baldwin was one of a talented group of junior officers with an Indian fighting acumen their superiors often lacked. A native of Michigan, he had enlisted as a second lieutenant in the Nineteenth Michigan Infantry on the outbreak of the Civil War, winning the Medal of Honor during the Atlanta Campaign.

After the war, he farmed and briefly attended Hillsdale College before reentering the army as a second lieutenant in the Nineteenth U.S. Infantry. He was soon transferred to the Fifth Infantry and, during the Red River War of 1874–75, was named chief of scouts.

On November 8, 1874, he was leading a small detachment of troops accompanying an empty wagon train when he stumbled onto a hostile Southern Cheyenne village near McClellan Creek, Texas. Although outnumbered, Baldwin ordered an attack, drove the Cheyennes from their camp, and recovered two captive white girls. For this, he received his second Medal of Honor, one of only four men ever to win two, and the only soldier so decorated for both the Civil War and Indian wars.[16]

Baldwin started eastward after Sitting Bull on December 1, 1876, arriving at Fort Peck four days later. There he found Johnny Bruguier, who advised him the Hunkpapa leader was camped about fifteen miles east of the agency.

Bruguier was ordered to take this information to Miles, but Baldwin doubted whether the colonel could arrive in time to support. Aware that he was risking his career by acting on his own, he nevertheless rationed his 112 officers and men for two days, with 100 rounds of ammunition in each man's pack and another 18,000 rounds in the mule train, and left Fort Peck at 8:00 P.M., December 6, hoping to catch the Indians at dawn. On the trail, he met scattered groups of Yanktons who, alarmed by the large number of Lakotas in the vicinity, were heading toward the Fort Peck Agency. They told him Sitting Bull had moved his camp to the Missouri, was regaining some of his following, and his strength had now grown to a hundred lodges.

The following day, the troops came upon Sitting Bull's initial campsite, where fires were still burning and the ground covered with litter, indicating the Indians had fled at the approach of the troops. They had left a wide, hard-packed trail, which the soldiers followed to the Milk River, near its confluence with the Missouri. Shortly before dawn, a band of Indians moved in among the mules, but were driven off by the train guard with one warrior killed. Baldwin immediately moved his troops into a stand of timber and prepared them for action. Although the day was bitterly cold, he refused to allow campfires for fear of giving the Indians a target.

At daybreak, the soldiers deployed along the north side of the frozen Missouri. The main group of Indians had just crossed to the south side, but the rear guard was still on the ice. The women and children could be seen in the distance, hurrying into the timbered foothills to the south. Noticing several camps of agency Yanktons on his own side, Baldwin ordered the soldiers not to fire on any Indians on the north bank.[17]

After the hostiles finished crossing, Baldwin sent the eighteen-year-old scout Joseph Culbertson and two other mounted men across to look around. No sooner did they reach the south bank than the Lakotas opened fire from the timber, forcing them back onto the ice. "I came near cashing in my checks at this fight, as the Indians had me cut off from the command," Culbertson later remarked.

Baldwin sent one company across to clear the timber while his second company provided covering fire from the north bank, and the third was held in reserve. The infantrymen crossed the ice and moved up the bank, driving the Indians out of the trees. Beyond the line of timber, however, they ran into a large body of warriors who pushed the soldiers back into the trees.

Baldwin now realized there were more hostiles than he anticipated. With the sun coming out, the ice was melting, and he feared it might break up, trapping his men on the south side. His problems were aggravated by a group of agency Yanktons who had gathered at his rear to watch. Not trusting them, he sent word that if they did not get out of the way, he would open fire on them; the Yanktons scattered.

By early afternoon, the position on the south bank was becoming untenable and, still worried about the Yanktons to the rear, Baldwin ordered his troops back. The defiant hostiles waved as the soldiers recrossed the river and collapsed on the north side, exhausted by the cold and by lack of sleep. The only casualties appear to have been the one Indian killed in the predawn move against the mule train, and one government mule killed during the fight on the river.[18]

The soldiers moved downriver, where they dug trenches, threw up breastworks of cottonwood logs, and tried to get some sleep. Aside from exchanging occasional shots with the pickets, the Lakotas expressed no interest in continuing the fight. About dusk, a blizzard blew in, sending the temperature down to minus forty-two. Realizing many of his men would freeze to death if they remained in camp, Baldwin started them back toward Fort Peck. The mules marched at the head of the column to break through the snow and pack it. Lifelines were run from the mule train and the soldiers were ordered to hold on. Occasionally, the mules were trotted, forcing the men to run and keep up their circulation. Three senior sergeants were placed in the rear to prod the soldiers onward at bayonet point. At one time, Baldwin himself went to sleep, fell off his horse, and could only be awakened by several jabs with a bayonet. The command finally staggered into Fort Peck the next afternoon, exhausted and frostbitten, having marched seventy-three miles in less than forty-eight hours. "Not once on that march (ever memorable to me) did I hear a soldier complain," Baldwin wrote. There was a certain satisfaction over and above the endurance of his men; by forcing Sitting Bull to hastily abandon his first camp, the soldiers had compelled the Indians to leave much of their provisions and equipment. No matter how badly the soldiers suffered, Baldwin knew the Indians were suffering more.[19]

Determined not to put his men through any such ordeals in the future, Baldwin assembled twenty-two wagons to transport them, and ordered an old howitzer reconditioned so that he might have some artillery support. He was obviously embarrassed by his failure on the Missouri, and notified Miles that he intended to cross the river in force, hopefully driving the Indians southward into Miles's troops. The colonel replied, "If you meet with ill-success I can take the responsibility of the movement; if you are successful it will be very creditable to you."

After feeding and resting his troops for three days, Baldwin loaded them into wagons and started them back east along the Missouri toward Sitting Bull. At the Wolf Point Agency, some Assiniboines told him Sitting Bull planned to consolidate with Crazy Horse on the Yellowstone. Successfully crossing the thinning ice of the Missouri, Baldwin pushed on to the valley of the Red Water.[20] On December 17, he rested his troops while Joe Culbertson scouted south along the Red Water.

About noon, Culbertson spotted a lone buffalo running through the snow. Suspicious, he waited until he saw an Indian chasing it. Certain the hostiles were near, he rode to a high hill from which he scanned the area in the direction of Ash Creek, a tributary of the Red Water. He saw the Indian pony herd feeding in the hollows along the creek. Beyond was Sitting Bull's camp, extending about 1,500 feet along the east side of the creek, between two lines of bluffs. Culbertson estimated the distance at about twenty miles south of Baldwin, and the strength at between 400 and 500 warriors. Keeping in a line of badlands where he would be hard to see, he rode back to report.[21]

Baldwin broke camp at 7:00 A.M., December 18, moving east, then south to avoid discovery. Morale was high. Even though many of the men were sick from exposure and privation, everyone joined his company. By 2:00 P.M. they were within four miles of the camp. Most of the warriors were out hunting. Struck by the terrain's resemblance to that of McClellan Creek in 1874, Baldwin deployed his troops in the same fashion, with one company as skirmishers in front of the wagons, another company on either side, and a small rear guard. Then he started them down the creek toward the Indian camp.

The Indians spotted the deploying soldiers, and those warriors still in camp moved out to circle the train in an effort to draw attention away from fleeing noncombatants. Baldwin scattered them with three rounds from his howitzer. Then the infantry moved in, saturating the tipis with rifle fire and forcing the Indians out.

"The whole camp was captured . . . with all the buffalo robes and dried meat," Culbertson recalled. "All they got away with was their saddle horses. A good many of the squaws and kids froze their feet and hands." Baldwin ordered the meat and supplies loaded on the wagons to sustain the troops, then burned whatever could not be taken.

Moving a short distance up to the divide between the Missouri and Yellowstone, the troops went into camp behind breastworks made from sacks of corn and oats, and hardtack boxes. The wagons were circled into a corral for the mules. The temperature dropped to minus forty, and captured buffalo robes were distributed among the men and used to cover the mules. During the night, about 400 warriors surrounded the bivouac and fired into it, but no one was injured.[22]

The next morning, the captured Indian animals, numbering some sixty horses, mules, and ponies, were killed, and the troops started south toward the Tongue River Cantonment to join Miles.[23]

Miles was pleased with Baldwin's success, but his pleasure was tinged with bitterness over a totally unrelated incident.[24] Baldwin's fight should have been the last action of the Great Sioux War. Sitting Bull's band was now as destitute as Dull Knife's, and, like the Cheyennes, it was heading toward Crazy Horse where it would put yet another strain on Oglala resources and render their situation hopeless. But the fortunes of war are perverse and sometimes take the field against both sides. Even as Baldwin prepared to move against Sitting Bull, the chance of an early peace had already been lost.

On December 16, five powerful Miniconjou chiefs and twenty or thirty warriors approached the cantonment under a flag of truce. They represented a peace faction that had gained strength among the remaining free-roaming bands largely congregated with Crazy Horse.[25] Anticipating such delegations, Miles had already instructed his Indian scouts to honor anyone approaching under a white flag.

He had not, however, anticipated his Crow scouts, who allowed old hatreds to overrule common sense. "It must be remembered," Trumpeter Brown wrote in his diary, "that the Sioux and the Crows are the most deadly enemies, and when they meet one or the other has to die."[26] As the Miniconjous passed the Crow camp, the scouts ambushed and massacred them before the soldiers in the nearby cantonment could intervene.

Reacting immediately, Miles ordered the remaining Crows disarmed, and confiscated twelve of their horses and other property, which were sent to the relatives of the dead Miniconjous as an indemnity. Explaining the situation to General Terry, he wrote, "It is to be hoped that the Sioux will understand that they fell into a camp of their ancient enemies, and did not reach the encampment of this command."

Miles believed that had this group of Miniconjous reached the cantonment and been received honorably, "it would have broken and reduced the influence and power of Sitting Bull, Crazy Horse and others, who are not yet disposed to accept the terms of the Government."[27] Instead they had been killed in the mindless act of an ancient blood feud, filling the free-roaming Indians with a new resolve against surrender. The peace faction lost face and the war faction again prevailed.

30

Wolf Mountain:
Crazy Horse Defeated

WHILE BALDWIN AND SITTING BULL MANEUVERED AROUND EACH other, Miles plotted his next course. He intended, as he later wrote Sherman, to "have a good fight with Crazy Horse."[1] Everything dictated a new expedition. No doubt stung by the attention given Mackenzie after the Dull Knife fight, Miles's ego demanded a decisive victory. Crazy Horse and the war faction, angered by the murder of the Miniconjou peace delegation, refused to consider any further negotiations, so Miles had justification for seeking his fight. Equally important was the urgent need to get his soldiers back into the field and under strict discipline because of a totally different enemy—alcohol.

Traders had set up shop in the vicinity during the autumn, and, while they brought necessities such as heavy winter clothing to supplement the inadequate government issue, they also brought barrels of liquor. This not only undermined discipline, it also presented a special danger to the troops. After several soldiers dropped dead going from a saloon to camp, Miles learned that the trader "manufactured his gin and different drinks in a cellar, and sold them at every opportunity to these unfortunate soldiers under the name of 'liquors,' though they were rank poison." Despite the best efforts of the officers to regulate the trade, the soldiers invariably contrived ways to get alcohol.[2]

Crazy Horse was rumored to be camped somewhere south of the cantonment, although no one was absolutely certain where. The Indians themselves provided a clue the day after Christmas, however, when they attacked the beef contractor's herd, running off 250 head of cattle. A force sent after them skirmished with part of the band, recovering over 100 head and finding a clear trail. On December 29, Miles marched out in pursuit. His command consisted of 436 men from the Fifth and Twenty-second Infantries, with two pieces of artillery disguised with wagontop bows and canvas, and placed in the train so that Indian observers would not recognize them for cannon. Some forty infantrymen were placed on captured ponies and designated as a mounted company. The scouts included Yellowstone Kelly, Tom Leforge, John Johnson, called "Liver-Eating" Johnson because of a dubious claim that he had once eaten the liver of an Indian he killed, Bob Jackson, and Johnny Bruguier, along with two Crows and a Bannock Indian.[3]

The temperature, minus twenty-eight at daybreak, had risen to minus ten by the time the command started out, and the day was dreary and overcast. The command marched south through the valley of the Tongue, in snow that averaged a foot deep and in hollows often deeper. It had been hard packed, however, by the constant passage of buffalo and Indian ponies pulling travois, and the wagons had little trouble keeping up. The soldiers followed the twisting river, crossing time and again over ice thick enough to support the wagons and artillery.

On New Year's Day, 1877, the bitter cold abated, but a chilling rain began to fall, lasting over the next several days and turning the road into a bog, hindering progress. Just before going into camp, the scouts exchanged shots with a small party of Indians, who quickly outdistanced them.[4]

The next day, the soldiers came across the site of an old camp that appeared to have been abandoned in a hurry. Several fresh trails were found, indicating the Indians had fled farther up the river toward the Bighorn Mountains, where they felt they might be safe.[5]

That night some cattle strayed from the beef herd, and when the command marched out the following day, two soldiers were detailed to remain behind and round them up. The troops were scarcely out of sight when the sound of gunfire reached them. One company rushed back but arrived too late; a party of fifteen or twenty Cheyennes concealed in the nearby bluffs had jumped the soldiers, killing one and wounding the other.[6]

On the afternoon of January 5, the command entered the Wolf Mountains between the Tongue and the Little Bighorn. "The deep canons [sic] of the mountains meeting the valley, break away into ravines, and these in their turn become as ramous [ramus] as the roots of a tree," Baldwin wrote. "Again we are visited with a severe and continuous rain, making the road heavy and everybody uncomfortable." Farther upriver, they found a campsite that had been occupied only a day or two before, because the ground was still warm from the fires. "This camp was a large one and extended for miles up the valley," Kelly noted. "The trail of the stolen cattle led to it, and some of them had been butchered."[7]

A blinding snowstorm blew in early the next morning, but the troops pushed on. They passed through several large Indian camps, whose fires were still smoldering, with many lodgepoles still standing and various utensils scattered about. In one, they found some emaciated ponies that had been abandoned as their owners fled. "We infer from this that the camp is aware of our presence, has been moving slowly, and is but a short distance in advance of us," Baldwin wrote. "The cold becomes intense, the mercury sinking many degrees below zero."[8]

As Baldwin surmised, the Indians were very much aware of the troops. Most of the Indians in the band were Oglalas, although there were also some Cheyennes who either had not been involved in the fight with Mackenzie or remained behind when Dull Knife moved on. At first, they had traveled slowly, hunting along the way. While the Cheyennes laid in a new supply of buffalo meat and obtained more hides for their lodges, the Oglalas met the immediate needs of the camp from the cattle taken in the raid on Miles's beef herd. Beyond that, the Indians were largely destitute because the constant movement to avoid various military columns forced them to abandon much of their equipment and travel lightly. They still had a few government horses captured at the Little Bighorn, but these, too, were starving for lack of forage.

Initially, the plan was to draw Miles into the field with a series of decoy raids, which had been the rationale behind the attacks on livestock both at the cantonment and on the trail. Once the soldiers were far away from their base, the chiefs hoped to ambush them among the rocks and canyons of the Tongue, drawing them into the badlands then turning on them, much as the Indians had done with Fetterman at Fort Phil Kearny and Crook at the Rosebud.

The plan was going wrong. Although Miles took the bait, he kept his troops together. The soldiers were well supplied and moving too rapidly. The Indians were no longer in condition to lead them on until the proper moment for ambush; in fact, the Oglalas and Cheyennes could barely keep ahead of them. With little in the way of food and equipment, the hostile camp was too large to support itself.[9]

On January 7, the chiefs decided to divide into smaller bands, with the Oglalas moving east while the Cheyennes continued southwest along the Tongue. A small group of Cheyennes, including Wooden Leg's sister, Crooked Nose, had already started toward the southwest. Just as the main bands were preparing to move out in their separate directions, scouts came in to report that the soldiers were coming. The two bands immediately came together again. Women, children, and the elderly moved the camp farther up the river while the warriors prepared to intercept the troops.

MILES WAS LESS THAN FIVE MILES AWAY. NOW ALMOST A HUNDRED miles southwest of the cantonment, he had broken camp at seven-thirty that morning. The trail along the twisting river was so bad that by noon they had covered just over two miles. Since there was little hope of further progress, they went into camp.[10]

Ahead, the scouts spotted a small group on horseback. Leforge and the Crows opened fire, and when the Indians failed to fight back, moved in on them. A warrior named Big Horse, who had been riding ahead of the others, managed to get back to the main Indian camp. The rest were captured and proved to be four women, two girls, and one that Leforge called "a boy," although he may have been of fighting age.[11] After bringing the prisoners to camp, the scouts were sent back out with instructions to locate the Indian village.

UP THE TRAIL, THE CHEYENNES WERE PREPARING FOR BATTLE when someone told Wooden Leg, "They have captured some women. Your sister is one of them." Wooden Leg jumped on his horse, lashing it as he raced down the trail taken by his sister's group. He came to the spot where Leforge and the Crows had captured the little group, and followed the tracks of the government horses to the river. Directly across was Miles's camp. Wooden Leg scanned the camp, trying to see them. When he couldn't—they had been placed in a tent under guard to protect them from the soldiers—he presumed they must have been killed. But Wooden Leg himself was seen, and some soldiers opened fire, forcing him to the foot of a ridge about a mile from the military camp, where he found some other warriors gathered.[12]

Leforge and the scouts had seen the Cheyenne warriors heading for the ridge. Spreading out, the scouts moved nervously toward the ridge. The Cheyennes jumped up and opened fire. As the scouts retreated, Leforge's horse took a mortal wound and fell, pitching him forward on his head. Stunned, he recovered to find his leg sprained, his horse dead, and his rifle lost. He crawled to a small gully, where he hid himself, hugging the ground while the soldiers crossed the river and scattered the Indians with rifle fire and shells from the three-inch Rodman gun.[13]

The first phase of the Battle of Wolf Mountain was over. "Several of our horses were killed," Trumpeter Brown noted in his diary. "None of the men were hurt but many of them had their clothing riddled by bullets; one of our scouts, Liver-Eating Johnson had a furrow cut through his long hair [by a bullet]; he said it was *close*."[14]

Certain now the Indians were within striking range, Miles ordered reveille at 4:00 A.M. It was snowing and the temperature was fourteen degrees. At daybreak, the soldiers began fixing breakfast. The Indian warriors, who had almost nothing to eat, were watching them hungrily from the heights up the valley.

Miles's camp was in a cottonwood grove on a bend in the river. Moving inland from the bend, the ground rose up to form a bench, which gave way to a bluff sloping up to perpendicular ridges about 400 yards away. Three hundred yards to the south, was a cone-shaped hill, which later became known as Battle Butte. Miles climbed up to the top of the butte and surveyed the area, ordering the Rodman gun moved up to the bluff to cover the troops as they prepared to get under way.[15]

"Just as we got ready to move out," Brown wrote, "our scouts came running in and reported a large body of Sioux coming in direction of Camp."[16]

Reacting swiftly, Miles ordered one company to cross the ice to the other side of the river, to avoid being surrounded. The Indians first attempted to charge down the valley and overrun the camp, but the crew of the Rodman gun opened fire from the bluff, and the heavy Napoleon field piece swept the ground along the valley floor. The Indians scattered among the ridges as the Rodman's shells exploded among them. Accustomed to solid shot, they were frightened by the explosive shells hurling shrapnel, and convinced—not unreasonably—that the guns fired twice with each shot.

As he watched, Miles was impressed by the changes in Indian tactics, probably acquired from almost a year of fighting the soldiers. "The Indians fought throughout as Infantry," he told Sherman, "using their horses only to carry them from one part of the field to another; they would dismount, leaving their horses behind bluffs and march down to meet this command or charge on foot. They also used whistles to communicate."[17]

Two companies of Fifth Infantry moved up along the ridge behind the camp, gaining command of that height before the Indians could reach it. But the warriors managed to secure Battle Butte and two adjacent hills, from which they now covered Miles's entire flank. The time had come for the infantry to move in with rifle and bayonet. Four companies, under Capts. James S. Casey, Edmond Butler, and Robert McDonald, and Lieutenant Baldwin moved against the almost perpendicular base of the butte, under steady fire from the Indians. Gaining the slopes, the infantrymen pushed through the snow and climbed over rocks, firing as they advanced.

The Indians poured down a heavy gunfire, but the steep slope made aiming difficult without exposing themselves. They were becoming unnerved by the steady push of the soldiers, and warriors with repeating rifles began levering shell after shell into their chambers, shooting rapidly without pausing to aim.

As bullets cut through the air around him, Baldwin "rode along the line and cheered up the men telling them to have courage and meet the enemy like men," Brown noted in his diary. "Capt Butler had his horse shot from under him, but this did not [re]tard their progress, for they went gallantly up and with the loss of two wounded they drove the Indians from it and held the hill in triumph."[18]

Wooden Leg was among the Indians hunkered in the rocks on Battle Butte, firing at the soldiers as they scaled the sides of the hill. He had a "soldier rifle"—a Springfield taken in an earlier fight—and plenty of ammunition. Crazy Horse was nearby. They stayed behind the rocks, peering out only to fire, and ducking the soldiers' bullets as they ricocheted off the rocks.

Big Crow, a Cheyenne chief with a conspicuous war bonnet, walked up and down the ridge defiantly, daring the soldiers to shoot him. He was firing a carbine captured at the Little Bighorn, and soon expended his ammunition. Replenishing his cartridge belt from Wooden Leg and several others, he went back up on the ridge, where he resumed his pacing until a bullet cut him down. Wooden Leg and two Lakotas dashed out and found him barely alive. They were carrying him back to safety when the concentrated fire from the approaching infantry forced them to abandon him and drove them back among the rocks. When there was a brief lull in the shooting, they went out for Big Crow once again. As they reached him, Wooden Leg's brother called out that they were abandoning the butte. Wooden Leg dropped his hold and ran to join his brother, leaving Big Crow for the two Lakotas to bring along.[19]

The Indians moved to the bluffs on the left and to the front, and again had to be forced out. Soldiers and warriors fired on each other point-blank, at distances of fifty to seventy-five yards. The soldiers had to win and they knew it. Miles later wrote:

> I think every officer and soldier realized the desperate nature of this encounter. . . . If they had met with disaster it would have been many weeks before any relieving command could have reached the ground from the nearest possible source of aid. Every officer and soldier knew that a mistake meant disaster, and disaster or defeat meant annihilation, and were therefore inspired to deeds of heroism and fortitude and a corresponding confidence.

About noon, a blizzard blew in, which, Miles wrote, "added an inexpressible weirdness to the scene."[20] The soldiers reached the top of the bluffs as the Indians ran out of ammunition. The warriors fought hand-to-hand, with spears, and using rifle butts as clubs while runners sped upriver to the camp to get the women and children moving. The blowing snow soon became so blinding that neither side could see, and fighting broke off. It made no difference, however—the Indians had had enough. They fled through the blizzard to join their families and move as far as possible up the Tongue, away from the troops.[21]

"Our loss is one killed and eight wounded, one of the latter dying on the return march," Baldwin wrote. "The Indian loss is unknown, but must have been considerable, for at several points where the fight raged the fiercest the snow is dyed with blood."

The camp was moved up to the high bluff, which gave better shelter from the weather and could be more easily defended. That night, the temperature rose slightly, and the snow gave way to a chilling rain. The next morning, the wagons were left under guard, and the troops continued up the river. Passing the battlefield, they saw several dead ponies, the trails where the Indian wounded had been carried away, and the dead dragged with lassos. From these, Brown estimated their losses at fifteen killed and twenty-five wounded. Beyond the deserted Indian camp, the trail separated, showing that the Indians had split into two groups and were no longer in the vicinity.[22]

Miles was anxious to return to the Tongue River Cantonment. He had inflicted a severe blow to the Indians, and his primary concern now was the safety of his command.

> I had two enemies worse than the Indians to contend with—very severe elements and a terrible country to move over and the danger of getting snowed up without food was my greatest anxiety.[23]

On January 10, the command started back downriver toward the cantonment, arriving eight days later after a bitter trek through snow, ice, and blizzard. They had marched 242 miles, crossing the Tongue more than a hundred times going to and from Wolf Mountain. "Enthusiasm knew no bounds when the ringing sound of the 5th Infantry Band greeted our ears, coming out over the flat to break the monotonous tread of the boys in blue," Brown wrote.[24]

Miles had mixed emotions. He was pleased with the expedition itself because, although Wolf Mountain was not a major engagement in the sense of the Little Bighorn or Rosebud,

> it demonstrated the fact that we could move in any part of the country in the midst of winter, and hunt the enemy down in their camps wherever they might take refuge. In this way, constantly pursuing them, we had made them realize that there was no peace or safety for them while they remained in a hostile attitude.[25]

Privately, however, he felt hindered by a total lack of support from General Terry. In a letter of outrage to Sherman, he wrote:

> Fifteen hundred troops could have been wintered here without the least trouble but there has been the worst management in the rear of this com[man]d that I have ever known in the volunteer or regular service. . . . I am satisfied that there is criminal neglect of duty at St Paul or there is a determination that I shall not accomplish anything.

Upon returning to the cantonment, he said he found an inexplicable set of orders from Terry "for the immediate discharge" of all but two scouts, his teamsters, wagonmaster, contract blacksmiths, and other support, and a reduction of his transportation to thirty wagons, "which is not enough to reach any camp of Indians." This order, Miles said, "compells [sic] me to do just what Sitting Bull wanted me to do—namely go into winter quarters."

Although the country between the Bighorn and Little Missouri Rivers as far as the Bighorn Mountains had been swept free of Indians, Miles said if he were not allowed to mount a new expedition during the winter, the government could anticipate more Indian troubles west of the Bighorns in the spring.

Then Miles came to the point:

> Now if I have not earned a command [of a department] I never will, and if I have not given proff [sic] of my ability to bring my command into a successful encounter with Indians every time I never will[.] Besides I now have a better knowledge of this country than any other white man and unless you can give me a command and it should be no less than a department you can order my Regt[.] out of this country as soon as you like for I have campaigned long enough for the benefit of thieves and contractors. If you will give me this command & *one half the troops now in it, I will end this sioux war once and forever in four months.*[26]

Although Sherman found such tirades exasperating, he was accustomed to them, having had to tolerate similar outbursts from Mackenzie for years. Besides, badly as he disliked Miles, there was merit in the demand. Crook and Terry had both proven disappointing in this war. Terry's personal conduct of the campaign in his department had been disastrous, and Crook's only real success was due entirely to Mackenzie.

Sherman was particularly unhappy with Crook, who complained about lack of transportation and other necessities. In an acid comment to Sheridan, he wrote, "General Crook was certainly empowered to provide for his command as liberally as any General that ever took the Field at any time. . . . If his men were not properly provided with Everything, it was his own fault."[27]

More to the point, Crook had failed to follow up on Mackenzie's victory by moving against Crazy Horse, whom Sherman considered within striking distance. In a subsequent telegram to

Sheridan, Sherman praised Miles for the Wolf Mountain fight, then pointedly failing to mention Crook by name, asked, "Would it not help to have [the] other detachment engaged in the same manner from the direction of fort Reno[?]"[28]

In short, of all the independent commanders (Mackenzie being directly under Crook), only Miles had shown any real ability in this war. With him in charge of all field operations, Sherman believed the conflict might be ended in a timely manner.

Sheridan, however, could not envision the Indians standing still long enough to be defeated in a single all-or-nothing battle as Miles appeared to visualize, and said the war would have to "peter out" by the attrition campaign then being waged. To counter the suggestion that Miles have overall command, the lieutenant general proposed expanding his area of operations to include the Powder River country, which would extend his jurisdiction into the Department of the Platte, although he would nominally remain under General Terry's command. Once Mackenzie was released from duty in Washington, he would resume command of the Black Hills and the areas of the Little Missouri and Belle Fourche Rivers, on Miles's eastern flank. Terry would ensure that Miles received adequate supplies through St. Paul, while Crook would continue to supply Mackenzie.

Sherman agreed, and sent Miles a reassuring letter that acknowledged the complaints but explained the existing political impossibility of a single departmental command. Although swayed by Sheridan's argument for continuing the attrition campaign, Sherman nevertheless appealed to Miles's vanity by reminding him that whoever ended the war would be well on his way to promotion.[29]

31

Surrender

THE MAIN BAND OF OGLALAS FLED SOUTHWARD TO THE LITTLE
Powder River, but had lost most of their food and equipment to
Miles. Their original plan to move east was, for the time being,
abandoned; they were simply trying to survive. "We were almost
as poor as Dull Knife's people were the day they came to us," Black
Elk remembered. They now existed only by eating their ponies.

Crazy Horse and another group of Oglalas opted to go with the
Cheyennes. They fled southwest along the Tongue, traveling all
night and the next day, until their scouts in the rear confirmed that
the soldiers were marching back toward the Yellowstone.[1] They finally located near the base of the Bighorn Mountains where, on
January 15, they were joined by Sitting Bull with about a hundred
lodges of Hunkpapas. There was an abundance of buffalo in the
area and, after hunting for a while, the Indians moved on to the
Little Bighorn.

Various other bands joined during the march, and the camp became immense. Many of the remaining free-roaming Northern
Cheyennes were present, as were Crazy Horse and Little Big Man
of the Oglalas, Black Shield and Lame Deer with their Miniconjous, Spotted Eagle and Red Bear of the Sans Arcs, and Sitting Bull
with his Hunkpapas.[2]

So many Indians in one spot strained the game resources, but soldiers controlled the surrounding areas. The defeat at Wolf Mountain gave new confidence to the previously discredited peace faction. Many of the chiefs began to talk more openly of surrender, and arguments broke out in the council sessions. Despite the murder of their chiefs by Miles's Crows, most of the Miniconjous and Sans Arcs were ready to turn themselves in. The Hunkpapas and Oglalas remained hostile. The Cheyennes, who had borne the worst of the fighting since Reynolds's attack almost a year earlier, mainly wanted to be left alone.

Finally, in the early part of February, it was agreed they had to split up, with each band acting according to its own best interests. The Oglalas and Cheyennes remained along the Little Bighorn. The Miniconjous and Sans Arcs turned east toward the agencies, while the Hunkpapas, with a few hard-line Miniconjous and Sans Arcs under Lame Deer, headed for Canada.[3]

On February 1, Miles ordered Johnny Bruguier to take Sweet Woman, one of the Cheyenne women captured at Wolf Mountain, find the Indians, and deliver an ultimatum to surrender. Bruguier located the Cheyenne-Oglala camp on the Little Bighorn, where he gave them Miles's demand for unconditional surrender, as well as subsequent obedience to any orders received from the government. Failure to do so would bring an immediate military operation against them. Sweet Woman, who was thin but healthy, assured the Cheyennes that the captives were alive and well treated, and that armed sentries protected the women from the attentions of the soldiers.[4]

The chiefs conferred and announced they would start in the direction of the Tongue River Cantonment, making a final decision one way or the other en route. As they moved north along the Tongue, Bruguier announced he was going to continue on to the cantonment. Nineteen chiefs, among them Two Moons, Sleeping Rabbit, Iron Shirt, Crazy Mule, Black Bear, Little Creek, White Thunder, Crazy Head, and the medicine man, White Bull, resolved to accompany him and ascertain what would happen to the Cheyennes when they came in. They started toward the cantonment, while the remaining Cheyennes and Oglalas turned eastward toward the Powder River. There, the Cheyennes would wait for word from their chiefs while the Oglalas continued on east. The Cheyenne camp was only a short distance above the spot where they had been attacked by Reynolds.[5]

A few miles south of the cantonment, Bruguier rode ahead of the chiefs, to advise the soldiers they were coming in. They were to follow him in the next day. On February 19, as the chiefs neared the cantonment, Bruguier and another scout met them with a message from Miles, assuring them they could ride into the post unmolested. When they reached the parade ground, the soldiers fell into line. Not understanding the custom of saluting defeated enemy leaders, White Bull told Two Moons, "Make up your mind now. Have courage, for here we are to be killed." If Two Moons replied, it is not recorded.

Miles, however, rode up on a gray horse, shook hands with Two Moons and White Bull, introduced his staff, and ordered tents set up for the chiefs. Once they had settled in, he summoned them to his quarters.

"Here you are in my house and I want to talk to you," he told them. "In some ways I am a mean man. In other ways I am a good man. I want you people to come here and surrender to me; give me your arms and horses, and turn them over to me. If you do as I tell you, I will be a good man to you, but if you do not do this, I will be mean to you."

There was no other option, and Two Moons realized it. He replied, "It is well; we will go back to our camp, and move right in to the post and surrender to you."

Miles then suggested that one chief remain behind as a hostage, and after some deliberation, White Bull agreed to stay. Informed of the decision, Miles brought White Bull into his quarters and offered him a chair.

"I will do no harm to this man whom you are leaving with me, but I shall enlist him now as a scout." He would begin drawing pay immediately.[6] Two Moons seemed pleased with the idea, but the news was received with displeasure among the Cheyennes camped on the Powder River. Understandably it appeared to them that White Bull had reconciled himself to the whites by "hunting Indians."[7]

Now a new complication arose. A band of Cheyennes arrived

from the Nebraska agencies, and advised them they would get a better deal from General Crook in Nebraska. With most of the fighting finished, Crook was still looking for as much prestige as possible—by negotiating the peace for instance. Scattered groups of Indians coming into the Red Cloud Agency had reported the dissension among the hostiles, and as early as January Crook sent emissaries urging the various bands to come south and surrender to him. Unlike Miles, he offered to let them retain their arms and ponies.[8]

Crook was assisted by Spotted Tail, who had returned from the Indian Territory completely unimpressed and ready to help negotiate the surrenders for a price—Crook was to use his influence in Washington against plans to relocate the Lakota agencies to the Missouri River. Spotted Tail was one of the few Indian leaders sophisticated enough to realize that the Missouri River plan was simply the first step in the eventual removal of the tribes to the Territory; if Crook blocked the move, this would effectively end any notions of ultimately resettling the Lakotas in Oklahoma. Crook, who needed Spotted Tail's influence as badly as the chief needed his, readily agreed.[9]

In the Cheyenne camp, minor fighting broke out between peace advocates and hard-liners who still wished to continue the war. Nevertheless, Little Wolf and most of the others decided to go to Crook. The great medicine man Charcoal Bear announced the medicine lodge would accompany them. A small faction headed by Two Moons opted for Miles, while the hard-liners moved westward to join Lame Deer's Miniconjous, who had left Sitting Bull and were camped on a tributary of the Rosebud.[10]

As Two Moons's band approached Miles's cantonment, a delegation of chiefs went ahead to see if they might secure more favorable terms. When Miles advised them there could be no conditions other than the ones he had previously stated, the Indians became silent. Miles remembered this silence "was the cause of the most painful anxiety on my part as the moments went slowly by."

Finally, Little Chief spoke. After describing the historic right of his people to the contested country, calling the whites invaders and aggressors, and telling Miles that the Cheyennes were victims of a war they had not sought, Little Chief capitulated:

We are weak, compared with you and your forces; we are out of ammunition; we cannot make a rifle, a round of ammunition, or a knife; in fact we are at the mercy of those who are taking possession of our country; your terms are harsh and cruel, but we are going to accept them and place ourselves at your mercy.

Relieved, Miles offered to send a delegation of their people to Washington. They declined. One chief commented he had been to Washington, and had been shown a map on which had been designated land to be theirs in perpetuity. Now this land had been taken from them, proving the officials in Washington had lied. "You have not lied yet," the chief told Miles, "and I am going to try you and am coming in here. I am going to surrender to you."

The leading chiefs were kept in the cantonment as hostages while the others went to bring in their people. Two Moons's band surrendered on April 22, 1877. They were allowed to camp in a grove of timber by the river, outside the military reservation. The men were disarmed. Their ponies were herded together by the soldiers and driven into the post, later to be sold, with the proceeds going to purchase cattle for the Indians. A few days later, thirty warriors were rearmed and enlisted as scouts.[11]

WHILE MILES DEALT WITH THE BANDS OF TWO MOONS AND VARious other chiefs coming into his cantonment, the majority of the Indians were pushing south toward Nebraska and Crook's more favorable proposition. On February 24, Little Wolf arrived at Camp Robinson with a Cheyenne vanguard of eight warriors, ten women, and about twenty children.[12]

In late February or early March, Spotted Tail took about 250 Brulé chiefs and subchiefs to the Oglala camp to confer with his nephew, Crazy Horse. Spotted Tail spoke bluntly. If they did not surrender before spring, when the soldiers could move about easily, a new expedition would be mounted against them. Not only would Crook be assisted by his traditional scouts, the Crows and Shoshones, but by Lakotas and Cheyennes as well. Now that their own people and ancient allies had gone over to the government side, the Oglala chiefs knew the end had come for them, too. Crazy

Horse symbolically untied the war bindings of his pony's tail and let it fall free. In April, when the grass was high enough for the ponies to travel, they would begin the trek south to Camp Robinson and the Nebraska agencies.[13]

Crook had deftly played the Indian factions against each other. Divided among themselves, the Lakotas and Cheyennes now faced a united nation. The election crisis had been resolved when the southern states threw their electoral votes behind Hayes in exchange for concessions that included the removal of the last Reconstruction forces. The peaceful inauguration of Hayes and the withdrawal of troops from the South released more soldiers—including Mackenzie—for frontier duty.

This was emphasized by Spotted Tail, as he moved among the camps along the Little Powder and Little Missouri Rivers during February and March. When he returned to the agency on April 5, he brought 917 people, with assurances that Crazy Horse would arrive within the next month. In recognition of his achievement, Crook commissioned Spotted Tail as a lieutenant in the Regular Army.[14]

Not to be outdone by Spotted Tail, Red Cloud offered to go out and hurry Crazy Horse along. Like Spotted Tail, he was related to Crazy Horse and contended that as an Oglala he would have more influence than would the Brulé relative. Crook, eager for any means to speed up the process, approved, although he said Red Cloud would go as an interested party and not as a government representative.

Nevertheless, Crook gave Red Cloud a message for Crazy Horse. He said he planned to prepare for a new expedition immediately, and would remain in the field all summer and into the next winter. He had delayed operations simply to give those who so desired a chance to surrender. When he resumed hostilities, he would have a large contingent of Cheyennes, Arapahos, Shoshones, Bannocks, Pawnees, and Utes. Every day that Crazy Horse delayed his surrender "was one day closer to the moment when the troops and their Cheyenne allies were to sally out and attack and kill his warriors wherever found." Crook continually emphasized Cheyenne participation, knowing the effect it would have not only on Crazy Horse but on Red Cloud as well. He and Spotted Tail both feared

Crook's growing influence among the Cheyennes and Arapahos, and understood that if they did not do something to gain the general's gratitude, the Lakotas would come off second best.[15]

On April 14, as Crook waited for Red Cloud, Spotted Tail brought an immense column of Miniconjous and Sans Arcs into Camp Sheridan, where they halted and waited until Crook and Mackenzie arrived from the Red Cloud Agency about twenty miles away. Joe Wasson from the San Francisco *Alta California* estimated their number at 1,200 to 1,300 people, with 1,600 to 1,800 ponies.

When Crook appeared he dramatically unfurled the guidon of Company I, Seventh Cavalry, taken at the Little Bighorn and recaptured at Slim Buttes. After announcing their intention to surrender, the Indians dropped their weapons on the ground, then continued on to the Spotted Tail Agency, where they set up camp. Troops searched the tipis in the camp for additional weapons then, despite Crook's assurances to the contrary, rounded up their ponies and took them back to the post. Looking over the inventory of weapons, Bourke noted Springfield carbines taken at the Little Bighorn.[16]

One week after the Miniconjous and Sans Arcs reported to Camp Sheridan, Dull Knife came into the Red Cloud Agency with 524 Cheyennes. The effects of the Mackenzie fight the previous November were vividly apparent to Bourke:

> They are almost entirely without blankets and with only a very scant supply of robes. They have many widows and many people with frozen feet. . . .
> Their apologies for lodges are made from old remnants of canvas, old hides and robes, and even pieces of gunny sacks—just such things as they could pick up in the old camps of General Crook's Expedition. I saw not one perfect lodge. The squaws are also compelled to carry water in skin bags, as they have not a single utensil of any description.

Many were also wounded. They surrendered 600 ponies, sixty-eight carbines and rifles, thirty-four pistols, and fourteen bows and arrows.[17]

Crook ordered the surgeons to tend to the wounded and those suffering from exposure. The following day he held a council with the chiefs and said there were ample provisions for their needs. When he finished, Mackenzie told them, "Gen. Crook gives you what you need now, not because you went off to fight us, but because he sees how poor you are, and pities you, and believes that hereafter you will do right."

Dull Knife told Crook, "When your messengers came to us, we listened to their words and came right in. From this time on, anything you say to my people will be heeded." Turning to Mackenzie, he said, "You were the one I was afraid of when you came here last Summer."[18]

The Cheyenne surrender left Crazy Horse as the only remaining holdout in Crook's jurisdiction. On April 23, however, Bourke wrote in his diary, "Couriers from Crazy Horse's camp came in last night and confirmed . . . that he is moving as fast as he can towards this Agency. He appears to be travelling eight or ten miles a day." His band was virtually intact; Red Cloud had managed to prevent any serious defections. On May 2, when the exhausted, hungry Oglalas were thirty miles from the agency, a detachment from Camp Robinson met them with ten wagonloads of rations and a hundred head of cattle. They ate and rested for two days, before resuming the march.[19]

Shortly after noon on May 6, Crazy Horse came into Camp Robinson with 889 Oglalas and 2,000 ponies. Crook was in Washington, and Mackenzie did not come out to meet them. The honor of accepting the great chief's long-sought surrender went to Lt. Philo Clark, a specialist in sign language, who communicated with the Indians directly.

Crazy Horse offered his left hand to Clark, explaining, "I shake with this hand because my heart is on this side; I want this peace to last forever." The other chiefs then shook hands. The Oglalas were allowed to go on to the Red Cloud Agency, where, as soon as they were settled in, Clark confiscated their firearms. After that, they were generally left alone. The same week that Crazy Horse surrendered, Sitting Bull crossed the border into Canada.[20]

* * *

IN THE TONGUE RIVER CANTONMENT, MILES HAD AUGMENTED his infantry with four companies of Second Cavalry from Fort Ellis. He was preparing to go after Lame Deer's Miniconjous, who were hunting near the headwaters of the Rosebud. They represented the only major band that was not either fleeing to Canada or moving toward the agencies.

On May 1, Miles left the cantonment with almost 500 officers and men, including four companies each of Second Cavalry and Twenty-second Infantry, two companies of Fifth Infantry, a mounted detachment from the Twenty-second Infantry, and scouts.

During the next five days, they moved south along the Tongue until, on May 5, they reached the pass through the divide separating the valleys of the Tongue and Rosebud. At 2:30 P.M., Miles left the infantry to guard the wagon train, and took the cavalry and pack mules west over the divide. Crossing the Rosebud shortly before sundown, they continued through the rainy night. Finally, about 3:00 A.M., May 6, Miles halted for an extended rest, resuming the march about dawn.[21]

Some Indian scouts and soldiers moved ahead until, coming to the top of a high ridge, they spied Lame Deer's camp some fifteen miles away. At first, the whites saw only what appeared to be a mist rising against the side of one of the mountains, but the Indians insisted it was smoke from the campfires. They also saw ponies grazing on the hillsides. The entire scenario was eerily similar to that on the Crow's Nest overlooking the Little Bighorn, with two exceptions—this time, the whites could see the pony herd; and Miles was not Custer.

Miles waited until dark, then moved the command through hills and ravines toward the Indian camp. With frequent halts to avoid premature encounters, they continued until they were within five miles.[22]

"The first streak of daylight discovers to us the Indian village in the valley . . . ," Baldwin wrote. "The smoke of last night's camp fires still hovers over the lodges of the sleeping Indians, and a large herd of ponies are seen grazing close by the village."[23]

The camp was situated in typical Indian fashion, along the banks of the stream under the protection of hills on the opposite side. A few women were up early to stir the cooking fires, and some boys were tending the ponies, but most were asleep. The Cheyenne scout White Bull spotted a lone rider watching them from across the creek. He moved toward the village and disappeared, but still there was no alarm.

The scouts surveyed the area, and Miles halted so the men could adjust their saddles and check their weapons. He organized the command for attack and ordered that there would be no shooting of women and children. When everything was ready, Lt. E. W. Casey led twenty scouts the last mile toward the village to stampede the pony herd while Lt. Lovell H. Jerome's company headed off the herd and rounded it up. The remainder of the battalion charged directly into the village.

The boys herding the ponies dropped into the grass and opened fire. The noise of the horses coming into camp awoke the warriors, who put up a fight while women grabbed children and ran for the hills, driving with them some ponies that had been tethered by the tipis. Meanwhile, Casey had driven off the herd guards and Jerome's company secured the livestock. Within a few minutes, the camp was deserted, the warriors having fled toward a high hill beyond. Capt. Randolph Norwood took a dismounted company through the camp and chased them up the hill, while Capt. George Tyler moved up the adjacent hill to catch the massing warriors in a cross fire, pushing them farther back as Norwood's men inched up the steep hill and secured the heights.[24]

Lame Deer, the leading warrior Iron Star, and several other warriors had become separated from the others and were cut off in the camp. Miles ordered the Indian scouts to tell them that if they surrendered their lives would be spared. The hostiles put their weapons on the ground and Miles rode over, calling out one of the few Lakota phrases he knew, "How-how-kola," indicating he came as a friend. He extended his hand, which Lame Deer took, while his nervous adjutant, Lt. George W. Baird, shook hands with Iron Star.

At that point a misunderstanding led to a tragic consequence. A young white scout came up and, apparently fearing for Miles's life, leveled his rifle at Lame Deer. Instinctively, the chief jerked away, while Iron Star broke loose from Baird. Lame Deer grabbed one of the carbines that the Indians had just put down and fired at Miles, who wheeled his horse around and ducked. The bullet passed over him and struck his orderly, Pvt. Charles Shrenger, in the chest, killing him instantly.[25]

During the confusion, Lame Deer and Iron Star dashed up the hill, where they were caught in the cross fire between the main group of warriors and Tyler and Norwood's companies. Lame Deer was hit seventeen times. Iron Star was cut down thirty yards beyond.[26]

By 9:00 A.M., Miles was in complete control of the camp, which he intended to occupy while he waited for the infantry. The Indians had abandoned everything except a few rifles. More than 450 ponies were captured, all in excellent condition, having fattened up on the lush spring grass.

Unlike their poverty-stricken kinsmen and allies who had been forced to surrender for survival, these Indians appeared to have avoided much of the conflict of the previous sixteen months. Miles called the camp "one of the richest I had ever seen. It was composed of fifty-one beautiful lodges, richly stored with robes, horse-equipments, and every other species of Indian property." Baldwin recorded tons of dried buffalo meat, several hundred saddles and "bead work in profusion." When the infantry arrived that afternoon, the men were allowed to take what they wanted as souvenirs. The rest was burned the following morning.[27]

Total army losses were four killed and eight wounded. Seventeen dead Indians were counted, including Lame Deer. Before moving out, Miles ordered some 200 ponies selected on which to mount the infantry. Several horses were found with Seventh Cavalry brands. At 10:30 A.M., May 8, the command marched back toward the Rosebud and the Tongue, arriving at the cantonment on May 14.

The Lame Deer fight was the last battle. For better or worse, the only remaining free-roaming band was now as destitute as the rest and would have no other choice but to go into the agencies and surrender.

The Great Sioux War was over.

32

Aftermath

The Great Sioux War was perhaps the most costly of all Indian conflicts. Army losses from February 1876 through December 1877 were 283 killed (the majority of whom died at the Little Bighorn) and 125 wounded. These figures are for soldiers alone, and do not include civilians and Indian auxiliaries, who were also killed or wounded in government service. No one knows how many private citizens—settlers, Black Hills miners, and others—died at the hands of Indians on the northern plains in 1876 and 1877.

The financially battered government, still recovering from the Civil War and in the midst of economic depression, spent $2,312,531.24 defeating the Lakotas and their allies.[1] The actual impact of such a figure may be determined by considering that the same amount of money would have built at least nine large steam warships, fully armed and equipped, and ready for sea.

Hostile Indian losses will never be accurately determined. Battle casualties included both warriors and noncombatants. Many also died of starvation or exposure after their villages were destroyed by the army. By their traditional reckoning of wealth, the economic loss to the Indians was prohibitive. Their historic way of life was gone forever.

The fate of those conquered in the Great Sioux War depended largely on where they surrendered. The Cheyennes who capitulated to Miles were enlisted as scouts and allowed to remain along the Tongue River, where they served the army faithfully for almost twenty years. Those who surrendered to Crook at Camp Robinson were not so fortunate; despite their belief in a better deal, they were marched almost immediately to the Indian Territory. The removal of the Camp Robinson Cheyennes created misgivings among the Lakotas, who began to suspect they were next, regardless of Spotted Tail's arrangement with Crook.[2]

Their suspicions were well founded. In the wake of the long, bloody war, the Lakotas had few friends in the government, and the general public tended to view them all the same, no matter which side they had taken during the conflict. Congress resisted pressure to send them to the Territory, adopting a course only slightly less detestable in Lakota eyes—relocation of the Red Cloud and Spotted Tail Agencies to the west bank of the Missouri, near the town of Yankton. There they could be easily and economically supplied by steamer, and troops could control them. Supply and control were not the only considerations; area politicians and businessmen realized the two giant agencies with their vast populations would be an economic boon to Yankton and surrounding communities.

The Ponca Indians, a minor tribe traditionally friendly to the government, were summarily uprooted and removed to the Indian Territory so their reservation could be given over to the new Lakota agencies.[3] The very thing that Spotted Tail had worked so hard to oppose was now coming to pass.

As early as May 1877, when the last of the hostiles were still coming into the Nebraska agencies and Miles was mopping up in Montana, the first group from the Spotted Tail Agency was sent east to the new agencies on the Missouri. But many still remained at the old agencies. Some looked to Crazy Horse as a potential leader. Others, exhausted by war, feared him. And there were other chiefs, including Red Cloud and Spotted Tail, who were jealous of the psychological hold he had on the whites.

These rival chiefs now acted. Rumors were planted among the troops that Crazy Horse intended to break out. Lt. Philo Clark was ordered specifically to watch Crazy Horse and his Oglalas and "to keep General Crook fully informed as to anything of interest." Many Lakotas were ready to assist the soldiers.[4] Crazy Horse was dogged by informers, both Indian and white. Frank Grouard, who nursed old hatreds from his period of Oglala captivity, aggravated the situation by repeating hearsay to Clark, including an outrageous story of a plot to murder himself and Clark, and take over the agency.[5]

Even as these suspicions became aggravated, the government provoked a war with the long-friendly Nez Percés of Oregon's Wallowa Valley. This now appeared an appropriate time to test the allegiance of Crazy Horse and his Oglalas as scouts. Clark called a council at the Red Cloud Agency with Crazy Horse and several other leaders, to discuss their scouting against the Nez Percés. Apparently eschewing sign language, he took Grouard and Louis Bordeaux to interpret.[6]

Crazy Horse listened, then replied, "We are tired of war; we came in for peace, but now that the Great Father asks our help, we will go north and fight until there is not a Nez Percé left."

Incredibly, Grouard translated this last statement, "We will go north and fight until not a white man is left."

The flabbergasted Bordeaux tried to correct Grouard. Clark, however, had already decided to accept the translation, and was exchanging recriminations with the chiefs. Grouard hurried out of the meeting, and the lieutenant sent for William Garnett to finish translating for the council. Angered by Grouard's error and Clark's snub, Bordeaux lapsed into silence. Still unaware of the mistranslation, Crazy Horse was listing conditions for participation in the Nez Percé War, amid growing acrimony on both sides. Clark was in no mood to talk, and finally Crazy Horse lost his temper and left the meeting.[7]

This misunderstanding was a turning point. Relations now deteriorated until finally on September 5, General Crook notified Sheridan that he had ordered Crazy Horse's arrest. Crook recommended the government send him to some remote place, possibly the ancient Spanish castle at Fort Marion, Florida, a notorious detention center for undesirable chiefs.[8]

Crazy Horse, meanwhile, had taken refuge at the Spotted Tail

Agency, where he was advised he would have to return to Red Cloud as a prisoner. The same day that Crook urged Sheridan to transport him, Crazy Horse's party was riding to Red Cloud, when a courier brought orders diverting them to Camp Robinson. Arriving at the post, Crazy Horse was taken to the guardhouse.

Initially, he did not seem to comprehend the situation. Once inside the rough log building, however, he saw the cells and several prisoners in irons, and suddenly realized what was happening. With a shout, he drew his knife, slashed at the officer of the day, and dashed out the door where Pvt. William Gentles, one of the sentries, instinctively lowered his rifle to the challenge position. Little Big Man, who was standing outside, grabbed Crazy Horse, trying to pinion his arms behind him and force him to the ground. Thrown off balance, Crazy Horse fell against Gentles's bayonet. The weapon went through his side, piercing both kidneys.

Dr. Valentine McGillycuddy, the agency surgeon, forced his way through the line of guards and found Crazy Horse lying on his back, grinding his teeth and frothing in pain. Blood trickled out of his mouth. His pulse was already weak and missing beats. McGillycuddy realized the wound was mortal. Crazy Horse was taken to the post adjutant's office, where he died about midnight.[9]

The boyhood prophecy was fulfilled. Crazy Horse had been stabbed to death, his arms held behind him. The adjutant, Lt. Frederic S. Calhoun, may have felt a grim satisfaction that the chief had died in his office. His brother was Jimmi Calhoun, the Custer in-law killed at the Little Bighorn.[10]

With Crazy Horse dead, the chiefs now moved rapidly to assert themselves. Winter was approaching and the government was determined to enforce the edict that they relocate on the Missouri River. The supplies for the new agencies were there and would not be shipped to the existing ones. The Indians would move or they would starve.[11]

Still unhappy over the move, the chiefs did what they did best now that they could no longer lead their warriors in battle—they obstructed and delayed. In an effort to win them over, the government invited them to Washington, to meet the new Great Father.

*   *   *

RUTHERFORD B. HAYES SAW HIMSELF AS A HEALER. HE HAD BEEN elected amid accusations of fraud, and presided over a nation still divided by the bitterness of civil war. His confirmation as president had been the first act in bringing the people together, and he apparently believed this process of healing should include Indians as well. Part of the credit for this must go to General Crook, who, true to his pledge to Spotted Tail, had been hounding the government since summer to allow the Lakotas to live on some portion of their traditional lands.

Arriving at the White House on September 27, Red Cloud, Spotted Tail, and the others found Hayes a sympathetic listener who saw their viewpoint. He patiently explained that they would have to move to the Missouri for the winter because of the rations waiting for them. In the spring, however, he would send a commission to the remaining lands of the Great Sioux Reservation, and the chiefs could select any point inside the reservation boundaries for their permanent agencies. They returned home much encouraged; Red Cloud kept a copy of the proceedings, on which he carefully marked Hayes's statements in blue pencil.[12]

The move, which began in October, was not without travail, particularly among the Red Cloud Indians, who refused to be herded. Some of the northern bands, primarily those associated with Crazy Horse, slipped away and managed to return to their old haunts along the Powder River, or cross the border to Canada. Nevertheless, most settled near the old White River agencies, close enough to the Missouri to satisfy the government.

In the meantime, Carl Schurz, Hayes's brilliant, aggressive secretary of the interior, successfully fought a move in Congress to overrule the president and transfer the Lakotas to the Indian Territory of Oklahoma. On June 20, 1878, Congress authorized the commission promised by Hayes and just in time; the Lakotas on the White River were already accusing the government of betrayal. Ultimately, they got agencies in their old domains, with Red Cloud at Pine Ridge, South Dakota, and Spotted Tail at Rosebud, South Dakota, some distance to the east.[13]

*   *   *

THIS SAME INTERVAL, UNPLEASANT FOR THE LAKOTAS, WAS DISAStrous for the defeated Cheyennes in the Indian Territory. Arriving at the Cheyenne-Arapaho Agency at Darlington, Oklahoma, in the malarial heat of July, many were soon ill. During the following winter, 41 of the 999 Cheyennes died. Rations were short and barely edible, and they went hungry. Conditions became so intolerable that in July the next year, Little Wolf and Dull Knife's bands broke camp at the agency and started for their old homeland.

In what became known as the Cheyenne Autumn, they pushed northward, skirmishing with troops along the way. Little Wolf headed toward the Powder River country, while Dull Knife pushed toward the Red Cloud Agency, unaware it had been closed. Little Wolf's people eventually were intercepted by troops from Fort Keogh, as Miles's Tongue River Cantonment was now called. Taken to the fort, they were promptly enlisted as scouts. Thus, ironically, they finally settled in their own country.[14]

Dull Knife's band, on the other hand, was captured and interned at Fort Robinson. Driven by desperation and hunger, they broke out on January 9, 1879. Sixty-five were rounded up and brought back by morning, along with the bodies of fifty who, weakened by starvation and exposure, had died during the night. Ultimately most were captured. About fifty-eight were sent to join the Lakotas at Pine Ridge, and about twenty were returned to the Indian Territory. Some drifted up to Fort Keogh, where they were welcomed by Miles. The remainder died in the hills beyond Fort Robinson. Dull Knife settled with his family in Pine Ridge, where he died in 1883.[15]

FOR SITTING BULL'S PEOPLE, CANADA WAS NOT ALL THEY HAD hoped for. The Canadian government was uneasy about harboring so many battle-hardened Indians. Their presence also strained relations with the United States. The Mounted Police restricted their movements and watched them constantly. Finally, in 1881, Sitting Bull returned to the United States and surrendered at Fort Buford, Dakota Territory. By then, the war had been over for four years. Tempers had cooled and the chief found himself a minor celebrity.

In Canada, he had learned to write his name, and his autograph was in great demand.[16] He settled down at the Standing Rock Reservation, where he waged an almost continual contest of wills with the autocratic agent, James McLaughlin. Later Sitting Bull performed with Buffalo Bill's Wild West Show, ultimately returning to Standing Rock and resuming his old feud with the agent.

GRADUALLY, THE PLAINS INDIANS OF THE UNITED STATES BEGAN adjusting to a new life. If their will to war was not completely broken, their ability to make war was, and no one realized this better than the chiefs. Keeping their people under control, they secured limited self-government by tribal councils and maintained order with uniformed tribal police.

Among the Lakotas, Spotted Tail emerged at the forefront, winning a vicious political struggle for supremacy. Already paramount chief of the agencies by government mandate, it appeared he would gain the title over all the Lakotas by common consent, becoming the most powerful man in the nation's history. But the political fight had won him bitter enemies and on the Fourth of July, 1881, Spotted Tail was assassinated by Crow Dog, leader of the opposition. The last and greatest Brulé leader, his death ended their importance as a Lakota tribe.[17]

With Spotted Tail gone, Red Cloud assumed the mantle of leadership. He had grown increasingly visionary and over the years completely reorganized the Oglalas, ultimately persuading them to abandon their communal lifestyle and settle down on individual farms. The Oglalas began to prosper, setting an example for the Lakota Nation as a whole.[18]

Yet, while individual agencies and reservations might be successful, the situation among the Plains Indians as a whole was desperate. Many tribes, including those historically friendly to the government, had been reduced to near poverty. Their land was continually subdivided and the reservations diminished to areas that could barely support the populations. They were idle much of the time, and alcoholism ran rampant.

The Lakotas' turn came in the late 1880s, when their reservation was cut down to a shadow of its former size. In 1889, and again in

1890, the Midwest suffered crop failures. Many white settlers migrated to the Pacific or abandoned farming for other pursuits. The Indian farmers, however, had no such options. Restricted to their reservations, they were helpless.[19] Hungry and reduced to idleness, the Lakotas were ready for a deliverer.

His name was Wovoka, and he was a Paiute mystic strongly influenced by the passive forms of Christianity. Many of his teachings parallel those of Jesus, whom he often cited as inspiration. He preached universal peace, when the living would be united with the dead, the buffalo again would roam the earth, and the Indian would be free. In the meantime, the people were to dance, pray, and celebrate in honor of the Almighty.

In retrospect, the Ghost Dance religion, as it came to be called, appears to allude to a heavenly paradise rather than an earthly one. Wovoka was a prophet of friendship and brotherly love toward all men, regardless of color. Whatever the source of his vision, the Ghost Dance in its original form accomplished something unprecedented in history: It abolished centuries-old tribal hatreds, brought a renunciation of the warrior heritage, and drew the Plains Indians together in religious ecstacy.[20]

The religion spread rapidly among the desperate Indians of the plains. The federal government became alarmed at this newfound unity among the tribes, particularly since the initial religious fervor was beginning to show signs of xenophobia. Agent McLaughlin took steps to suppress it at Standing Rock, as did Agent J. G. Wright at Rosebud.

Some believed the government was overreacting. Indians belonging to established Christian churches said the Ghost Dance phenomenon was only temporary and advised letting it run its course.[21]

So did Nelson Miles. Now a major general and commander of the Military Division of the Missouri, he understood perfectly the desperation of the tribes.

"We have taken away their land and the white people now have it," he wrote his wife. "The Indians have been half fed or half starved. Neither I nor any other official can assure the Indians that they will receive anything different in the future. They say, and very justly, that they are tired of broken promises."[22]

Meeting with the new Oglala agent, Daniel F. Royer, on October 27, 1890, Miles speculated that the Ghost Dance would die out on its own. The following day he told the Indian leaders that the dance must stop, then left them to ponder his words in the slow, deliberate Indian fashion.

Miles realized that a decision to end the dance might take days or weeks, and returned to his headquarters in Chicago. The incompetent Royer, however, was frightened and bombarded the Indian Bureau with pleas for troops. Initially, cooler heads prevailed and Royer's requests were ignored. But on November 15, Agent Wright at Rosebud added his voice to the chorus, advising the bureau that his Indian police were rapidly losing control of the situation. Two days later, Miles ordered Brig. Gen. John R. Brooke, commander of the Department of the Platte, to occupy Pine Ridge and the Rosebud Agency. Brooke was specifically cautioned to keep his troops a safe distance from the Indian settlements and not allow them to become involved with the people. This way, Miles hoped to awe the Indians by a show of force while he pressured the Indian Bureau to upgrade agency rations and alleviate other grievances.[23]

At Standing Rock, the capable McLaughlin viewed Sitting Bull as the source of most Ghost Dance trouble, but did not consider him or the movement threats to peace at the agency. On the contrary, he was more concerned about a series of directives from the Indian Bureau, ordering him to "separate the well-disposed from the ill-disposed Indians," and stressing military involvement in suppressing the cult. Although McLaughlin enjoyed cordial relations with the military command at nearby Fort Yates, he felt he already had the agency under control, and soldiers would only aggravate the tensions. He therefore decided to obey the separation order by arresting Sitting Bull, but the job would be done by Indian police.[24]

On December 14, 1890, McLaughlin ordered forty-three Indian officers to surround Sitting Bull's house and bring him in. They rode out the next morning and at daybreak took him into custody. They also confiscated several weapons.

A crowd had gathered and, as Sitting Bull was brought out, two of his followers opened fire on the police. A vicious fight began. When it was over, Sitting Bull and seven Indian civilians were killed, along with five Indian police officers. The well-trained police held off the crowd for two hours until they were rescued by soldiers from Fort Yates.[25]

TROOPS HAD ALREADY OCCUPIED PINE RIDGE AND ROSEBUD, around the middle of November. Many alarmed Indians stampeded to what is now the Badlands National Park, some fifty miles to the northwest. General Brooke, however, had cordoned off the region, and the line of troops confined them to the general vicinity. At the same time, he assured them that the army did not want a war, and the military command intended to protect their rights and interests. Just after Christmas, most of the refugees broke camp and began moving back toward Pine Ridge, trailed at a distance by several detachments of troops. A large band of Lakota refugees from the Cheyenne River Agency under the chief Big Foot was intercepted by a detachment of Seventh Cavalry and escorted to Wounded Knee Creek. Big Foot had 106 warriors with their dependents, who pitched their tipis on an open plain west of Wounded Knee, just north of a dry ravine that led into the creek. To make certain they would remain, the camp was ringed on three sides by soldiers, with a fourth line of troops facing the Indians from the opposite side of the ravine. Four heavy-caliber Hotchkiss rapid-fire guns—each capable of firing fifty rounds a minute—were placed on a nearby rise and trained directly into the camp where the Indians had hoisted a white flag. All together there were 470 soldiers and scouts.

Brooke intended to disarm Big Foot's people, and send them back to their own agency. Shortly after 8:00 A.M., December 29, the warriors were ordered to assemble and turn over their weapons. As the soldiers searched, a young warrior named Black Fox pulled a rifle from under his blanket and opened fire. Instantly, a line of soldiers moved forward, raised their rifles, and fired point-blank into the crowd, their muzzles almost touching the Indians immediately in front. That first volley is believed to have killed about half the warriors. The survivors rushed the troops.

"For a few minutes," ethnologist James Mooney wrote in his report of the fight, "there was a terrible hand to hand struggle, where every man's thought was to kill. Although many of the warriors had no guns [i.e., rifles], nearly all had revolvers and knives in their belts under their blankets, together with some of the murderous warclubs still carried by the Sioux. The very lack of guns made the fight more bloody, as it brought the combatants to closer quarters."

The women and children rushed up to see what was happening. At that moment, the four Hotchkiss guns opened up with two-pound shrapnel shells. The flying fragments of exploding steel literally tore the spectators to pieces.

Within minutes 60 soldiers and 200 Indians were dead. The surviving Lakotas fled into a ravine. The Hotchkiss guns were shifted and swept the ravine with shrapnel.

"There can be no question that the pursuit was simply a massacre, where fleeing women, with infants in their arms, were shot down after resistance had ceased and when almost every warrior was stretched out dead or dying on the ground," Mooney reported.

The federal government ordered an immediate investigation. It determined that neither the Indians nor the soldiers anticipated trouble, and that both sides had gathered that morning in good faith. While it noted that the first shot was fired by an Indian, and that the soldiers behaved correctly in returning fire against the warriors, "the wholesale slaughter of women and children was unnecessary and inexcusable."[26] Wounded Knee has remained a bloody stain on the national conscience, the very name coming to mean massacre.

For all practical purposes, the Indian wars ended on that frozen, windswept plain in the newly created state of South Dakota on December 29, 1890.

That same year, the superintendent of census declared the American frontier was no longer a relevant factor in national development.

NOTES

INTRODUCTION

1. Connell, *Son of the Morning Star,* 332.
2. Gray, *Centennial Campaign,* 6; Plumb, "Victorians Unbuttoned," 20–21.
3. W. T. Sherman to John Sherman, September 23, 1868, qtd. in Athearn, *William Tecumseh Sherman,* 223.
4. Some might argue that Vietnam is an exception. In Vietnam, however, the weaponry of the Communist forces was comparable to the U.S., and Communist strategy and tactics were more sophisticated.
5. For a general overview of the Indian war soldier see Don Rickey, Jr., *Forty Miles a Day on Beans and Hay.*
6. Utley, *Frontier Regulars,* 11, 14–15.
7. Rickey, *Forty Miles a Day,* 221–22.
8. Ibid., 217–19; Hunt and Hunt, *I Fought With Custer,* 92; Wilson, *Peacemakers,* 23.
9. Fox, *Archaeology,* 41–45.
10. Jordan, "Ghosts on the Little Bighorn," 797; Wilson, *Peacemakers,* 33–34; Robinson, *Bad Hand,* 234.
11. W. P. Clark to AG, Platte, September 14, 1877, in RG 393, Special File, Military Division of the Missouri, Sioux Wars, hereinafter cited as "Special File—Sioux."
12. Connell, *Son of the Morning Star,* 308.

1: THE INDIANS AND THE LAND

1. "The Black Hills," 305.
2. Ibid.
3. Mooney, *Calendar History of the Kiowa Indians*, 156–57.
4. Hassrick, *The Sioux*, 3, 6.
5. Not connected with the Piegan Blackfeet of the far north.
6. Hassrick, *The Sioux*, 7.
7. Ibid.
8. Hyde, *Red Cloud's Folk*, 3–4.
9. Ibid., 17.
10. Grinnell, *Cheyenne Indians*, 1:1, 7–10.
11. Hassrick, *The Sioux*, 13–14.
12. Grinnell, *Cheyenne Indians*, 1:1.
13. Ibid., 2:48–50; Hassrick, *The Sioux*, 91.
14. Catlin, *Letters and Notes*, 1:208–11.
15. DeLand, *Sioux Wars*, 15:33.
16. Parkman, *California and Oregon Trail*, 137.
17. DeLand, *Sioux Wars*, 15:33–34; Hyde, *Red Cloud's Folk*, 58.
18. Olson, *Red Cloud*, 4–5.
19. Parkman, *California and Oregon Trail*, 136.
20. Olson, *Red Cloud*, 6–7.
21. For a detailed study of the Grattan Massacre, see Lloyd E. McCann, "The Grattan Massacre," *Nebraska History*, 37:1, March 1956, available in reprint.

2: DEFEAT AND DUPLICITY

1. Nickerson, "Major General George Crook," 20.
2. Jesse M. Lee to Walter M. Camp, May 13, 1910, Camp Collection.
3. DeBarthe, *Frank Grouard*, 117.
4. Bourke, *On the Border*, 414–15; Louis Bordeaux to Eli Ricker, Ricker Papers.
5. Michno, "Crazy Horse," 42.
6. Sandoz, *Crazy Horse*, 103–5.
7. William Garnett to Eli Ricker, Ricker Papers. This conflicts with Black Elk's account, which says Crazy Horse tied his pony's tail. See Neihardt, *Black Elk*, 139.
8. DeLand, *Sioux Wars*, 15:43–45; Olson, *Red Cloud*, 9–10; Brown, *Fetterman Massacre*, 13–15.
9. Olson, *Red Cloud*, 14; Brown, *Fetterman Massacre*, 16.
10. Carrington, *Ab-sa-ra-ka*, 79.
11. For a detailed study of Red Cloud, see George Hyde, *Red Cloud's Folk*, and James C. Olson, *Red Cloud and the Sioux Problem*.

12. Carrington, *Ab-sa-ra-ka*, 110–18; Brown, *Fetterman Massacre*, 74–77.

13. Carrington, *Ab-sa-ra-ka*, 120–21.

14. The figure is from the muster roll of Fort Phil Kearny for August 31, 1866, and is quoted in Brown, *Fetterman Massacre*, 106.

15. DeLand, *Sioux Wars*, 15:126–27; Olson, *Red Cloud*, 58–60.

16. The full text of the treaty with signatures is reprinted in Lazarus, *Black Hills*, 433–99.

17. Qtd. in Gray, *Centennial Campaign*, 15.

3 : BLACK HILLS FEVER

1. Department of the Interior, *Annual Report—1877*, 19; Hyde, *Red Cloud's Folk*, 190–91, 200.

2. Hyde, *Spotted Tail's Folk*, 150; Lazarus, *Black Hills*, 65.

3. Lazarus, *Black Hills*, 66.

4. Grant, Second Inaugural Address, March 4, 1873, in Richardson, *Messages and Papers*, 6:4176.

5. Qtd. in Lazarus, *Black Hills*, 64.

6. Marquis, *Wooden Leg*, 178.

7. Sitting Bull's life is recounted in two significant books. Stanley Vestal's classic *Sitting Bull, Champion of the Sioux,* tells the story of the first coup on pp. 9–13. A more recent work is *The Lance and the Shield: The Life and Times of Sitting Bull,* by Robert Utley, who describes Sitting Bull's elevation to the paramount chieftaincy on pp. 85–87.

8. DeLand, *Sioux Wars*, 15:257–58.

9. King, *Campaigning With Crook*, 16.

10. The best work on Sheridan's career in the west is Paul Andrew Hutton's *Phil Sheridan and His Army.*

11. Gray, *Centennial Campaign*, 16; Lazarus, *Black Hills*, 69.

12. Alfred H. Terry to George Armstrong Custer, May 30, 1874; Custer to Terry, May 30, 1874, both in RG 393, Special File, Military Division of the Missouri, Citizens Expedition to the Black Hills, hereinafter cited as "Special File—Citizens."

13. Custer is one of the most extensively studied individuals in the English language, with dozens of new books appearing each year. The classics include Elizabeth Custer's *Boots and Saddles,* Frederick F. Van de Water's *Glory Hunter,* and Evan Connell's *Son of the Morning Star.* Among the numerous recent works is Robert Utley's *Cavalier in Buckskin.*

14. Sioux City *Daily Journal*, September 4, 1874.

15. Captain R. H. Offly, Fort Sully, to AAG DptDak, December 21, 1874; Terry to AAG MilDivMo, March 9, 1875, Special File—Citizens.

16. William D. Whipple, AG USA to Sheridan, March 17, 1875, ibid.

17. *New York Herald,* July 1, 1875; ibid., July 5, 1875.

18. Undated and unattributed newspaper clippings in John Gregory Bourke, Diary, Vol. 2.

4: THE ROAD TO WAR

1. Department of War, *Annual Report—1876,* 498. In preparing his annual report for 1876, the always thorough Crook often referred back to the preceding report, submitted on September 15, 1875, to give a general overview of the situation in his department. Although Colorado was in the Department of the Missouri, commanded by Gen. John Pope, the raids into that territory originated in Crook's jurisdiction.

2. Hyde, *Red Cloud's Folk,* 240; Bourke, Diary, 3:40. Bourke heard the story of Sitting Bull's refusal from scout Louis Richaud, who delivered the message to the chief and received the answer.

3. DeLand, *Sioux Wars,* 15:272–75; Utley, *Frontier Regulars,* 245; Hyde, *Red Cloud's Folk,* 240–45; Department of Interior, *Annual Report—1876,* 33–34.

4. Department of War, *Annual Report—1876,* 28.

5. Bourke, *On the Border,* 287; Anderson, "A Challenge," 46.

6. Department of War, *Annual Report—1876,* 440; Anderson, "A Challenge," 48.

7. Department of the Interior, *Annual Report—1876,* xv; extract of Burke's letter in Chandler to secretary of war, January 25, 1876, Special File—Sioux War; Anderson, "A Challenge," 48.

8. J. Q. Smith to secretary of the interior, January 21, 1876, Special File—Sioux.

9. Sheridan to Sherman, January 4, 1876, ibid.

10. Gray, *Centennial Campaign,* 32.

11. Custer to AAG, DptDak, March 3, 1875, Special File—Citizens.

12. Department of Interior, *Annual Report—1876,* iv–v, 33; Butler, *Daughters of Joy,* 10.

13. J. Q. Smith to Chandler, January 21, 1876, Special File—Sioux.

14. Sheridan, Sherman, endorsements to ibid.

15. C. W. Darling to Huston, February 15, 1876; Maj. Orlando H. Moore to Huston, n.d., both ibid.

16. Athearn, *William Tecumseh Sherman,* 308–9; Chandler to secretary of war, February 1, 1876, Special File—Sioux.

17. Department of War, *Annual Report—1876,* 440.

18. Gray, *Centennial Campaign,* 36–37.

19. Terry to AAG, MilDivMo, February 8, 1876, Special File—Sioux.

20. Sheridan to Terry, February 8, 1876, ibid.

5 : THE ARMY TAKES THE FIELD

1. Department of the Interior, *Annual Report—1876,* xiv.
2. Gibbon, "Gibbon on the Sioux Campaign," 64.
3. The Territory of Dakota was partitioned into north and south for admission as two separate states in 1889. Bismarck is now the capital of North Dakota.
4. Brown, *Plainsmen,* 241.
5. Hutton, *Phil Sheridan,* 130–31; Boatner, *Civil War Dictionary,* 831.
6. Stewart, "Major Brisbin's Relief," 116–18.
7. Ibid., 118–19; Department of War, *Annual Report—1876,* 458–59.
8. Gibbon, "Gibbon on the Sioux Campaign," 4–5.
9. Gibbon to Terry, March 8, 1876, Special File—Sioux.
10. Bourke, Diary, 3:1–2.
11. At the time of the campaign, the Indians also knew Crook as "Lone Star," a reference to the rank insignia of a brigadier general. Sometimes he was called "Three Stars," apparently because of the various placements of a brigadier general's star about the uniform. See De Barthe, *Frank Grouard,* 485–86.
12. O'Neal, *Fighting Men,* 96–97; Mills, *My Story,* 407; Hutton, *Phil Sheridan,* 124–25; Robinson, *Bad Hand,* 212; Nickerson, "Major General George Crook," 15, 19; Bourke, Diary, 3:95–96.
13. Bourke, Diary, 3:2–3; Brown, *Plainsmen,* 241.
14. Bourke, Diary, 3:3–4.
15. Robert Strahorn, Denver *Rocky Mountain News,* February 24, 1876.
16. Bourke, Diary, 3:2.
17. The city of Laramie is forty miles west of Cheyenne, while Fort Laramie is about ninety miles to the northeast. Both are named for their proximity to the meandering Laramie River, which flows into the North Platte by Fort Laramie.
18. Strahorn, Denver *Rocky Mountain News,* undated clipping in Bourke, Diary, 3.
19. Bourke, Diary, 3:6; Hedren, *Fort Laramie,* 58.
20. De Barthe, *Frank Grouard,* 504.
21. Frank Grouard's life is told in De Barthe, *Life and Adventures of Frank Grouard.* The story that Grouard was half Oglala was told by Mrs. Nettie Goings, an Oglala woman who claimed to be his half-sister through the same father, and by William Garnett, both of whom were interviewed by Judge Eli Ricker. Their statements are in the Ricker Papers.
22. De Barthe, *Frank Grouard,* 178–79; Gilbert, *"Big Bat,"* 45.
23. Bourke, Diary, 3:38; Hedren, *Fort Laramie,* 60.
24. Bourke, Diary, 3:11–13; Cheyenne *Daily Leader,* February 24, 1876.
25. Bourke, Diary, 3:27.

6: COLLISION COURSE

1. Department of War, *Annual Report—1876,* 1:502.
2. Robinson, *Bad Hand,* 52–53, 192–93; Werner, *"The Soldiers Are Coming!"* 10; Bourke, *On the Border,* 270; Mills, *My Story,* 163.
3. Knight, *Following the Indian Wars,* 169–71.
4. Dobak, "Yellow-Leg Journalists," 89. This situation was commonplace in the nineteenth-century army. During the Civil War, Confederate officers often got their best information on Union military and naval movements from the New York newspapers.
5. O'Neal, *Fighting Men,* 47–48.
6. Marquis, *Wooden Leg,* 155.
7. Ibid., 3–5.
8. Ibid., 159–61.
9. Strahorn, Denver *Rocky Mountain News,* March 16, 1876.
10. Bourke, Diary, 3:28–32.
11. Strahorn, Denver *Rocky Mountain News,* March 16, 1876.
12. Ibid.; Bourke, Diary, 3:37–38.
13. Strahorn, Denver *Rocky Mountain News,* undated clipping in Bourke, Diary, 3.
14. Bourke, Diary, 3:41–42.
15. Strahorn, undated clipping in Bourke, Diary, 3; Bourke, ibid., 3:44ff.
16. Bourke, Diary, 3:44ff.
17. Ibid., 3:56–61, 67.
18. Bourke, *On the Border,* 259.
19. De Barthe, *Frank Grouard,* 180.
20. Bourke, Diary, 3:67ff.
21. Marquis, *Wooden Leg,* 159–63.
22. Ibid., 163; Two Moons, in Hardorff, *Lakota Recollections,* 131–32.
23. Marquis, *Wooden Leg,* 163–64.
24. Schmitt (ed.), *General George Crook,* 191; Bourke, Diary, 3:64ff.
25. Bourke, Diary, 3:34ff, and *On the Border,* 269–70; Schmitt, *General George Crook,* 191.

7: "THE SOLDIERS ARE RIGHT HERE!"

1. De Barthe, *Frank Grouard,* 188; Bourke, *On the Border,* 270–71; Strahorn, Denver *Rocky Mountain News,* undated clipping in Bourke, Diary, 3; Werner, *"The Soldiers Are Coming!"* 19.
2. Bourke, Diary, 3:102–3; Strahorn, Denver *Rocky Mountain News,* undated clipping, ibid., 3.
3. Marquis, *Wooden Leg,* 164.
4. Bourke, Diary, 3:105–9; De Barthe, *Frank Grouard,* 190–91.
5. Bourke, Diary, 3:108–9.
6. Ibid., 3:109.

7. Anson Mills to Lt. Charles Morton, March 27, 1876, qtd. in Werner, *"The Soldiers Are Coming!"* 65–66; Hutton, *Phil Sheridan,* 303.

8. Bourke, Diary, 3:110–13, and *On the Border,* 273.

9. Marquis, *Wooden Leg,* 164–65; Strahorn, Denver *Rocky Mountain News,* undated clipping in Bourke, Diary, 3.

10. Marquis, *Wooden Leg,* 165–66.

11. Strahorn, Denver *Rocky Mountain News,* undated clipping in Bourke, Diary, 3; Bourke, ibid., 3:113ff.

12. Marquis, *Wooden Leg,* 166–67.

13. Mills to Morton, March 27, quoted in Werner, *"The Soldiers Are Coming!"* 66–67.

14. Marquis, *Wooden Leg,* 167–68; Two Moons, in Hardorff, *Lakota Recollections,* 132.

15. Marquis, *Wooden Leg,* 165.

16. Mills to Morton, March 27, 1876, reprinted in Werner, *"The Soldiers Are Coming!"* 68–69.

17. Strahorn, Denver *Rocky Mountain News,* undated clipping in Bourke, Diary, 3; Bourke, ibid., 3:120–24.

18. Bourke, Diary, 3:122–23; Reynolds to AAG, Platte, April 15, 1876, reprinted in Werner, *"The Soldiers Are Coming!"* 62.

19. Bourke, Diary, 3:123–24.

20. Ibid., 3:126–28.

21. Ibid., 3:130.

22. Ibid; Schmitt, *General George Crook,* 192; Nickerson, "Major General George Crook," 21–22.

23. Secretary of War, *Annual Report—1876,* 1:502.

24. Bourke, Diary, 3:131ff; Schmitt, *General George Crook,* 191–92.

8: THE INDIANS CONSOLIDATE

1. Marquis, *Wooden Leg,* 168–70, and *Custer on the Little Bighorn,* 82; Two Moons, in Hardorff, *Lakota Recollections,* 132.

2. Sandoz, *Crazy Horse,* 303–5; Marquis, *Wooden Leg,* 170.

3. Two Moons, in Hardorff, *Lakota Recollections,* 132–33.

4. Sandoz, *Crazy Horse,* 307–8; Vestal, *Warpath,* 182–83; Marquis, *Wooden Leg,* 170–72, 177; Utley, *Lance and Shield,* 132.

5. Vestal, *Warpath,* 185, and *Sitting Bull,* 141.

6. Department of the Interior, *Annual Report—1876,* iv–v; Hyde, *Red Cloud's Folk,* 259.

7. Cheyenne *Daily Leader,* April 5, 1876; *New York Tribune,* April 7, 1876.

8. Cheyenne *Daily Leader,* April 7, 1876.

9. Crook to Sheridan, March 24, 1876, Special File—Sioux.

10. Olson, *Red Cloud,* 217–18.

11. Gibbon to Terry, March 30, 1876; Terry to Gibbon, March 31, 1876, Special File—Sioux.
12. Lt. George Ruhlen to Terry, April 19, 1876, with endorsements, ibid.
13. Gray, *Centennial Campaign,* 335; Hyde, *Red Cloud's Folk,* 259.
14. Reno to AAG DptDak, April 27, 1876; Reno to Col. George Ruggles, May 2, 1876, Special File—Sioux.

9: BLUNDERING ALONG THE YELLOWSTONE

1. Marquis, *Wooden Leg,* 179–84.
2. Ibid., 185–86; Sandoz, *Crazy Horse,* 308–9.
3. Hampton, "Battle of the Big Hole," 4.
4. Gibbon to G. D. Ruggles, AAG, DptDak, October 17, 1876, reprinted in Overfield, *Little Big Horn, 1876,* 78–79; Gibbon to Terry, April 3, 1876, in Special File—Sioux; Gibbon, "Gibbon on the Sioux Campaign," 5.
5. Geant, "Journal," April 7, 1876.
6. O'Neal, *Fighting Men,* 50. Bradley was killed during the Nez Percé War in 1877.
7. Leforge, *Memoirs,* 206–9; Bradley, *Montana Column,* 48–49. This Curly is not to be confused with Crazy Horse.
8. Gray, *Centennial Campaign,* 73; Gibbon, "Gibbon on the Sioux Campaign," 5.
9. Gray, "Captain Clifford's Story," 1:75–76.
10. Bradley, *Montana Column,* 67–68; Gibbon to Ruggles, October 17, 1876, in Overfield, *Little Big Horn, 1876,* 79–80.
11. Johnson, "With Gibbon," 9:1:1.
12. McClernand, *On Time for Disaster,* 43.
13. Bradley, *Montana Column,* 85; Gibbon, "Gibbon on the Sioux Campaign," 12.
14. Buecker, "A Surgeon at the Little Big Horn," 128.
15. Bradley, *Montana Column,* 87–88; Leforge, *Memoirs,* 212–13.
16. Bradley, *Montana Column,* 89–93.
17. Gray, "Captain Clifford's Story," 1:77.
18. Leforge, *Memoirs,* 221–22.
19. Gray, "Captain Clifford's Story," 1:77; Bradley, *Montana Column,* 95–96; McClernand, *On Time for Disaster,* 138.
20. Bradley, *Montana Column,* 96–97.
21. Ibid., 99–102.
22. Geant, "Journal," April 17, 1876; Bradley, *Montana Column,* 102–4; Schneider, *Freeman Journal,* 45; Gray, *Centennial Campaign,* 80–81; Gibbon to Ruggles, October 17, 1876, in Overfield, *Little Big Horn, 1876,* 80.
23. Geant, "Journal," April 17, 1876.

24. Bradley, *Montana Column,* 104–5; Gibbon, "Gibbon on the Sioux Campaign," 14–15.

25. Bradley, *Montana Column,* 107; Gray, *Centennial Campaign,* 81.

26. Bradley, *Montana Column,* 107–11.

27. Ibid., 119–22.

28. Leforge, *Memoirs,* 229–30.

29. Bradley, *Montana Column,* 122–24; Gibbon, "Gibbon on the Sioux Campaign," 18.

30. DeLand, *Sioux Wars,* 15:346–47.

10: THE MARCH OF THE DAKOTA COLUMN

1. Utley, *Cavalier in Buckskin,* 156–57.

2. Ibid., 157; Custer, *Boots and Saddles,* 210–14.

3. Gray, *Centennial Campaign,* 59–60; Stewart, *Custer's Luck,* 122.

4. Gray, *Centennial Campaign,* 68; Utley, *Cavalier in Buckskin,* 161–62.

5. R. C. Drum, AAG, MilDivMo, to Terry, May 5, 1876, reprinted in Whittaker, *General George A. Custer,* 555–56.

6. DeLand, *Sioux Wars,* 15:427–28.

7. Officially, Col. Samuel Sturgis was commander of the Seventh Cavalry. However, he was kept perpetually on detached duty, in part because of a poor service record during the Civil War, and partly to give Custer a free hand with the regiment.

8. Terry to AG, MilDivMo, May 6, 1876, in Whittaker, *General George A. Custer,* 559–60.

9. DeLand, *Sioux Wars,* 15:430–31.

10. Hunt and Hunt, *I Fought With Custer,* 56.

11. Custer, *Boots and Saddles,* 218.

12. Ibid., 216–17; Buecker, "Frederic S. Calhoun," 22. Emma Reed later married Jimmi Calhoun's younger brother, Fred, doubling the relationship between the Custers and the Calhouns.

13. Terry, Annual Report, qtd. in *Field Diary,* 2; Mark Kellogg, *New York Herald,* June 19, 1876.

14. Gray, *Centennial Campaign,* 98; Reynolds, Diary.

15. Custer, *Boots and Saddles,* 220; Hunt and Hunt, *I Fought With Custer,* 53.

16. Utley, *Cavalier in Buckskin,* 168; O'Neal, *Fighting Men,* 41–42; Connell, *Son of the Morning Star,* 33, 39, 40–41; DeWolf to wife, May 14, 1876, in Luce, "Diary and Letters," 72; Thompson, "Custer's Last Fight," Belle Fourche, S.D., *Bee,* February 19, 1914; Hunt and Hunt, *I Fought With Custer,* 50.

17. *St. Paul Pioneer-Press,* May 27, 1876.

18. Terry, *Field Diary,* 15–19; *St. Paul Pioneer-Press,* June 15, 1876.

19. Terry, *Field Diary,* 16; Gray, *Centennial Campaign,* 98–99.

20. Terry, *Field Diary,* 19; Gray, *Centennial Campaign,* 99.

21. Dunlay, *Wolves for the Blue Soldiers,* 54; Connell, *Son of the Morning Star,* 15.

22. George Armstrong Custer to Elizabeth B. Custer, May 30, 1876, qtd. in Custer, *Boots and Saddles,* 268; George Ruggles, AAG, DptDak, to AG, MilDivMo, June 10, 1876. Special File—Sioux; Luce, "Diary and Letters," 77.

23. Terry, *Field Diary,* 19.

24. Ibid.; Custer to Elizabeth B. Custer, May 31, 1876, qtd. in Custer, *Boots and Saddles,* 269–70; Gray, *Centennial Campaign,* 101.

25. Terry, *Field Diary,* 19.

26. *St. Paul Pioneer-Press,* June 24, 1876.

11: CROOK TRIES AGAIN

1. Bourke, *On the Border,* 283–85, and Diary, 4:220; Headquarters, Department of the Platte, General Court Martial Orders No. 29, May 2, 1876, copy in Bourke, Diary, 4.

2. Maj. Edwin F. Townsend to Sheridan, May 30, 1876, Special File—Sioux War; Chicago *Inter-Ocean,* May 18, 1876.

3. Crook to Sheridan, May 29, 1876. Special File—Sioux.

4. Chicago *Inter-Ocean,* May 11, 1876; Cheyenne *Leader,* May 11, 1876.

5. Chicago *Inter-Ocean,* May 11, 1876; Bourke, *On the Border,* 287.

6. Crook to Sheridan, May 17, 1876. Special File—Sioux; Hutton, *Phil Sheridan,* 312; King, *War Eagle,* 153–54.

7. Bourke, *On the Border,* 286.

8. New York *Sun,* May 10, 1876.

9. *Omaha Herald,* May 19, 1876.

10. Bourke, Diary, 4:314–15; and *On the Border,* 291.

11. O'Neal, *Fighting Men,* 187–89.

12. Mills's life is told in his autobiography, *My Story.*

13. Mills, ibid., 397.

14. Knight, *Following the Indian Wars,* 168–73; Finerty, *War-Path,* 4–5.

15. R. Williams, AAG, Platte, to Sheridan, June 5, 1876. Special File—Sioux.

16. Neihardt, *Black Elk,* 92–94.

17. Vestal, *Sitting Bull,* 142.

18. Marquis, *Wooden Leg,* 186–88.

19. Ibid., 178–79.

20. Utley, *Lance and Shield,* 135.

21. Ibid., 136–37.

22. Bourke, Diary, 4:317, 335–37; Capron, "Indian Border War," 7.

23. Mills, *My Story,* 397–98.

24. Bourke, Diary, 4:340–41.

25. Ibid., 4:346, and *On the Border*, 293.

26. Capron, Diary, June 5, 1876; Finerty, *War-Path*, 78–79.

27. Bourke, *On the Border*, 294–95; Finerty, *War-Path*, 87–88.

28. Finerty, *War-Path*, 88.

1 2 : THE MARCH TO THE ROSEBUD

1. Sherman to Sheridan, June 5, 1877. Special File—Sioux.

2. Hedren, *Fort Laramie*, 63–65.

3. Ibid., 106–7; Merritt to Sheridan, June 7, 1876. Special File—Sioux.

4. P. H. Sheridan to Michael V. Sheridan, various telegrams, June 12–18, 1876. Special File, ibid.; Hutton, *Phil Sheridan*, 312–13.

5. Quoted in King, *War Eagle*, 155.

6. Capron, Diary, June 8, 1876; Bourke, Diary, 4:357.

7. Neihardt, *Black Elk*, 95.

8. Marquis, *Custer on the Little Bighorn*, 83.

9. Ibid., *Wooden Leg*, 187–92.

10. Grinnell, *Fighting Cheyennes*, 328–89; Marquis, ibid., 190–91, 193–95.

11. Finerty, *War-Path*, 89–90; Vaughn, *With Crook*, 16–17.

12. Finerty, *War-Path*, 92–95; Bourke, Diary, 4:368–69.

13. Crook to Sheridan, June 15, 1876, Special File—Sioux; Vaughn, *With Crook*, 19.

14. Bourke, Diary, 4:371, 375–76; Capron, Diary, June 12, 1876.

15. Neihardt, *Black Elk*, 95–96.

16. Ibid., 96–98; Hassrick, *The Sioux*, 282–83.

17. Neihardt, *Black Elk*, 98.

18. Utley, *Lance and Shield*, 137–38.

19. Bourke, Diary, 4:379–83; Capron, Diary, June 14, 1876; Finerty, *War-Path*, 98–100.

20. Bourke, Diary, 5:384–85.

21. Ibid., 5:383; G. L. Luhn, letter to wife, June 15, 1876, Luhn, Diary and Letters.

22. Bourke, Diary, 5:386–87; Crook to Sheridan, June 15, 1876. Special File—Sioux.

23. Bourke, Diary, 5:388, 396; Finerty, *War-Path*, 102. Bourke called the Shoshones "Snakes," which was another name for the tribe at the time, not meant as derogatory.

24. Bourke, Diary, 5:388–91; Old Crow's speech in Finerty, *War-Path*, 104.

25. Bourke, Diary, 5:391–92; Nickerson, "Major General George Crook," 23.

26. Capron, Diary, June 14, 1876.

27. Crook to Sheridan, June 15, 1876. Special File—Sioux.
28. Bourke, *On the Border,* 304.

13: CROOK DEFEATED

1. Nickerson, "Major General George Crook," 23–24.
2. Luhn, Diary, 9; Capron, Diary, June 15, 1876; Bourke, Diary, 5:393–94; Finerty, *War-Path,* 114.
3. Bourke, Diary, 5:394.
4. Ibid., 5:397.
5. Ibid., 5:398; Capron, Diary, June 16, 1876; Finerty, *War-Path,* 115–17.
6. Mills, *My Story,* 398.
7. Bourke, Diary, 5:400–1; Capron, Diary, June 16, 1876.
8. Bourke, Diary, 5:403–4; Capron, Diary, June 16, 1876; Finerty, *War-Path,* 121; Mills, *My Story,* 399–400.
9. Bourke, Diary, 5:404; Finerty, *War-Path,* 122.
10. Bourke, Diary, 5:404.
11. Grinnell, *Fighting Cheyennes,* 330–32; Vestal, *Warpath,* 185; Neihardt, *Black Elk,* 99; Marquis, *Wooden Leg,* 198.
12. Marquis, *Wooden Leg,* 198–99; Neihardt, *Black Elk,* 99.
13. Luhn, Diary, 9; Finerty, *War-Path,* 124–25; Nickerson, "Major General George Crook," 25.
14. Finerty, *War-Path,* 126; Vaughn, *With Crook,* 47–48, 188; Lemly, "Fight on the Rosebud," 13.
15. Grinnell, *Fighting Cheyennes,* 333; Marquis, *Warpath,* 187.
16. Marquis, *Wooden Leg,* 199; Grinnell, *Fighting Cheyennes,* 333; Marquis, *Warpath,* 187.
17. Nickerson, "Major General George Crook," 25; Vaughn, *With Crook,* 48–49; Finerty, *War-Path,* 126; Mills, *My Story,* 401.
18. Mills, *My Story,* 401; Bourke, Diary, 5:405.
19. Van Vliet to Maj. A. W. Evans, June 20, 1876, reprinted in Vaughn, *With Crook,* 235.
20. Bourke, Diary, 5:405–6.
21. Neihardt, *Black Elk,* 100–1.
22. Mills, *My Story,* 402; Grinnell, *Fighting Cheyennes,* 333.
23. Stands in Timber and Liberty, *Cheyenne Memories,* 188–89.
24. Marquis, *Wooden Leg,* 199–200.
25. Vestal, *Warpath,* 188.
26. Lemly, "Fight on the Rosebud," 14.
27. Nickerson, "Major General George Crook," 27.
28. Royall to AAAG, Big Horn and Yellowstone Expedition, June 20, 1876, reprinted in Vaughn, *With Crook,* 231–32; Guy V. Henry to H. R. Lemly, June 20, 1876, ibid., 228–29; Bourke, Diary, 5:409;

Lemly, "Fight on the Rosebud," 15; Brady, *Indian Fights,* 206–8. Towne's account of Marshall's death differs slightly from Lemly's. Towne claimed Marshall had been mortally wounded, and he alone stayed with him. He also contended his effort to save the sergeant caused his own capture and near death. Unlike Lemly, who recorded his impressions only three days after the fight, Towne's recollections came almost thirty years later, when he was seeking a Medal of Honor. Towne also felt his disability pay was inadequate for the injuries he received at the Rosebud.

29. Stands in Timber and Liberty, *Cheyenne Memories,* 186–87.
30. Royall to AAAG, Big Horn and Yellowstone Expedition, June 20, 1876, reprinted in Vaughn, *With Crook,* 231–32; Bourke, Diary, 5:409; Lemly, "Fight on the Rosebud," 15.
31. Bourke, Diary, 5:408–9; Vaughn, *With Crook,* 110.
32. Nickerson, "Major General George Crook," 27; Mills, *My Story,* 403–4.
33. *Helena Independent,* June 30, 1876, reprinted in *New York Herald,* July 11, 1876.
34. Bourke, *On the Border,* 311.
35. Bourke, Diary, 5:412.

14: THE "UNKNOWN QUANTITY"

1. Crook to AAG, MilDivMo, June 20, 1876, reprinted in Vaughn, *With Crook,* 217; Mills, *My Story,* 404–5; Iron Hawk, quoted in Neihardt, *Black Elk,* 101.
2. Crook, to AAG, MilDivMo, June 20, 1876, reprinted in Vaughn, *With Crook,* 216; Lemly, "Fight on the Rosebud," 16–17.
3. Finerty, *War-Path,* 146; *New York Times,* July 13, 1876.
4. *New York Times,* July 13, 1876; Bourke, *On the Border,* 316–17.
5. Bourke, Diary, 5:413–14, and *On the Border,* 317; Finerty, *War-Path,* 146–48.
6. Nickerson, "Major General George Crook," 29. Henry recovered and returned to service, rising to general.
7. Bourke, *On the Border,* 317; Finerty, *War-Path,* 149–50.
8. Bourke, Diary, 5:424; Crook to Sheridan, June 19, 1876, reprinted in Vaughn, *With Crook at the Rosebud,* 214.
9. Capron, Diary, June 17, 1876; Mills, *My Story,* 406.
10. Bourke, Diary, 5:427–28; Finerty, *War-Path,* 151.
11. Bourke, Diary, 5:429–30.
12. *New York Herald,* June 27, 1876.
13. Crook to Sheridan, July 26, 1876, Special File—Sioux; Bourke, Diary, 5:621.

14. Bourke, *On the Border*, 311; Hardorff, Lakota Recollections, 27; Neihardt, *Black Elk*, 99.
15. Neihardt, *Black Elk*, 103–4.
16. Marquis, *Wooden Leg*, 202–3.
17. Marquis, *Custer on the Little Bighorn*, 83.
18. Marquis, *Wooden Leg*, 203–5.
19. Neihardt, *Black Elk*, 106–8.
20. Stands in Timber and Liberty, *Cheyenne Memories*, 191–92.
21. Ibid., 192; Marquis, *Custer on the Little Bighorn*, 83.

15: TERRY CHANGES PLANS

1. Terry, *Field Diary*, 20–21; *St. Paul Pioneer-Press*, June 24, 1876; *New York Herald*, June 27, 1876; Headquarters, Department of Dakota, Special Field Orders No. 11, June 10, 1876, in Overfield, *The Little Big Horn, 1876*, 20–21; Gray, *Centennial Campaign*, 126.
2. Luce, "Diary and Letters," 40–41; Thompson, "Custer's Last Fight," Belle Fourche *Bee*, February 19, 1914; Gray, *Centennial Campaign*, 132–33.
3. Thompson, "Custer's Last Fight," Belle Fourche *Bee*, February 19, 26, 1914; Gray, *Centennial Campaign*, 134.
4. Arikara narrative in Graham, *Custer Myth*, 29; Custer, in *New York Herald*, July 11, 1876.
5. Custer in *New York Herald*, July 11, 1876.
6. Gray, *Centennial Campaign*, 136–37; Terry, *Field Diary*, 22–23.
7. Ruggles to AG, MilDivMo, July 4, 1876. Special File—Sioux.
8. Terry, Annual Report, qtd. in *Field Diary*, 4.
9. Custer in *New York Herald*, July 11, 1876.
10. Terry's instructions appear in original and in various reports in the Special File—Sioux, and, following the disastrous battle of the Little Bighorn, were reprinted in many metropolitan newspapers. They have also been quoted in many works, including Overfield, *The Little Big Horn, 1876*, 23–24.
11. Gibbon, "Gibbon on the Sioux Campaign," 22.
12. Ibid., 23; Bradley, *Montana Column*, 143–44.
13. Gibbon, "Gibbon on the Sioux Campaign," 22–23.
14. The number of scouts carried by the command was forty, but sixteen of these were performing other duties, such as delivering mail or dispatches. See Carroll, *Custer's Chief of Scouts*, 59–60.
15. Gibbon to Terry, qtd. in Brady, *Indian Fights*, 223; Gibbon, "Gibbon on the Sioux Campaign," 23.

16: THE TRAIL TO DISASTER

1. Thompson, "Custer's Last Fight," Belle Fourche *Bee*, February 26, 1914.

2. Wagner, *Old Neutriment,* 142–43.

3. Benteen, narrative, in Carroll, *Benteen-Goldin Letters,* 162.

4. Francis Gibson to Katherine Gibson, July 4, 1876, qtd. in Fougera, *With Custer's Cavalry,* 267–68; George D. Wallace, Report, January 27, 1877, in War Department, *Annual Report—1877,* 1377; Edward S. Godfrey in Graham, *Custer Myth,* 134–35. The recollections of Gibson and Godfrey concerning the possibility of Custer's death are virtually identical.

5. Fougera, *With Custer's Cavalry,* 275–77.

6. Gray, *Centennial Campaign,* 154.

7. Wagner, *Old Neutriment,* 144–45; Arikara, narrative, in Graham, *Custer Myth,* 30.

8. Luce, "Diary and Letters," 41.

9. Arikara, narrative, in Graham, *Custer Myth,* 30.

10. Gray, *Centennial Campaign,* 159–60; Herendeen in Graham, *Custer Myth,* 262.

11. Carroll, *Custer's Chief of Scouts,* 61.

12. Arikara, narrative, in Graham, *Custer Myth,* 30–33.

13. Wallace, Report, January 27, 1877, in Department of War, *Annual Report—1877,* 1377.

14. Grinnell, *Fighting Cheyennes,* 348; Stands in Timber and Liberty, *Cheyenne Memories,* 193–94.

15. Marquis, *Wooden Leg,* 215.

16. Indian accounts do not absolutely agree on the layout of the village, other than the Cheyennes were at the north end, and Hunkpapas in the south between the Oglala camp and the river. The arrangement given here is that most commonly remembered.

17. Marquis, *Wooden Leg,* 215–16; Neihardt, *Black Elk,* 108; Red Feather in Hardorff, *Lakota Recollections,* 81.

18. The record does not specify which tribe of Lakotas was involved, but it was probably the Oglalas, since they had regular contact with the Cheyennes. See Stands in Timber and Liberty, *Cheyenne Memories,* 195n.

19. Ibid., *Cheyenne Memories,* 194–95.

20. Marquis, *Wooden Leg,* 216.

21. McLaughlin, *My Friend the Indian,* 166–67.

22. Carroll, *Custer's Chief of Scouts,* 61.

23. Stories persist among the Lakotas that the boy was killed by the soldiers, but the man escaped. They are identified as a Sans Arc father and son named Ozo Gila and Wicohan, respectively. If this is true then fourteen-year-old Wicohan, whose name translates loosely as "Deeds," became the first casualty of the Little Bighorn. See Hardorff, *Hokahey!* 17ff.

24. Carroll, *Custer's Chief of Scouts,* 62–64.

25. Godfrey, narrative, in Graham, *Custer Myth,* 137–38; Benteen, narrative, in Carroll, *Benteen-Goldin,* 167.
26. The letter "J" was not included in army designations because it could be too easily confused with "I."
27. Godfrey, in Graham, *Custer Myth,* 138; Benteen, in Carroll, *Benteen-Goldin,* 168.
28. Reno to E. W. Smith, AAG, DptDak, July 5, 1876, in Overfield, *Little Big Horn, 1876,* 43.
29. Herendeen, in Graham, *Custer Myth,* 263; Arikara narrative, ibid., 39–40, Graham, "Come On!" ibid., 293.
30. Sgt. Daniel Kanipe, in Graham, *Custer Myth,* 249; White Man Runs Him, ibid., 13.
31. Reno to Smith, July 5, 1876, in Overfield, *Little Big Horn, 1876,* 43–44; Girard qtd. in Gray, *Custer's Last Campaign,* 273–75.
32. McLaughlin, *My Friend the Indian,* 167–68.
33. Reno to Smith, July 5, 1876, in Overfield, *Little Big Horn, 1876,* 44.
34. Carroll, *Custer's Chief of Scouts,* 65.
35. Pvt. William C. Slaper in Brininstool, *Troopers with Custer,* 48; Crow King, Cincinnati *Commercial,* undated clipping, author's collection; Hammer, *Custer in '76,* 118; Thomas O'Neill, *Washington Post,* July 12, 1897.

17: THE LITTLE BIGHORN

1. Red Feather, in Hardorff, *Lakota Recollections,* 81.
2. Marquis, *Wooden Leg,* 217.
3. Neihardt, *Black Elk,* 108–9.
4. Red Horse, in Graham, *Custer Myth,* 57.
5. Marquis, *Wooden Leg,* 217–18; Neihardt, *Black Elk,* 109; Hardorff, *Lakota Recollections,* various entries.
6. Neihardt, *Black Elk,* 109–10.
7. Graham, *Little Big Horn,* 38; Neihardt, *Black Elk,* 109–10; Gall, in Graham, *Custer Myth,* 88; Vestal, *Warpath,* 193.
8. McLaughlin, *My Friend the Indian,* 168–69.
9. Gall, in Graham, *Custer Myth,* 90.
10. Graham, ibid., 88; Neihardt, *Black Elk,* 110.
11. Standing Bear, in Hammer, *Custer in '76,* 215.
12. Graham, *Little Big Horn,* 145.
13. Slaper, in Brininstool, *Troopers with Custer,* 48.
14. Carroll, *Custer's Chief of Scouts,* 65; Varnum, in Brininstool, *Troopers with Custer,* 100.
15. Carroll, *Custer's Chief of Scouts,* 61; Vestal, *Warpath,* 193.
16. Graham, *Little Big Horn,* 41.
17. Ibid., 145.

18. Slaper, in Brininstool, *Troopers with Custer,* 51; Sgt. John M. Ryan, in Graham, *Custer Myth,* 242; O'Neill, *Washington Post,* July 12, 1897.
19. Ryan, in Graham, *Custer Myth,* 242; Herendeen, ibid., 261; Graham, *Little Big Horn,* 43.
20. Ryan, in Graham, *Custer Myth,* 242.
21. Varnum, in Brininstool, *Troopers with Custer,* 107–8; O'Neill, ibid., 131; Ryan, in Graham, *Custer Myth,* 242; Carroll, *Custer's Chief of Scouts,* 123.
22. Iron Hawk, in Hardorff, *Lakota Recollections,* 64–65.
23. Graham, *Little Big Horn,* 45–46.
24. Luther Hare, in Denison, Texas, *Daily News,* July 15, 1876.
25. Hammer, *Custer in '76,* 119.
26. Graham, *Little Big Horn,* 46–47.
27. Slaper, in Brininstool, *Troopers with Custer,* 52.
28. Neihardt, *Black Elk,* 112.
29. Two Eagles, in Hardorff, *Lakota Recollections,* 143.
30. DeRudio, in Graham, *Custer Myth,* 252–53; O'Neill, *Washington Post,* July 12, 1897.
31. Two Eagles, in Hardorff, *Lakota Recollections,* 143.

18: CATASTROPHE ON THE RIDGES

1. Gray, *Custer's Last Campaign,* 278.
2. Kanipe, in Graham, *Custer Myth,* 249; Graham, "Come On!" ibid., 290; Gray, *Custer's Last Campaign,* 279.
3. Curley, in Graham, *Custer Myth,* 13.
4. Graham, "Come On!" ibid., 290.
5. Sherman, "The Bugler," 19.
6. Curley, in Graham, *Custer Myth,* 14.
7. Godfrey, narrative, in Graham, ibid., 138–39; Benteen, narrative, in Carroll, *Benteen-Goldin,* 168–70; Hunt and Hunt, *I Fought With Custer,* 80–81.
8. Kanipe, in Graham, *Custer Myth,* 249.
9. Benteen, narrative, *Benteen-Goldin,* 170; Benteen to Smith, July 4, 1876, in Overfield, *Little Big Horn, 1876,* 40–41.
10. Fox, *Archaeology,* 139–42; various accounts in Hardorff, *Lakota Recollections,* and Hammer, *Custer in '76.*
11. Fox, "A New View," 37.
12. Fox, *Archaeology,* 139, and "A New View," 35, 37; Marquis, *Custer on the Little Bighorn,* 85; Stands in Timber and Liberty, *Cheyenne Memories,* 200.
13. Lame White Man was originally a Southern Cheyenne who lived with the Northern Cheyennes.

14. Hardorff, *Lakota Recollections,* various entries; Marquis, *Wooden Leg,* 230–31, 234, and *Custer on the Little Bighorn,* 87–89; Neihardt, *Black Elk,* 115–16.

15. Two Moons, in Hardorff, *Lakota Recollections,* 137; Fox, *Archaeology,* 228; Bourke, Diary, 21:69–70. Bourke accompanied the reburial detail in 1877, and surmised what happened by the positions of the bodies.

16. Hardorff, *Lakota Recollections,* various entries; Marquis, *Custer on the Little Bighorn,* 89; Neihardt, *Black Elk,* 116–17.

17. Bourke, Diary, 21:70.

18. Marquis, *Custer on the Little Bighorn,* 89.

19. Hunt and Hunt, *I Fought With Custer,* 96.

20. Benteen, narrative, in Carroll, *Benteen-Goldin,* 170–71.

21. Hunt and Hunt, *I Fought With Custer,* 97.

22. Fox, "A New View," 35–36.

23. Bourke, Diary, 21:67–68; Knight, *Following the Indian Wars,* 211–12; Hammer, *Custer in '76,* 199, 215; Marquis, *Custer on the Little Bighorn,* 89–90, and *Wooden Leg,* 237; Neihardt, *Black Elk,* 122–23; Stands In Timber and Liberty, *Cheyenne Memories,* 200–2; Hardorff, *Hokahey!* 71; Leforge, *Memoirs,* 311–12; Fox, *Archaeology,* 227. Tom Leforge, who camped in the area over the ensuing years, said he found remains of soldiers as much as twenty-five miles from the scene of the fight, which he believed accounted for a substantial discrepancy between the body count and the number of men known to have been with Custer.

24. Marquis, *Wooden Leg,* 237–38, and *Custer on the Little Bighorn,* 90; Bourke, Diary, 21:69; Gray, *Custer's Last Campaign,* 397.

19: VALLEY OF THE DEAD

1. Marquis, *Custer on the Little Bighorn,* 91; Utley, *Lance and Shield,* 154–55.

2. Neihardt, *Black Elk,* 124.

3. Marquis, *Wooden Leg,* 243.

4. Ibid., 262–63; Two Eagles, in Hardorff, *Lakota Recollections,* 150; Grinnell, *Fighting Cheyennes,* 355; Bradley, *Montana Column,* 173–74; Jordan, "Ghosts on the Little Bighorn," 790–800; Fox, *Archaeology,* 200–1.

5. Marquis, *Custer on the Little Bighorn,* 91.

6. Grinnell, *Fighting Cheyennes,* 354.

7. Marquis, *Wooden Leg,* 239–43, 245.

8. Hardorff, *Hokahey!* 130.

9. Neihardt, *Black Elk,* 125–27.

10. DeRudio in Graham, *Custer Myth,* 254; O'Neill, in Brininstool, *Troopers with Custer,* 133–34.

11. O'Neill, in Brininstool, *Troopers with Custer,* 134.

12. Ibid., 134–38; DeRudio, in Graham, *Custer Myth,* 254; Girard, ibid., 251.

13. Hunt and Hunt, *I Fought With Custer,* 102–3; Benteen, narrative, in Carroll, *Benteen-Goldin,* 209–10; Wagner, *Old Neutriment,* 170.

14. Hunt and Hunt, *I Fought With Custer,* 102; Benteen, narrative, in Carroll, *Benteen-Goldin,* 173; Godfrey, in Graham, *Custer Myth,* 144; Graham, *Little Big Horn,* 137.

15. Benteen, narrative, in Carroll, *Benteen-Goldin,* 210; Goldin to Johnson, January 6, 1932, ibid., 34–35; Godfrey, in Graham, *Custer Myth,* 144. Long after Reno and Benteen were dead, the story arose that Reno himself wanted to flee during the night, abandoning the wounded, and that Benteen had vetoed the idea. Trooper Goldin, who corresponded extensively with Benteen after both had left the service, flatly denied the allegation, saying, "Reno was inexperienced as an Indian fighter, but he was not a coward."

16. Marquis, *Custer on the Little Bighorn,* 91.

17. No connection with the Hunkpapa White Bull.

18. Marquis, *Wooden Leg,* 255–57, 267; Little Robe Woman, in Hardorff, *Lakota Recollections,* 96; Hardorff, *Hokahey!* Appendix B.

19. Benteen, narrative, in Carroll, *Benteen-Goldin,* 173.

20. Godfrey, in Graham, *Custer Myth,* 144–45; Hunt and Hunt, *I Fought with Custer,* 104–5.

21. Marquis, *Wooden Leg,* 269–70.

22. Hunt and Hunt, *I Fought With Custer,* 106.

23. Ibid., 107; Marquis, *Wooden Leg,* 270; Godfrey, in Graham, *Custer Myth,* 145–46.

20: "SO DIFFERENT FROM THE OUTCOME WE HAD HOPED FOR"

1. Bradley, *Montana Column,* 148–54.

2. Ibid., 154; McClernand, *On Time,* 146.

3. Bradley, *Montana Column,* 154–59; McClernand, *On Time,* 57–58.

4. McClernand, *On Time,* 147.

5. Bradley, *Montana Column,* 160–62.

6. McClernand, *On Time,* 59; Hammer, *Custer in '76,* 139.

7. Bradley, *Montana Column,* 172.

8. McClernand, *On Time,* 60–61.

9. Hammer, *Custer in '76,* 249–50; Bradley, *Montana Column,* 172–73.

10. Fougera, *With Custer's Cavalry,* 276.

11. Terry to AG, MilDivMo, June 27, 1876, in Overfield, *Little Big Horn, 1876,* 26–30.
12. Sgt. James E. Wilson to Chief Engineer's office, DptDak, January 3, 1877, in McClernand, *On Time,* 176; Hammer, *Custer in '76,* 139–40.
13. *New York Times,* July 6, 1876.
14. Sheridan to Drum, July 6, 1876, Special File—Sioux; Overfield, *Little Big Horn, 1876,* 34n; Hutton, *Phil Sheridan,* 315.
15. Terry to Sheridan, in Overfield, *Little Big Horn, 1876,* 36–38.
16. Hutton, *Phil Sheridan,* 315–16; Reno to Smith, July 5, 1876, in Overfield, *Little Big Horn, 1876,* 51.
17. Wagner, *Old Neutriment,* 164–65.
18. Whittaker, *Custer,* 590, 606.
19. Graham, *Little Big Horn,* 142. Libbie Custer always blamed Reno for her husband's death, and in 1926 successfully blocked army plans to memorialize Reno on the fiftieth anniversary of the battle.
20. Reno to Benét, July 11, 1876, in Overfield, *Little Big Horn, 1876,* 60–62. General Benét was grandfather to the poets Stephen Vincent and William Rose Benét.
21. Fox, *Archaeology,* 237–41. Reno himself was a member of the 1872 board of officers that selected the Springfield for government use.
22. *New York Times,* July 17, 1876.

21: "CONGRESS IS . . . WILLING TO GIVE US ALL WE WANT"

1. Sheridan to Drum, July 7, 1876; Pope to Drum, July 7, 1876, both in Special File—Sioux.
2. Pope to Sheridan, July 16, 1876; Sherman to Sheridan, July 15, 1876; James B. Fry, AAG, MilDivAtlantic, to AAG, MilDivMo, July 9, 1876, all ibid.
3. Bourke, Diary, 5:432–33.
4. Ibid., 5:437.
5. Finerty, *War-Path,* 159, 163.
6. Sibley to AAG, Big Horn and Yellowstone Expedition, July 12, 1876, Special File—Sioux; Crook to Sheridan, July 16, 1876, in Bourke, Diary, 6:602; Brady, *Indian Fights,* 298.
7. Finerty, *War-Path,* 194–95; Bourke, *On the Border,* 332.
8. Crook to Sheridan, July 16, 1876, in Bourke, Diary, 6:602; Bourke, *On the Border,* 332–34.
9. Crook to Terry, July 16, 1876, Special File—Sioux.
10. Bourke, *On the Border,* 338.
11. Gray, *Centennial Campaign,* 198.
12. Qtd. in ibid., 256–57.
13. Athearn, *William Tecumseh Sherman,* 310–11.

14. Sherman to Sheridan, July 14, 1876, Special File—Sioux.
15. Ibid. (two telegrams), July 22, 1876.

22: "FIRST SCALP FOR CUSTER"

1. Gray, *Centennial Campaign,* 205.
2. Crook to Sheridan, July 23, 1876, Special File—Sioux.
3. King, *War Eagle,* 158.
4. O'Neal, *Fighting Men,* 166–67.
5. King, *Campaigning With Crook,* 19–21; Merritt to Sheridan, July 5, 1876, Special File—Sioux; Hedren, *First Scalp,* 50–52; Sgt. John Powers, in Dobak, "Yellow-Leg Journalists," 99; Frew, Diary, July 5, 1876.
6. Townsend to Merritt, July 12, 1876; Merritt to Sheridan (three telegrams) July 15, 1876, all Special File—Sioux; Powers, in Dobak, "Yellow-Leg Journalists," 100; Frew, Diary, July 14–15, 1876.
7. King, *Campaigning With Crook,* 25; Hedren, *First Scalp,* 58–59.
8. Davies, *Ten Days,* 83.
9. Cody, *Life,* 340–42.
10. Powers, in Dobak, "Yellow-Leg Journalists," 100; King, *Campaigning With Crook,* 26; Hedren, *First Scalp,* 60–61.
11. King, *Campaigning With Crook,* 27.
12. Ibid., 27–32.
13. Powers, in Dobak, "Yellow-Leg Journalists," 100; King, *Campaigning With Crook,* 33–34.
14. The warrior's Cheyenne name was Hay-o-wei, which translates as "Yellow Hair," referring to a scalp he carried as a trophy. Little Bat mistranslated the name as "Yellow Hand," and that mistake has been carried over into most histories of the fight, as well as motion pictures (see Hedren, *First Scalp,* 63n). This Yellow Hair was a different person from Wooden Leg's brother, Yellow Hair.
15. Cody, *Life,* 343–44.
16. James Frew to A. E. Long, August 8, 1928, Frew, Papers; ibid., Diary, July 17, 1876; King, *Campaigning With Crook,* 34; Powers, in Dobak, "Yellow-Leg Journalists," 100.
17. Powers, in Dobak, "Yellow-Leg Journalists," 100; Frew, Diary, July 17, 1876.
18. Merritt to Sheridan, July 19, 1876, Special File—Sioux.
19. Hedren, *First Scalp,* 83–84.

23: THE LONG, TERRIBLE SUMMER

1. Marquis, *Wooden Leg,* 275–77.
2. Vestal, *Warpath,* 206–8.
3. Pope to Sheridan, July 24, 1876, and July 25, 1876, Special File—Sioux.

4. Ibid., July 25, 1876 (second telegram of that date).

5. Ibid., July 26, 1876; Robinson, *Bad Hand,* 198.

6. Sherman to Sheridan, July 25, 1876, and July 31, 1876, both Special File—Sioux.

7. Scott, *Some Memories,* 40.

8. Qtd. in King, *Campaigning With Crook,* 53–54.

9. Finerty, *War-Path,* 237–46; Bourke, *On the Border,* 349–50.

10. Finerty, *War-Path,* 247–48; Walter Schuyler, Letter, November 1, 1876.

11. Schuyler, Letter, November 1, 1876; Bourke, *On the Border,* 351.

12. King, *Campaigning With Crook,* 72–73.

13. King, ibid., 79–80; Bourke, *On the Border,* 352–53.

14. Finerty, *War-Path,* 253; Bourke, *On the Border,* 354.

15. Marquis, *Wooden Leg,* 279–80; Neihardt, *Black Elk,* 132; Hardorff, *Hokahey!* 13–14.

16. Robinson, *Bad Hand,* 235.

17. Neihardt, *Black Elk,* 133; Finerty, *War-Path,* 255–56; King, *Campaigning With Crook,* 81.

18. Before returning to the East, Cody scouted briefly for Nelson Miles in Montana, but did nothing significant during that campaign.

19. Bourke, *On the Border,* 357–59; King, *Campaigning With Crook,* 88.

20. Finerty, *War-Path,* 263.

21. Neihardt, *Black Elk,* 133; Utley, *Lance and the Shield,* 166.

22. King, *Campaigning With Crook,* 91–92.

23. Bourke, *On the Border,* 363–65.

24. King, *Campaigning With Crook,* 93–94.

25. Finerty, *War-Path,* 275–76; Bourke, *On the Border,* 365.

26. Schuyler, Letter, November 1, 1876.

27. Ibid.; Bourke, *On the Border,* 367, 369.

28. Schuyler, Letter, November 1, 1876.

24: BLOODY RETRIBUTION AT SLIM BUTTES

1. Greene, *Slim Buttes,* 46; Mills to Lt. George F. Chase, Battalion AG, Third Cavalry, September 9, 1876, Special File—Sioux.

2. Greene, *Slim Buttes,* 48; Mills, *My Story,* 166.

3. Mills, *My Story,* 166; Mills to Chase, September 9, 1876, Special File—Sioux.

4. Hyde, *Red Cloud's Folk,* 275; Sandoz, *Crazy Horse,* 339–40; Greene, *Slim Buttes,* 49. The number of lodges is not certain, with estimates by soldiers ranging from twenty-five to forty.

5. Greene, *Slim Buttes,* 51; Mills, *My Story,* 166; Mills to Chase, September 9, 1876, Special File—Sioux.

6. De Barthe, *Frank Grouard,* 303; Mills qtd. in Greene, *Slim Buttes,* 54.

7. Greene, *Slim Buttes,* 57; Mills, *My Story,* 166–67; Mills to Chase, September 9, 1876, Special File—Sioux.

8. Mills, *My Story,* 167; Mills to Chase, September 9, 1876, Special File—Sioux; Greene, *Slim Buttes,* 60–63.

9. Greene, *Slim Buttes,* 65–66; Mills, *My Story,* 167.

10. Bourke, Diary, 9:866–69.

11. De Barthe, *Frank Grouard,* 306; Mills, *My Story,* 167–68; Bourke, *On the Border,* 371.

12. Schuyler, letter, November 1, 1876; Richard Stirk to Eli Ricker, Ricker, Papers, 8:7; Finerty, *War-Path,* 309.

13. Baptiste Pourier to Eli Ricker, Ricker, Papers, 13:34.

14. Pourier, ibid.; Stirk, ibid., 8:11–13.

15. Stirk to Eli Ricker, Ricker, Papers, 8:7–10; Bourke, Diary, 9:873–76.

16. Bourke, Diary, 9:876–77.

17. Mills, *My Story,* 168.

18. Stirk to Ricker, Ricker, Papers, 8:13; Schuyler, Letter, November 1, 1876; Capron, "Indian Border War," 28; Neihardt, *Black Elk,* 133; Alfred McMackin, in Dobak, "Yellow-Leg Journalists," 104; King, *Campaigning With Crook,* 98; McGillycuddy, *Blood on the Moon,* 58–59.

19. Luhn, Letter, September 10, 1876.

20. McMackin, in Dobak, "Yellow-Leg Journalists," 104.

25: SHOWDOWN AT THE AGENCIES

1. Finerty, *War-Path,* 334.

2. Grant, *Personal Memoirs,* 2:541.

3. For a comprehensive biography of Mackenzie, see Robinson, *Bad Hand.*

4. Mackenzie to Sheridan, August 1, 1876, Special File—Sioux.

5. Wilson, *Peacemakers,* 112; Frasca and Hill, *The .45-70 Springfield,* 2; Mackenzie to AG, USA, August 31, 1871, RG 391 Series 757, Fourth Cavalry Expedition Records, Powder River Expedition, hereinafter referred to as Expedition Records.

6. Williams to AAG, MilDivMo, September 1, 1876; Mackenzie to Sheridan, September 2, 1876, both Special File—Sioux.

7. Gray, *Centennial Campaign,* 309–10.

8. Mackenzie to Sheridan, September 2, 1876; Mackenzie to AAG, Platte, September 2, 1876, both in Special File—Sioux; Mackenzie to unspecified general (probably Sheridan), September 8, 1876, Mackenzie, Letterbook, 52–53, hereinafter cited as "Letterbook."

9. Prucha, *Great Father,* 212; Gray, *Centennial Campaign,* 261.

10. Gray, ibid., 260–62.

11. Ibid., 261.

12. Hyde, *Sioux Chronicle,* 5; Mackenzie to Crook, September 9, 1876, Letterbook, 53–54; Robinson, *Bad Hand,* 190.

13. Bourke, *On the Border,* 378.

14. King, *Campaigning With Crook,* 149–150.

15. Bourke, *On the Border,* 377–79; Neihardt, *Black Elk,* 133–34; McGillycuddy, *Blood on the Moon,* 60–61.

16. Williams to AAG, MilDivMo, September 9, 1876, Special File—Sioux; Robinson, *Bad Hand,* 202.

17. Schuyler, Letter, November 1, 1876.

18. Robinson, "Horse Meat March," 32; Neihardt, *Black Elk,* 134.

19. Prucha, *Great Father,* 212; Hyde, *Spotted Tail's Folk,* 202.

20. DeLand, *Sioux Wars,* 17:186, 362–67; Hedren, *Fort Laramie,* 170–71; Robinson, *Bad Hand,* 202–3.

21. Robinson, *Bad Hand,* 203–4; North, *Man of the Plains,* 202–3; Wheeler, *Buffalo Days,* 116–17.

22. Wasson in *Alta California,* October 14, 1876.

23. Cheyenne *Leader,* October 24, 1876.

24. Crook to AAG, MilDivMo, October 30, 1876, with Sheridan, endorsement, November 6, 1876, Special File—Sioux; Hutton, *Phil Sheridan,* 325–26.

25. Hyde, *Red Cloud's Folk,* 285–86, and *Spotted Tail's Folk,* 258.

26: "THE BEGINNING OF THE END"

1. Johnson, "With Gibbon," 9.

2. Miles to Mary Sherman Miles, August 20, 1876, qtd. in Pohanka, *Nelson A. Miles,* 89.

3. For a current and comprehensive biography of Miles, see Robert Wooster, *Nelson A. Miles and the Twilight of the Frontier Army.* The Mackenzie-Miles rivalry is detailed in Robinson, *Bad Hand.*

4. Wooster, *Nelson A. Miles,* 82; Pohanka, *Nelson A. Miles,* 89; Greene, *Yellowstone Command,* 69; Terry to AAG, MilDivMo, September 5, 1876, Special File—Sioux.

5. Miles, *Personal Recollections,* 1:218–19; Pohanka, *Nelson A. Miles,* 90.

6. Greene, *Yellowstone Command,* 71–72.

7. Gray, "What Made Johnnie Brugier [sic] Run?" 35–36.

8. Vestal, *Warpath,* 217–19; Wheeler, *The Scouts,* 106.

9. Miles, *Personal Recollections,* 1:221–22.

10. Ibid., 1:222; Otis, report, October 13, 1876, qtd. in DeLand, *Sioux Wars,* 17:191–92; Vestal, *Warpath,* 219; Utley, *Lance and Shield,* 169.

11. Otis, report, October 27, 1876, and Miner, report, both qtd. in DeLand, *Sioux Wars,* 17:193–95; Greene, *Yellowstone Command,* 83–87.

12. Vestal, *Warpath,* 220–21.

13. Miner, report, qtd. in DeLand, *Sioux Wars,* 17:196.

14. Brady, *Indian Fights and Fighters,* 321–22; Vestal, *Sitting Bull,* 191–92; Utley, *Lance and Shield,* 169–70.

15. Otis, report, October 27, 1876, qtd. in DeLand, *Sioux Wars,* 17:197–98; Vestal, *Sitting Bull,* 192–93; Utley, *Lance and Shield,* 170; Greene, *Yellowstone Command,* 90.

16. Greene, *Yellowstone Command,* 90–91; Miles, *Personal Recollections,* 1:224–25; Kelly, *Yellowstone Kelly,* 154.

17. Edwin M. Brown, Diary, 4.

18. Brown, ibid., 4–5; Miles, *Personal Recollections,* 1:225.

19. Miles to Terry, October 28, 1876, Special File—Sioux; Vestal, *Sitting Bull,* 193–94.

20. Miles, *Personal Recollections,* 1:226.

21. Miles, report, October 25, 1876, qtd. in DeLand, *Sioux Wars,* 17:201.

22. Miles, *Personal Recollections,* 1:225–26.

23. Brown, Diary, 6; Vestal, *Sitting Bull,* 198; Greene, *Yellowstone Command,* 98; Utley, *Lance and Shield,* 172.

24. Brown, Diary, 6–7; Miles, *Personal Recollections,* 1:227; Utley, *Lance and Shield;* Greene, *Yellowstone Command,* 99.

25. Brown, Diary, 7.

26. Vestal, *Warpath,* 223.

27. Brown, Diary, 7; Miles, *Personal Recollections,* 1:226–28; Wooster, *Nelson A. Miles,* 84–85; Greene, *Yellowstone Command,* 100–3.

28. Brown, Diary, 7–8.

29. Kelly, *Yellowstone Kelly,* 157.

30. Miles, *Personal Recollections,* 1:226–28; Wooster, *Nelson A. Miles,* 84–85; Greene, *Yellowstone Command,* 100–3; Vestal, *Warpath,* 225.

31. Miles, *Personal Recollections,* 1:228. Although Miles had successfully mounted infantrymen on captured Indian ponies during the Red River War, this was contingent on having a convenient supply of saddles and equipment, as well as experienced horsemen who could train the soldiers. These were readily available in the extensive network of forts and depots on the southern plains, but not in the nearly empty Yellowstone region.

32. Kelly, *Yellowstone Kelly,* 157–58; Brown, Diary, 9.

33. Miles to AAG, DptDak, October 27, 1876, and Miles to Terry, October 28, 1876, Special File—Sioux.

34. Vestal, *Warpath,* 224–25.

27: THE NOOSE TIGHTENS

1. Sherman to Sheridan, November 19, 1876, Special File—Sioux.

2. Carlin to Ruggles, September 12, 1876, ibid.

3. Sheridan to Drum, September 17, 1876, ibid.

4. Greene, *Yellowstone Command,* 111; Utley, *Lance and Shield,* 176–77.

5. Utley, *Lance and Shield,* 177; Greene, *Yellowstone Command,* 122–23; Kelly, *Yellowstone Kelly,* 165; Miles, *Personal Recollections,* 1:228–29.

6. Sherman to Sheridan, November 10, 1876, Special File—Sioux.

7. Crook to AAG, MilDivMo, January 8, 1877, ibid.

8. Ibid., 14:1355, and "Mackenzie's Last Fight," 3.

9. Headquarters, Powder River Expedition, General Orders No. 7, November 4, 1876, copy in Bourke, Diary, 14:1353–54.

10. Bourke, Diary, 14:1367–74.

11. Ibid., 14:1374–76.

12. Ibid., 14:1377.

13. Ibid., 14:1380; Dodge, Diary, November 11, 1876.

14. Dodge, Diary, November 14, 1876.

15. Ibid., November 16, 1876.

16. Ibid.

17. Bourke, Diary, 14:1389–90; Buecker, "Journals," 28.

18. Bourke, Diary, 14:1401–2; Dodge, Diary, November 19, 1876.

19. Crook to Sheridan, November 20, 1876, copy in Bourke, Diary, 14:1402.

20. Bourke, ibid., 14:1403–4.

21. Crook to Sheridan, November 21, 1876, in Bourke, ibid., 14:1406.

22. Bourke, ibid., 14:1409; Dodge, Diary, November 22–23, 1876.

23. Crook to AAG, MilDivMo, January 8, 1877, Special File—Sioux.

24. Dodge, Diary, November 23, 1876.

25. Bourke, Diary, 14:1410; North, *Man of the Plains,* 211; Buecker, "Journals," 29.

26. Bourke, Diary, 14:1411–12; Buecker, "Journal," 29; Smith, *Sagebrush Soldier,* 64; Wheeler, *Buffalo Days,* 130.

27. Smith, *Sagebrush Soldier,* 64; Bourke, Diary, 14:1412–13.

28. North, *Man of the Plains,* 211.

29. North, ibid., 212; Bourke, Diary, 14:1413; Smith, *Sagebrush Soldier,* 64–65; Buecker, "Journals," 29.

30. Smith, *Sagebrush Soldier,* 65; Wheeler, *Buffalo Days,* 131.

31. Bourke, Diary, 14:1414–15.

32. Buecker, "Journal," 29.

33. Bourke, Diary, 14:1415.

28: THE END FOR THE CHEYENNES

1. The noise was probably from the iron shoes and equipment of the government horses.

2. Grinnell, *Fighting Cheyennes,* 370–74; Stands in Timber and Liberty, *Cheyenne Memories,* 214–16.

3. The Cheyennes never forgave Last Bull for goading them into the subsequent disaster. Ultimately, the Fox Soldiers deposed him, and he eventually went to live among the Crows. See Stands in Timber and Liberty, ibid., 216n.

4. Brady, *Indian Fights,* 314.

5. Grinnell, *Fighting Cheyennes,* 375; Stands in Timber and Liberty, *Cheyenne Memories,* 216.

6. Grinnell, *Fighting Cheyennes,* 377.

7. Bourke, Diary, 14:1415–16; Smith, *Sagebrush Soldier,* 72.

8. Grinnell, *Fighting Cheyennes,* 375; Stands in Timber and Liberty, *Cheyenne Memories,* 216.

9. Smith, *Sagebrush Soldier,* 72.

10. Bourke, Diary, 14:1416–17.

11. Ibid., 14:1417–19; Robinson, *Bad Hand,* 218–19; Grinnell, *Fighting Cheyennes,* 376.

12. Grinnell, *Fighting Cheyennes,* 375–78.

13. Bourke, Diary, 14:1423–24.

14. Bourke, ibid., 14:1425–26; Mackenzie to AAG, Powder River Expedition, November 26, 1876, Expedition Records.

15. Bourke, Diary, 14:1425–26, 1429; Robinson, *Bad Hand,* 220.

16. Bourke, Diary, 14:1426–27; Smith, *Sagebrush Soldier,* 80.

17. Smith, *Sagebrush Soldier,* 88, 91; Robinson, *Bad Hand,* 110, 221–22.

18. Buecker, "Journals," 29.

19. Grinnell, *Fighting Cheyennes,* 381–82; Robinson, *Bad Hand,* 222–23.

20. Marquis, *Wooden Leg,* 282–86.

21. Ibid., *Custer on the Little Bighorn,* 95.

22. Bourke, "Mackenzie's Last Fight," 44–45. Lieutenant McKinney's body was shipped to his family in Tennessee.

23. Dodge, Diary, November 29–30, 1876.

24. Sherman's telegram qtd. in Bourke, "Mackenzie's Last Fight," 44.

29: OPPORTUNITY LOST

1. Stands in Timber and Liberty, *Cheyenne Memories,* 217–18.

2. Ibid., 218; Marquis, *Wooden Leg,* 287–88; Grinnell, *Fighting Cheyennes,* 382.

3. Robinson, *Bad Hand,* 226.

4. Neihardt, *Black Elk,* 136.

5. Robinson, *Bad Hand,* 234.

6. Neihardt, *Black Elk,* 136.

7. Robinson, *Bad Hand,* 228.

8. Dodge, Diary, December 3, 1876.

9. Ibid., various entries; Bourke, Diary, various entries; "Troops are slowly . . ." R. H. Day to Frank Baldwin, December 15, 1876, Baldwin, Collection.

10. Dodge, Diary, December 21, 1876; Robinson, *Bad Hand,* 232.

11. Vestal, *Warpath,* 223. In December 1879, Bruguier was acquitted of the murder.

12. Miles to Sherman, November 18, 1876, Sherman, Unofficial Correspondence.

13. Brown, Diary, 14; Miles, *Personal Recollections,* 1:229–31; Greene, *Yellowstone Command,* 125–27.

14. Utley, *Lance and Shield,* 177.

15. Greene, *Yellowstone Command,* 131–32; Wooster, *Nelson A. Miles,* 87; Miles, *Personal Recollections,* 1:230.

16. O'Neal, *Fighting Men,* 38–39.

17. Baldwin, "The Fights at Bark Creek and Ash Creek," 159; Baldwin to Alice Baldwin, December 8, 1876, Baldwin, Collection.

18. Baldwin, "The Fights at Bark Creek and Ash Creek," 159–60; Greene, *Yellowstone Command,* 136–37; Utley, *Lance and Shield,* 178; Brown, Diary, 16; Culbertson, *Joseph Culbertson,* 72.

19. Culbertson, *Joseph Culbertson,* 72; Greene, *Yellowstone Command,* 198; Baldwin qtd. in Miles, *Personal Recollections,* 1:230; Miles to Terry, December 20, 1876, Special File—Sioux.

20. Greene, *Yellowstone Command,* 140; Utley, *Lance and Shield,* 178; Miles to Baldwin, December 11, 1876, Baldwin, Collection.

21. Culbertson, *Joseph Culbertson,* 72–73.

22. Ibid., 74; Greene, *Yellowstone Command,* 143–44.

23. Culbertson, *Joseph Culbertson,* 74–75; Miles to Terry, December 20, 1876, Special File—Sioux; Greene, *Yellowstone Command,* 141–42; Miles, *Personal Recollections,* 1:230.

24. Miles to Terry, December 20, 1876, Special File—Sioux.

25. Utley, *Lance and Shield,* 179.

26. Brown, Diary, 17.

27. Miles to AAG, DptDak, December 17, 1876, Special File—Sioux.

30: WOLF MOUNTAIN: CRAZY HORSE DEFEATED

1. Miles to Sherman, January 20, 1877, Sherman, Unofficial Correspondence.

2. Miles, *Personal Recollections,* 1:232.

3. Brady, *Indian Fights and Fighters,* 326; Miles, *Personal Recollections,* 1:236.

4. Kelly, *Yellowstone Kelly,* 166–67; Baldwin, *Memoirs,* 79–81; Greene, *Battles and Skirmishes,* 187, 194.

5. Kelly, *Yellowstone Kelly,* 167; Miles, *Personal Recollections,* 1:236.

6. Baldwin, *Memoirs,* 81.

7. Ibid., 82–83; Kelly, *Yellowstone Kelly,* 167. "Wolf Mountain," rendered singular refers to the mountain range in which the battle was fought rather than to a specific mountain.

8. Baldwin, *Memoirs,* 83.

9. Marquis, *Wooden Leg,* 288–89; Anderson, "Indian Peace-Talkers," 237.

10. Baldwin, *Memoirs,* 83.

11. Leforge, *Memoirs,* 271; Brown, *Plainsmen of the Yellowstone,* 301–2. Miles (*Personal Recollections,* 1:236) describes the boy as a "young warrior."

12. Marquis, *Wooden Leg,* 289–90; Neihardt, *Black Elk,* 137; Leforge, *Memoirs,* 272.

13. Leforge, *Memoirs,* 272–74.

14. Brown, Diary, 23. Miles (*Personal Recollections,* 1:236) later claimed the fight was an attempt by some 300 warriors to free the prisoners. Other contemporary accounts, however, speak only of the fight involving the scouts.

15. Neihardt, *Black Elk,* 137; Kelly, *Yellowstone Kelly,* 172; Baldwin, *Memoirs,* 84–85; Greene, *Yellowstone Command,* 165–66.

16. Brown, Diary, 23.

17. Miles to Sherman, January 20, 1877, Sherman, Unofficial Correspondence.

18. Brown, Diary, 23–24; Baldwin, *Memoirs,* 85; Greene, *Battle and Skirmishes,* 201.

19. Marquis, *Wooden Leg,* 290–91.

20. Miles, *Personal Recollections,* 1:238.

21. Neihardt, *Black Elk,* 137.

22. Brown, Diary, 24–25; Baldwin, *Memoirs,* 85–86.

23. Miles to Sherman, January 20, 1877, Sherman, Unofficial Correspondence.

24. Brown, Diary, 25; Baldwin, *Memoirs,* 86.

25. Miles, *Personal Recollections,* 1:238–39.

26. Miles to Sherman, January 20, 1877, Sherman, Unofficial Correspondence.

27. Crook to AAG, MilDivMo, January 8, 1877; Sherman to Sheridan, February 2, 1877, Special File—Sioux.

28. Sherman to Sheridan, February 6, 1877, ibid.

29. Wooster, *Nelson A. Miles,* 90–91; Athearn, *William Tecumseh Sherman,* 313–14.

31: SURRENDER

1. Neihardt, *Black Elk*, 137–38; Marquis, *Wooden Leg*, 292–93.
2. Wooden Leg, who gave his recollections to Thomas B. Marquis almost fifty years later, remembered the four old man chiefs, including Dull Knife, as being present. Contemporary military sources, however, have Dull Knife leading his people in the wake of Crook, scavenging what they could from abandoned military camps, and nearing starvation when they surrendered in April. Also, there was now bad blood between Dull Knife's people and Crazy Horse, making it unlikely the two groups would have remained long in camp together unless absolutely essential for survival.
3. Utley, *Lance and Shield*, 179–80; Marquis, *Wooden Leg*, 293–94; Anderson, "Indian Peace-Talkers," 238.
4. Marquis, *Wooden Leg*, 295–96; Miles, *Personal Recollections*, 1:239.
5. Marquis, *Wooden Leg*, 296–97; Miles, *Personal Recollections*, 1:240; Grinnell, *Fighting Cheyennes*, 384.
6. Grinnell, *Fighting Cheyennes*, 385–86.
7. Ibid., 386; Marquis, *Wooden Leg*, 297.
8. Marquis, *Wooden Leg*, 298; Greene, *Yellowstone Command*, 187; Miles, *Personal Recollections*, 1:241; Anderson, "Indian Peace-Talkers," 239.
9. Hyde, *Spotted Tail's Folk*, 264–65; Anderson, "Indian Peace-Talkers," 244.
10. Marquis, *Wooden Leg*, 299; W. P. Clark to John G. Bourke, February 24, 1877, Special File—Sioux.
11. Miles, *Personal Recollections*, 1:241–47; Grinnell, *Fighting Cheyennes*, 387.
12. Clark to Bourke, February 24, 1877, Special File—Sioux.
13. DeLand, *Sioux Wars*, 17:313; Neihardt, *Black Elk*, 138–39.
14. DeLand, *Sioux Wars*, 17:314.
15. Hyde, *Spotted Tail's Folk*, 268–69; Bourke, Diary, 19:1885–86.
16. San Francisco *Alta California*, April 21, 1877; Hyde, *Spotted Tail's Folk*, 269; Bourke, Diary, 19:1887–88.
17. Bourke, Diary, 19:1905–10.
18. *New York Tribune*, April 23, 1877.
19. Bourke, Diary, 19:1913–14; Anderson, "Indian Peace-Talkers," 252–53; Olson, *Red Cloud*, 239.
20. DeLand, *Sioux Wars*, 17:314; Olson, *Red Cloud*, 239; Bourke, *On the Border*, 412–13; Utley, *Lance and Shield*, 182.
21. Greene, "Lame Deer," 12–13, and *Yellowstone Command*, 203; Baldwin, *Memoirs*, 91.
22. Miles, *Personal Recollections*, 1:249; Baldwin, *Memoirs*, 92.

23. Baldwin, *Memoirs,* 92.

24. DeLand, *Sioux Wars,* 17:308; McBlain, "Lame Deer," 207–8; Baldwin, *Memoirs,* 92–93.

25. Miles, *Personal Recollections,* 1:250–51; DeLand, *Sioux Wars,* 17:309–10; McBlain, "Lame Deer," 209.

26. McBlain, "Lame Deer," 209; DeLand, *Sioux Wars,* 17:310.

27. Miles, *Personal Recollections,* 1:251–52; Baldwin, *Memoirs,* 93.

32: AFTERMATH

1. Greene, *Yellowstone Command,* 233.

2. Bourke, *On the Border,* 417–18; Stands in Timber and Liberty, *Cheyenne Memories,* 231–32.

3. Hyde, *Sioux Chronicle,* 3–4n; Lazarus, *Black Hills/White Justice,* 94.

4. Schmitt, *General George Crook,* 218; Clark, *Killing of Chief Crazy Horse,* 28; DeLand, *Sioux Wars,* 17:316; McGillycuddy, *Blood on the Moon,* 76.

5. De Barthe, *Frank Grouard,* 337–39.

6. Clark, *Killing of Chief Crazy Horse,* 28–29.

7. DeLand, *Sioux Wars,* 17:319–20; McGillycuddy, *Blood on the Moon,* 79–80; Clark, *Killing of Chief Crazy Horse,* 29–30.

8. Crook to Sheridan, September 5, 1877, Special File—Sioux; McGillycuddy to Garnett, June 24, 1927, reprinted in Clark, *Killing of Chief Crazy Horse,* 126. Fort Marion, at St. Augustine, is now known by its original Spanish name, Castillo de San Marcos.

9. McGillycuddy to Garnett, June 24, 1927, reprinted in Clark, *Killing of Chief Crazy Horse,* 121–26; DeLand, *Sioux Wars,* 17:329–30; Carroll, "Man Who Killed Crazy Horse," 41. Fearing Indian reprisal, Bradley ordered Private Gentles's immediate transfer to Sidney Barracks. He was secretly taken there the same night.

10. Buecker, "Frederic S. Calhoun," 22.

11. Olson, *Red Cloud,* 246; Hyde, *Sioux Chronicle,* 5.

12. Hyde, *Sioux Chronicle,* 5–6, and *Red Cloud's Folk,* 299; Olson, *Red Cloud,* 247–48.

13. Hyde, *Sioux Chronicle,* 6ff.

14. Grinnell, *Fighting Cheyennes,* 400ff.

15. Ibid., 414ff.

16. Utley, *Lance and Shield,* 236–37.

17. Hyde, *Spotted Tail's Folk,* 325–30.

18. Olson, *Red Cloud,* 306–8.

19. Mooney, *Ghost Dance Religion,* 834; Neihardt, *Black Elk,* 231.

20. The Ghost Dance movement is thoroughly examined by James Mooney in *The Ghost Dance Religion and Wounded Knee.*

21. Eastman, *Sister to the Sioux,* 146.
22. Miles to Mary Miles, December 20, 1890, qtd. in Pohanka, *Nelson A. Miles,* 186.
23. Mooney, *Ghost Dance Religion,* 848–49; Pohanka, *Nelson A. Miles,* 186.
24. McLaughlin, *My Friend the Indian,* 200–1.
25. Mooney, *Ghost Dance Religion,* 855–59; McLaughlin, *My Friend the Indian,* 217–21.
26. Mooney, *Ghost Dance Religion,* 867–70.

BIBLIOGRAPHY

MANUSCRIPTS

Baldwin, Frank D. Collection. Henry E. Huntington Library and Art Gallery, San Marino, California.

Bourke, John Gregory. Diary. United States Military Academy Archives, West Point, New York.

Brown, Edwin M. Diary. Small Collection 476. Montana Historical Society Archives, Helena, Montana.

Camp, Walter Mason. Collection. Little Bighorn Battlefield National Memorial, Crow Agency, Montana.

Capron, Cynthia. "The Indian Border War of 1876." Department of Commerce, Cultural Resources Division, Wyoming State Museum, W.P.A. Collection, Cheyenne.

Capron, Thaddeus. Collection. American Heritage Center, University of Wyoming, Laramie. MS 1694.

Dodge, Richard Irving. Diary of the Powder River Campaign, 1876–1877. Everett D. Graff Collection, the Newberry Library, Chicago, Illinois. MS 1110.

Dustin, Fred. Collection. Little Bighorn Battlefield National Memorial, Crow Agency, Montana.

Frew, James. Diary and Letters. Nebraska Historical Society, Lincoln, Nebraska. MS 4229.

Geant, Eugene. "Journal of Private Geant, H C[ompany]., 7th U.S. Infantry." Typescript. Little Bighorn Battlefield National Memorial, Crow Agency, Montana.

Luhn, Gerhard L. Diary and Letters. Typescript. American Heritage Center, University of Wyoming, Laramie. MS 3954.

Mackenzie, Ranald Slidell. Letterbook. Thomas Gilcrease Institute, Tulsa, Oklahoma.

Nickerson, Azor H. "Major General George Crook and the Indians." Walter Schuyler Collection, Henry E. Huntington Library and Art Gallery, San Marino, California.

Reynolds, Charles. Diary. Minnesota Historical Society, St. Paul, Minnesota.

Ricker, Eli. Collection. Nebraska Historical Society, Lincoln, Nebraska. MS 0008.

Schuyler, Walter E. Collection. Henry E. Huntington Library and Art Gallery, San Marino, California.

Sherman, William T. Unofficial Correspondence. Library of Congress, Washington, D.C.

United States Department of War. Office of the Adjutant General. Fourth Cavalry Expedition Records, Letters and endorsements sent and orders issued, 1871–1881, RG 391, Series 757. Powder River Expedition.

————. Special File. Military Division of the Missouri. RG 393. As follows:

————. Citizens Expeditions to the Black Hills, 1874.

————. Sioux War, 1876–77.

White, William H. Diary, 1876. Typescript. Little Bighorn Battlefield National Memorial, Crow Agency, Montana.

BOOKS

Athearn, Robert G. *William Tecumseh Sherman and the Settlement of the West*. Norman: University of Oklahoma Press, 1956.

Baldwin, Alice Blackwood. *Memoirs of the Late Frank D. Baldwin, Major General, U.S.A.* Los Angeles: Wetzel Publishing Co., 1929.

Boatner, Mark, III. *Civil War Dictionary*. Revised ed. New York: Random House, 1988.

Bourke, John Gregory. *On the Border with Crook*. New York: Charles Scribner's Sons, 1891. Reprinted by Time-Life Books, Alexandria, Va., 1980.

Bradley, James H. *The March of the Montana Column: A Prelude to the Custer Disaster*. Norman: University of Oklahoma Press, 1961. Reprint, 1991.

Brady, Cyrus Townsend. *Indian Fights and Fighters*. McClure, Philips & Co., 1904. Reprinted by University of Nebraska Press, Lincoln, 1971.

Brininstool, E. A. *Troopers with Custer: Historic Incidents of the Battle of the Little Big Horn.* Harrisburg, Pa.: Stackpole Co., 1952. Reprinted by University of Nebraska Press, Lincoln, 1989.

Brown, Dee. *The Fetterman Massacre.* Originally published as *Fort Phil Kearny: An American Saga.* New York: G. P. Putnam's Sons, 1962. Reprinted by University of Nebraska Press, Lincoln, 1971.

Brown, Mark H. *The Plainsmen of the Yellowstone: A History of the Yellowstone Basin.* New York: G. P. Putnam's Sons, 1961. Reprinted by University of Nebraska Press, Lincoln, 1969.

Butler, Anne M. *Daughters of Joy, Sisters of Misery: Prostitutes in the American West, 1865–1890.* Urbana: University of Illinois Press, 1985.

Carrington, Margaret. *Ab-sa-ra-ka, Home of the Crows: Being the Experience of an Officer's Wife on the Plains.* Philadelphia: J. B. Lippincott & Co., 1868. Reprinted by Time-Life Books, Alexandria, Va., 1984.

Carroll, John M. (ed.). *The Benteen-Goldin Letters on Custer and His Last Battle.* New York: Liveright, 1974. Reprinted by University of Nebraska Press, Lincoln, 1991.

———. *Custer's Chief of Scouts: The Reminiscences of Charles A. Varnum, Including his Testimony at the Reno Court of Inquiry.* Glendale, Calif.: Arthur H. Clark Co., 1982. Reprinted by University of Nebraska Press, Lincoln, 1987.

Catlin, George. *Letters and Notes on the Manners, Customs, and Conditions of North American Indians.* 2 vols. London: 1844. Reprinted by Dover Publications, New York, 1973.

Clark, Robert A. (ed.). *The Killing of Chief Crazy Horse: Three eyewitness views by the Indian, Chief He Dog, the Indian-white, William Garnett, the White doctor, Valentine McGillycuddy.* Glendale, Calif.: Arthur H. Clark Co., 1976. Reprinted by University of Nebraska Press, Lincoln, 1988.

Cody, William F. *The Life of the Hon. William F. Cody Known as Buffalo Bill, the Famous Hunter, Scout and Guide.* Hartford, Conn.: Frank E. Bliss, 1879. Reprinted by Time-Life Books, Alexandria, Va., 1980.

Connell, Evan S. *Son of the Morning Star.* San Francisco: North Point Press, 1984.

Culbertson, Joseph. *Joseph Culbertson, Famous Indian Scout Who Served Under General Miles in 1876–1895.* Wolf Point, Mont.: Privately printed, 1958.

Custer, Elizabeth B. *"Boots and Saddles" or, Life in Dakota with General Custer.* New York: Harper and Brothers, 1885. Reprinted by University of Oklahoma Press, Norman, 1961.

Davies, Henry E. *Ten Days on the Plains.* New York: Crocker & Co., n.d. (1871). Reprinted by Southern Methodist University Press, Dallas, 1985.

De Barthe, Joe. *The Life and Adventures of Frank Grouard, Chief of Scouts, U.S.A.* St. Joseph, Mo.: Combe Printing Company, 1894. Reprinted by Time-Life Books, Alexandria, Va., 1982.

DeLand, Charles E. *The Sioux Wars.* Vol. 15. *South Dakota Historical Collections.* Pierre, S.D.: State Department of History, 1930.

———. *The Sioux Wars.* Vol. 17. *South Dakota Historical Collections.* Pierre, S.D.: State Historical Society, 1934.

Dodge, Richard Irving. *Our Wild Indians: Thirty-Three Years' Personal Experience Among the Red Men of the Great West.* Hartford, Conn.: A. D. Worthington and Co., 1882.

Dunlay, Thomas W. *Wolves for the Blue Soldiers: Indian Scouts and Auxiliaries with the United States Army, 1860–90.* Lincoln: University of Nebraska Press, 1982. Reprint, 1987.

Eastman, Elaine Goodale. *Sister to the Sioux: The Memoirs of Elaine Goodale Eastman, 1885–91.* Lincoln: University of Nebraska Press, 1978. Reprint, 1985.

Finerty, John F. *War-Path and Bivouac: The Big Horn and Yellowstone Expedition.* Originally published as *War-Path and Bivouac or The Conquest of the Sioux.* Chicago: Privately printed, 1890. Part I reprinted by University of Nebraska Press, Lincoln, 1966.

Fougera, Katherine Gibson. *With Custer's Cavalry.* Caldwell, Idaho: Caxton Printers, 1942. Reprinted by University of Nebraska Press, Lincoln, 1968.

Fox, Richard Allan, Jr. *Archaeology, History, and Custer's Last Battle: The Little Big Horn Reexamined.* Norman: University of Oklahoma Press, 1993.

Frasca, Albert J., and Robert Hill. *The .45-70 Springfield.* Northridge, Calif.: Springfield Publishing Company, 1980.

Gilbert, Hila. *"Big Bat" Pourier.* Sheridan, Wyo.: The Mills Company, 1968.

Graham, W. A. (comp.). *The Custer Myth: A Source Book of Custeriana.* Harrisburg, Pa.: Stackpole Co., 1953. Reprinted by University of Nebraska Press, Lincoln, 1986.

———. *The Story of the Little Big Horn, Custer's Last Fight.* New York: Century Co., 1926. Reprinted by University of Nebraska Press, Lincoln, 1988.

Grant, U. S. *Personal Memoirs.* 2 vols. New York: Charles A. Webster & Co., 1885.

Gray, John S. *Centennial Campaign: The Sioux War of 1876.* Fort Collins, Colo.: The Old Army Press, 1976. Reprinted by University of Oklahoma Press, Norman, 1988.

————. *Custer's Last Campaign: Mitch Boyer and the Little Bighorn Reconstructed.* Lincoln: University of Nebraska Press, 1991.

Greene, Jerome A. (comp.). *Battles and Skirmishes of the Great Sioux War, 1876–1877: The Military View.* Norman: University of Oklahoma Press, 1993.

————. *Slim Buttes, 1876: An Episode of the Great Sioux War.* Norman: University of Oklahoma Press, 1982. Reprint, 1990.

————. *Yellowstone Command: Colonel Nelson A. Miles and the Great Sioux War 1876–1877.* Lincoln: University of Nebraska Press, 1991.

Grinnell, George Bird. *The Cheyenne Indians.* 2 vols. New Haven: Yale University Press, 1923. Reprinted by University of Nebraska Press, Lincoln, 1972.

————. *The Fighting Cheyennes.* New York: Charles Scribner's Sons, 1915. Reprinted by University of Oklahoma Press, Norman, 1956.

Hammer, Kenneth (ed.). *Custer in '76: Walter Camp's Notes on the Custer Fight.* Provo: Brigham Young University, 1976. New edition, Norman: University of Oklahoma Press, 1990.

Hardorff, Richard G. *Hokahey! A Good Day to Die! The Indian Casualties of the Custer Fight.* Spokane: The Arthur H. Clark Company, 1993.

———— (comp.). *Lakota Recollections of the Custer Fight: New Sources of Indian-Military History.* Spokane: The Arthur H. Clark Company, 1991.

Hassrick, Royal B. *The Sioux: Life and Customs of a Warrior Society.* Norman: University of Oklahoma Press, 1964.

Hedren, Paul L. *First Scalp for Custer: The Skirmish at Warbonnet Creek, Nebraska, July 17, 1876.* Glendale, Calif.: The Arthur H. Clark Company, 1980. Reprinted by University of Nebraska Press, Lincoln, 1987.

————. *Fort Laramie in 1876: Chronicle of a Frontier Post at War.* Lincoln: University of Nebraska Press, 1988.

Hunt, Frazier, and Robert Hunt. *I Fought with Custer: The Story of Sergeant Windolph, Last Survivor of the Battle of the Little Big Horn.* New York: Charles Scribner's Sons, 1947.

Hutton, Paul Andrew. *Phil Sheridan and His Army.* Lincoln: University of Nebraska Press, 1985.

Hyde, George. *Red Cloud's Folk: A History of the Oglala Sioux Indians.* Norman: University of Oklahoma Press, 1975.

————. *A Sioux Chronicle.* Norman: University of Oklahoma Press, 1956.

————. *Spotted Tail's Folk: A History of the Brule Sioux.* Second ed. Norman: University of Oklahoma Press, 1974.

King, Charles. *Campaigning With Crook.* New York: Harper and Brothers, 1890. Reprint, Norman: University of Oklahoma Press, 1964.

King, James T. *War Eagle: A Life of General Eugene A. Carr.* Lincoln: University of Nebraska Press, 1963.

Knight, Oliver. *Following the Indian Wars: The Story of the Newspaper Correspondents Among the Indian Campaigners.* Norman: University of Oklahoma Press, 1993.

Lavender, David. *Fort Laramie and the Changing Frontier.* Washington: U.S. Department of the Interior, 1983.

Lazarus, Edward. *Black Hills/White Justice: The Sioux Nation Versus the United States, 1775 to the Present.* New York: HarperCollins Publishers, 1991.

Leforge, Thomas H. *Memoirs of a White Crow Indian (Thomas H. Leforge) as Told by Thomas B. Marquis.* New York: The Century Co., 1928. Reprinted by University of Nebraska Press, Lincoln, 1974.

McClernand, Edward J. *On Time for Disaster: The Rescue of Custer's Command.* Originally published as *With the Indian and the Buffalo in Montana, 1870–1878.* Glendale, Calif.: Arthur H. Clark Company, 1969. Reprinted by University of Nebraska Press, Lincoln, 1989.

McGillycuddy, Julia B. *Blood on the Moon: Valentine McGillycuddy and the Sioux.* Originally published as *McGillycuddy, Agent.* Palo Alto, Calif.: Stanford University Press, 1941. Reprinted by University of Nebraska Press, Lincoln, 1990.

McLaughlin, James. *My Friend the Indian.* Boston: Houghton Mifflin, 1910. Reprinted, with chapters omitted from original edition, by University of Nebraska Press, Lincoln, 1989.

Marquis, Thomas B. *Custer on the Little Big Horn.* Second rev. ed. Algonac, Mich.: Reference Publications, Inc., 1987.

———— (interpreter). *Wooden Leg, a Warrior Who Fought Custer.* Originally published as *A Warrior Who Fought Custer.* Minneapolis: The Midwest Company, 1931. Reprinted by University of Nebraska Press, Lincoln, n.d.

Miles, Nelson A. *Personal Recollections and Observations of General Nelson A. Miles.* Chicago: Werner Company, 1896. Reprinted in 2 vols. by University of Nebraska Press, Lincoln, 1992.

Mills, Anson. *My Story.* Second ed. Washington: Press of Byron S. Adams, 1921.

Mooney, James. *Calendar History of the Kiowa Indians.* Seventeenth Annual Report of the American Bureau of Ethnology, 1895–96. Washington: Government Printing Office, 1898. Reprinted by Smithsonian Institution Press, Washington, 1979.

————. *The Ghost-Dance Religion and Wounded Knee.* Fourteenth Annual Report (Part 2) of the Bureau of Ethnology, 1892–93. Washington: Government Printing Office, 1896. Reprinted by Dover Publications, New York, 1973.

Neihardt, John G. (comp.). *Black Elk Speaks, Being the Life Story of a Holy Man of the Oglala Sioux.* New York: William Morrow & Company, 1932. Reprinted by University of Nebraska Press, Lincoln, 1979.

North, Luther. *Man of the Plains: Recollections of Luther North, 1856–1882.* Lincoln: University of Nebraska Press, 1961.

Olson, James C. *Red Cloud and the Sioux Problem.* Lincoln: University of Nebraska Press, 1965.

O'Neal, Bill. *Fighting Men of the Indian Wars: A Biographical Encyclopedia of the Mountain Men, Soldiers, Cowboys, and Pioneers Who Took Up Arms During America's Westward Expansion.* Stillwater, Okla.: Barbed Wire Press, 1991.

Overfield, Loyd J., II (comp.). *The Little Big Horn, 1876: The Official Communications, Documents and Reports with Rosters of the Officers and Troops of the Campaign.* Glendale, Calif.: Arthur H. Clark Company, 1971. Reprinted by University of Nebraska Press, Lincoln, 1990.

Parkman, Francis, Jr. *The California and Oregon Trail: Being Sketches of Prairie and Rocky Mountain Life.* New York: George P. Putnam, 1849. Reprinted by Time-Life Books, Alexandria, Va., 1983.

Pohanka, Brian C. (ed.). *Nelson A. Miles: A Documentary Biography of His Military Career 1861–1903.* Glendale, Calif.: The Arthur H. Clark Company, 1985.

Prucha, Francis Paul. *The Great Father: The United States Government and the American Indians.* Abridged ed. Lincoln: University of Nebraska Press, 1986.

Richardson, James D. (comp.). *A Compilation of the Messages and Papers of the Presidents.* Vol. 6. Washington: Bureau of National Literature and Art, 1897.

Rickey, Don, Jr. *Forty Miles a Day on Beans and Hay: The Enlisted Soldier Fighting the Indian Wars.* Norman: University of Oklahoma Press, 1963.

Robinson, Charles M., III. *Bad Hand: A Biography of General Ranald S. Mackenzie.* Austin, Tex.: State House Press, 1993.

Sandoz, Mari. *Crazy Horse, the Strange Man of the Oglalas.* New York: Alfred A. Knopf, 1942. 50th anniversary ed., Lincoln: University of Nebraska Press, 1992.

Schmitt, Martin F. (ed.). *General George Crook, His Autobiography.* Norman: University of Oklahoma Press, 1946. Reprint, 1986.

Schneider, George A. (ed.). *The Freeman Journal: The Infantry in the Sioux Campaign of 1876.* San Rafael, Calif.: Presidio Press, 1977.

Scott, Hugh Lenox. *Some Memories of a Soldier*. New York: The Century Co., 1928.

Smith, Sherry L. *Sagebrush Soldier: Private William Earl Smith's View of the Sioux War of 1876*. Norman: University of Oklahoma Press, 1989.

Stands in Timber, John, and Margot Liberty. *Cheyenne Memories*. New Haven: Yale University Press, 1967. Reprinted by University of Nebraska Press, Lincoln, 1972.

Stewart, Edgar I. *Custer's Luck*. Norman: University of Oklahoma Press, 1955.

Terry, Alfred H. *The Field Diary of General Alfred H. Terry: The Yellowstone Expedition—1876*. Second ed. Bellevue, Neb.: The Old Army Press, 1970.

Time-Life Books, Editors of, with Keith Wheeler. *The Scouts*. The Old West. Alexandria, Va.: Time-Life Books, 1978.

United States Department of the Interior. *Report of the Commissioner of Indian Affairs to the Secretary of the Interior, 1876*. Vol. 1. Washington: Government Printing Office, 1876.

———. *Report of the Commissioner of Indian Affairs to the Secretary of the Interior, 1877*. Washington: Government Printing Office, 1877.

United States Department of War. *Report of the Secretary of War: Being Part of the Message and Documents Communicated to the Two Houses of Congress at the Beginning of the Second Session of the Forty-Fourth Congress*. Vol. 1. Washington: Government Printing Office, 1876.

Utley, Robert M. *Cavalier in Buckskin: George Armstrong Custer and the Western Military Frontier*. Norman: University of Oklahoma Press, 1988.

———. *Frontier Regulars: The United States Army and the Indian, 1866–1891*. New York: Macmillan, 1973. Reprinted by University of Nebraska Press, Lincoln, 1984.

———. *The Lance and the Shield: The Life and Times of Sitting Bull*. New York: Henry Holt and Company, 1993.

Van de Water, Frederic F. *Glory-Hunter: A Life of General Custer*. Indianapolis: Bobbs-Merrill Co., 1934. Reprinted by University of Nebraska Press, Lincoln, 1988.

Vaughn, J. W. *With Crook at the Rosebud*. Harrisburg, Pa.: Stackpole Co., 1956. Reprinted by University of Nebraska Press, Lincoln, 1988.

Vestal, Stanley (Walter Stanley Campbell). *Sitting Bull, Champion of the Sioux*. Boston: Houghton Mifflin Co., 1932. Reprinted by University of Oklahoma Press, Norman, 1989.

———. *Warpath: The True Story of the Fighting Sioux Told in a Biography of Chief White Bull*. Boston: Houghton Mifflin Co., 1934. Reprinted by University of Nebraska Press, Lincoln, 1984.

Wagner, Glendolin Damon. *Old Neutriment.* Boston: Ruth Hill, 1934. Reprinted by University of Nebraska Press, Lincoln, 1989.

Werner, Fred H. *"The Soldiers are Coming!" The Story of the Reynolds Battle March 17, 1876.* Greeley, Colo.: Werner Publications, 1982.

Wheeler, Homer W. *Buffalo Days: The Personal Narrative of a Cattleman, Indian Fighter and Army Officer.* Indianapolis: Bobbs-Merrill, 1925. Reprinted by University of Nebraska Press, Lincoln, 1990.

Whittaker, Frederick. *A Complete Life of Gen. George A. Custer, Major-General of Volunteers, Brevet Major General U.S. Army, and Lieutenant-Colonel Seventh U.S. Cavalry.* New York: Sheldon & Company, 1876.

Wilson, R. L. *The Peacemakers: Arms and Adventure in the American West.* New York: Random House, 1992.

Wooster, Robert. *Nelson A. Miles and the Twilight of the Frontier Army.* Lincoln: University of Nebraska Press, 1993.

ARTICLES

Anderson, Harry H. "A Challenge to Brown's Indian War Thesis." Paul L. Hedren, ed. *The Great Sioux War 1876–77: The Best from* Montana, the Magazine of Western History. Helena: Montana Historical Society Press, 1991: 39–52.

———. "Cheyennes at the Little Big Horn—A Study of Statistics." *North Dakota History,* vol. 27, no. 2 (Spring 1960): 81–93.

———. "Indian Peace-Talkers and the Conclusion of the Sioux War of 1876." *Nebraska History,* vol. 44, no. 4 (December 1963): 223–254.

Baldwin, Frank D. "The Fights at Bark Creek and Ash Creek, December 1876." Jerome A. Greene, comp. *Battles and Skirmishes of the Great Sioux War, 1876–1877: The Military View.* Norman: University of Oklahoma Press, 1993: 157–166.

"The Black Hills, Once Hunting Grounds of the Red Men." *National Geographic,* September 1927: 305–329.

Bourke, John Gregory. "Mackenzie's Last Fight with the Cheyennes, A Winter Campaign in Wyoming and Montana." Vol. 11, *Journal of the Military Service Institution of the U.S.* 1890. Reprinted by Argonaut Press, New York, 1966.

Buecker, Thomas R. "Frederic S. Calhoun, A Little-Known Member of the 'Custer Clique.'" *Greasy Grass,* vol. 10 (1994): 16–25.

——— (ed.). "The Journals of James S. McClellan, 1st Sgt., Company H. 3rd Cavalry."

Carroll, John. "The Man Who Killed Crazy Horse." *Old West,* vol. 27, no. 4 (Summer 1991): 38–41.

Dobak, William A. "Yellow-Leg Journalists: Enlisted Men as Newspaper Reporters in the Sioux Campaign, 1876." *Journal of the West,* January 1974: 86–112.

Fox, Richard Allan, Jr. "A New View of Custer's Last Battle." *American History Illustrated,* vol. 28, no. 4 (September/October 1993): 30–37, 64–66.

Gibbon, John. "Gibbon on the Sioux Campaign of 1876." *American Catholic Quarterly Review,* April 1877, October 1877. Reprint. Second ed. Bellevue, Neb.: Old Army Press, 1970.

Gray, John S. "What Made Johnnie Bruguier Run?" *Montana: The Magazine of Western History,* vol. 14, no. 1 (Spring 1964): 34–49.

Greene, Jerome A. "The Lame Deer Fight, Last Drama of the Sioux War of 1876–1877." *By Valor and Arms: Journal of American Military History,* vol. 3, no. 3 (1979): 11–21.

Hampton, Bruce. "Battle of the Big Hole." *Montana: The Magazine of Western History,* vol. 44, no. 1 (Winter 1994): 2–13.

Johnson, Barry C. (ed.). "With Gibbon Against the Sioux in 1876: The Field Diary of Lieutenant William L. English." *English Westerners' Brand Book,* vol. 8, no. 4 (July 1966): 7–12; vol. 9, no. 1 (October 1966): 1–10.

Jordan, Robert Paul. "Ghosts on the Little Bighorn: Custer and the Warriors of the Plains." *National Geographic,* December 1986: 787–813.

Lemly, H. R. "The Fight on the Rosebud." John M. Carroll (ed.). *The Papers of the Order of Indian Wars.* Fort Collins, Colo.: Old Army Press, 1975: 13–18.

Luce, Edward S. (ed.) "The Diary and Letters of Dr. James M. DeWolf, Acting Assistant Surgeon, U.S. Army; His Record of the Sioux Expedition of 1876 as Kept Until His Death." *North Dakota History,* vol. 25, nos. 2–3 (April–July, 1958): 33–81.

McBlain, John F. "The Lame Deer Fight, May 7, 1877." *Journal of the United States Cavalry Association,* 10 (June 1897). Reprint. Jerome Greene, comp. *Battles and Skirmishes of the Great Sioux War, 1876–1877: The Military View.* Norman: University of Oklahoma Press, 1993: 204–212.

McCann, Lloyd E. "The Grattan Massacre." *Nebraska History,* vol. 37, no. 1, March 1956. Reprint. N.d., n.p.

Michno, Gregory F. "Crazy Horse, Custer, and the Sweep to the North." *Montana: The Magazine of Western History,* vol. 43, no. 3 (Summer 1993): 42–53.

Plumb, J. H. "The Victorians Unbuttoned." *Horizon,* vol. 11, no. 4 (Autumn 1969): 16–35.

Robinson, Charles M., III. "The Horse Meat March." *True West,* vol. 39, no. 1 (January 1992): 28–32.

Sherman, R. Joshua. "The Bugler—Unsung Hero!" *True West,* vol. 40, no. 11 (November 1993): 14–19.

Stewart, Edgar I. "Major Brisbin's Relief of Fort Pease." Paul L. Hedren, ed. *The Great Sioux War 1876–77: The Best from* Montana, The Magazine of Western History. Helena: Montana Historical Society Press, 1991: 115–121.

Thompson, Peter. "Custer's Last Fight." Belle Fourche, S.D., *Bee.* Feb. 19, Feb. 26, March 5, March 12, March 19, March 26, April 2, April 9, 1914.

NEWSPAPERS

Cheyenne *Daily Leader*
Cheyenne *Sun*
Chicago *Inter-Ocean*
Cincinnati *Commercial*
Denison, Texas, *Daily News*
Denver *Rocky Mountain News*
Helena Independent
New York Herald
New York Sun
New York Times
Omaha Herald
Omaha *Republican*
San Francisco *Alta California*
St. Paul Pioneer-Press and *Minneapolis Tribune*
Sioux City, Iowa, *Daily Journal*
Washington Post

INDEX

Note: *Italicized* page numbers refer to maps.

Two Moons *(cont'd)*
  and the Dull Knife fight, 291
  and Gibbon's march, 98
  and the Indian decision for war,
    86–87
  and the Little Bighorn battle, 192
  and the Oglala-Cheyenne council,
    86–87
  surrender of, 326, 327, 328, 329
  welcomes the Cheyennes, 86
Tyler, George, 334

Ute scouts, 237, 241

Varnum, Charles A., 109, 167, 170,
  173, 174, 176, 181, 183
Vestal, Stanley, 30
Vliet, Frederick van, 142
Vroom, Peter, 144–45

Wallace, George D., 166, 181, 209,
  210
War Bonnet Creek, skirmish at the,
  230–33
War Department, U.S., 106–7, 119
Washakie, 133, 222
Washington, D.C., Indians invited to,
  339, 340
Washita River, Battle of, 7, 34, 110,
  165–66, 210
Wasson, Joe, 121, 265–66, 331
Watkins, E. C., 41, 223
Weir, Thomas, 189, 194
westward movement. *See* Oregon
  Trail
Wheeler, Homer, 290, 300
"Where the Girl Saved Her Brother"
  battle, 143
Whipple, Henry, 261
White Antelope, 222
White Bird, 138–39, 142
White Bull, 143, 202, 234–35, 273,
  277, 278, 279, 326, 327, 334
White, Charley "Buffalo Chips," (aka
  Jonathan White), 228, 231–32,
  251, 253
White Eyebrows, 173
White Man Runs Him, 103

White River Agency, 94
White Shield, 142, 145
White Swan, 207
White Thunder, 326
Whittaker, Frederick, 215
Wild Hog, 291
Williamson, John W., 95
Windolph, Charles, 111, 189, 194,
  201, 205
Wolf Mountain, fight at, 314–24, 326
Wolf Point Agency, 45, 311
Wooden Leg
  amd miseries of the Indians, 85,
    240, 302
  and the Big Horn Expedition, 64,
    77, 78–79, 80
  and consolidation of the Indians, 87
  and the Dull Knife fight, 301–2
  and the Little Bighorn battle, 178,
    191, 192, 198–99, 202–3
  and the Little Bighorn camp, 172,
    173
  at the Rosebud River camp, 123
  on Sitting Bull's reputation, 123
  social life of, 171
  and souvenirs of Little Bighorn, 234
  and the Wolf Mountain fight, 318,
    320
Wounded Knee massacre, 345–46
Wovoka, 343
Wrapped Hail, 295
Wright, J. G., 343, 344

Yankton Nakota Sioux, 4, 8, 21–23,
  128, 172, 309, 310
Yarnell, 133–34
Yates, George W., 174, 188, 190,
  191, 195
Yellow Eagle, 138–39, 298
Yellow Hair, 173, 178, 199, 232–33
Yellow Robe, 121–22
Yellowstone Command
  Indian attacks on the, 272–74
  map of the, 270
  See also Miles, Nelson
Young Two Moons, 293–94, 296,
  298, 301
Young-Man-Afraid-of-His-Horses, 39